MARTIN

BARRÉ

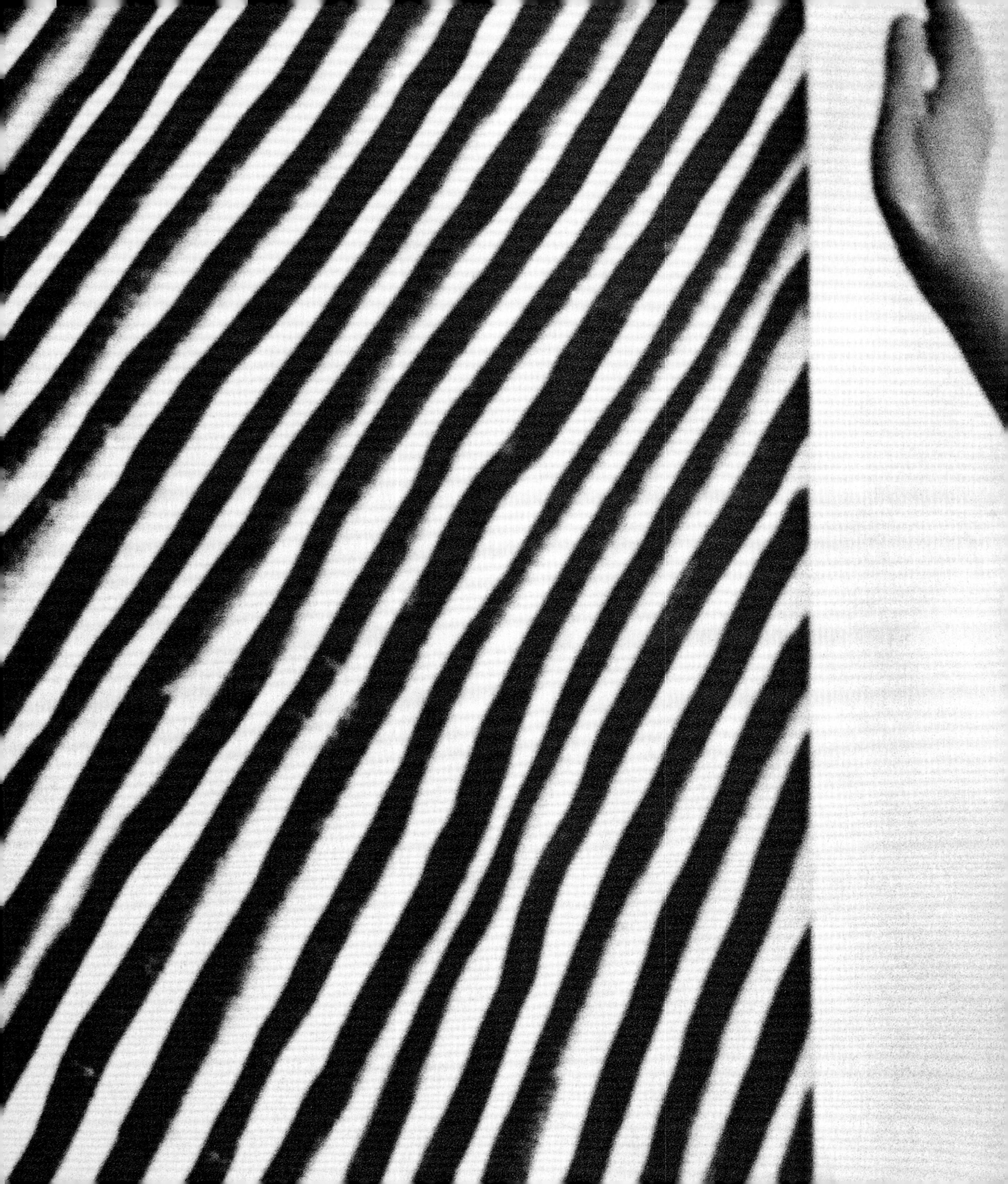

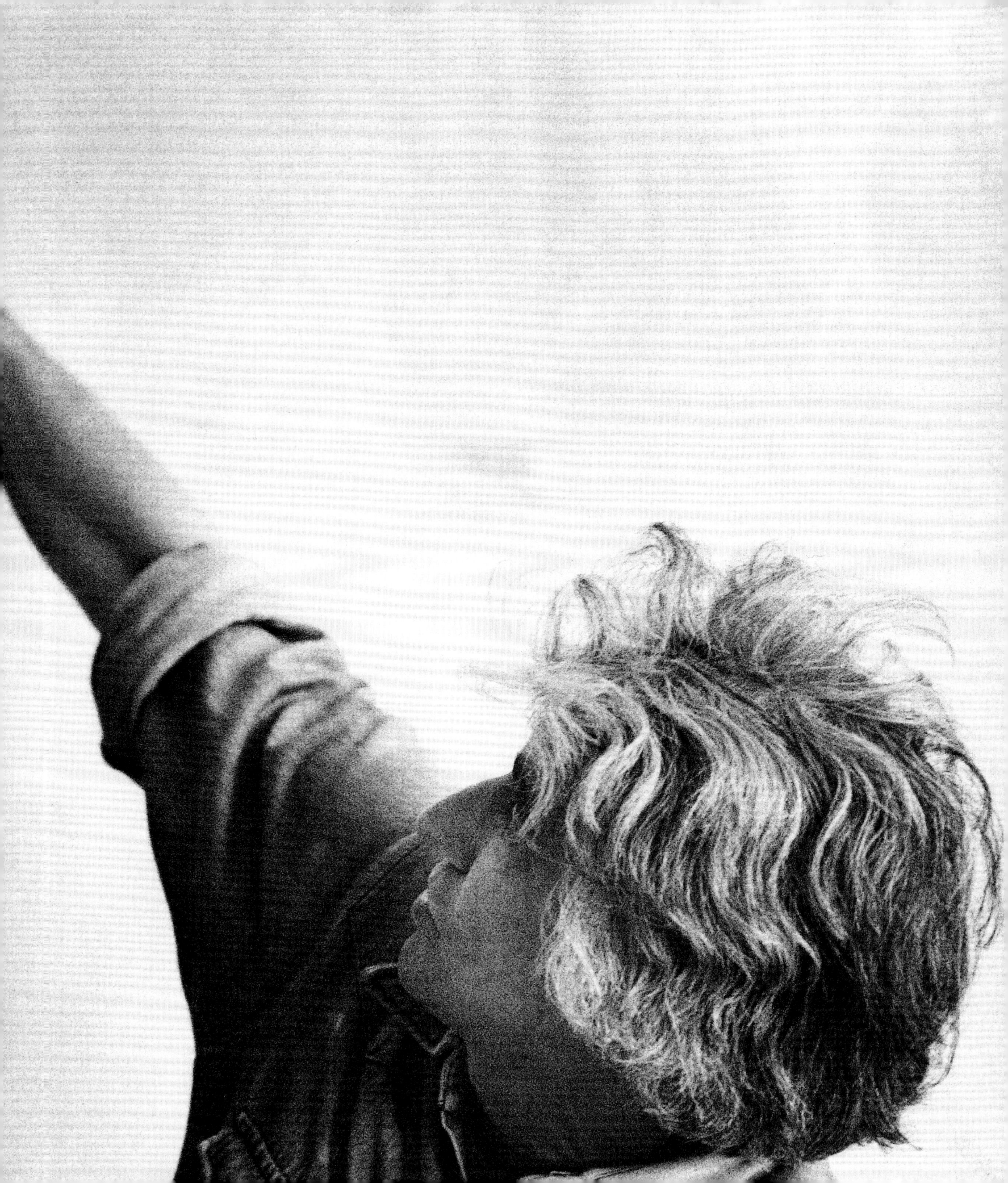

This publication is edited by
Clément Dirié and Michel Gauthier.

It is published on the occasion of the exhibitions *Martin Barré* held at MAMCO Geneva, from October 9, 2019, to February 2, 2020, curated by Clément Dirié, and at the Musée National d'Art Moderne, Centre Pompidou, Paris, from October 14, 2020, to January 4, 2021, curated by Michel Gauthier.

—

The exhibition at MAMCO received the support of the Fondation Gandur pour l'Art and the French Embassy in Switzerland.

The exhibition at the Centre Pompidou received the support of the Fonds de Dotation Emerige.

pp. 2–3
Martin Barré in his studio,
Rue Dauphine, Paris, 1977

Serge Lasvignes

President,
Centre Pompidou

Bernard Blistène

Director,
Musée National
d'Art Moderne

The Centre Pompidou is delighted to present today a retrospective of Martin Barré's oeuvre after having, over the past few years, devoted exhibitions to Pierre Soulages, Simon Hantaï, François Morellet, and Jesús Rafael Soto, other major figures of the French scene, all belonging to the same generation. It is an opportunity for people to discover or rediscover a demanding, radical oeuvre, like no other, a fundamental milestone in the history of pictorial abstraction.

It was with enthusiasm and perseverance that Michel Gauthier, curator at the Musée National d'Art Moderne, set about conceiving an exhibition that would help us understand the logic behind the development of Barré's oeuvre. In the mid-1950s, Barré paved the way for a profoundly original abstract painting, neither lyrical nor geometric. From the lines he drew on the canvas in the 1960s, first with a paint tube and then with an aerosol can, to the colored figures of the late series in the 1990s, to the paintings of the 1970s, with their grids and hatching, Barré's painting, constantly at the peak of its idiom, offers to our gaze objects both of reflection and contemplation, where concept and beauty are inseparably combined.

We would like to thank the individuals and institutions who have kindly entrusted us with their works for the duration of the exhibition. Our special thanks go to Michèle Gozland-Barré for her constant receptiveness and commitment alongside the Centre Pompidou team. We also salute the work accomplished by the Association des Amis de Martin Barré, which has done so much over the last fifteen years to enhance the appreciation and dissemination of his oeuvre.

This exhibition is also the fruit of a welcome cooperation with MAMCO (Museum of Modern and Contemporary Art) in Geneva, with its director Lionel Bovier, and with Clément Dirié, the curator of the *Martin Barré* exhibition on which the Swiss museum worked in parallel. It is gratifying to see two European cultural institutions showing the work of one of the greatest painters of his time and joining forces to produce the reference work that is this publication.

Lionel Bovier

Director,
MAMCO Geneva

Martin Barré belongs, biographically, to a generation of artists in whom MAMCO has rarely taken an interest. Indeed, the museum's narrative is rather that of the "short time" that separates us from the textual and phenomenological turning point of the 1960s. Conceptual art and its legacy, as well as minimalism and its aftermath, are the true foundations on which the institution has built its work since its founding in 1994, and from which it has sketched the contours of contemporary art history.

However, when Clément Dirié suggested that we organize the exhibition which this book charts and which it complements, Martin Barré's painting seemed to us to be perfectly consistent with this program. It is probably because the radicality of *gestures*—understood in the sense of forms that are also forms of thought—that Barré invented resonates with the practices of a generation that MAMCO has constantly studied and presented to the public.

Barré's relationship to a painting's construction through a system of rules is reminiscent of those laid down by the likes of Sol LeWitt and François Morellet in the second half of the 1960s, although Barré allowed himself the freedom to modify them according to the pictorial result. His understanding of the painting as part of a series and his relationship to the installation of his works as a determining factor in their perception could also evoke minimalist approaches or those linked to the crisis encountered by the "painting-object" in the 1970s. Barré's short "conceptual episode" in 1968–71 made explicit this fundamental questioning of the work's constituent parts, which he continually applied to all dimensions of his pictorial enterprise. But it also invites us to rediscover the beginnings of that enterprise in the preceding bodies of work and to reinterpret them in the light of this methodical investigation into what makes not only a painting, but also a *good* painting.

I am therefore particularly pleased that the Martin Barré retrospective—conceived in Geneva by Clément Dirié in collaboration with Michèle Gozland-Barré—can be presented in two versions that are sufficiently different to take into account the specificities of the institutions organizing the exhibition, MAMCO and the Centre Pompidou, but also to produce contrasting insights into this practice. I am indebted to the Centre Pompidou in Paris, to its president, Serge Lasvignes, the director of its Musée National d'Art Moderne, Bernard Blistène, and to Michel Gauthier, the curator in charge of the project in Paris, for offering us this opportunity for a union that is more than the sum of its parts and to which this book bears testimony.

Finally, I would like to warmly thank the Fondation Gandur pour l'Art and its president, Jean-Claude Gandur, for their generous support of this project.

**“FOR ME, NEITHER
THE *CONSTRUCTIVE*,
NOR THE *USEFUL*,
NOR THE *FUNCTIONAL*
ARE IN ANY WAY OPPOSED
TO THE *POETIC*,
TO THE *SENSORY*;
ON THE CONTRARY,
ONE *ENGENDERS*
THE OTHER.”**

Martin Barré, 1976

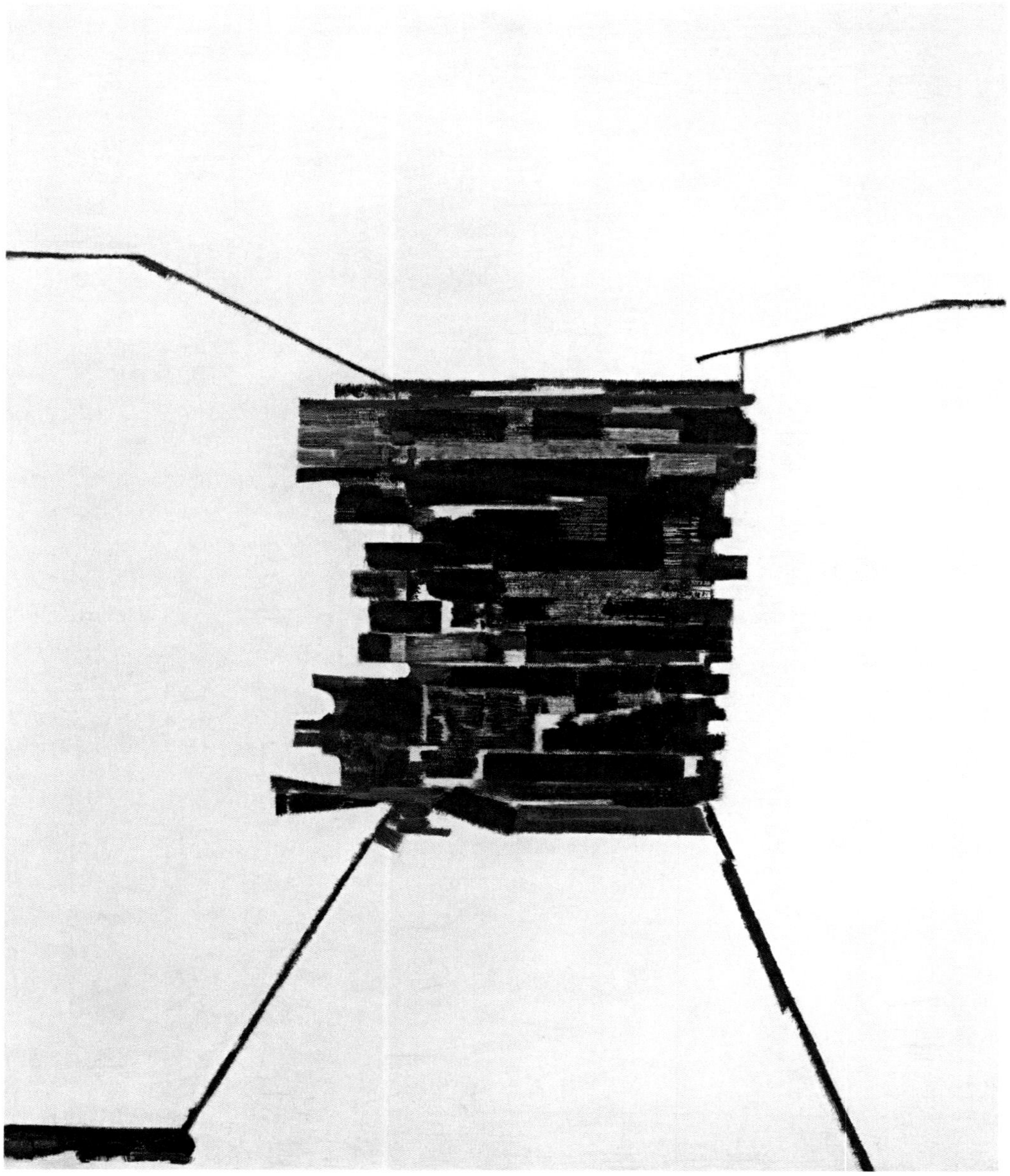

Peinture, 1955
73 × 60 cm

MARTIN BARRÉ: OF SPACE AND NEGATION

Michel Gauthier

Born in 1924, Martin Barré belongs to the generation of Simon Hantaï, Jesús Rafael Soto, François Morellet, and Ellsworth Kelly. He distinguished himself in mid-1950s Paris by avoiding the two great idioms that structured pictorial production at the time. His abstraction was neither lyrical nor geometric. From this moment forward, it harbored an extravagance, an eccentricity that we should be wary of diminishing. Right when the second École de Paris (School of Paris) was coming to an end, Barré's paintings were characterized by their dissimilarity—soon to be immeasurable—from the works of the abstract painters of the period. The lines he drew on the canvas during the 1960s, first directly from a tube and then with a spray can, confirmed the specificity of his poetics. As for the paintings he created from 1972 to 1977, consisting of superimposed, covered-up, repositioned, and hatched grids, both ruled and unruled, they were unequaled in the pictorial modernity of the time. And beneath their manifest geometric and chromatic reasoning, the last series, which spanned the 1980s and the beginning of the following decade up until his death in 1993, proved to be disconcerting objects of reflection and contemplation.

It was hence from 1954, and even more so from 1955, that Barré's painting took an unexpected turn: a reduction of the palette to three colors—red ochre, white, and Prussian blue; an assemblage of forms with rectilinear edges, whose armature sometimes tended to stand alone in a single line; the quantitative and qualitative importance of the ground, which was white or very light-colored. Michel Ragon, his friend since 1945, devoted a few lines to him in an entry in a small 1956 book, prefaced by the Belgian polygraph Hubert Juin.[1] In it, a connection was made between his painting and what was then known as the Jeune École de Paris (Young School of Paris) and which appeared to be a simple replica of the major trends of the second École de Paris. Barré seems like a real intruder in this selection. How, indeed, could the modestly sized *Peinture* (*Painting*, 73 × 60 cm) from 1955, displaying a more or less rectangular form in its center, which consists of an accumulation of marks of different colors possessing

1 Apart from Martin Barré, the book *Seize peintres de la Jeune École de Paris* (Paris: Le Musée de Poche, 1956) presented the work of Pierre Alechinsky, François Arnal, Gianni Bertini, Huguette Arthur Bertrand, Camille, Oscar Chelimsky, Corneille, Jacques Doucet, Roger-Edgar Gillet, Robert Lapoujade, John Levee, Maryan, Wilfrid Moser, Louis Nallard, and Kumi Sugaï.

a rather dark overall tonality, and which four lines connect, or should one instead say, lash to the left, right, and lower edges, be related to the aesthetics of the Jeune École de Paris? Most certainly, such a painting seems to veer toward Kazimir Malevich more than it does to gestural, informal, and lyrical outpourings.[2] With *57-60-B*[A] (1957), the form of 1955 is multiplied and crosses the whole canvas diagonally: the approximate quadrangles link to each other by varying their dimensions and by establishing a lively tension between, on the one hand, their respective formal individuations and, on the other, the line that they form together. Another pictorial heterodoxy is *57-100×100-A*,[B] one of the most striking paintings the artist produced during this period. One of these forms, predominantly brown —resulting from the aggregation of different marks, which had characterized Barré's painting since 1955— is obscured by a white square whose upper part merges with the ground of the canvas. In the same period, Hans Hofmann seemed to be moving toward a similar pictorial formula, with paintings such as *Yellow Burst* (1956), *Flowering Swamp*, *Golden Splendor*, and *Autumn Gold* (all 1957): thoroughly orthogonal quadrangles stand out against a very *painterly* ground. A world, not just an ocean, nevertheless separates *57-100×100-A*[B] from Hofmann's paintings. In the latter, the quadrangles, in number and color, are part of a composition seeking balance and not devoid of a representative weight. In Barré's canvas, the white square seems to redact the form that still links the artist's painting to the second École de Paris and, beyond it, to the heritage of cubism. Above all, the white square appears to signify a veritable tectonic uplift of the ground. The white of the ground seems to engulf the form, both by substituting itself for it and by threatening its very principle.

Such painting proved to be radically foreign to the French pictorial abstraction of the time—whether one thinks of the contemporary calligraphy of Jean Degottex, Pierre Soulages, Georges Mathieu, or Simon Hantaï— while it also heralded the 1959 and 1960 paintings with which Barré, no longer having to negotiate any kind of breaking away, would embark on such an unusual path. But what was the nature of this strangeness? What were the sources of the oeuvre that would develop over a little more than three decades?

THE SPACE RATHER THAN THE FORM

In 1959, Barré produced a few quite exceptional paintings, including *59-140×130-A*.[C] The work is, as Yve-Alain Bois[3] noted, one of the rare examples of a rectangular painting hung from one of its corners, echoing the diamond-shaped

A → p.30

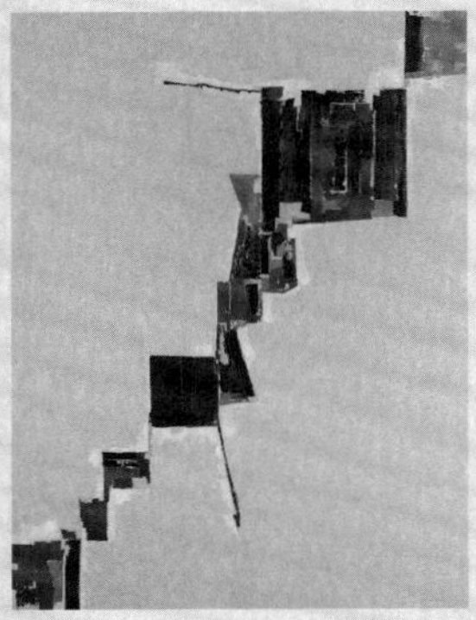

B → p.33

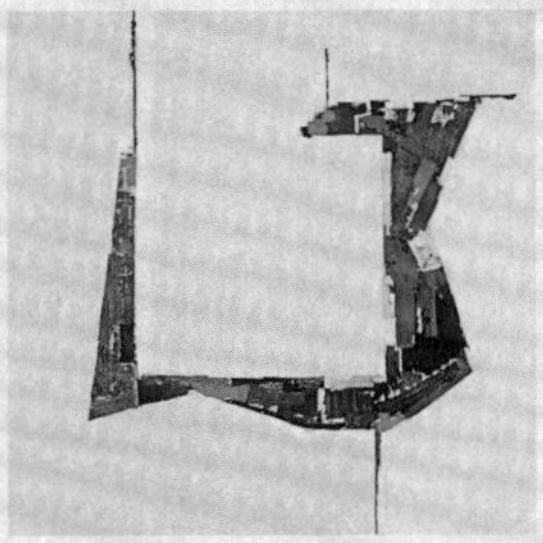

C → p.39

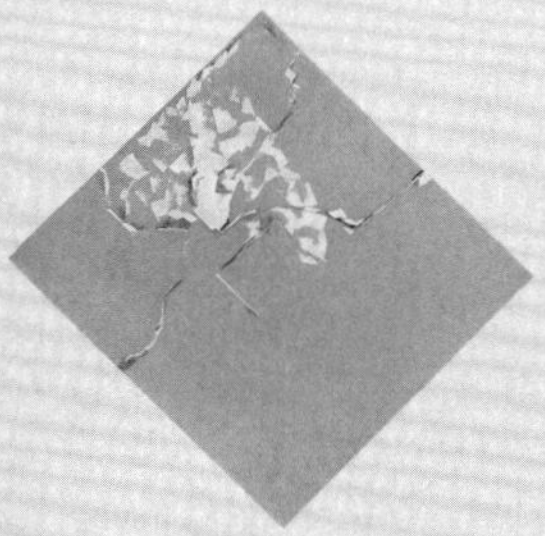

2 Other than in reproduction, Barré first saw paintings by Malevich in 1958 in Amsterdam, before visiting the retrospective at the Louisiana Museum (Humlebæk, Denmark) at the beginning of 1960.

3 Yve-Alain Bois, *Martin Barré* (Cologne, New York, and Paris: Galerie Daniel Buchholz, Andrew Kreps Gallery, Galerie Nathalie Obadia, and Thea Westreich/Ethan Wagner, 2008), 18.

D → p.37

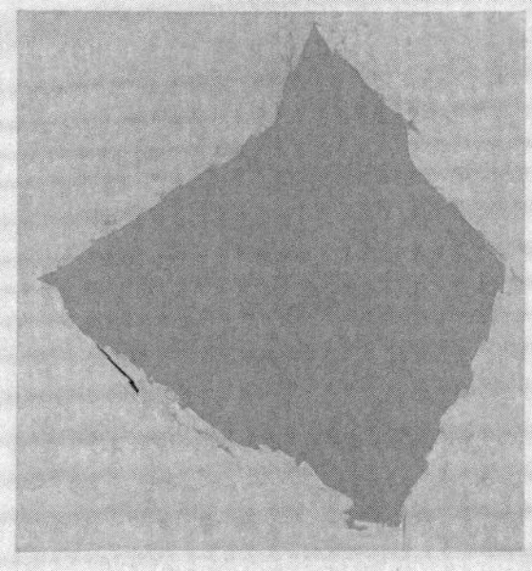

E → p.40

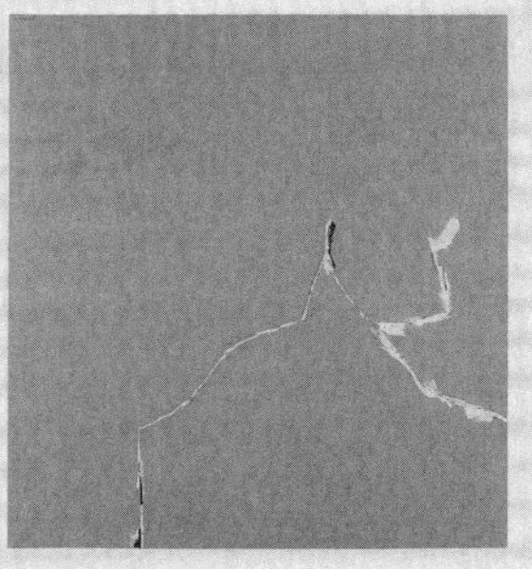

F → p.34

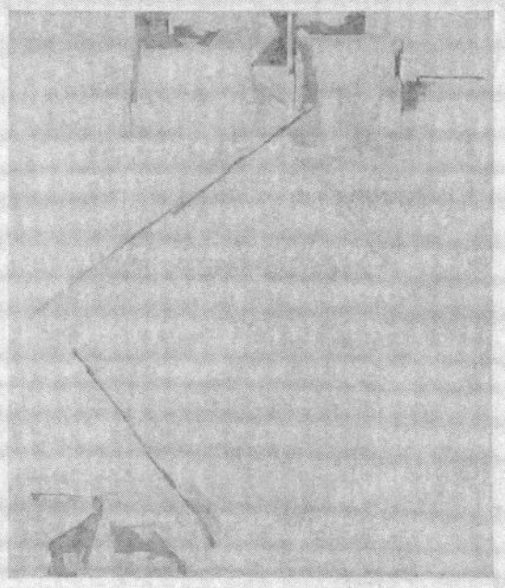

G → p.35

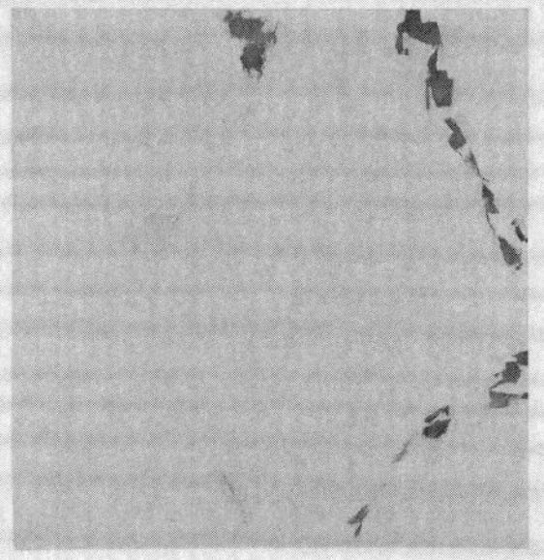

H → p.126

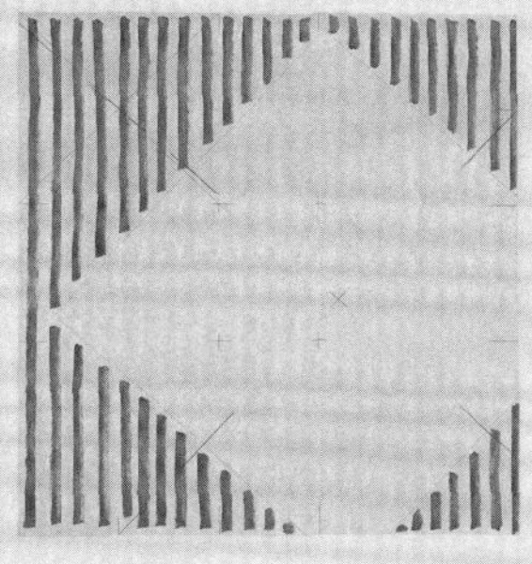

paintings by Piet Mondrian. A white form seems to have disintegrated within it—its armature having even lost its rectilinearity. It is the unpainted ground of unbleached canvas that takes on importance here. Two other paintings from the same year relate to this work: *59-120×110-C*[D] and *59-120×110-B*.[E]

With *59-120×110-C*,[D] a portion of unpainted canvas, vaguely diamond-shaped, fills the center of the painting, the four corners of which are painted white. This diamond, or at least this tilted quadrangle, displaying its emptiness in the center of the canvas, would reappear several times in the artist's productions: for example, with *59-116×97-A*,[F] *60-T-20*,[G] *75-76-A-157×145*[H] and in the "86-87" series.[→ pp.174–79] In *59-120×110-C*[D] we can see an inversion of the relationship between the figure and the ground, since it is the unpainted part of the canvas, self-evidently the ground, which acts as the figure. But isn't it more interesting to observe here the way space resists being filled up, or the gaping openness at the heart of the pictorial expanse? From this viewpoint, it is tempting to relate such a painting to the *Tagli* that Lucio Fontana had just started creating as part of the vast undertaking of the *Concetto spaziale*.[I → p.14] Fontana opened the pictorial space by incising the painted canvas. Barré, for his part, opened it by making the unpainted canvas active. *60-T-17*, with its wide indentation on a red-brown surface, and *60-T-23*, with its unsutured incision allowing the same red to be seen, justify even more readily the relationship with Fontana's *Tagli*.

59-120×110-B[E], another major work from 1959, again leaves a very large part of the canvas unpainted. A form does not even attempt to take shape. Having lost all rectitude, only the lines of the armatures, now without object, remain. White, punctuated here and there with black, these lines are marked by an irregular, unpredictable stroke, which no gesture, no expressiveness can explain. The two paintings *1944-N No. 1* and *1944-N No. 2*[J → p.14] (1944) by Clyfford Still show marks, made with a knife, which are relatively similar, but on a black ground and in bright colors—red, yellow, green—that weigh down the painting with an emotional charge not sought by Barré's canvas. Beyond the formal proximity with certain works by Still, and more profoundly, *59-120×110-B*,[E] like some other paintings of the transitional period, straddling 1959 and 1960, testifies to a strategy of breaking away from the then dominant abstraction which was not unrelated to that borrowed by other European painters, especially some in the ZERO movement,[4] during the same period.

A small book by Michel Ragon, with its beautiful Bachelardian title *Martin Barré et la poétique de l'espace* (*Martin Barré and the Poetics of Space*), reproduces

4
Like, for example, Hermann Goepfert and his *Weissbilder* of 1960.

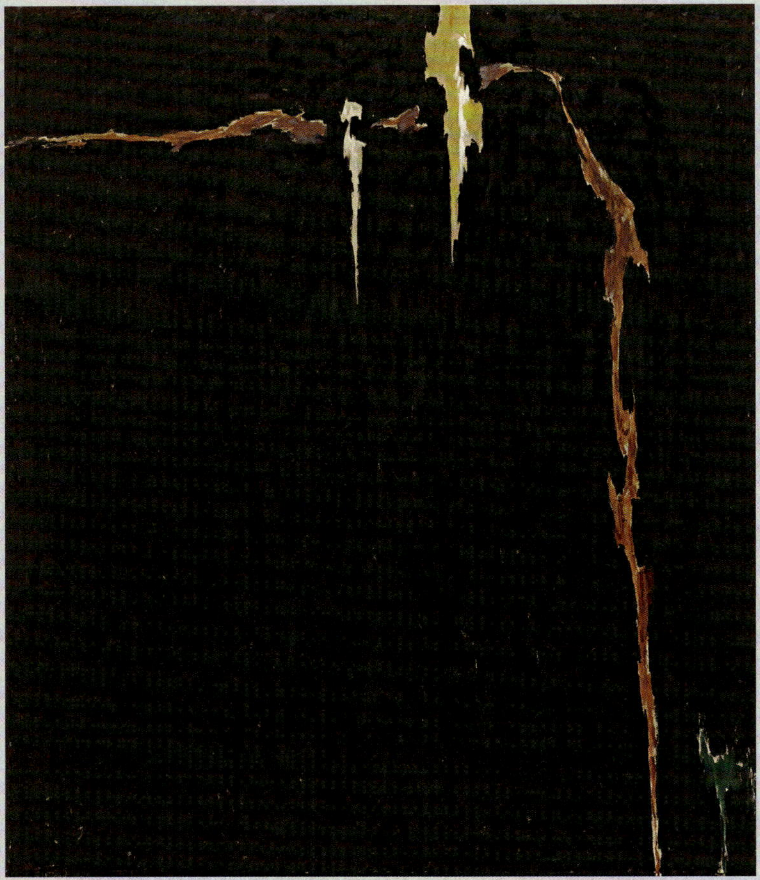

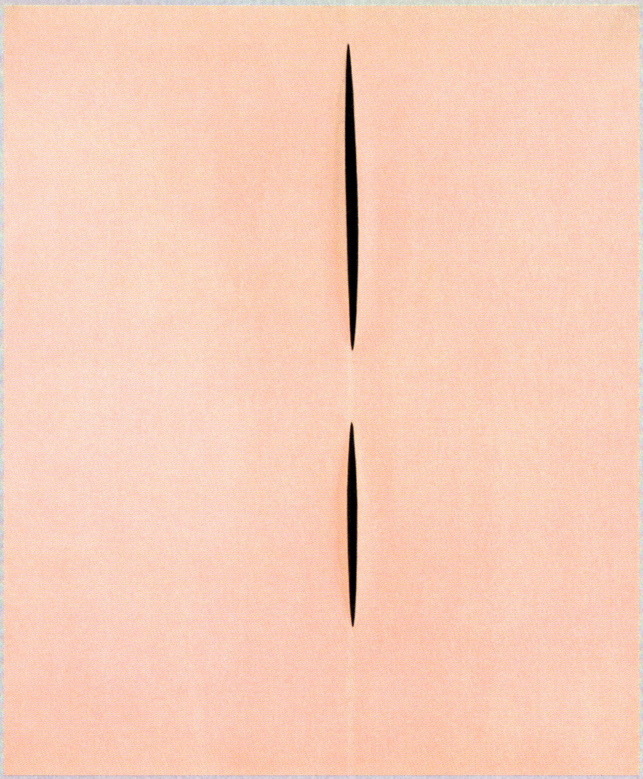

J ↑
Clyfford Still
1944-N No. 2, 1944
Oil on canvas, 264.5×221.4 cm
The Museum of Modern Art,
New York

I →
Lucio Fontana
Concetto spaziale,
Attese (T.104), 1958
Vinyl paint on canvas,
incisions, 125×100.5 cm
Musée National d'Art Moderne/
Centre Pompidou, Paris

O →→
Stefan Gierowski
XCVII, 1960
Oil on canvas, 135×100 cm
Stefan Gierowski Foundation,
Warsaw

an enlightening remark by the painter: "And in this monochromy which is already *space*—or expanse, which is an even better word for it—I *carelessly* introduce the forms. . . . Their existence is perilous because the space, that their intrusion causes, matters to me as much as they do."[5] Barré here reveals, as of 1960, one of the foundations of his art: the form is worth less for itself than as an engenderer of space. With *59-120×110-B*,[E] he came across a solution that meant he no longer had to recklessly introduce forms which would be endangered as soon as they found life on the canvas: the line.

From 1960 to 1967, from tube-painted to spray-painted canvases—the first of which date from 1963—Barré seems largely to have entrusted the fate of his oeuvre to the line. In the large polyptych *60-T-43*,[K] there is no single pictorial element that does not consist of a line. Admittedly, in the lower part of the right-hand central panel, a gray line turns back on itself in zigzags a few centimeters long to deliver a small doodle to our gaze; it is nonetheless a line. The lines can be long, crossing the entire pictorial field—the "lasso" line of *61-T-36*[L] runs about two meters; they can also be very short, as in some sprayed canvases (*65-H-L-113×86*,[M] *65-A-73×54*[N]), where they only appear on the canvas edges. In the pictorial creations of this period, it is perhaps only in Stefan Gierowski's work that the line plays a comparable role. A black line crosses the pictorial rectangle horizontally in *LXXX* (1959) and diagonally in *XCVI* (1960). Paintings such as *XCVII*[O] (1960)—a long oblique line on the left edge of the canvas—or *CI* (1961)—a short, thick line in the lower right-hand part of the canvas—are the most tempting to relate to Barré's oeuvre, and more particularly to the sprayed canvases.[6]

The line was certainly not absent from the pictorial aesthetics of the turn of the 1960s, and more particularly from informal painting which, in one or another of its variants, had been dominant for a decade. Thus, the line was, at that time, a major resource in Hans Hartung's oeuvre. Whether one thinks of *T55-28* (1955)—a black line swelling in its middle section obliquely crosses a celestial blue—or even more so of *P1961-31*, *P1961-35* (both from 1961), and *T1962-H28* (1962)—a single line crossing a large rectangle from top to bottom, which is given depth by the play of darkness in its center and the brightness at the sides, and, by the same token, is imbued with a representative role. However, Barré's line and the line of gestural or informal painting differ significantly. Bois has characterized this difference: if the gesturality of informal painting and lyrical abstraction is *iconic*, insofar as the pictorial marks it produces are given as a "pure subjective seismograph,"[7] in other words as a representation, the lines of Barré's paintings reveal their production process and can therefore

5

Michel Ragon, *Martin Barré et la poétique de l'espace / Martin Barré and the Poetics of Space* (Paris: Galerie Arnaud, 1960), 75.

K → pp. 48–49

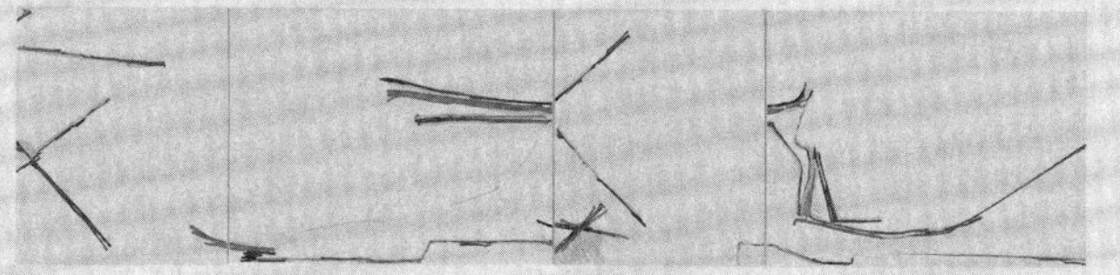

L → p. 55

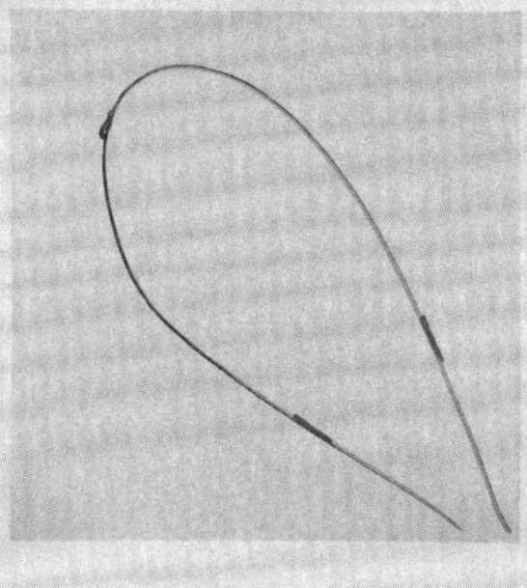

M → p. 85

N → p. 87

6

On these paintings by the Polish artist, I take the liberty of referring to my study "Zero-Dynamo-Cosmos," in Michel Gauthier (ed.), *Deep Impact: Stefan Gierowski and European Avant-Gardes in the 60s*, exh. cat. (Warsaw: Stefan Gierowski Foundation, 2019), 9–83.

7

Bois, *Martin Barré*, 20.

be declared *indexical*.[8] Referring to the paintings of 1960 and 1961, Bois defined the indexical content of the line as follows: “The line is to be read as a unidimensional, unambiguous movement in space (it started here, ended there) and as a temporal unfolding. The thickness of the line is an indicator of speed, either that of the paint coming out of the tube—submitted to various degrees of pressure—or that of the artist’s movement (both instances coincide when the gesture stops: the artist’s movement ends when the tube is empty).”[9] In the same way, the mossy aspect of the lines drawn with spray paint indicate the gesture and the instrument from which they proceed. At the same moment, Morris Louis’s *Unfurled* paintings (1960–61), for example, also participated in this indexical revolution: the thick, oblique lines that fill the edges of the canvas are immediately identified as drips and thus refer to the manner in which they were produced. Although this mutation of pictorial gesturality, this indexical turn could also be detected in the work of certain gestural painters during the period (Hartung and Degottex in particular), in Barré’s painting it fell to the line to embrace it with unparalleled radicality.

However, the line in Barré’s work cannot be reduced to its indexical dimension alone. Its effectiveness is not only due to the latter. The line does not travel through space just to indicate the gesture that produced it. Or should it be said more correctly that the line’s indexical value —the designation of movement made by the producing instrument—reinforces the dynamism inherent to the line. This is indeed a mark whose singularity is not to fill this or that portion of the pictorial field, but to transform it into space, into expanse, as a result of the trajectory that it draws therein. A painting like *60-T-53* [P] even bears witness to a dream of reducing painting to the pure tracing of the line: this vertical painting is twelve centimeters wide, the dimension of the widest twist described by the line. Scarcely five paintings—*Untitled (Number 1 to 5)*—from 1950, in which Barnett Newman tended to confuse the *zip* and the canvas (the widest is fifteen centimeters, the narrowest nine centimeters), can be mentioned as a precedent.

But if there was one line in Barré’s painting that definitely intended to make itself the trajectory, suggest movement, and indicate a meaning, it is that of the “Flèches” (“Arrows”), a series begun in 1963 and resumed in 1967, this time using a stencil larger than the canvas so that the artist no longer controlled the exact placing of the arrow. → p. 82, pp. 94–96 Hence, indifferent to its position in the pictorial field, the arrow asserted itself even more as a simple sign of movement in space.

8

While the icon signifies because of its resemblance to its referent, the indexical signifies because of its relationship of material contiguity with its referent. Hence, the breaks or interlacings of a line can resemble the movements that agitate the artist’s psyche. By being more or less thick, by mobilizing more or less pictorial matter, a line, as in Martin Barré’s work, refers to the actual instrument of its production.

9

Bois, *Martin Barré*, 21.

P → p. 52

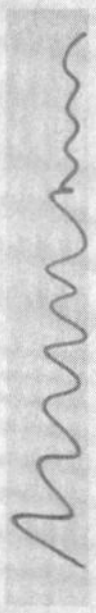

The line replaced the forms that Barré said he carelessly introduced into his paintings, insofar as space interested him just as much, if not more, than they did. Although, more often than not, the line did not close in on itself, this was in a sense less to prohibit the birth of a form than to preclude the space being transformed into a ground. Put another way, it was less a matter of preventing the intrinsically illusionist hierarchization of the pictorial field—a form detaching itself from a ground—than it was a reduction in the spatiality of the pictorial field: the form, by constituting itself, automatically deprives space of a part of itself.

"At the end of the 1950s, the artist had planned to exhibit a continuous line running around the walls of a gallery."[10] Bois noted that this unfinished project was very close, timewise, to Yves Klein's exhibition nicknamed *Le Vide* in 1958.[11] The line that would have gone round the Galerie Arnaud's walls was also contemporary with the series of *Linee* (Lines) undertaken by Piero Manzoni in 1959. Although Barré could not fulfil his desire to forsake the traditional painting-format with the long line that the gallery owner rejected, it was manifested in such works as *60-T-45*[Q] (1960): the same line runs between four paintings that the artist then spaced apart from each other.[12] We find the line jumping from canvas to canvas in two 1962 polyptychs (*62-4*, *62-5* → p. 74), as well as in two astonishing diptychs from 1961 (*61-T-15*,[R] *61-T-16*[S]) where the line seems to keep the two elements against each other and thus acts as an agent of an enlargement of the pictorial field. With works like these, it is clear that the line is more of an enabler of space than the vector of an indexical activity.

But, of course, Barré's line reveals its spatial efficacity the most in the way it creates the beyond-the-frame of the painting. The lines, especially those executed with spray paint, often seem to come from outside the painting or to exit from it. Of the ten arrows, mostly dextro-ascending, in *63-F-A*,[T] some originate outside the canvas, two begin and end within the boundaries of the painting, and the tip of one is beyond the frame. The canvas is perceived all the more as a space, or rather as a fragment of space, as it is the site of a movement that, on the one hand, is indifferent to its orthogonality and, on the other, exceeds its surface, both on the left and the right. In other sprayed paintings, the line is visible only on the edge of the canvas and for a few small centimeters (*65-H-L-113×86*,[M] *65-A-73×54*[N]): this is another way of powerfully suggesting the existence of the beyond-the-frame. Similar paintings attest to the passion for the edge that runs through all of Barré's oeuvre—from the tube-painted lines of *60-T-41*, *60-T-42*, and *60-T-46*, which remain far from the center,

10
Jean Clay, "La peinture en séton," in Suzanne Pagé et al., *Martin Barré*, exh. cat. (Paris: ARC – Musée d'Art Moderne de la Ville de Paris, 1979), 11.

11
Bois, *Martin Barré*, 22.

12
On this masterpiece, see Jean-Pierre Criqui's analysis, "Painting (Split) into Four," in the present publication, pp. 69–76.

Q → pp. 44–45

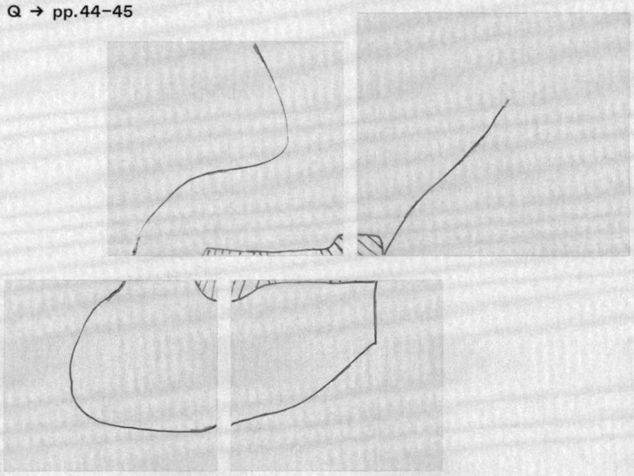

R → p. 56

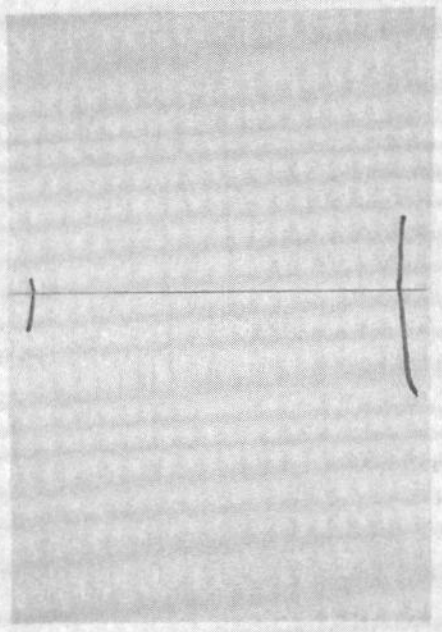

S → p. 57

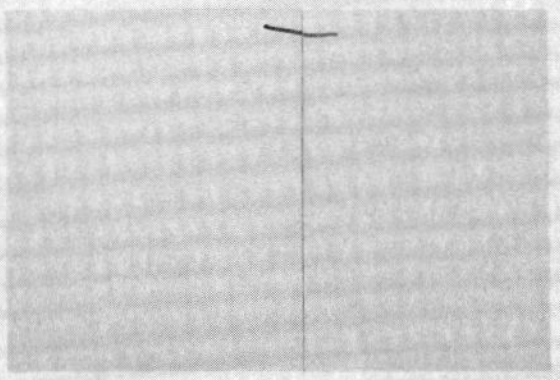

T → p. 82

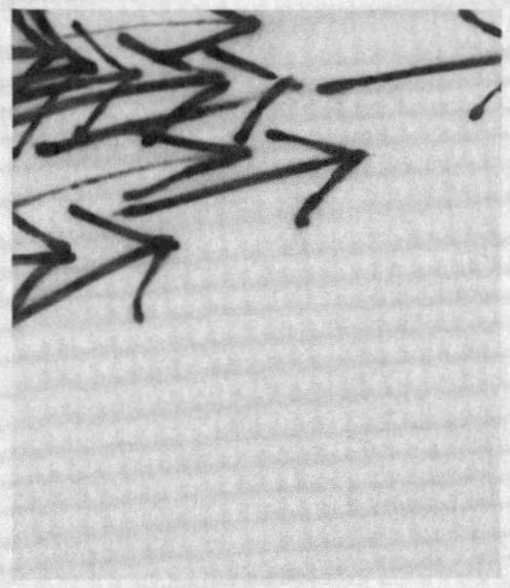

U → p.105

to the final "92A" and "92B" series,[→ pp.194–200] whose figures are firmly anchored to the upper and lower edges of the canvas, as well as a number of sprayed paintings and certain paintings from the 1970s, including the extreme *72-73-D-130×120*.[U] A way of not filling the space, while confronting it with the reality of its limits.

Extending to the edges of the canvas, the grids that structure the space of the paintings from the 1970s denote a space larger than the painting, whose orientation they moreover do not respect. In Piet Mondrian's work the possibility of expanding the grid outside the limits of the painting was understood as the declaration of the disappearance of painting, destined to take over as décor into the spaces of life. There is nothing of the sort in Barré's work. The centrifugal tropism of the grid does not participate in the modernist utopia of an art that questions the border which separates it from life. Like the trajectory described by the line, its function is to activate space.

The space surrounding the painting is not only the beyond-the-frame where lines and grids continue virtually; it is also the very real surface where the paintings are hung. As early as 1960, at the Galerie Arnaud, perhaps because he was unable to draw his long line on the walls, Barré played with the respective heights at which the different paintings were hung on the same wall.[B → p.63] Forgetting the supposed neutrality of hanging, which places the center of the painting at eye level, the artist spatialized his painting. He would later return to this question to explore new ways of spatializing it. Hence, at the Galerie Ricke in Cologne in 1979,[→ p.223] he hung the "79" series paintings in such a way that the turquoise-green strip bordering one or more sides of one painting was aligned, horizontally or vertically, with the strip of another painting, which would lead to peculiarities, with paintings placed very low or very high. During the 1980s and until his last exhibition in 1993 Barré again played with the hanging height of his works. His spatialist[13] conception of painting necessarily had to take into account this space that is the hanging wall.

When Barré's painting didn't put at stake, in one way or another, the space beyond itself, it strove to punctuate, to map out its own with a whole system of dashes and other marks, as can be seen in many works from the 1970s and, even more clearly, in the series "79," "80A," and "80B," "82-84," and "84-85." While these marks participated in the structural game that we will return to later, they also served to conjure the space of the painting by demonstrating the extent of it.[14]

13
On the understanding that it is appropriate here not to lend the term the exact meaning it was accorded in the first two spatialist manifestos (of 1947 and 1948) accompanying the movement created around Lucio Fontana.

14
If one had to compare these paintings with other works of the same period, it would perhaps be with those by the British artist Alan Uglow: they too make painting a marking of space more than a production of form.

V → p.195

Line-trajectory, the suggestion of the beyond-the-frame, marking out the field: these are some of the main ways in which Barré made his painting a revealer of space. But what, at first glance, makes the spatial dimension of such painting palpable is undoubtedly the importance of the void. From *57-100×100-A*[B] to *92B-124×128-D*[V] —three quadrangles aligned at the top of the canvas, leaving most of it vacant—Barré's painting was one of those with the lowest margin of occupancy of the surface by forms. Klein's example was decisive for Barré, not only because it contributed to freeing him from the tyranny of form, but also undoubtedly because it prevented him from embarking on the adventure of the monochrome. A surface uniformly covered with the same color is a full space, not an empty one. With canonical monochrome, the pictorial field is saturated. The feeling of emptiness can only come from the minimum space occupancy. The monochromes of spatialist painters such as Otto Piene and Francesco Lo Savio were not really monochromes. It is precisely on this account that their emptiness is spatializing. Barré's painting, perhaps more than any other, makes the space of the void palpable.

THE NEGATIVE

Although the void in Barré's painting is indicative of a spatialist aspiration, it also signals the powerful hold of the negative in his poetics. The fundamental extravagance of his painting is to a large extent due to the way in which negativity asserts itself as one of the main avenues of creation. It has been said that Barré's line is reluctant to close in on itself so as not to give birth to a form. There is, however, one line that two sprayed canvases —*63-0*[W] and *65-S-8*—chose to loop. And it was to draw a zero that the painter broke his rule. Between Simon Hantaï's *Peinture* (1957) loop, in which the stroke is imbued with the alternately positive and negative[15] moods of the informal, and the two hundred identical paintings created by Olivier Mosset from 1966 onwards, which display the mechanical figure with a Warholian indifference, Barré's zero seems to emblematize the awareness of a fundamental intercourse with the negative.

W → p.80

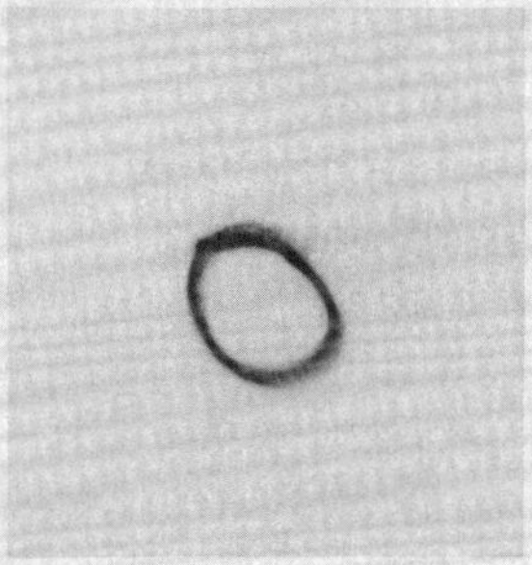

15 Another work painted by Simon Hantaï in the same year shows the + sign.

However, emptiness is not the only manifestation of negativity at work. It is also indicated by the two procedures of overlaying and crossing-out. As we have seen, the white square that occurs in the center of *57-100×100-A*[B] conceals a pre-existing form, as if the painter's work consisted in partially undoing what he had just done. From 1956 to 1960, which is to say until the moment when, for the next seven years, the line imposed itself as the almost unique element of Barré's language, the permanent feature in his painting was the partial overlaying of the "carelessly" introduced forms, their whitening. Insofar as, here, the blacking-out is done in white, overlaying is also one of the modalities of clearing the space. But effacing, as practiced by Barré, always let some of the effaced form appear. In this, it differed markedly from the *Übermalung* practiced by Arnulf Rainer during the same period: the almost complete overlaying, in black or red, of an earlier version of the painting. In Barré's work, a dialectical relationship was established between what effaced and what was effaced. It is like Gerhard Richter's first opus, *Tisch* (1962), in which the reproduced image of a table was smeared by the painter but remains identifiable. And when the tube or spray paint would trace only lines on Barré's canvases and the tool of negation became the crossing-out, the relationship between the pictorial mark and its deletion drew even closer. This is demonstrated by *61-T-2*[X]: while the rest of the canvas is empty, on the upper edge, two red lines that a brown broken line erases, unless it is the other way around. The "spray" *65-H-L-78×74*[Y] is a close relative. The erasure can sometimes reach a very high degree of sophistication, as in *62-F*,[Z] a peak of pictorial "folly," where lines, smudges, and strikethroughs combine into a sumptuous scribble wherein the distinctions between a mark and its cancellation become blurred. In front of such paintings, one is reminded of Walter Benjamin's definition of romantic irony: "that destruction of form that makes every work into the work absolutely speaking."[16] *60-T-31*[α]: a white canvas whose upper left corner is filled by an inextricable skein of black lines that seem to have no other ambition than to strike through those previously drawn. A central position would almost have conferred a fully fledged status of form to this tangle. But, placed in its corner, the latter can only be a doodle.[17] Such a painting twice destroys the form: by the vacant space of most of its surface and by the doodle that fills one of its corners. But, through the visual tension it sets up between these two attributes of negativity—the doodle in a corner, as though straddling the edges of the canvas, makes the void active, not a ground—this double destruction of form generates a formal event in the full sense of the word.

When Barré returned to painting in 1972, after a gap of four years devoted to photo-conceptualism, the reductionist vein of his painting was reversed. As Bois wrote about the five series[18] that emerged over the next five years: "The huge reduction resulting from indexical procedures is suddenly replaced by an overflow ... that ... forces [the] beholder to admit that even though all the pieces of evidence are readily at hand, he or she will

X → p. 52

Y → p. 84

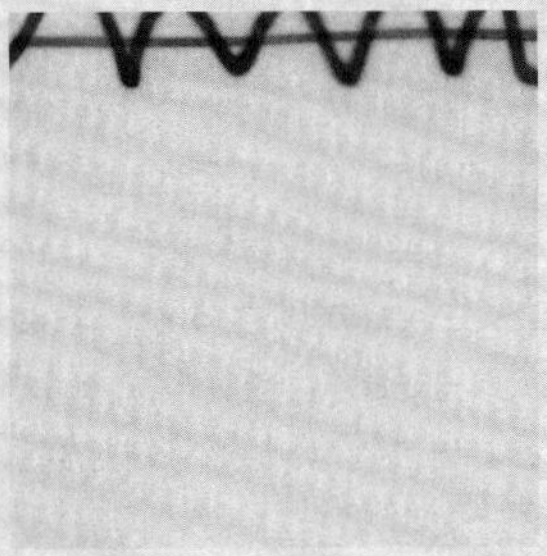

Z → p. 60

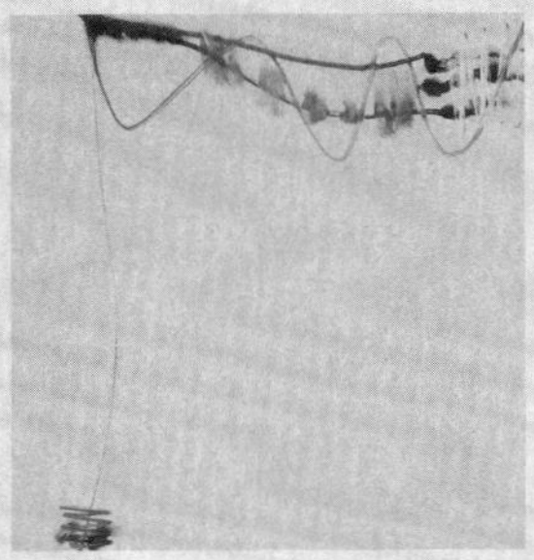

α → p. 51

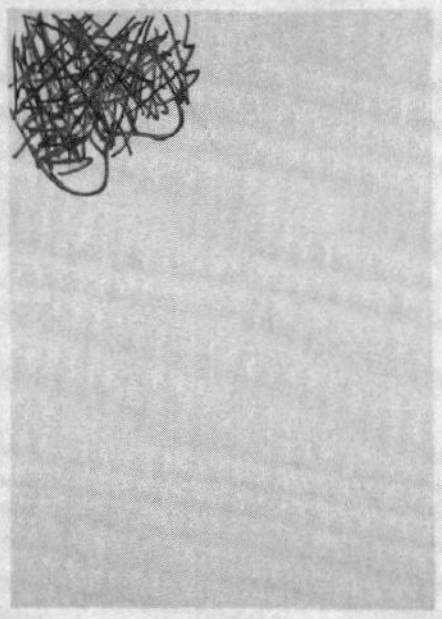

16
Walter Benjamin, "Der Begriff der Kunstkritik in der deutschen Romantik" (thesis defended in 1919), as noted in Philippe Lacoue-Labarthe and Jean-Luc Nancy, *The Literary Absolute: The Theory of Literature in German Romanticism* [1978] (Albany: State University of New York Press, 1988), 78.

17
One could practically mention Cy Twombly's oeuvre alone as a precedent for such a pictorial assumption of doodling and scribbling, and it was not until the second half of the 1980s and some of Jonathan Lasker's paintings that another one was found.

18
On these series from the 1970s, see the text by Molly Warnock, "Martin Barré Returns to Painting, 1972–1977," in this volume, pp. 133–39.

never crack the code, will always be lost somewhere in the labyrinth of painting."[19] The negative now worked differently, no longer by default but through excess. The painter's method in these five series was always the same. After being colored, a ground is overlaid with several off-white layers, upon which three operations are carried out in this order: 1. the oblique tracing of a grid fragment —the structure is shown; 2. hatching (or marking by some other means) of all or some of the squares[20]—a space is marked out and not filled by a form; 3. the addition of a more or less white veil (in *73-74-E-123×114*,[β] the "juice" used is rather brown)—a subtle dialectic of overlapping and transparency, of overshadowing and revelation takes place. And the sequence can be repeated several times, with the grid changing position or not, the hatching filling other squares or the same ones, and in this case with the same or different orientation, before a new veil is overlaid.[21] When the process is interrupted, either unobscured hatching may cover most of the canvas, as in *75-76-D-157×145*,[γ] or it is overlaid by a white veil, as in *75-76-C-157×145*.[δ] But in most cases, local, indeed very local hatching coexists with veiled areas creating a tension between the system's multiple possibilities, one of whose most beautiful and disconcerting examples is offered by *76-77-B-170×160*[ε]: a few small hatchings on part of the edge of two squares, the major portion of the field revealing a bluish, foliated plane, whose different strata are superimposed in dissonant harmonies. Without necessarily going into the procedural details of each of these series and paintings, it is possible to understand that Barré is here pursuing his ironic activity, but by other means. Instead of erasing, he veils; instead of doodling, he piles up grids and hatching. A new dimension is added, however. A system exposes itself by means of profuse lines, continuous or dotted, and dashes, and through the transparency of the accumulated veils.[22] But, in Barré's work, despite its revelation, the system thwarts any effect of control. The work is serial, not to reveal the power of the system but to accentuate its excessiveness. Here is a style of painting which stages the impossible completion of the program opened by the system that painting has given itself. Such "reflexive awareness of the incompleteness of the work"[23] is one of the directions that romantic irony takes.

Barré's painting would never wager to such an extent on excess to undermine structure, but irony nevertheless remains, as in the "84-85" series, which questions the place and color of the figures and, more fundamentally, the capacity of a system to provide an unimpeachable response. The works in the series show right-angled triangles on the one hand and dashes on the other. The position

19 Bois, *Martin Barré*, 40.

20 Hatching as a sign of marking space and not as a means of producing a form also appears in some of Giorgio Griffa's contemporary works.

21 One can imagine what Bernard Piffaretti's painting (the artist reiterates, on one side of the canvas, the process that gave rise to the forms visible on the other side) owes to these Barré series, which also show the reiteration of the process.

22 In 1971 and 1972, Claudio Verna, a major player in the Pittura Analitica movement, produced a series of paintings in which the systematicity, if not the system, was also displayed.

23 Laurent Van Eynde, *Introduction au romantisme d'Iéna: Friedrich Schlegel et l'Athenäum* (Brussels: Ousia, 1997), 172.

β → p. 112

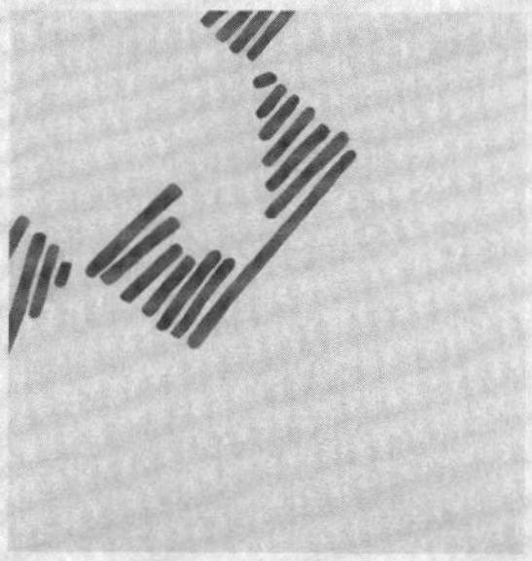

γ → p. 125

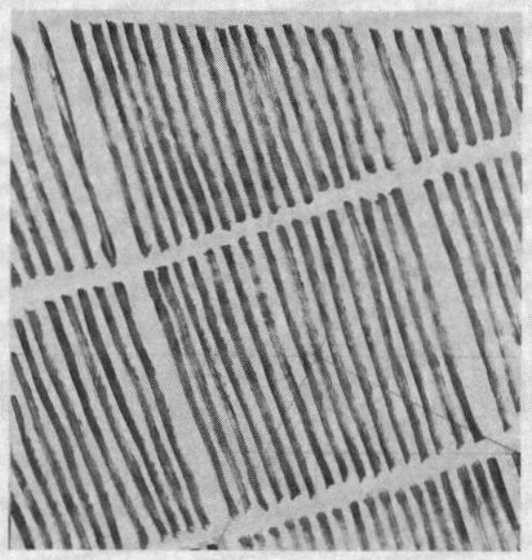

δ → p. 124

ε → p. 130

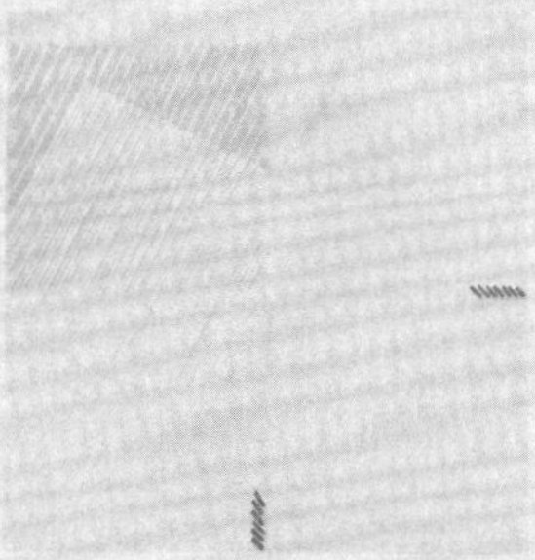

of the dashes and triangles, at least one side of which is always parallel to an edge of the canvas, is determined by the dimensions of the figure's three sides. Dashes and triangles are often aligned with each other. But not obligatorily. These dashes, which it would be tempting to see as marks indicating the placement of the triangles, are in fact separate from them. With regard to color, the rule is as follows: when two sides of a triangle are parallel to the edges of the canvas, its color is red or green; when only one of its sides is parallel to one side of the canvas, it is yellow. As can be imagined, the possibilities for placing figures and allocating colors are vast. Barré actualized only a few of them. The very power of the system generates arbitrariness in its utilization. We then better understand the reason for the dashes: they are like the emblems of a futile systematicity. The fact that, among the few actualizations of the possibilities offered by combinatorics, Barré chose one, for *84-85-144×132-A*,[ζ] which irresistibly calls to mind an origami hen,[24] only illustrates and adds spice to the series' fundamental irony.

Perhaps even beauty should, in Barré's work, be attributed to negativity, as the late series ("87-89," "89-90," "90-91," "91," "91-92," "92A," and "92B") demonstrate.[25] Different rules determine the relationships between figures, places, and colors. Yet the deciphering or impenetrability of the rules in question seem of little importance in the experience of the work. The presence in itself of the "color-figure," on a ground whose slight hue arrests the gaze, relativizes the calculation from which it results. In the same way that, in the series from the 1970s, Barré had to cover and conceal under several layers of white the colored ground he had nevertheless painted, the color test supposes the prior imposition and then the vacancy of the rule. Thus, insofar as it is the fruit not of a completeness but of a defect in the system, beauty has in Barré's work something of a vanitas. This makes it all the more disturbing.

·

The way in which Barré's painting articulates a spatialist aspiration and negativity at work gives it a place that cannot be confused with the manifestation of a pictorial materialism or an essentialist positivity. The names of Malevich and Klein, evoked very early on by the artist, are particularly enlightening in this respect. Space (and the time it takes to travel through it) rather than form, immediately present to itself. Negation and its agents (voiding, erasure, incompleteness) rather than the affirmative. This hardly corresponds to the idea of painting preoccupied with the epiphany of its elementary constituents.

ζ → p. 172

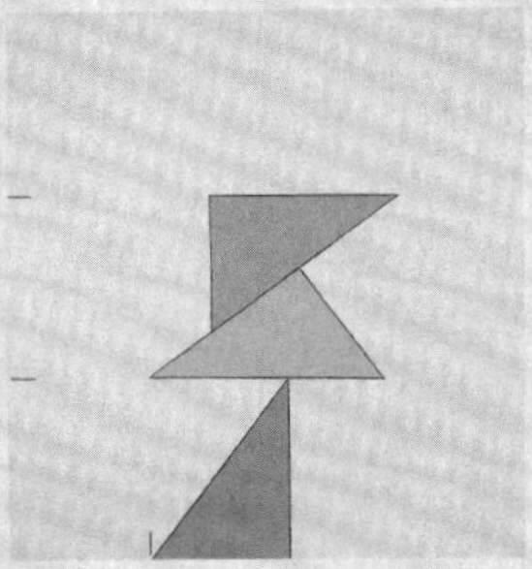

24 In 1987, Olivier Mosset painted several paintings very explicitly reproducing origami hens.

25 See, in this volume, the text by Clément Dirié about the 1980–90 series, "Audacity, Confidence, and Mayhem," pp. 201–9.

26

Paul Cézanne, letter to Émile Bernard, May 26, 1904, in *Correspondance* (Paris: Grasset, Les Cahiers Rouges coll., 1978), 394.

In Barré's work, painting's meditation on itself develops not in the illusion of a processual, formal, or perceptive parousia, but in the mode of a transcendental irony. "I owe you the truth in painting, and I will tell it to you,"[26] Paul Cézanne wrote. Barré shows us that painting is the space where the very possibility of its truth is defeated.

1954
1960

“IT WAS IN THE MIDDLE OF THE 1950s THAT I REALLY STARTED BEING ACTIVE. THE FIRST CANVASES FROM THOSE YEARS WERE UNLIKE BOTH GEOMETRIC ABSTRACTION AND LYRICAL ABSTRACTION; I WAS TRYING TO POSITION MYSELF, LET’S SAY, *ELSEWHERE*.”

Martin Barré, 1985

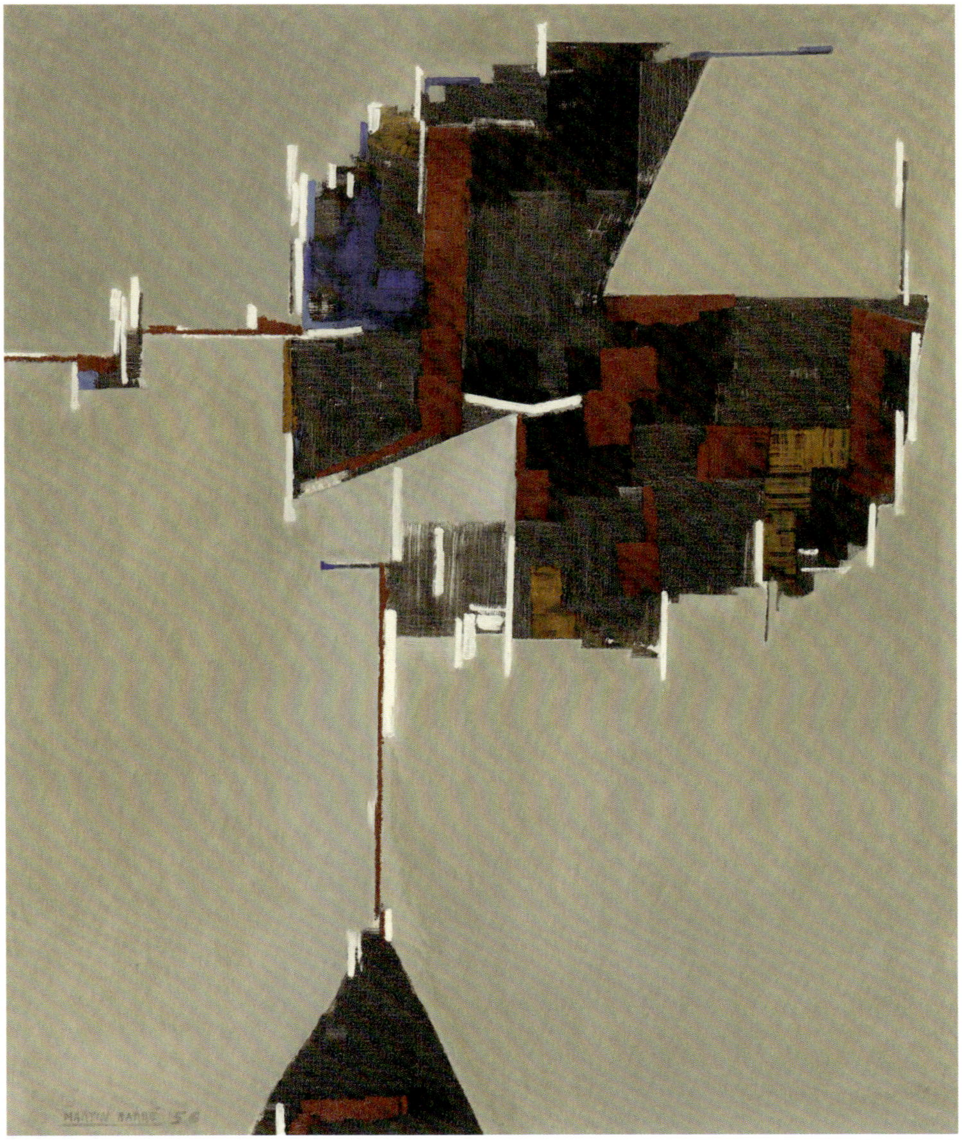

56-40-F, 1956
100 × 81 cm

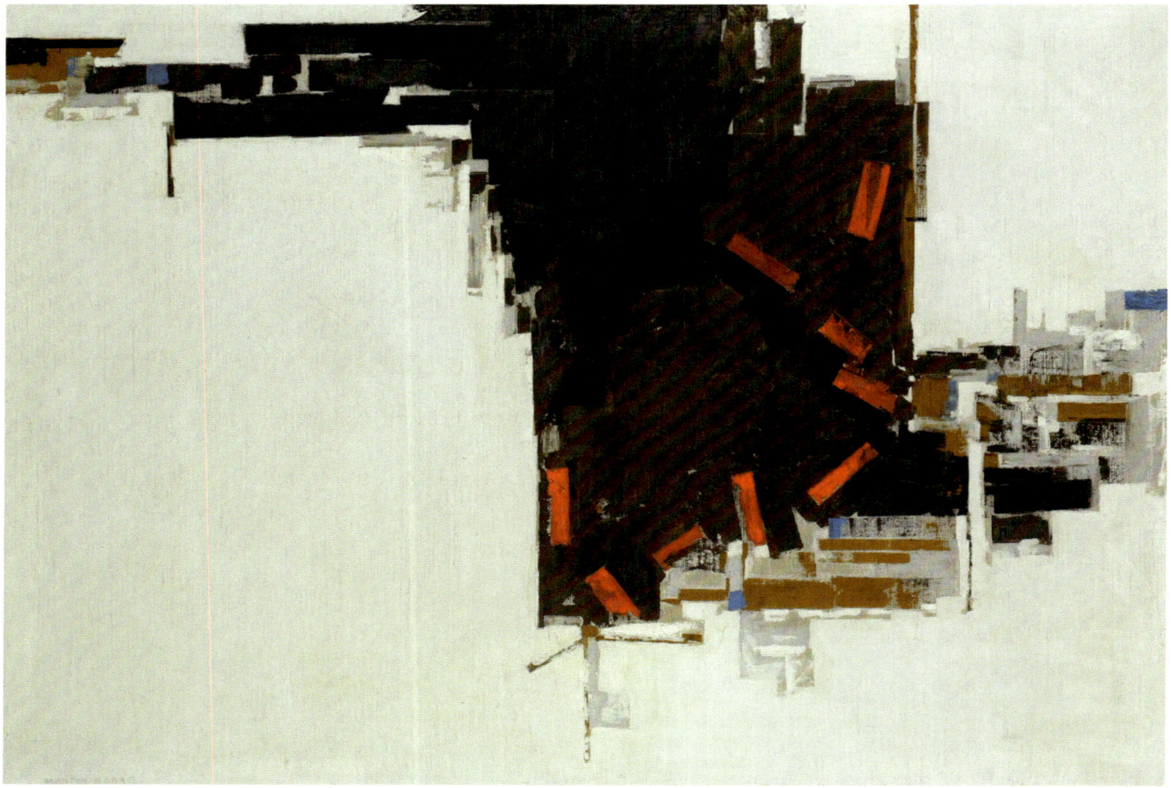

Grenam, 1957
81×116 cm

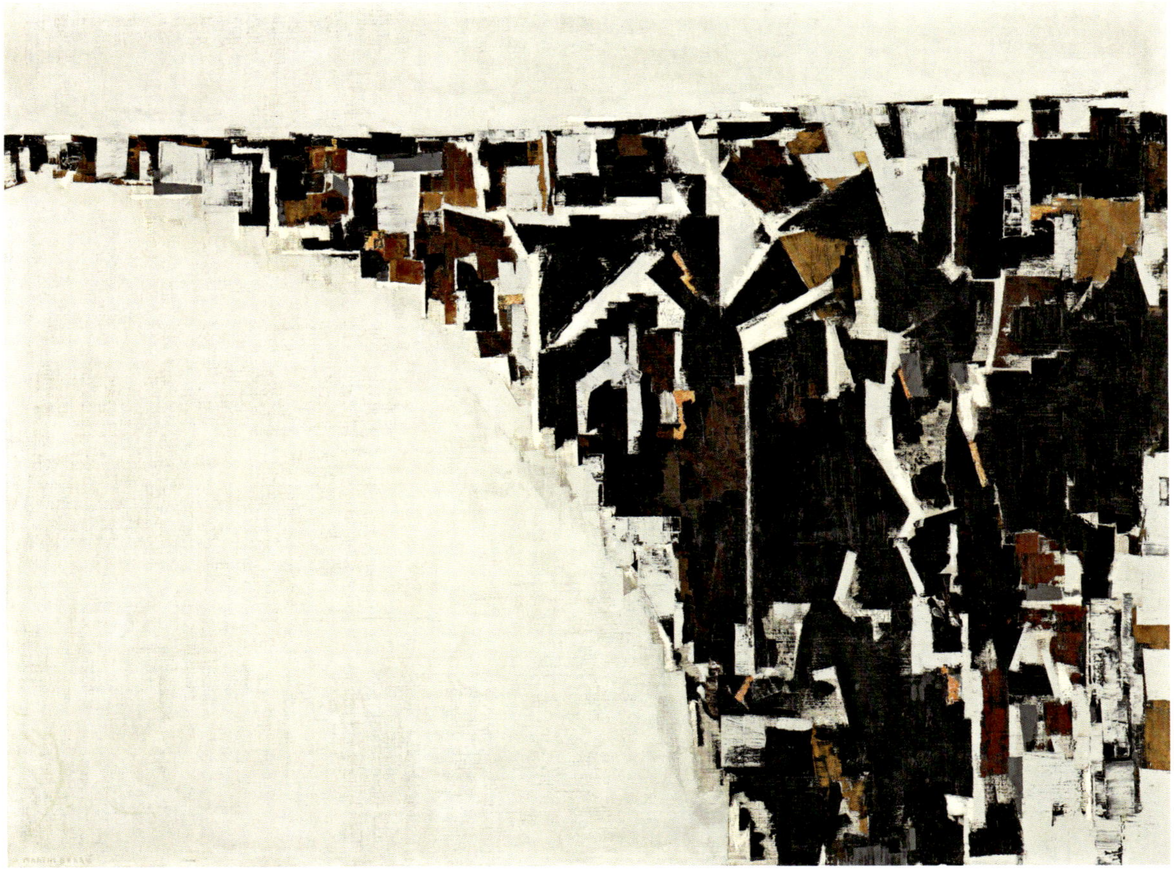

57-50-B, 1957
89 × 116 cm

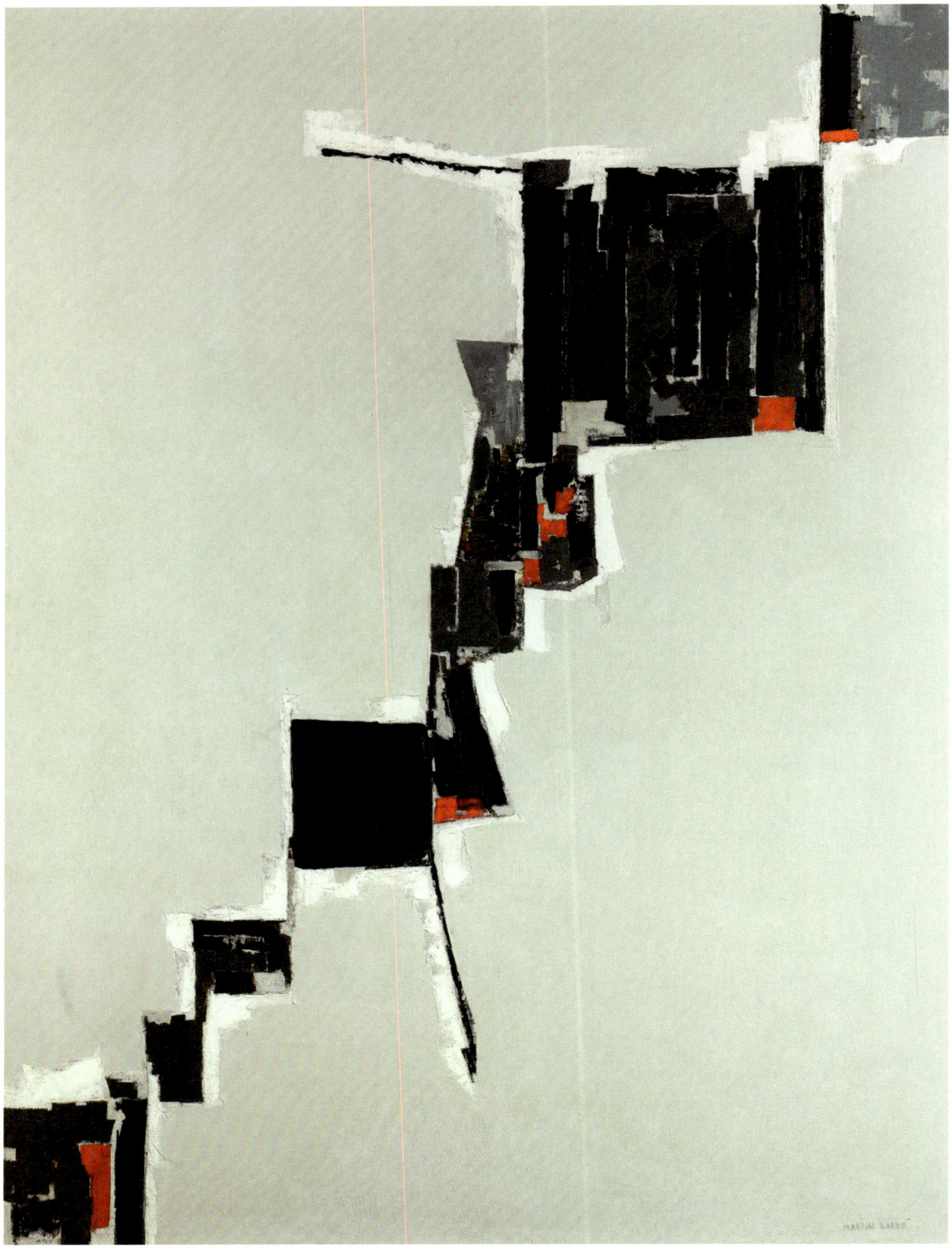

57-60-B, 1957
130 × 97 cm

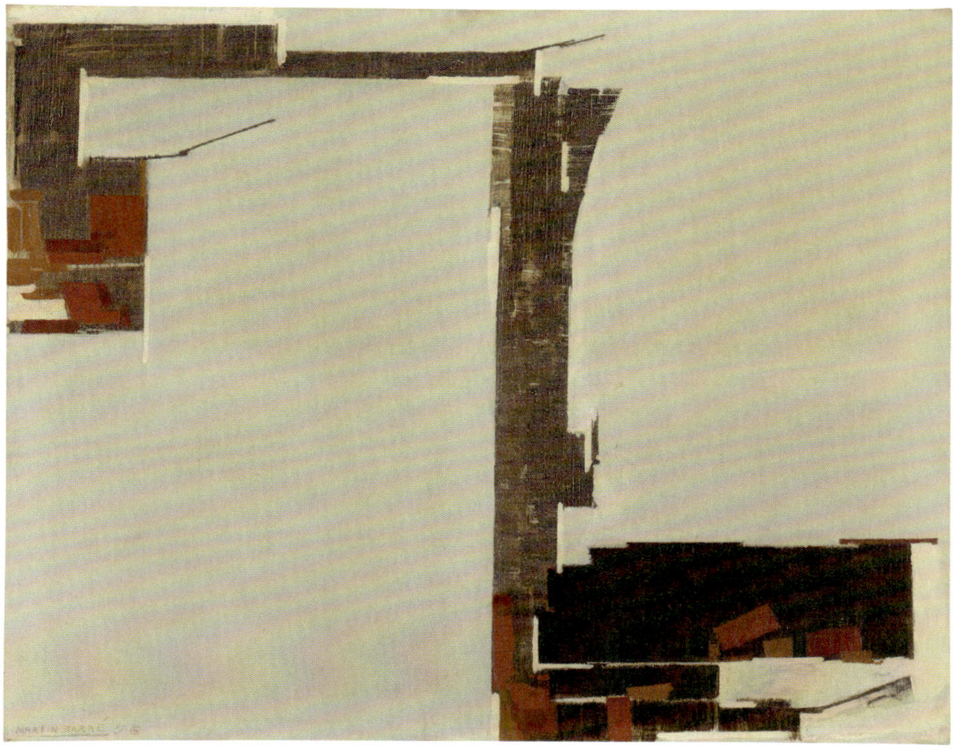

Peinture, 1956
65 × 81 cm

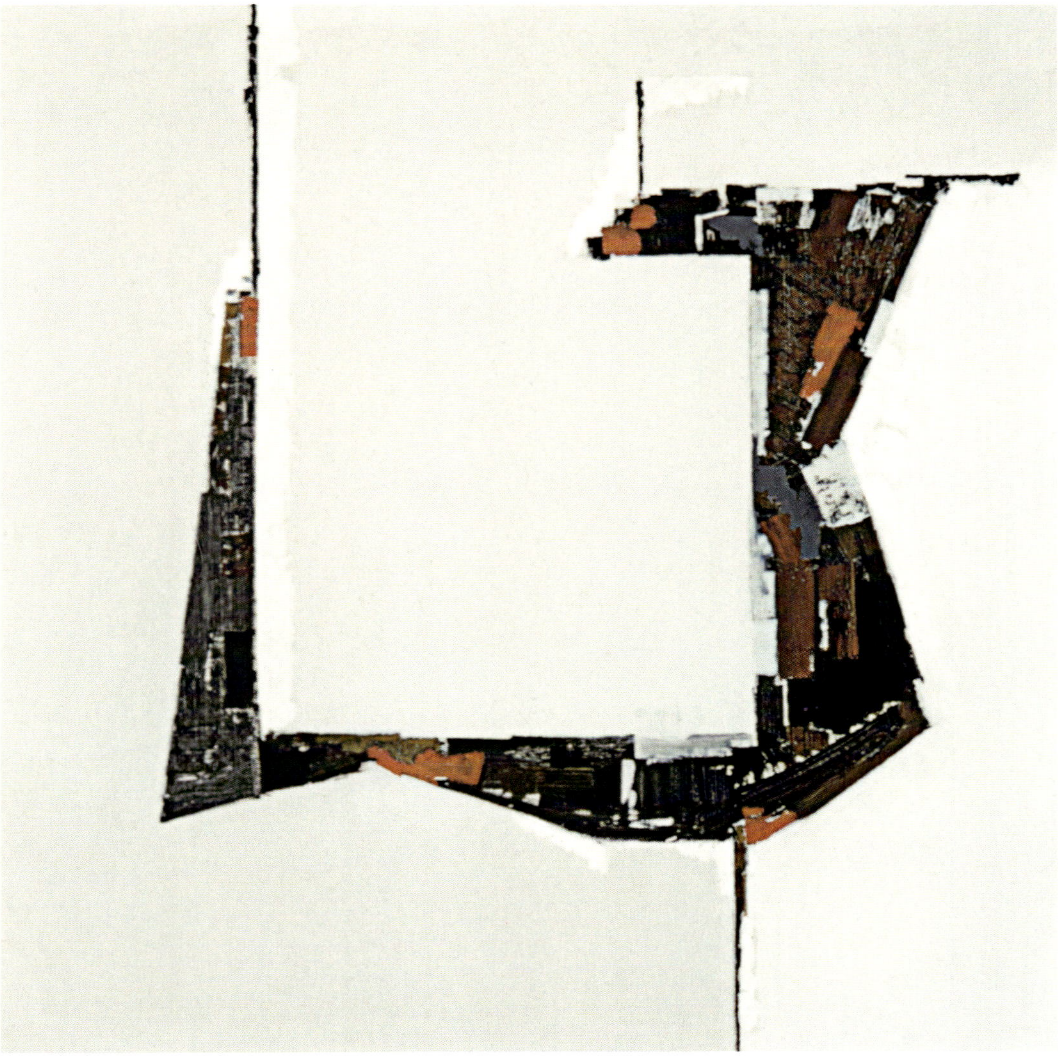

57-100×100-A, 1957

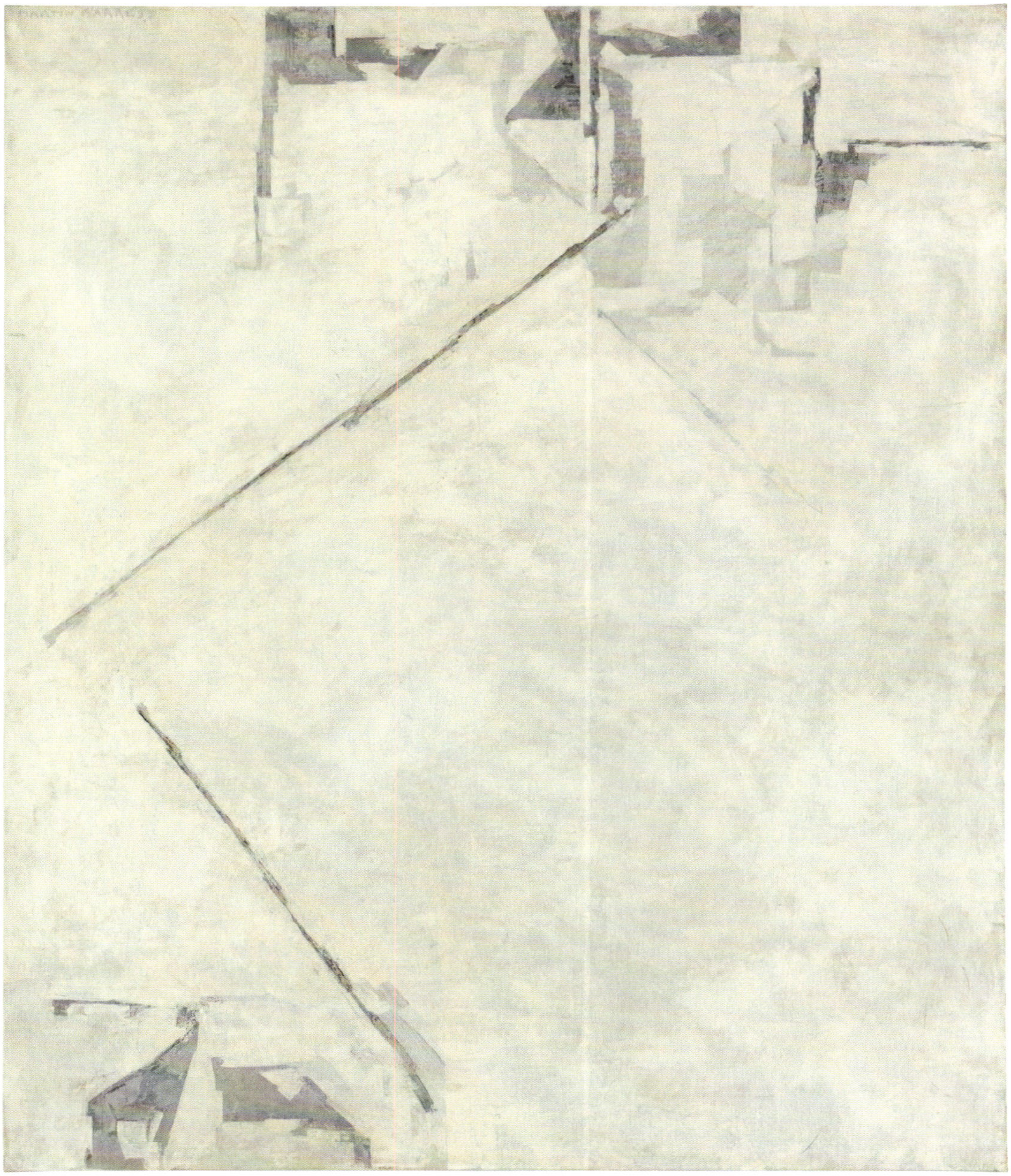

59-116×97-A, 1959

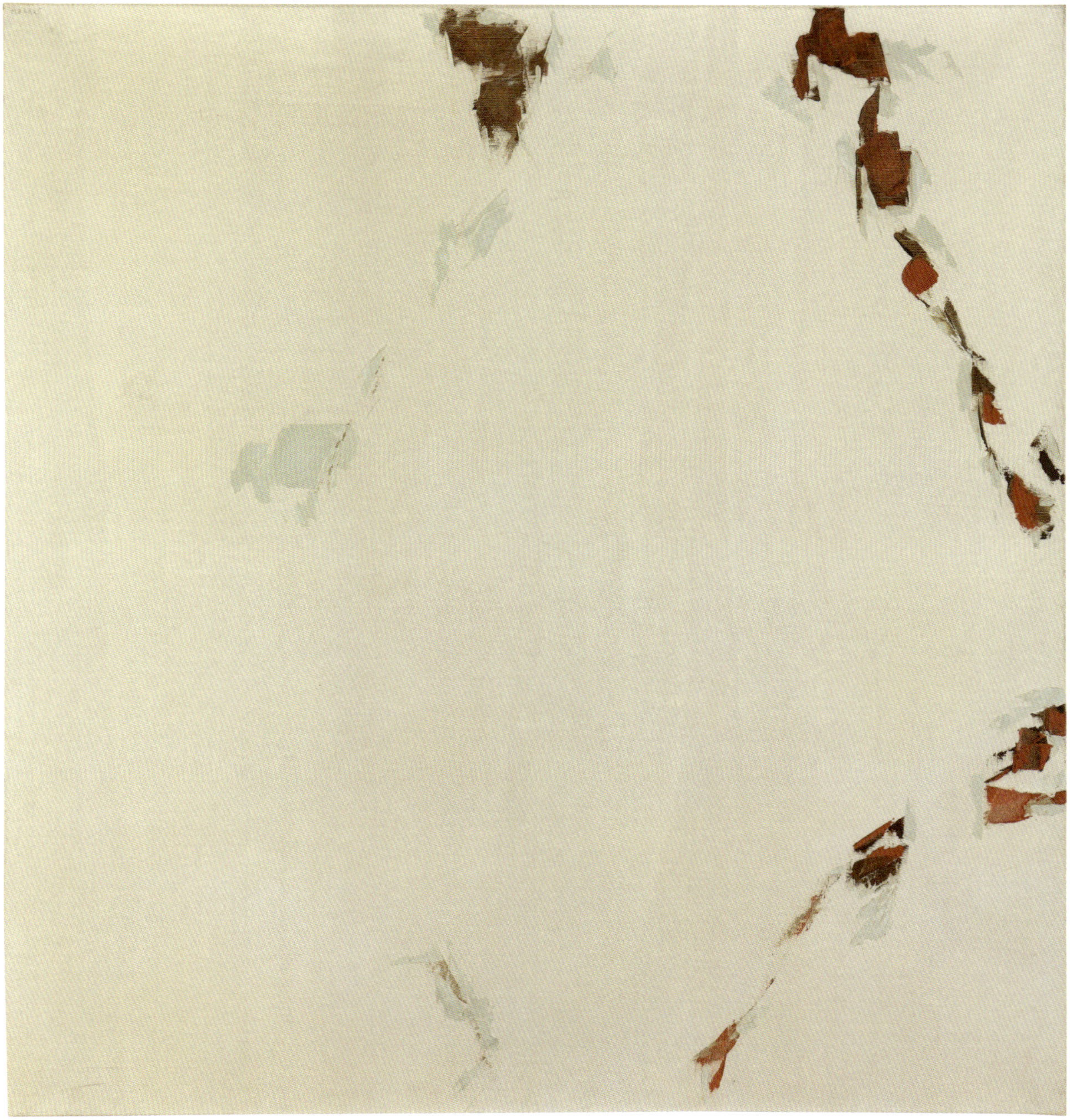

60-T-20, 1960
140 × 130 cm

59-120×110-C, 1959

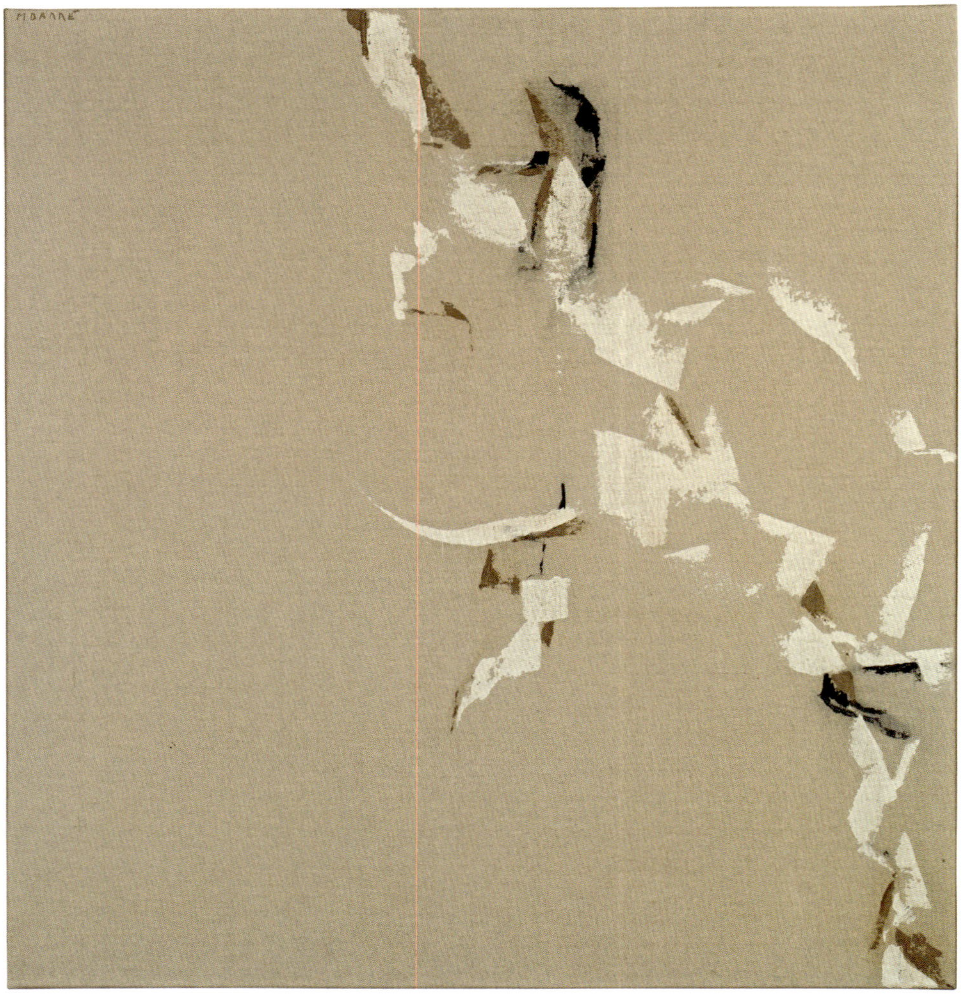

59-80×75-C, 1959

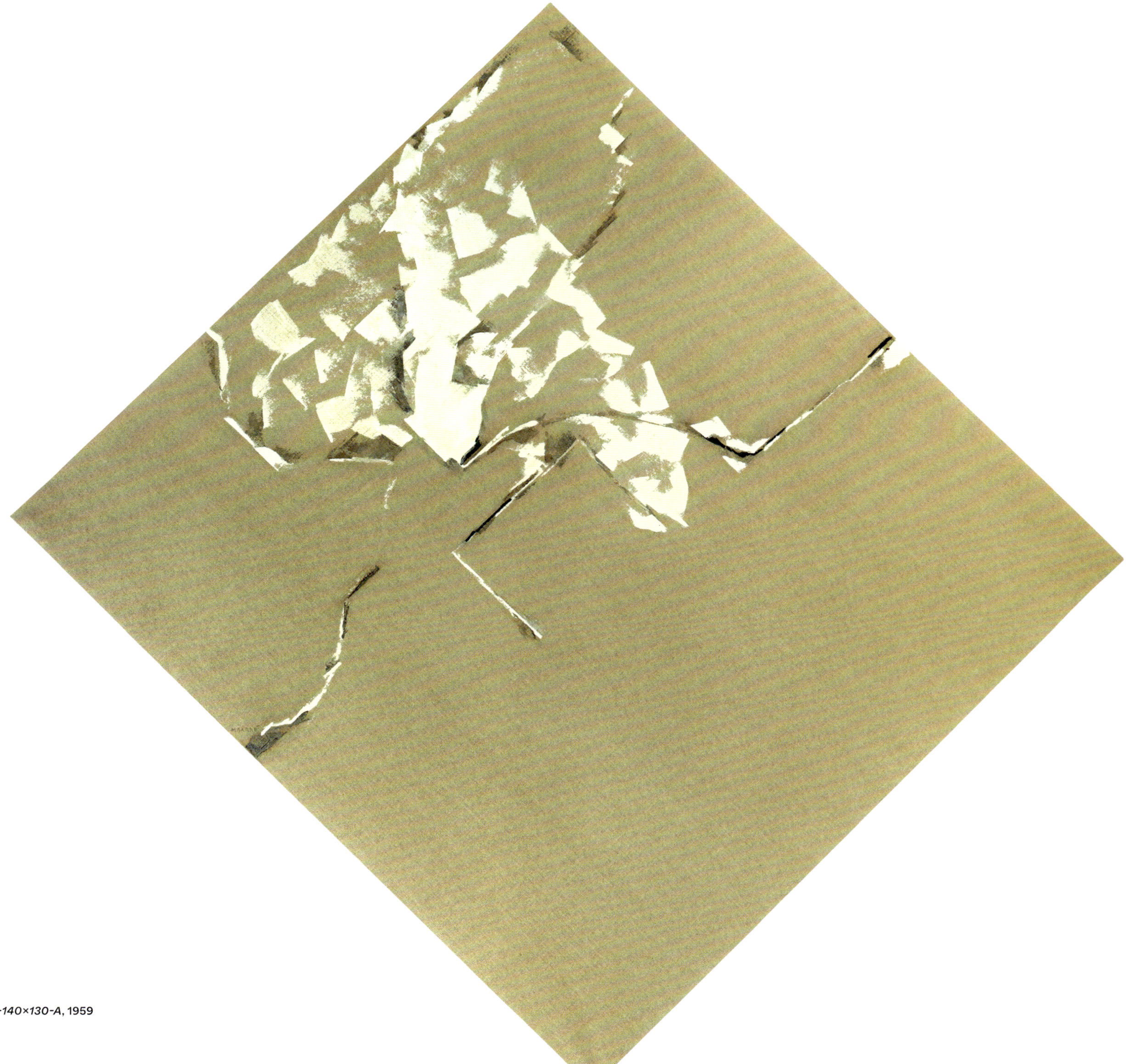

59-140×130-A, 1959

59-120×110-B, 1959

1960
1962

"WHEN I PAINTED DIRECTLY WITH THE TUBE, IT WASN'T THE TUBE THAT INTERESTED ME, BUT THE FACT OF GETTING RID OF THE BRUSH AND PALETTE KNIFE THAT I HAD USED BEFORE: ALL THIS TOWARDS A GREATER *REDUCTION-CONCENTRATION.*"

Martin Barré, 1974

60-T-47, 1960
73 × 120 cm

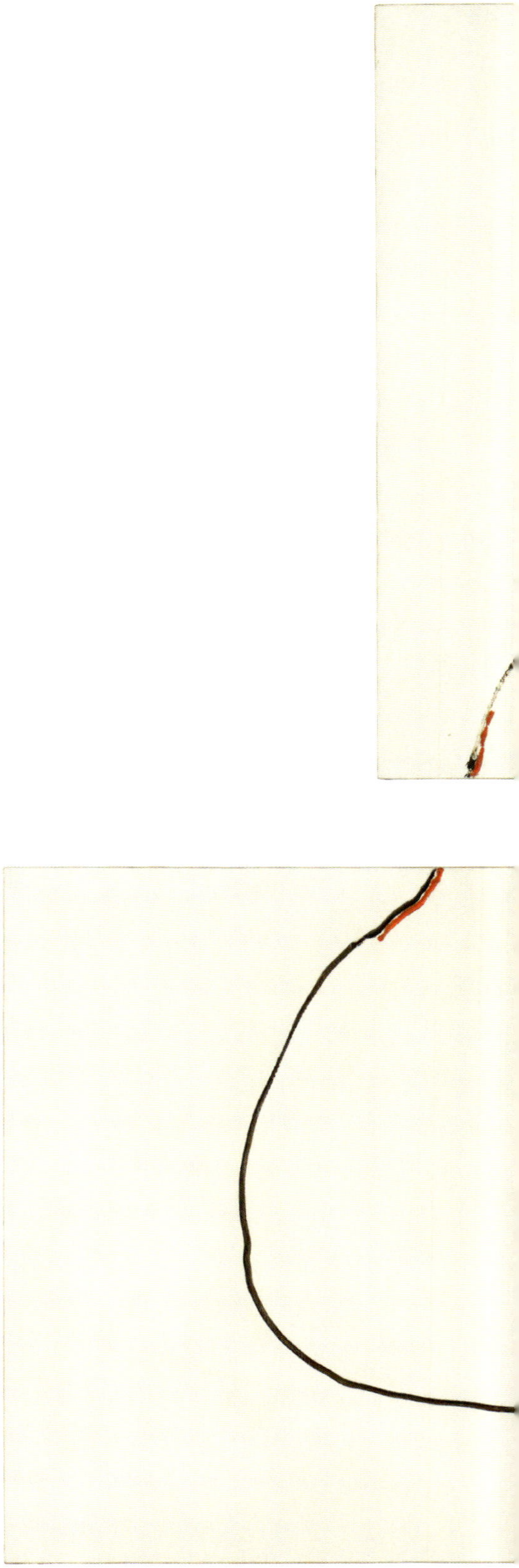

60-T-45, 1960
192 × 253 cm

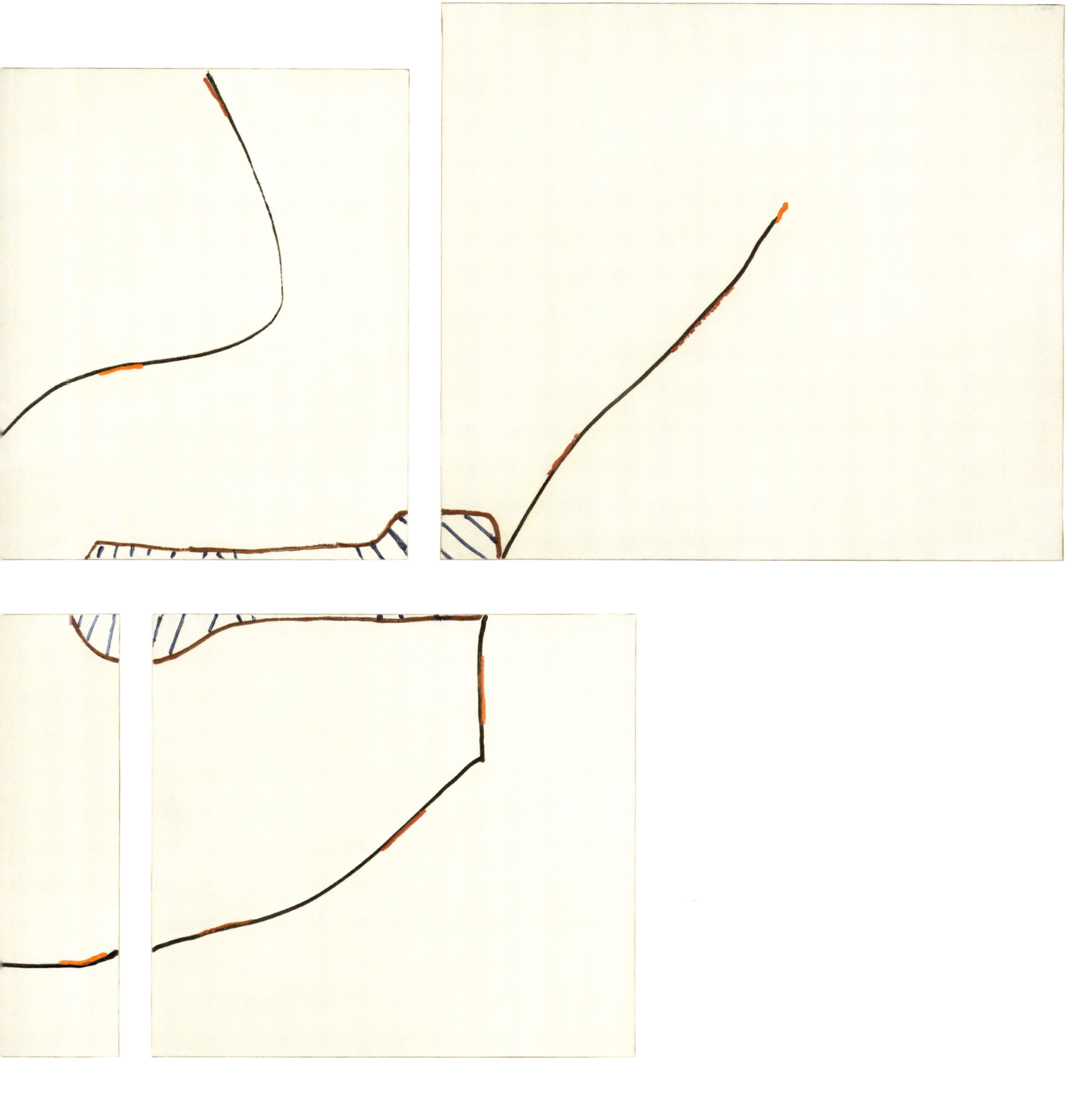

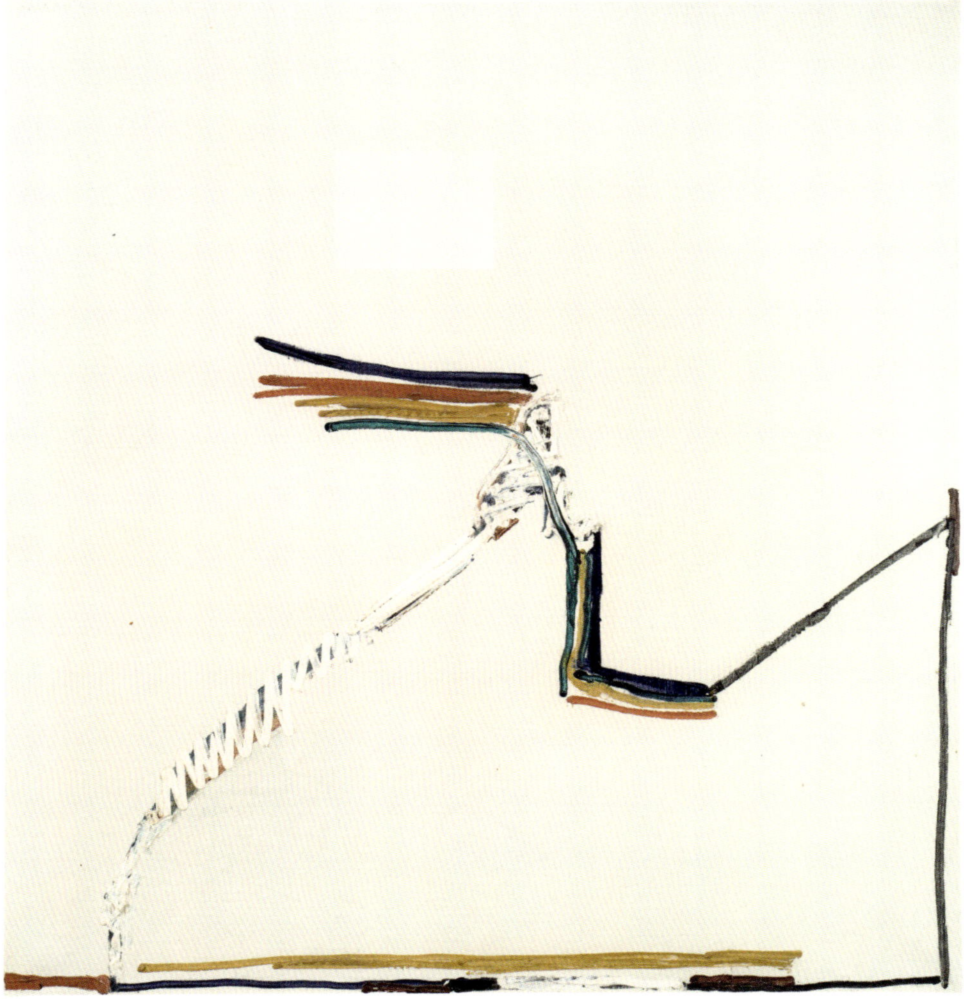

60-T-37, 1960
86 × 80 cm

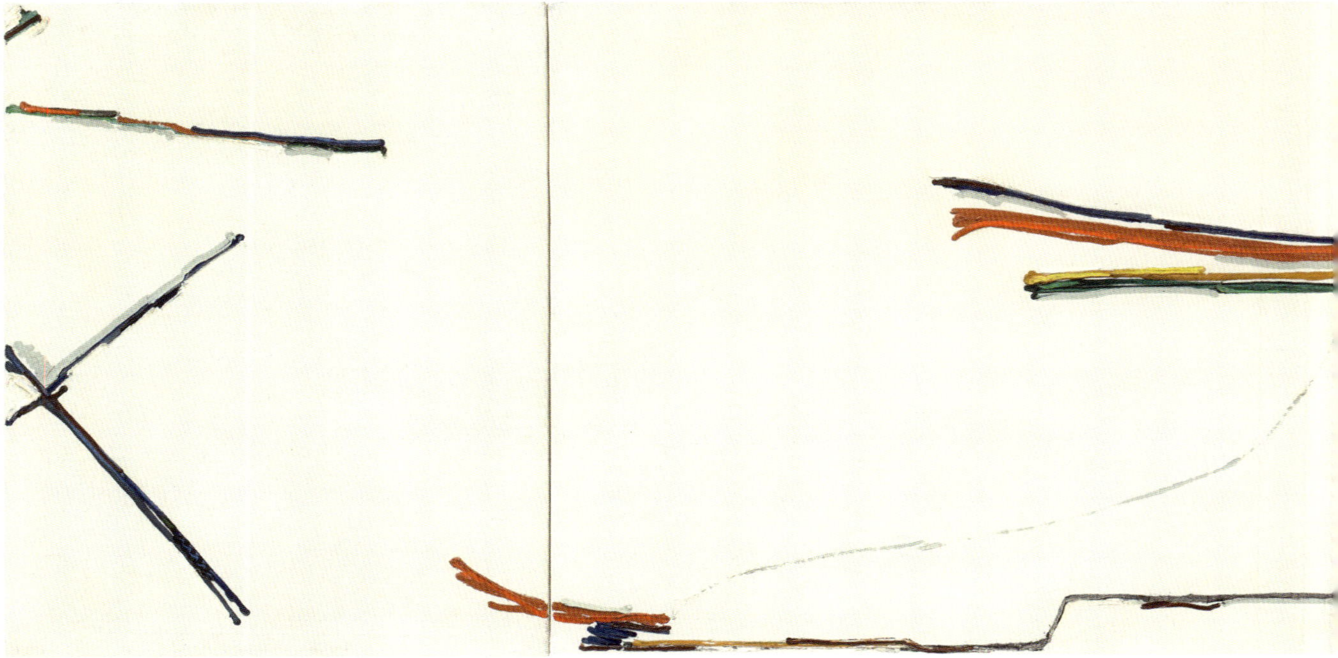

60-T-43, 1960
81 × 330 cm

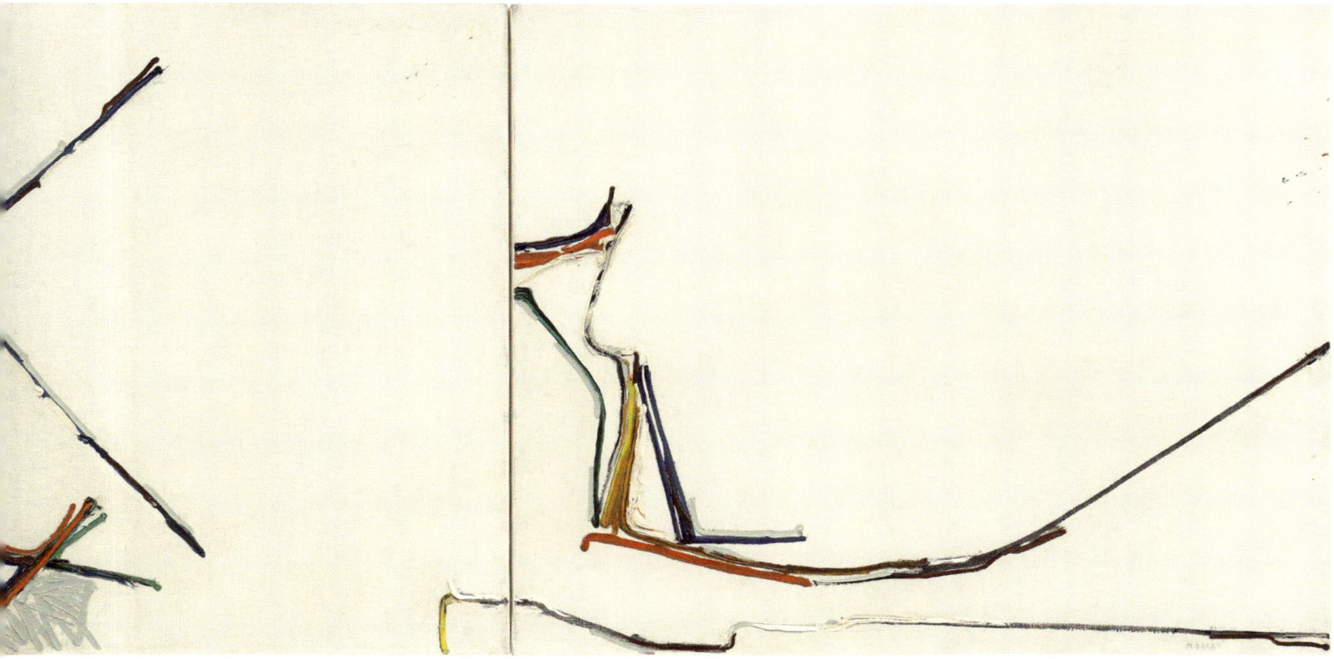

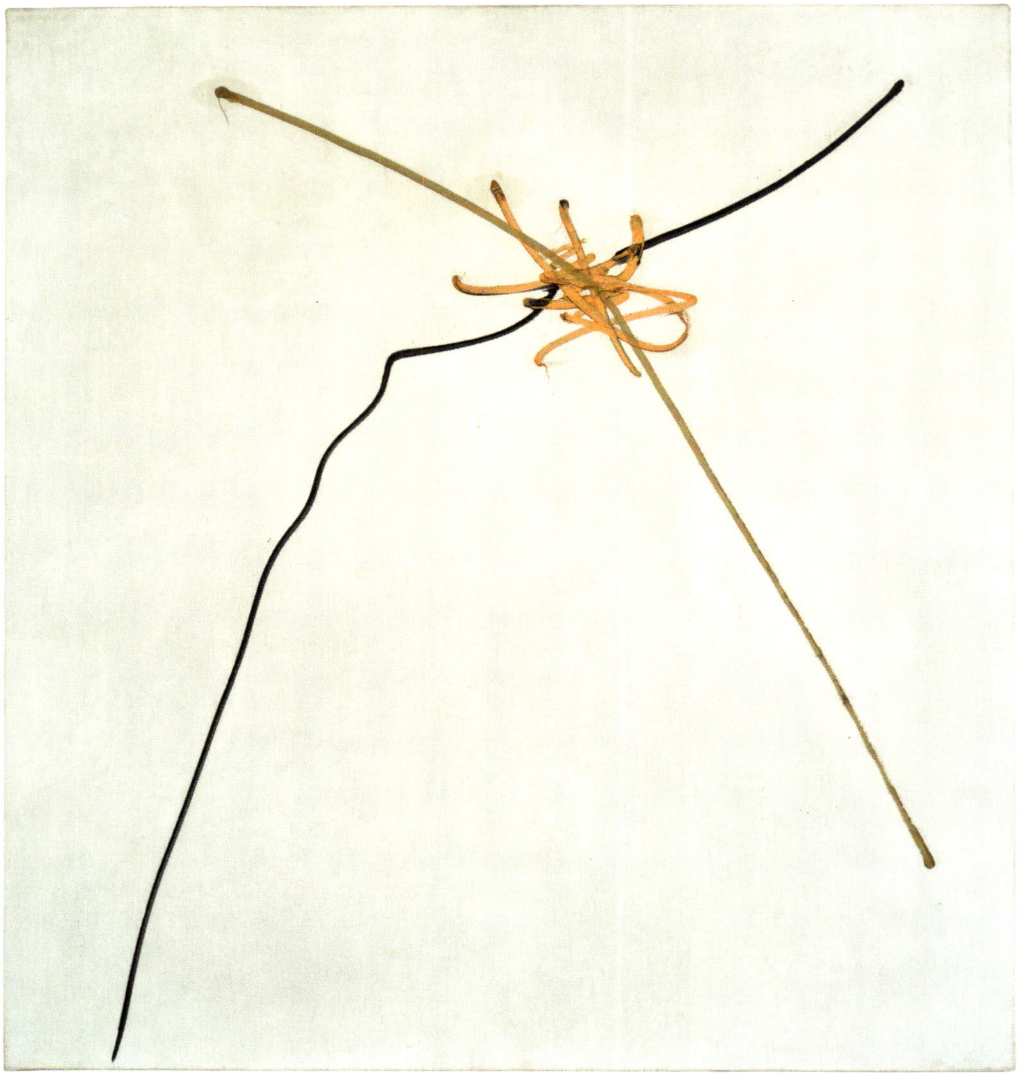

60-T-51, 1960
98 × 88 cm

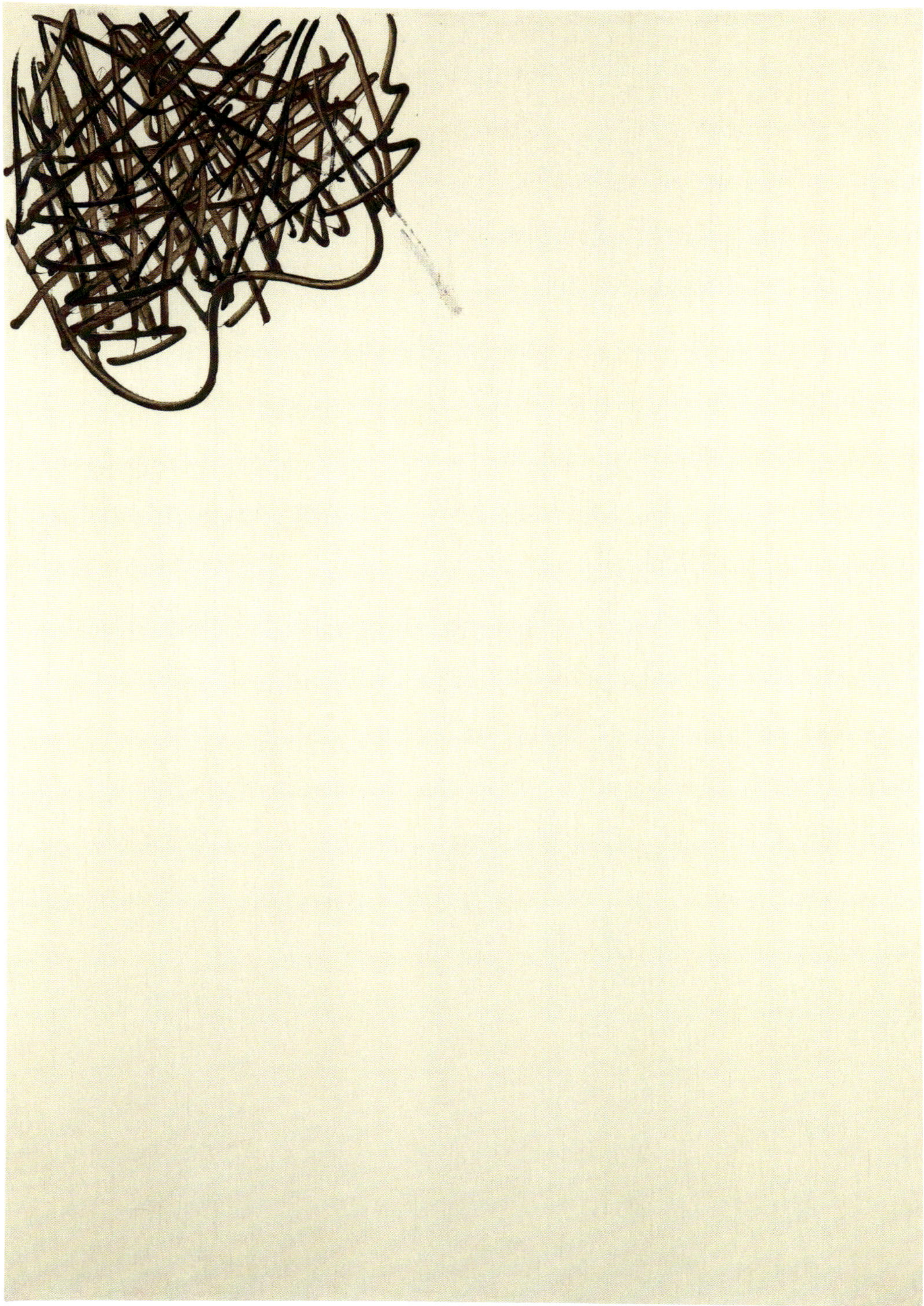

60-T-31, 1960
30 × 89 cm

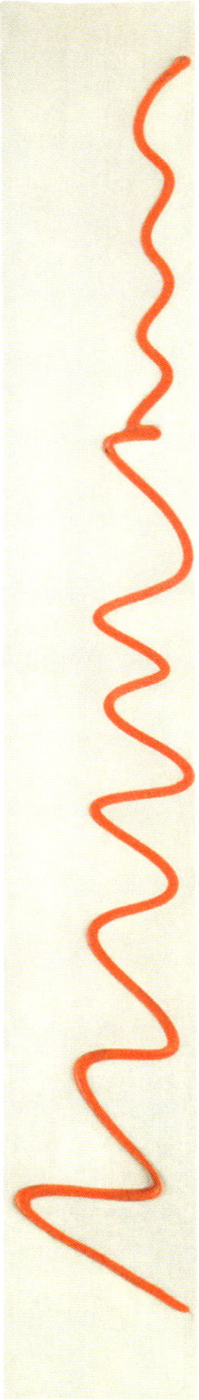

↑
60-T-53, 1960
89 × 12 cm

→
61-T-2, 1961
81 × 54 cm

61-T-5, 1961
92 × 65 cm

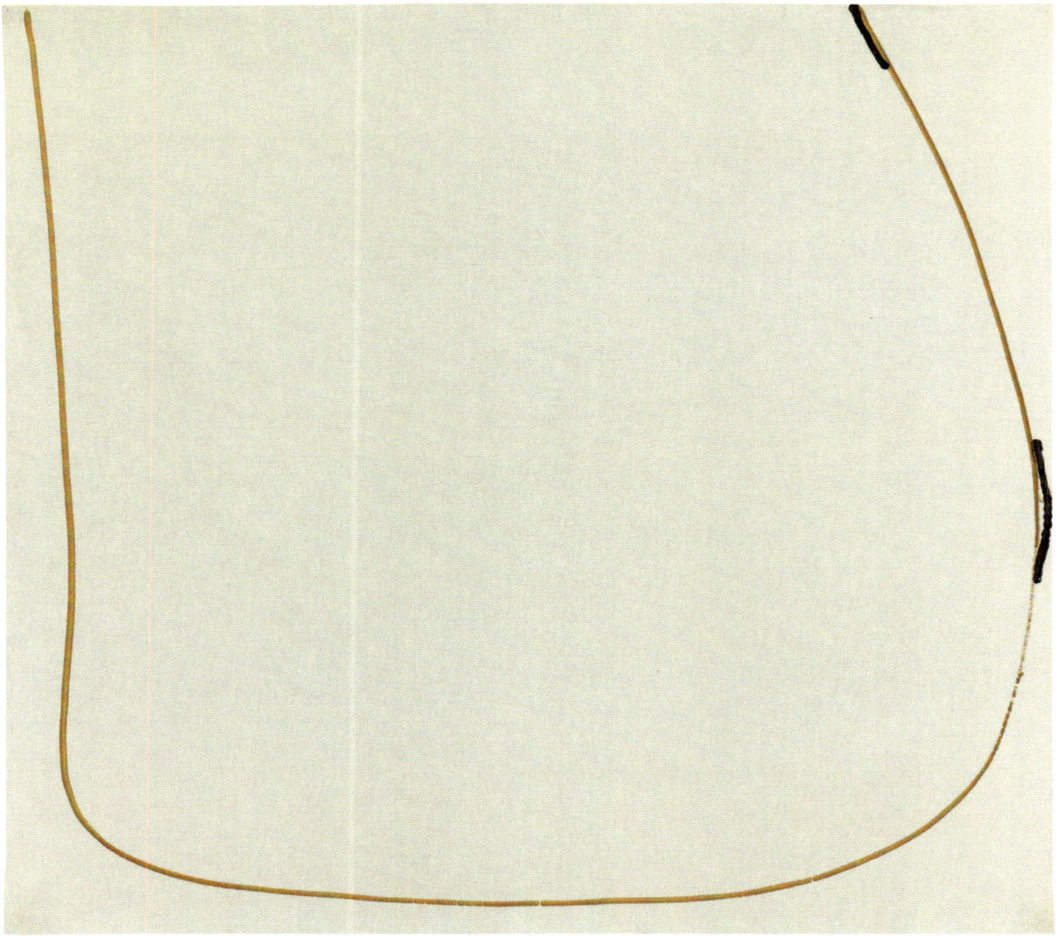

61-T-10, 1961
88 × 96 cm

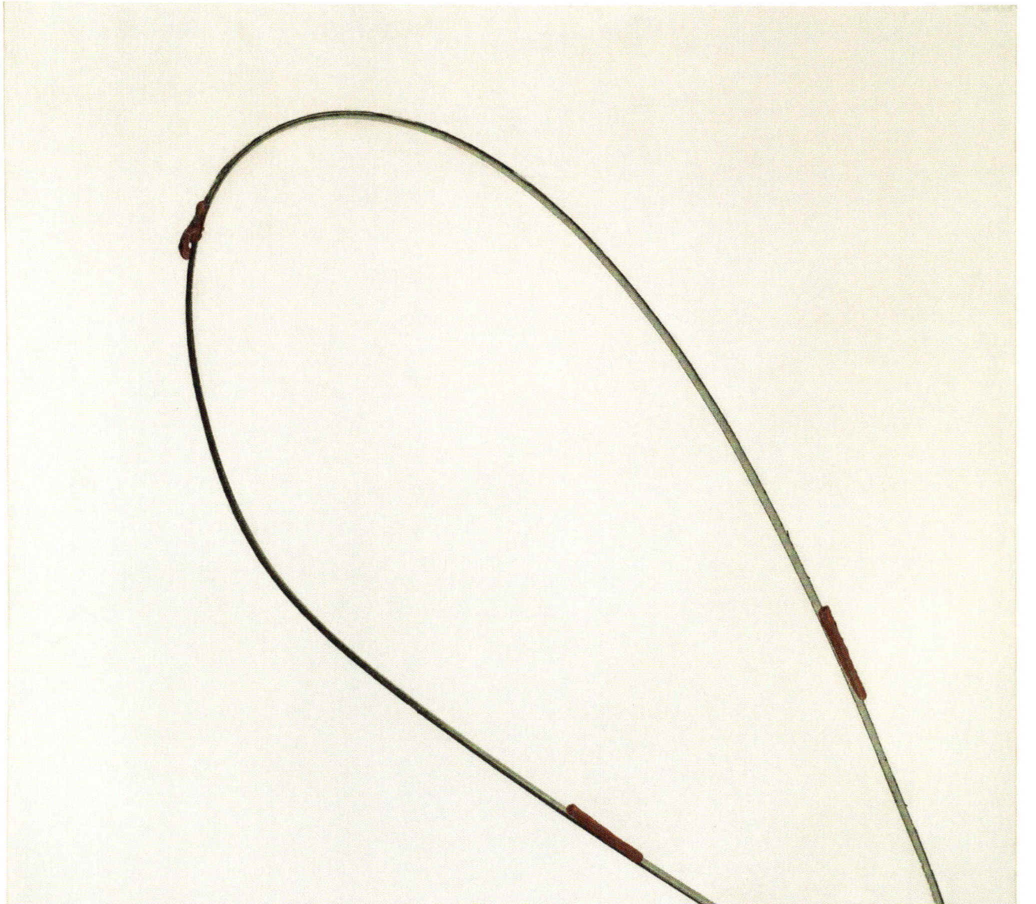

61-T-36, 1961
96 × 88 cm

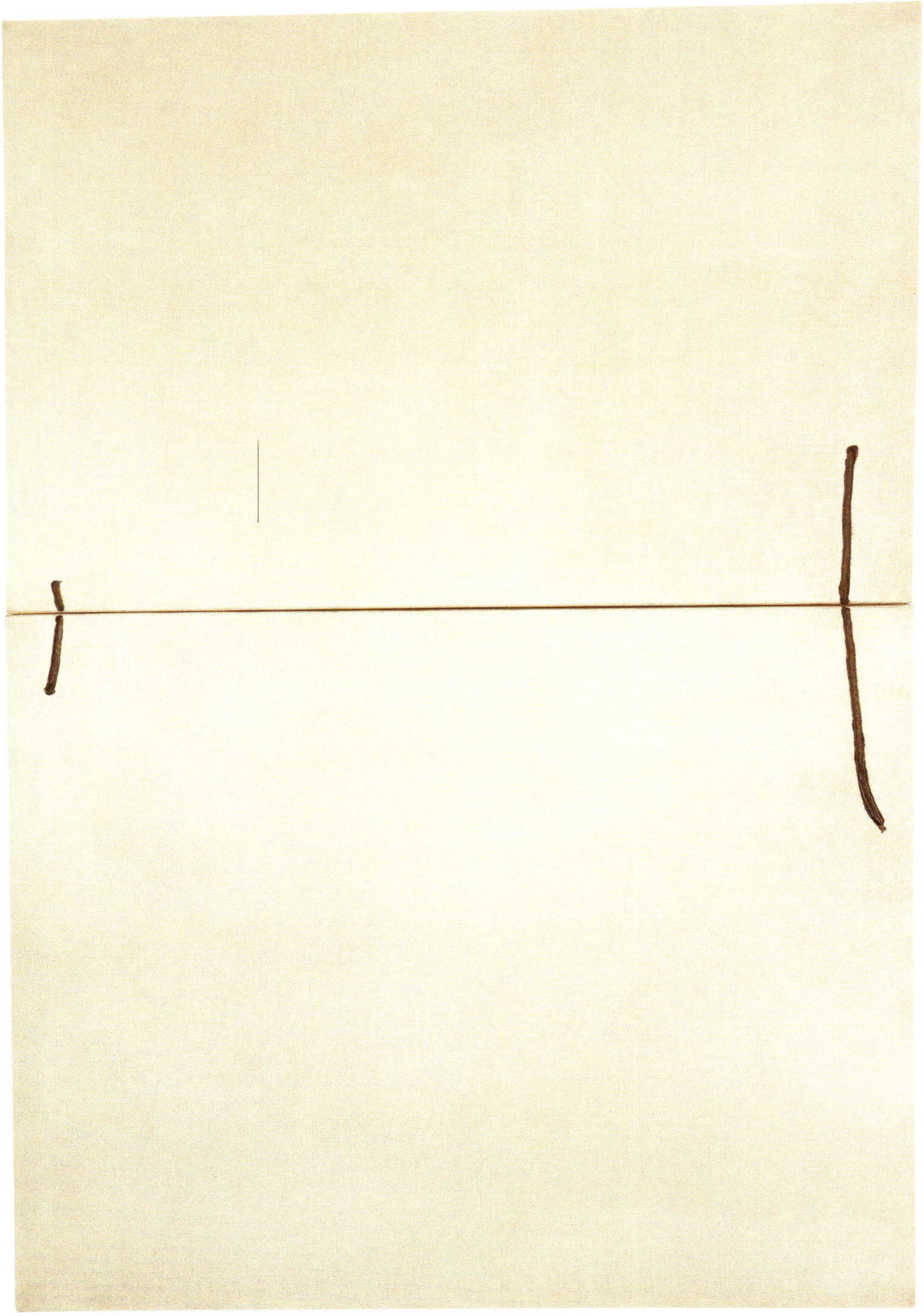

61-T-15, 1961
119 × 81 cm

61-T-16, 1961
81 × 119 cm

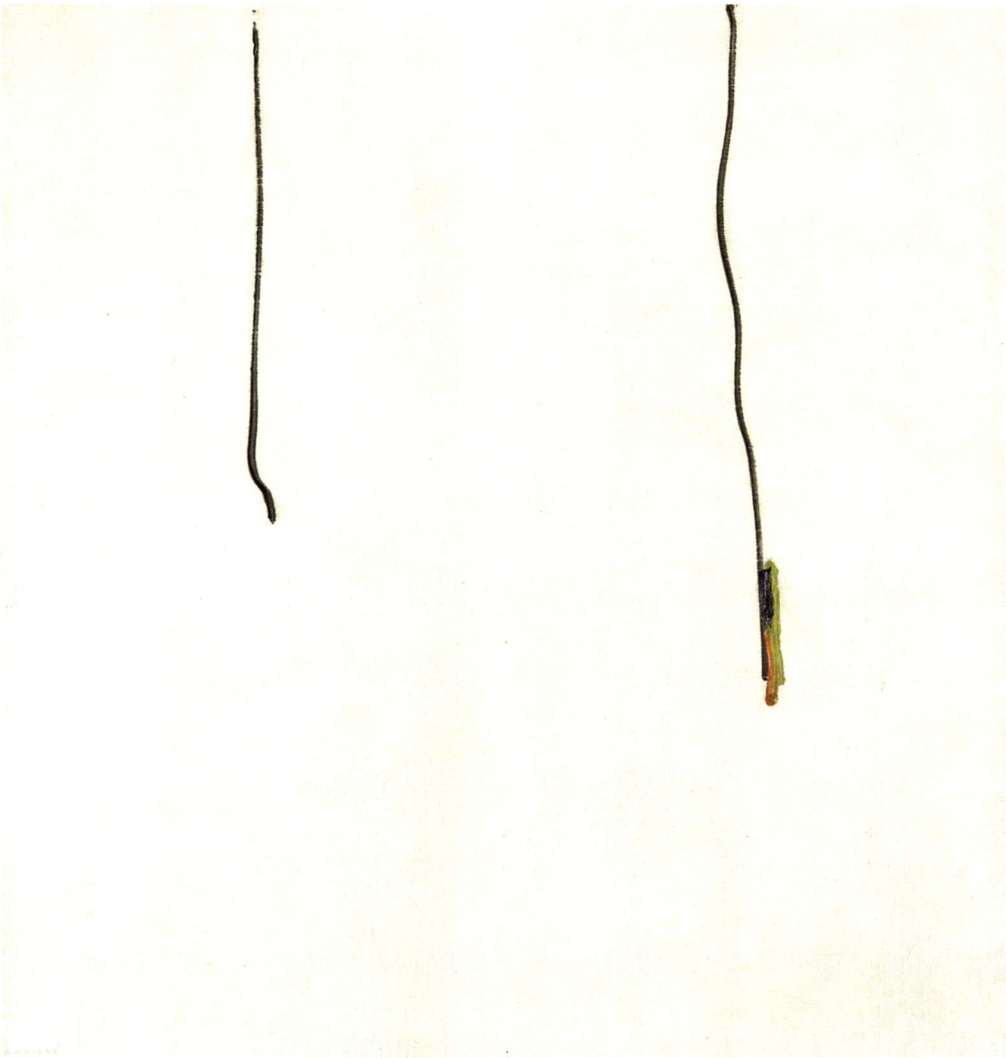

61-T-18, 1961
96 × 88 cm

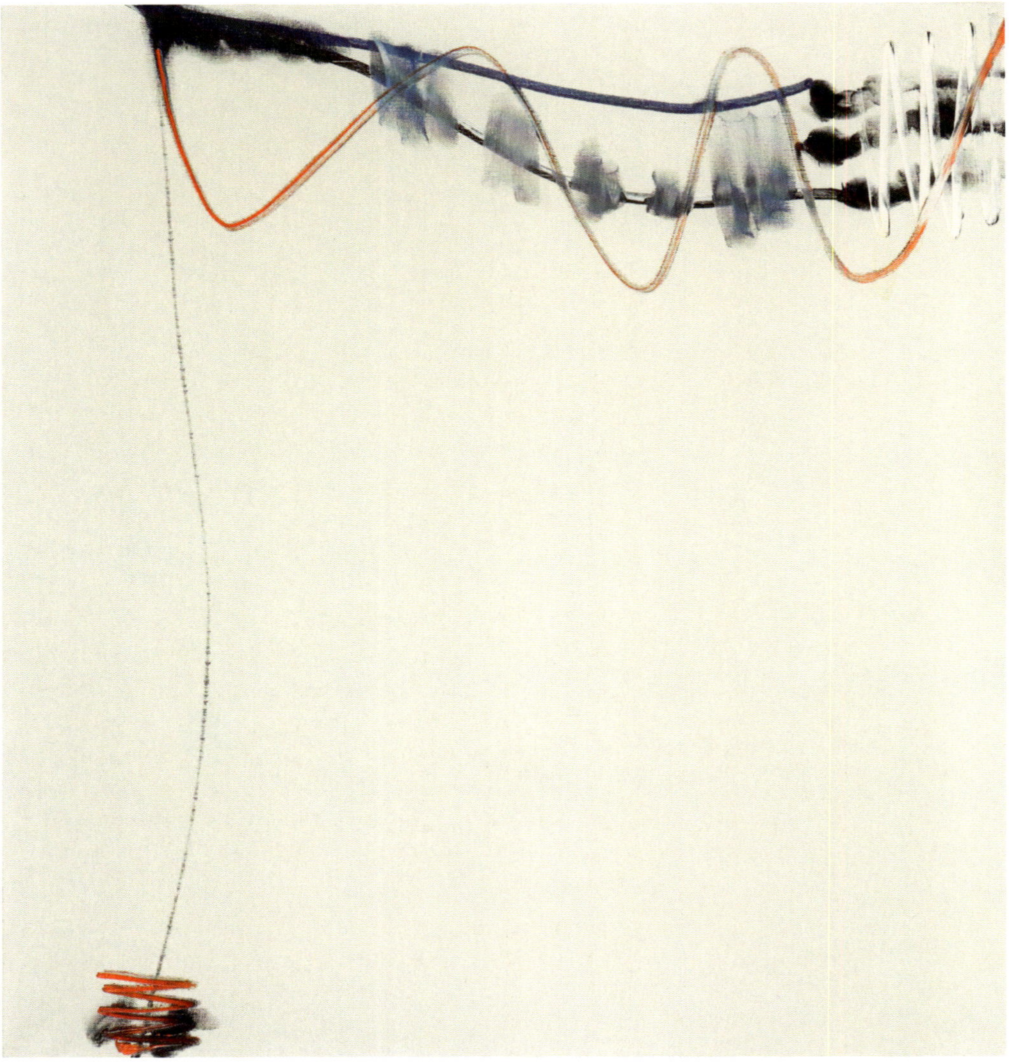

62-F, 1962
96 × 88 cm

THE TUBE PAINTINGS, 1960–1962

Yve-Alain Bois

In 1824, the young Eugène Delacroix was to write, "The main thing is to avoid this infernal ease of the brush. Make the material as hard to work as marble, rather —now, that would be totally new. . . . Make the paint rebel against us so as to conquer it with patience."[1] The first sentence of this quotation has been made famous by Paul Signac, and this is fitting considering his own pictorial technique (although it does not fit so well with the technique of Delacroix).[2] The rejection of "the finely crafted [*la belle facture*]" was to quickly become a rallying cry for the neo-impressionists. As early as 1886, Félix Fénéon, their most eloquent defender, used these words to introduce Georges Seurat's *A Sunday Afternoon on the Island of La Grande Jatte*: "Here indeed the hand [*la patte*] is useless, and trick effects impossible, there is no place for bravado; let the hand be clumsy but let the eye be nimble, perspicacious and well learned."[3] As Thierry de Duve reminds us, for Marcel Duchamp, it was the elimination of the gesture, the subjective touch, of "all that work of the hand," that saved Seurat from his retinal sin.[4]

But what about the second part of the Delacroix quotation, to which Signac was careful to avoid making any allusion? With its reek of heroism, it would have been of no use to him. It certainly took a lot of patience to paint a divisionist picture, but there was no great struggle to put on, no need to make the paint rebel so as to have the self-satisfaction of having conquered it, and this was because, according to the program at least, it was all about annihilating matter optically. Delacroix did seem to set hand against paint, but his aim was above all their reconciliation—wanting the substance of the paint to rebel and the work of the brush to be more difficult only so that the mastery of the artist would be that much more obvious. Hand and paste [*la patte et la pâte*]: Seurat turned his back on both of them.

Much has been written about the hand in twentieth-century art (most often in the context of the "gestural"), but there is rather little on the substance of the paint, at least as far as concerns the first half of the century. No doubt because the glorification of the paint matter itself

1 Eugène Delacroix, *Journal*, ed. Michèle Hannoosh (Paris: José Corti, 2009), 1:173–74, entry for Tuesday, July 20, 1824.

2 Surprisingly, Paul Signac refers to Delacroix here to add support to a whole series of quotations from John Ruskin's *Elements of Drawing*, translated by Signac's divisionist sidekick Henri-Edmond Cross. Paul Signac, *De Delacroix au néo-impressionnisme* [1899, p. 95], ed. Françoise Cachin (Paris: Hermann, 1964), 117.

3 Félix Fénéon, *Les Impressionnistes en 1886*, repr. in *Œuvres plus que complètes*, ed. Joan U. Halperin (Geneva: Droz, 1970), 36.

4 Thierry de Duve, "Le readymade et le tube de couleur," in *Résonances du readymade* (Nîmes: Jacqueline Chambon, 1989), 155–56. I am indebted to this remarkable essay for the detour by way of Eugène Delacroix, Paul Signac, and Félix Fénéon.

was quite marginal—the great totemic figures of modernity scarcely ever had recourse to it (there is very little impasto in Matisse, and Picasso's use of it was rare, always targeted and ironic; there is almost none in the work of the "pioneers of abstraction"—the most remarkable exception in this group being Władysław Strzemiński). Seeing themselves as the worthy successors of Vincent van Gogh, certain German expressionists sometimes painted their very gestural works with a lot of impasto (but less often than is frequently thought), and Paul Klee also, although he was interested in paste in the same way that he was interested in all the other little tricks of the artist's trade. Before the arrival of "Art Informel" there was really only Chaim Soutine, it seems, who was to remain unwavering in his commitment to the cult of hand and paste.

At the beginning of his career, Martin Barré inherited the pictorial culture of Art Informel, but it had by that time softened with age. Jean Dubuffet, Wols, and Jean Fautrier's audacious forays into materiality had become an accepted part of the scene, and those of Jackson Pollock were still poorly understood, if even known at all, on this side of the Atlantic. The "brush" had resumed its bristle, was firmly on top, and the entire Young School of Paris (YSP) sang praises in unison to its versatility. It is hard to tell when Barré became thoroughly tired of it. In 1956, he discovered the palette knife, adding it to his arsenal, but without completely abandoning the brush. Over the course of the following three years, we discern an obvious reduction in his use of this traditional tool, and he gives himself over with growing delight to the more fleshly pleasures of the knife. A new Courbet, he becomes such a virtuoso of the spatula that we have to look very closely at the paintings from 1959 and the beginning of 1960 to see that not a single line has been traced by a brush. If he did not exactly offer up this skillful ease as a show for the viewer, he was nonetheless very much within the line of thought of Delacroix. To want to paint a line with a knife is a bit like "eating oysters with boxing gloves," to borrow the incongruous pairing imagined by Rem Koolhaas in his *Delirious New York*.[5] Just try it and see! Anglo-Saxon criticism has given a word to this approach (untranslatable into French), and this is "deskilling," itself often only the preface to the dialectical riposte of "reskilling."[6]

Perhaps there was something slightly absurd about this "boxing gloves" procedure that played its part in Barré's abrupt decision, around 1960, to definitively hang up his collection of small trowels—why deprive oneself of the "ease of the brush" if it is only to imitate it with a cruder instrument? If such was the case, then it was an epiphenomenon that, sowing doubt, led him to put

5

Rem Koolhaas created this astonishing image in the context of his articles praising New York's Downtown Athletic Club, built in 1931. See *Delirious New York* (New York: Monacelli Press, 1994), 155.

6

On the origin of the concept of "deskilling," developed in 1981 by Ian Burn, see Benjamin Buchloh, "Hans Haacke: Memory and Instrumental Reason," in *Neo-Avantgarde and Culture Industry* (Cambridge: MIT Press, 2000), 210–11. On the dialectic of "deskilling/reskilling," see, by the same author, his introduction to *Formalism and Historicity* (Cambridge: MIT Press, 2015), xxiiff. We might define "deskilling" as the voluntary abandonment of an historically acquired technique, e.g. the handling of the artist's brush, to the benefit of procedures that are coarser and for which the artist has no expertise (for example, the drip technique for Jackson Pollock), but which is nonetheless an expertise that is very quickly acquired—thus called "reskilling."

his finger on the essential phenomenon which was that the whole aesthetic of the YSP, and this was true in spite of abstraction, was an aesthetics of representation. The YSP painter created pictures (often offered up as a seismographic expression of the state of the artist's psyche, and as if giving access, beyond their scratched or spotted surfaces, to a purely subjective and therefore directly inaccessible psychological depth). The artist's very gesturality was a form of representation: a scar here, a cloud there, a form uncertain or precise here again, and all of it hung against an atmospheric background by which the gaze can become engulfed. Barré never fully adhered to the postulates of the YSP, as we can see quite clearly in the way that, in the climate of that period, he stood by Piet Mondrian and Kasimir Malevich, models who were rejected by the defenders of "lyrical abstraction"—this false antagonism being called at the time the battle between "style" and "scream." But up to that point, he had not really been able to identify why he was feeling more and more like an ugly duckling among his peers, and this was because, in spite of himself, his art was still following the post-cubist canon that underpinned the entire rhetoric of the YSP.

It was at his solo exhibition at the Galerie Arnaud,[A, B] in November–December 1960, that Barré was to show his tube paintings, created over the course of the previous months, and in doing so he broke definitively with the YSP among whom he had become a rising star. Needless to say, his usual defenders, who were at the very least disorientated, turned their backs on him, some even going so far as to accuse him of imposture. The only critic to come to his defense was Pierre Restany, anathema to the champions of the YSP for his militancy in support of their nightmare, Yves Klein: "Martin Barré, with all the intellectual courage implied in the absolutist development of an authentic approach, and in just one go, got rid of all kinds of outmoded paraphernalia, a whole vocabulary of anachronistic forms he had been trying in vain to revive."[7] Moreover, Restany put Klein's monochrome painting in parallel with what he saw in Barré's work as a burgeoning monolinearity, and he declared to all those who saw in those canvases nothing but the work of a fraud: "I will rule out the objection that there is nothing left to see: for me there is still too much."

Towards the end of his "palette knife" period, Barré had already started to simplify his painter's panoply by adopting just as they came the pre-primed, gessoed canvases (most often white) that were available on the market (he also used, more rarely, unprepared canvas), thus eliminating one entire part of what he neatly called the "over/under business"[8] of traditional painting practice. Yet it was only with the tube

A → p. 215

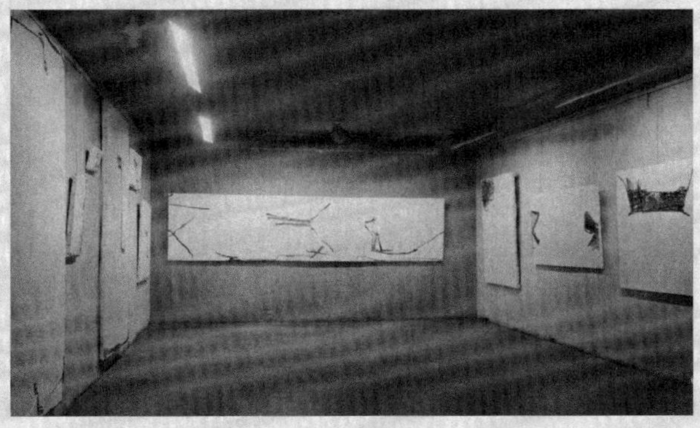

B → p. 215

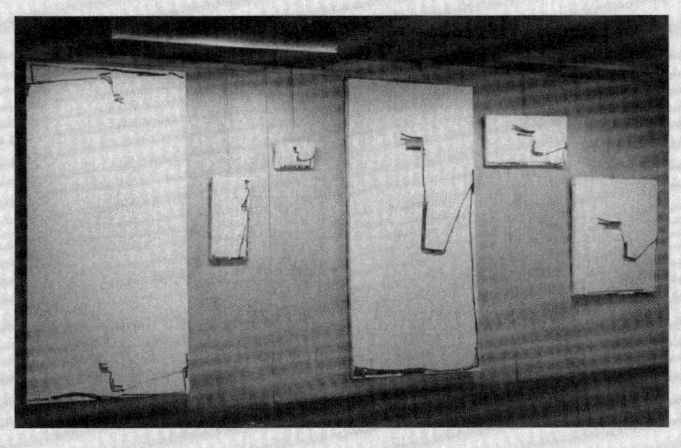

7
Cited in Yve-Alain Bois, *Martin Barré* (Cologne, New York, and Paris: Galerie Daniel Buchholz, Andrew Kreps Gallery, Galerie Nathalie Obadia, and Thea Westreich/Ethan Wagner, 2008), 15.

8
Ibid., 260.

paintings that this abandonment of the chromatic and textural subtleties of the background against which figures or gestures might stand out was revealed in all its rawness, and this was quite simply because it was from then on emphasized by another rawness, that other "deskilling" that was the tube-traced line. It might appear that this was just a simple extension of the logic of the "ready-made" that Barré had applied when he gave up preparing his own canvases (Duchamp pointed out, of course, that the tube of paint sold in stores was nothing but a ready-made, perhaps even the first one[9]). But there is something else going on here, as the painter himself was to indicate. When Catherine Millet asked him if it was his interest in using unmixed color that had motivated his tube technique, he replied: "No. That held no interest for me. On the contrary, I eventually managed to obtain empty tubes that I could fill with the mixture of my choice, and before filling them I filed away at the opening because I wasn't happy with the thinness of the line."[10] In certain cases, quite rare ones, the mixing can be seen because it was imperfect—several colors had been shoved into the tube without having been completely homogenized beforehand, and they are strung out the length of a single line traced on the canvas. Canvas becomes palette. We have to go back to Cézanne and his portraits of Uncle Dominique to find an historical precedent for this sort of contraction.[11]

The appeal of the ready-made was to come later for Barré, during the short but crucial "conceptual" period in 1968–71 when he abandoned painting.[12] But the tube paintings were to signal rather an apotheosis of process, i.e. of what was not "ready" in the "made." For several years, he had resisted what, in an interview with Jean Clay,[13] he called "the before-market," and he had rebelled in particular against the standard stretcher measures available on the market. Using the strategy of "defamiliarization" (made famous by the Russian formalists) to signal his rejection of these ready-made formats that were surreptitiously imposed upon painters, he had created two rectangular paintings that were to be hung diagonally, on the tip —rectangular and not square, and therefore necessarily arranged asymmetrically, unlike Mondrian's canvases that the latter called "losangiques." Still, it was only during the preparatory work for the 1960 exhibition that Barré came to understand that everything connected, i.e. that his revolt against traditional formats and his desire for new forms of hanging were all of a piece with the disgust he felt for the "over/under business," and this realization could be put down to, or was at least contemporary with, his move to the tube as an instrument of marking.

9 See Thierry de Duve's analysis of this idea, "Le readymade," 143ff.

10 Cited in Bois, *Martin Barré*, 263.

11 I am grateful to Paul Galvez for having pointed out to me the "palette-strokes" in what is known as Paul Cézanne's "ballsy" period, and for having shared with me the chapter that he devotes to them in his forthcoming book on Gustave Courbet. The most noticeable case of this is Cézanne's *Portrait of Uncle Dominique in a Turban* from 1866–67 (private collection, no. 407 of the online catalogue raisonné), where we see strokes of the palette knife each involving several colors (for example, beige-yellow-white-red or blue-yellow-white). No reproduction can faithfully render this phenomenon.

12 The conceptual episode was an essential turning point in the artist's career, and it was to result in an impasse from which he extricated himself by returning to the point of departure, at least as far as the basic instrument was concerned, i.e. the artist's brush. He was to go back to the brush in 1972, as he was to do moreover with the "over/under business," but this time laid bare in broad daylight, not as secret craftsmanship. The photographic interval, critical and theoretical in nature, allowed him to consciously reset the deck and to engage again with the game of painting that he had temporarily thought a lost cause.

13 See Jean Clay, "Questions à Martin Barré," *Macula* 2 (1977): 78. See, also, on pages 79–81, Jean Clay's fine analysis of the "Convergence des formats et tracés dans la peinture de Martin Barré [Convergence of format and line in Martin Barré's painting]."

To be sure, the instrument itself is never as important as the way in which it is used. Barré was not the first to practice "tubism." Georges Mathieu, the inventor of this neologism, had even made a great show of it.[14] In his case, to say that gesture was being represented would be an understatement —the painter literally put himself on stage, playing the role of an artist in the throes of inspiration. The choice of instrument was of no consequence; indeed, there is no formal difference between Georges Mathieu's tube paintings and his other works: it is always a case of a very centered composition with a star-like cluster of lines, most often anchored onto an orthogonal skeleton, bursting multidirectional spurts of paint whose essential function is to convey the painter's fulgurating energy—an absolute racket; to use Fénéon's term, pure "bravado."

There is an obvious contrast here with Barré's ascesis. For Barré, replacing the knife with the tube meant above all the abolition of transcendence: the gesture became purely indicial, referring only to its own process of production, possessing in itself no sort of grandiloquence. There is no furor, no puffing of the ego; the process is unidimensional, univocal, transparent; the line is the trace of a gesture whose stages can be reconstituted in their entirety (as indeed can be the time required to make it) without any need to make a song and dance out of it. A line starts from there, ends here, is more or less fat and thick depending upon the pressure of the hand on the tube and the speed of movement. There is no state of mind involved, only elementary physics. Everything is *alla prima*, with no possibility of correction. Or rather if there is correction, it is only on condition that the changes of mind be themselves visible as such in the form of white zig-zag hatching, striking out this or that line (*60-T-37*[C]), or as appears in very exaggerated form in various canvases from 1962 (*62-F*[D]) a stumping that is falsely but very obviously clumsy (there is quite a treatise that remains to be written on the visible erasure in Barré, a technique that was to become an essential part of his work in the 1970s). Erasure becomes its opposite, enacting a genuine dialectical reversal. In *61-T-2*,[E] four lines compete one with another, upping the ante as they cross, from one side to the other, the top of a blank canvas. The first line is white (the color of erasure), but this line is crossed out by a brown zig-zag line (the graphical sign of erasure), and this in its turn is struck out by two lines in sienna.

Was it the facticity peculiar to the process of tube painting that led Barré to question the compositional aesthetic of the YSP, an entirely arbitrary method of which he was himself a past master? Just as with his new interest in hanging, we might ask which came first (chicken or egg?). The tube-traced line was an immanent fact: *what you see is*

14
The most ghoulish surviving example is a video from 1959 in which we see Georges Mathieu performing in public. He has paint tubes arranged around him like sardines in cans on the floor, and he discharges their contents onto a canvas that is first laid flat on the stage and then raised up vertically. Smearing the paint with various other instruments as well, such as cloths, a jerrican of turpentine, various brushes, and a bowl, he is all the time gesticulating to the improvised music of Pierre Henry (not recorded), and eventually he gives birth to a work entitled *Hommage au Connétable de Bourbon, auteur du sac de Rome*—quite a program! Like the gangsters in the films of John Woo or Wong Kar-wai, who casually throw down their guns when they run out of bullets or don't need them anymore, having seen off their adversaries, Georges Mathieu throws his tubes to the floor, only to tread all over them in the heat of the action. The video is available at https://georges-mathieu.fr/hommage-au-connetable-de-bourbon-auteur-du-sac-de-rome-1959.

C → p. 47
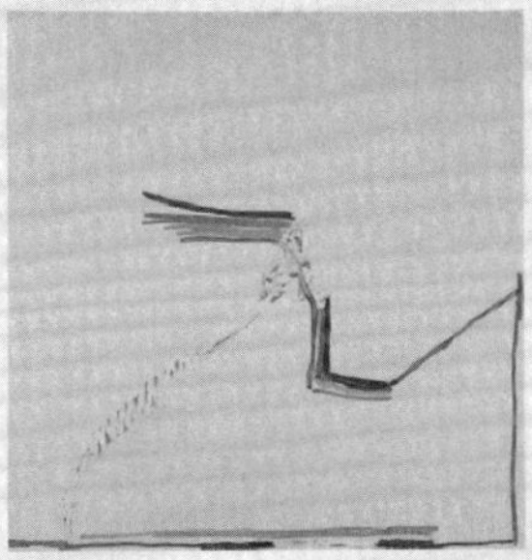

D → p. 60
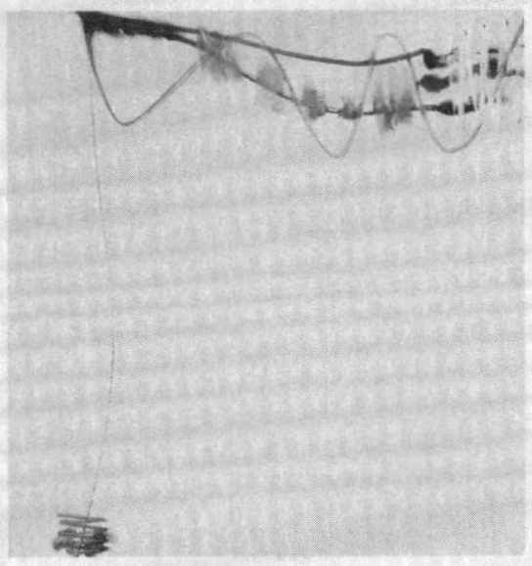

E → p. 52

what you see; there is nothing beyond, no thought behind it. Be that as it may, but why did the line take a particular direction? Where did the decision come from, and in what way was it less subjective than the least tiny manipulation of the "over/under business"? It is true that this sort of question was in the air at the time, at least for all of the artists opposed to the YSP or to the neo-Wagnerian circus of someone like Georges Mathieu. However, instead of adopting one or another of the most radical strategies used by others in reply, e.g. the modular grid, or the monochrome in the case of Klein, which had made a strong impression on Barré, the latter chose not to abolish compositional arbitrariness, but to put it in relief, to demonstrate its own arbitrary character. To carry out this indirect questioning, he made use of the two elements of pictorial practice that I have already referred to (elements generally little explored because taken for granted): format and hanging.

As Jean Clay brilliantly saw, already some time ago now, it was by redirecting the structure of the polyptych that Barré first came upon what were to be some of his most productive discoveries, and they are all there in his 1960 exhibition. Standing before the large polyptych *60-T-43*,[F] the viewer sees quite quickly that it is the result of a permutation (Clay: "this is two paintings [each one consisting of two panels] painted separately and then combined. AB and CD become in the new configuration: DACB. Furthermore, C is hung upside down."[15]). The same is true of the diptych *60-T-47*,[G] and here we can see that the initial design was a sort of pinned butterfly or a clover leaf (with four leaves!) divided in the middle by the junction of the two panels. The right/left reversal of the panels separates the wings or the leaves, pushing them out to the periphery and leaving in the middle a flat emptiness that is almost comical. In fact, there is a cartoonish side to many of the tube paintings. Another example of it is the scrunched-up scribbling at the upper left corner of *60-T-31*[H] (also included in the 1960 exhibition); but the most striking instance of this deadpan humor—the only sort of humor that is of any use against pretentiousness—is the narrow, vertical painting *60-T-53*[I] that did not figure in the 1960 exhibition. Through a single corkscrew line in red (like the whitewashed scribbles that bricklayers use to alert people to the presence of a pane of glass on a building site so that they won't break it by accident) the painting seems to be saying: this is the least effort required to cross out and take control of an entire surface.[16]

This comical side can also be seen in what we might call Barré's first series, standing out all the more by being

F → pp. 48–49

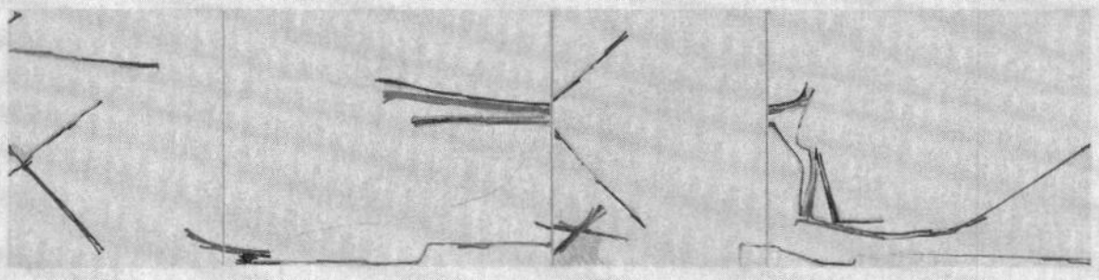

G → p. 43

H → p. 51

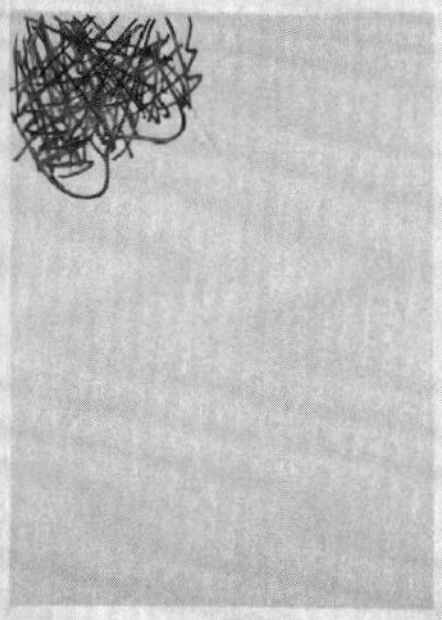

I → p. 52

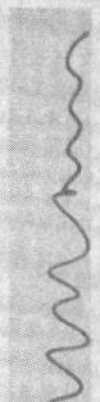

15
Jean Clay, "La peinture en séton," in Suzanne Pagé et al., *Martin Barré*, exh. cat. (Paris: ARC – Musée d'Art Moderne de la Ville de Paris, 1979), 11. It is true that to some extent Barré did cover his tracks if he chose to. Jean Clay adds: "There are lines added that 'consolidate' the new presentation" [lines that delay perhaps the perception of the permutation]. "The work is *at once* the product of an aleatory procedure and a unifying gesture: it is *at once* an accumulation of disparate fragments and a canvas."

16
This is off-topic, but no matter: whoever knew Barré personally can attest to his very dry humor (so much the more effective in that it came out only occasionally, and notably when he was alluding to the art world). Perhaps it is no accident that he often adopted facetious nicknames for his tube paintings (or willingly accepted suggestions from others): he called *60-T-32* (hung next to *60-T-47* in the 1960 exhibition) "the basket." *60-T-16* became "the staple," *61-T-36* and two other paintings with a similar loop became "the lassoes," the large painting in the collection of the Solomon Guggenheim Museum, *60-T-44*, was "the tie," etc.

J → pp. 44–45

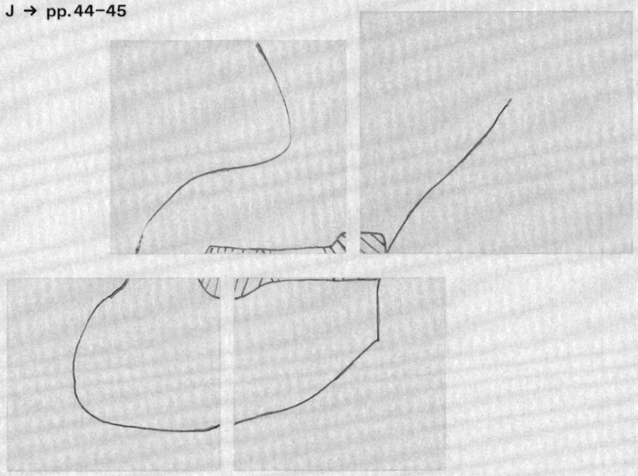

K → p. 215

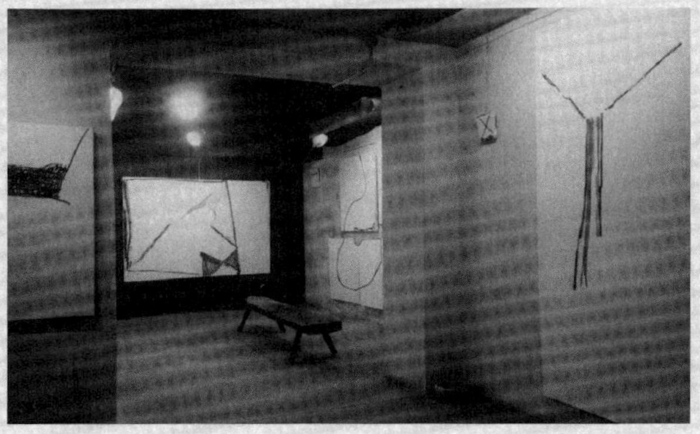

hung comic-strip fashion on the wall adjoining the one bearing the large polyptych.[A, B] Taken separately, any one of these six paintings (they have an almost identical motif) would already be rather droll. In the center of each of them, there is a funny-looking flag or feather duster in euphoric rainbow colors (*60-T-37*), but the effect from one canvas to another is something of a stutter. Looking closer, there is not really a repetition here: the quasi-identity of the motif is only there to accentuate the agency of the format, and therefore difference. If you want to trace the same gesture on supports of varying formats, then whatever you do, you will not be able to avoid adapting your markings proportionally: the same thing cannot be the same thing on a square, a small vertical rectangle, or a wide horizontal space. Quite apart from the fact that you will not see in the same way a painting hung near to the ceiling and one hung at floor level.

The huge gap from floor to ceiling was made part of the work on other walls, and for paintings hung next to each other having no serial relationship. This was the first time that Barré disrupted so forcefully the type of hanging typically used in museums and galleries (another code of the "before-market"), a hanging based on a horizontal baseline running through all of the paintings at their mid-point (the height of this line corresponding supposedly with the eye height of an average viewer). After this audacious first move, none of the solo exhibitions for which Barré designed the hanging was laid out following this ideal line—henceforth, the installation was always a function of the ways in which the works answered each other, going so far as to extend into each other and, by invitation, into the real, contingent surrounding space. But to take up again Clay's terminology, Barré was able to apply the principle of "lateralization" within a single work, provided it was composed of several separate panels. His first "divided polyptych," the great *60-T-45*,[J] dominated one of the walls of the 1960 exhibition.[K] With its curved lines and hatching going from one canvas to another across the thin interstice of wall-space separating them, it reveals (instead of secretly domesticating it) the active agency of the in-between. In making itself a simple sign (a marking of the surface, a measuring of time), paint categorically abolishes the hand and opens out onto real space. But this is only a reprieve. The next step will be the spray canister, where the paint as paste will be sent up in smoke.

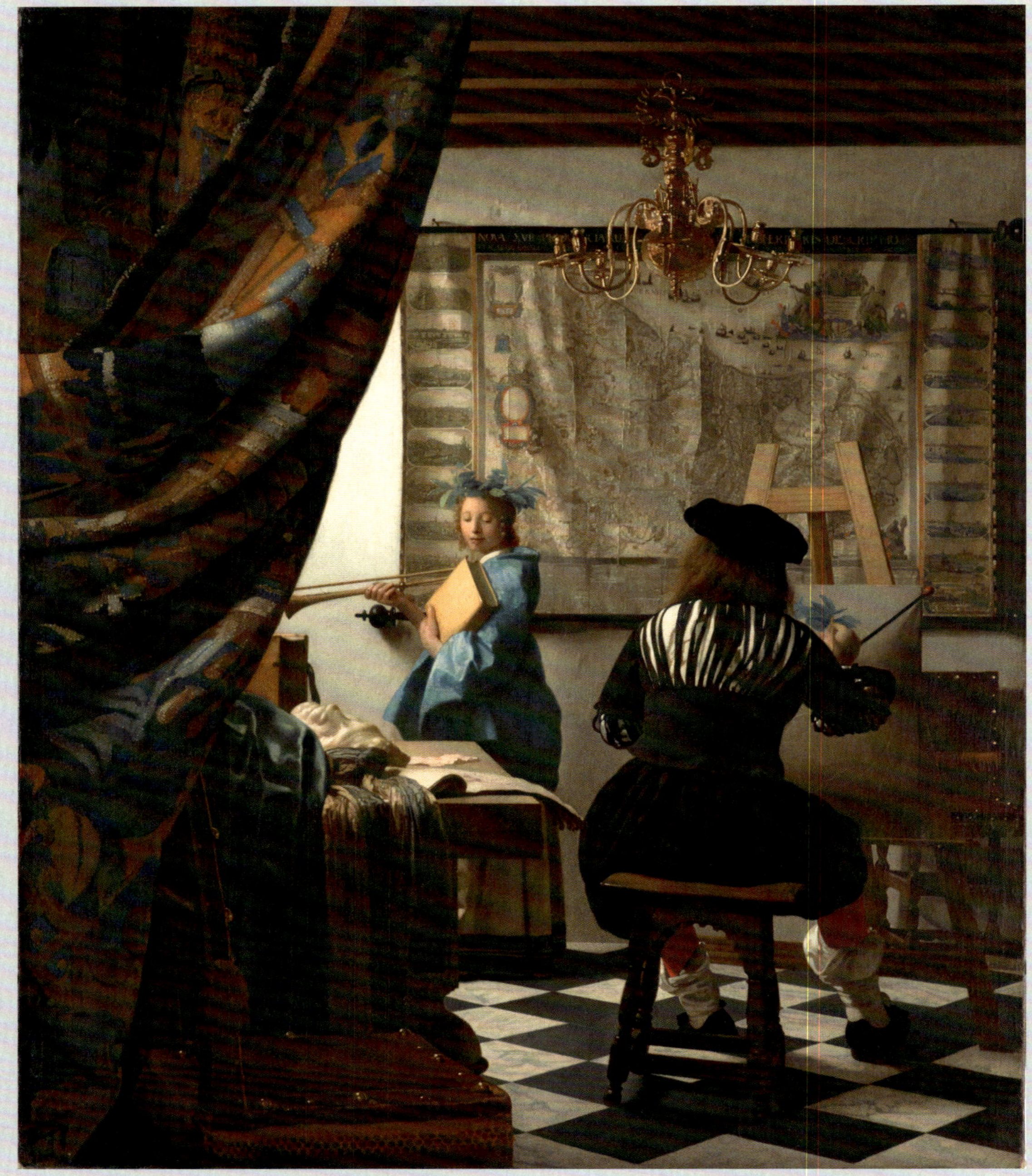

K
Johannes Vermeer
The Art of Painting, c. 1666–68
Oil on canvas, 120 × 100 cm
Kunsthistorisches Museum, Vienna

PAINTING (SPLIT) INTO FOUR

Jean-Pierre Criqui

"The thing to avoid, I don't know why, is the spirit of system. People with things, people without things, things without people, what does it matter, I flatter myself it will not take me long to scatter them, whenever I choose, to the winds. I don't see how. The best would be not to begin. But I have to begin. That is to say I have to go on."

Samuel Beckett, *The Unnamable*, 1949

1.

Between 1960 and 1962 Martin Barré painted four polyptychs, each with four elements. Four "quadriptychs," to use a word which, like many others in French and English, conjugates without too much thought given to the mash-up of Latin and Greek. In a different way, each of these works testifies to an "exigency of discontinuity," an expression coined by Maurice Blanchot to describe a thought where questioning is paramount, and ultimately contributes to thwarting any desire for affirmation,[1] in keeping with the aim that Barré recognized as the foundation of his practice: "I paint paintings, proposals in paint, questions about/to painting."[2] This deliberately interrogative position has some consequences for the viewer, whose function is thus itself questioned. In their apparent bareness, their irreducibility to preconceived ideas or categories, Barré's paintings first leave us *disconcerted* (discourse disorder: What am I looking at? What is there to say about it?), even *dislocated* (spatial disorder, by which we are dislodged from our habits—divided, split—in relation to art). This gives rise to a sort of tacit contract that we have to honor or not: to enter into the painter's game, to accept that something escapes us, to assume an active role in the elaboration of what the work deposits in us. Nothing very different from what art has been demanding since the dawn of time, perhaps, but exacerbated here by the reduction of what we can resort to: no explicit referent, no history (small or large, individual or collective), no expression of feelings. This is what separates, say, a pre-Socratic fragment or a paragraph by Gertrude Stein from a fable by La Fontaine or André Gide's *Journal*.

1 Maurice Blanchot, "Thought and the Exigency of Discontinuity," in *The Infinite Conversation*, trans. Susan Hanson (Minneapolis: University of Minnesota Press, 1969), 3–10. And notably this (p. 8): "... any language where it is a matter of questioning rather than responding is a language already interrupted—even more, a language wherein everything begins with the decision (or distraction) of an initial void."

2 1976 interview with Christian Bonnefoi, cited by Jean Clay, "Le dispositif Martin Barré," *Macula* 2 (1977): 68.

Faced with such a task, some will always prefer to do nothing —because "you can't fool them"—and rely on the cult of common sense or the virtue of hard work, even if it means ending up covering the object of their irritation with vengeful graffiti, a snub which Barré, like so many others, had to endure. It is not immaterial that such behavior, which ultimately appears to be a form of anxiety, actually stems from contempt for the commentary: "One begins by mocking the critic who does not create, and ends up finding that the creator could have created more."[3]

As Yve-Alain Bois pointed out in his monograph, 1960 marked a decisive moment in Barré's oeuvre.[4] It was the year in which Barré, who had just turned thirty-six, presented his third solo exhibition at the Galerie Arnaud in Paris in November and December. Two of the quadriptychs we are concerned with here, dated the same year, were included. *60-T-43*[A] is the only one of the four whose elements—twice two panels of identical dimensions, small and large, interspersed—fit together without spacing between them: the solution of continuity in this case is internal, which is immediately apparent from the way the lines of the canvas on the left flee beyond the frame, making an interruption subsequent to their inscription noticeable. The painting also astonishes when first glimpsed because of its format, a variable to which Barré would always pay extreme attention. Of average height (81 cm), it is four times as wide (barely more, in fact, to the nearest 6 cm, which, as was often the case with the artist, deviates from the comfort of round figures), thereby manifesting in another way the 1:4 ratio that serves as its principle. It is a composite ribbon, a frieze which, if examined, wouldn't take much to generate, in the viewer's mind, the fiction of an artifact that has been discovered in fragments and then reassembled somehow or other by a curator who lacks an instruction manual. For all practical purposes, Jean Clay restored the order of operations: "This is two paintings [each one consisting of two panels] painted separately and then combined. AB and CD become in the new configuration: DACB. Furthermore, C is hung upside down. There are lines added that 'consolidate' the new presentation. The work is *at once* the product of an aleatory procedure and a unifying gesture: it is *at once* an accumulation of disparate fragments and a canvas."[5] (Quotation marks around the verb "consolidate" are intended to convey the bewilderment that these additions actually cause through linking together parts that were originally separate. See thus the connection at the bottom of the first and second canvases, as well as at the bottom of the third and fourth: the hypothesis of a left-to-right organization, to which our reading habit also invites us, is a delusion.)

3
Jean Paulhan, *F. F. ou le critique* [1945] (Paris: Éditions Claire Paulhan, 1998), 86.

4
Yve-Alain Bois, *Martin Barré* (Cologne, New York, and Paris: Galerie Daniel Buchholz, Andrew Kreps Gallery, Galerie Nathalie Obadia, and Thea Westreich/Ethan Wagner, 2008), chapter "1960."

A → pp. 48–49

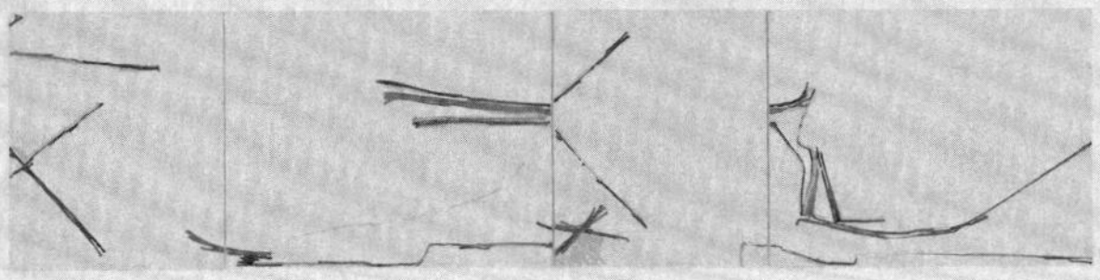

5
Jean Clay, "La peinture en séton," in Suzanne Pagé et al., *Martin Barré*, exh. cat. (Paris: ARC – Musée d'Art Moderne de la Ville de Paris, 1979), 11.

Through its slightly Frankenstein-like aspect, *60-T-43* [A] instils in us an idea of enigma, which, through a kind of secondary reflexivity, entrusts to us, like a hidden object passing from hand to hand, our share of "questions about/to painting." And to the question that we might want to be the ultimate one is linked yet another question. This is undoubtedly one of the most powerful resources of Barré's art. As in Henry James's short stories and novels, and at the extreme opposite of a "key" painting, this undecidable depth, which persists beyond any attempt at elucidation, is what matters most.

B → pp. 44–45

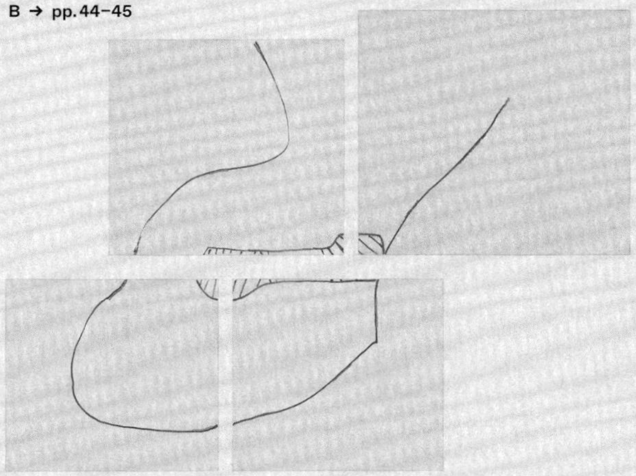

2.

I first saw *60-T-45* [B] at the Louvre in 1990, in the *Polyptyques* exhibition, subtitled "The multiple painting from the Middle Ages to the twentieth century"—important, among other things, for its determination, still too rare today, to free itself from hallowed chronological divisions. Insofar as they allow the identification of differences as well as similarities, unexpected, or not entirely expected rapprochements always produce enlightening effects, and indeed *60-T-45*, [B] although a "multiple painting," did not fail to appear in its full singularity at the exhibition. This was the second quadriptych painted by Barré in 1960 and was also presented at the end of the same year at the Galerie Arnaud. As was already the case with *60-T-43*, [A] Barré used the paint tube, previously filled with oil paint prepared by himself, as a marking tool, according to a method characteristic of the period spanning 1960 through 1962. But the four panels were now separated and tiered in a literally *quartered* arrangement. In the manner of a triplet in a binary rhythm, an odd element was introduced here by the formats of the canvases, three in number: the two lower panels, the only ones identical in this respect, measure 80 cm (height) by 86 cm (width); the upper left panel measures 90 × 96 cm (with the same gap between the two dimensions), the right panel 102 × 110 cm.

When in front of *60-T-45* [B] rather than the previous quadriptych, it is easy to understand the process from which the painting drew its final appearance: the canvases were brought together edge to edge to be painted, then moved apart, thus transforming the unitary block of the motif traced on their surface into a sort of archipelago. The feeling of disjunction is further reinforced by the panels' misalignment. A painter more fond of symmetry would have preserved the intersection of the spacing: Barré canceled it out by the panels' lateral gap at the moment he painted them, and accentuated the aforementioned disjunction, which is already noticeable on account of the variety of formats and by means of which something ternary happens again (the result is two portions of wall left vertically visible within the whole, but only one horizontally), by finally choosing *two* measures of spacing (5 cm between left and right edges, 10 cm between lower and upper edges). The violence of the procedure lies in the fact that it attempts to attack, in a manner of speaking, the principles of binocular vision: the temptation to try to make the two vertical axes coincide is irrepressible, as in those orthoptic exercises where we initially see a bear with a broom next to a bucket and where by squinting our eyes very hard we manage after a while to put the broom in the bucket—but it is impossible because the image that we are trying to reconstruct mentally contradicts this in an indisputable way.

We know that Barré first imagined dissociating the *60-T-45*[B] panels in order to disseminate them in as many exhibitions or collections as possible.[6] A way of prolonging their discontinuity by removing the latter from view, but also, as visitors to the *Polyptyques* exhibition could not help but notice, by ballasting it, not without a possible irony, with the weight of history relating to the fate of many of these "multiple paintings," which were to be dismantled, dispersed, and, in the best case scenario, reconstructed. One of the oldest works assembled for the Louvre exhibition, an Italian triptych by the Cesi Master, probably executed at the end of the thirteenth century, offered an edifying example of these vicissitudes: "The triptych by the Cesi Master was dismantled in the 1920s at the request of its owner, Béatrice Ephrussi de Rothschild; preoccupied with the interior design of the villa 'Île de France' that she had built between 1906 and 1912 in a pseudo-Florentine style, the work was used to make up the panels of a door called the "Siena Door" (their style is obviously not Sienese!). The two panels were thus separated from the central panel, lined on the reverse with fifteenth-century Spanish panels (a *Saint Peter* and a *Saint Bernard*) and small landscapes of mediocre quality, all set in a gilded wood frame."[7] Even if a return to a hypothetical original state remains unthinkable (it would be advisable, in this regard, to begin by reinstalling the work in the site for which it was conceived, which has undoubtedly changed as well), the adventures of our altarpiece had a happy ending: it's a "comedy of reassembly," one could argue, while saluting the memory of an eminent philosopher.[8] In any event, Barré's decision to keep the parts of his quadriptych together—simultaneously joined and separated, assembled and disassembled—was clearly the most relevant. What is gained is the visible tension that the artist strove to create in other proposals of the same period, such as in the diptych *60-T-47*,[C] where the central motif was broken up by inverting the panels once the painting process was completed. The right half passes to the left: from this simple gesture, added to the execution,

6

This is reported by Jean Clay in the "Repères iconographiques" ["Iconographic Landmarks"] (we will ponder all the appeal of this epithet) to which he associated about twenty of the artist's paintings: Pagé et al., *Martin Barré*, 44.

7

I quote here the entry relating to this work by Dominique Thiébaut, one of the curators of the exhibition, in the *Polyptyques* catalogue: Marie-Claude Chaudonneret et al., *Polyptyques: le tableau multiple du Moyen Âge au vingtième siècle* (Paris: RMN, 1990), 52.

8

See Stanley Cavell, *Pursuits of Happiness: The Hollywood Comedy of Remarriage* (Cambridge, MA: Harvard University Press, 1981).

C → p. 43

an object is created that goes in opposite directions, and splits the gaze (and thus the viewer). The image of a division where what most obstinately "stares" at us is ultimately the thin vertical slit marking the center of the painting with its shadow. In the Louvre exhibition, which highlighted a general longing for unity, for the ideal overcoming of the fragmentation peculiar to the polyptych, even a work as divergent as Jasper Johns's *Voice 2* (1971), composed of three non-joining panels of identical size and in which the title, fractured and split, extends from one end of the triptych to the other, in no way approached the disjunctive force of Barré's *60-T-45*.[B]

Pondering the kind of colored drawing that *60-T-45*[B] presents would, for example, be among a hundred other questions that such a painting, in a manner of speaking and with a smile, leaves to the discretion of whoever dares seek in it a pretext for discourse. What are we dealing with? Is there any prerequisite—observed, remembered, preconceived—to this drawing? I don't know. "All invention consists in making something out of nothing," Racine wrote in his preface to *Bérénice*, a play "so little charged with intrigue" that he was criticized for its "simplicity." Guided by the intuition that Barré would have allowed himself for his drawing of such an inaugural "nothing," we will hazard the supposition that he initially moved through the space of his joined canvases starting at the top of the upper left panel and continued his line toward the two lower panels and then back to the two on the left, and finally on the upper right panel, thus completing the circumscription of the central enclosure and completing this first delimitation, as if with a flourish, by the ascending line which is interrupted two-thirds into the largest painting. It is a stroke of wit, if you like, which leaves open this vast loop whose eye, or knot, has then been hatched in blue (hatching, a conventional sign of cartography to designate a relief, as if the painter were establishing himself as the geographer of his own territory). Another later gesture was the doubling, or indeed the extension, in red and always with the paint tube, of certain segments of the said loop: dabbing, accents added here and there along the initial line (a cosmetic gesture with no apparent object or motive, which again contributes to misleading our reconstruction effort). As for the distance finally arranged by Barré between each of his four panels, it confers an active and, to say the least, singular function to the wall: implicitly lured into the artwork, the wall brings its share of drawing to the whole, and in so doing complicates the flatness that presided over the painting's conception.[9]

9
Flatness, which of course constitutes an essential element of Barré's reflections on painting, in the thread (and via the sublation) of various cardinal moments in modern art. See in this regard the article by Claire Salles, "Le polyptyque *60-T-45* de Martin Barré: convoquer le mur d'accrochage pour dévoyer le sujet" in the online review *exPosition*, no. 3, 2017.

D

62-4, 1962
Quadriptych; 25×65 cm, 25×55 cm, 19×48 cm, 19×65 cm (from top left to bottom left, clockwise), overall dimensions: 68×140 cm

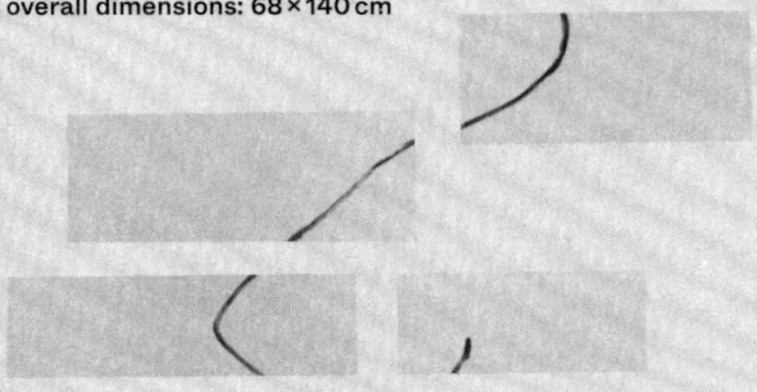

E

62-5, 1962
Quadriptych; 60×81 cm, 54×81 cm, 60×92 cm, 54×81 cm (from top left to bottom left, clockwise), overall dimensions: 157×184 cm

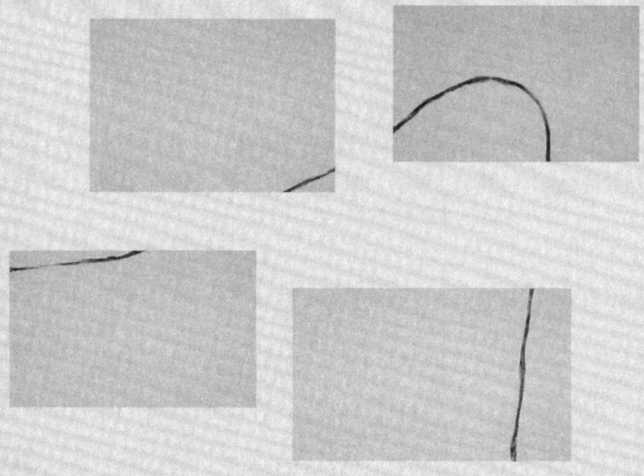

3.

In the two 1962 quadriptychs, we find the exploration of the asymmetry that was noticeable in those of 1960, as well as the quartered arrangement of the elements that already distinguished *60-T-45*.[B] *62-4*,[D] the smallest of the works in this quartet, plays with a different type of tiering than the previous one, notably by raising the upper right panel in relation to the left one, so that the gap between the two upper canvases in *60-T-45*,[B] which was due to their different sizes, is this time repeated between two canvases of equal height. Looking, like listening, is also counting, doing a little mental arithmetic, and here we quickly spot a certain ratio of dimensions. If, starting at the top left and going clockwise, we name the canvases of *62-4*[D] A, B, C, and D, it appears that A and B are of equal height, but not of the same width; B and C are of different height and width; C and D are of equal height, but of different width; D and A are of equal width, but of different height. Consequently, a very concerted combination of identities and differences. While again avoiding the junction of the vertical and horizontal, the spacing of the panels, as in *60-T-45*,[B] is equal from left to right and differs from the spacing between top and bottom panels —except that there are now *two* differences in the vertical: one between A, C, and D, somewhat less than the left/right spacing; the other between B and C, *equal in height to A and B*, and by far the largest. I wouldn't swear that I have kept hold of any reader's attention at this stage, but it is nevertheless worth adding what constitutes the most notable feature of *62-4*,[D] namely, another mark of discontinuity, this gap in the drawing that one cannot help noticing between panels C and D. As before, Barré indeed painted his canvases by bringing them together, but he broke off his line toward the bottom. The interruption is thus squared in *62-4*.[D] Painted shortly afterwards, *62-5*[E] reversed the logic that had prevailed until then by proposing a line inscribed on the four canvases kept separate, according to a spacing that perpetuates their hanging. Try to bring them together in your imagination, and the supposed continuity of the line is irretrievably shattered.

A composite number is a natural number other than zero that has a positive divisor other than one or itself. The smallest is four, which can also be divided by two. Often associated with an odd element, the number four is one of the bases of the rhythmic play that runs through Barré's work. It was already present in some of the properties of the conventional support which, as a painter, he never renounced, namely the four sides and the four corners of the canvas mounted on a stretcher. Let us look at the spray paintings of the mid-1960s, where his intervention was more than once limited to a few brief intrusions, and sometimes only one, on the paintings' edges: *65-A-30×30* [F] (one mark on one side), *65-S-1-96×90* [G] (two marks on one side), *65-A-73×73* [H] (three marks on two sides), *65-S-12* [I] (four marks on three sides). Like Herman Melville's Bartleby, Barré preferred not to overdo it, but it is better to distrust this: from the 1970s onward, his calculations, inseparable from what he concealed of them, would sometimes be extremely complex, and we have seen that already the 1960–62 quadriptychs were not to be outdone in this respect. A final example from this period: in its apparently disarming terseness, *60-T-50* [J] seems to be limited to crossing out the canvas (*X marks the spot*, as they say in English). What could be less *finished* than such a painting? But the sheer variety of traces recorded on its surface, the multiplicity of effects that they set against attempts at summary description, belie any univocity and impose on us the notion—the *cipher*—of a superior subtlety. Barré, as simple as it may seem, always did at least two things at once, with the contradictory power that such an attitude carried with it: learned negligence, attentive carelessness with regard to the rule observed and circumvented, which the Italian language calls *sprezzatura*, a word whose fortune was established in the Renaissance in books on good manners as well as in treatises on art.[10]

4.

Asked in 1985 about a possible "tradition of abstraction," Barré replied: "In Ancient Greece and Rome there was a cohabitation of abstraction and figuration, so I don't see abstraction as an invention of the twentieth century, but more as a rediscovery of non-representation. Near Pompeii, in a villa they began to excavate in 1964, I saw these abstract paintings made with stripes. In what have been called my 'Zebras' (the first of which dates from 1963) there were things very similar to that. So, there was a man who did that about two thousand years before me—and in my view he did it better! I think that's fantastic. Maybe the history of abstract painting needs to be rewritten."[11] The evident enthusiasm of these words encourages us to think of their author's oeuvre in conjunction with others. Contemporary, as can be attempted firsthand without too much difficulty.[12] But also, of course, more distant in time, as his remarks above invite us to do. From the standpoint of comparative painting, another reflection by Barré during the same interview regularly comes to mind. ("I often think of Vermeer. I made a calculation that is fairly simple because there aren't many paintings: his entire oeuvre could fit into a square measuring 3.97 by 3.97 meters."[13]) Firstly because the strangeness of the undertaking—why measure the total surface area

F
65-A-30×30, 1965

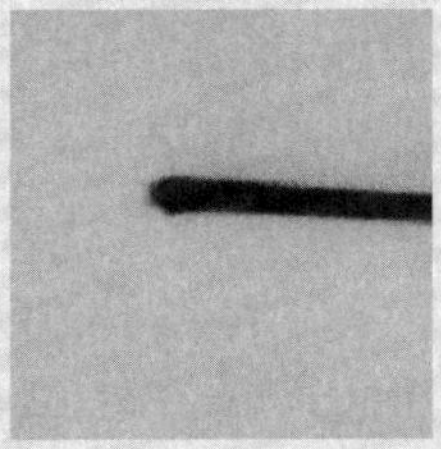

G
65-S-1-96×90, 1965

H → p. 86

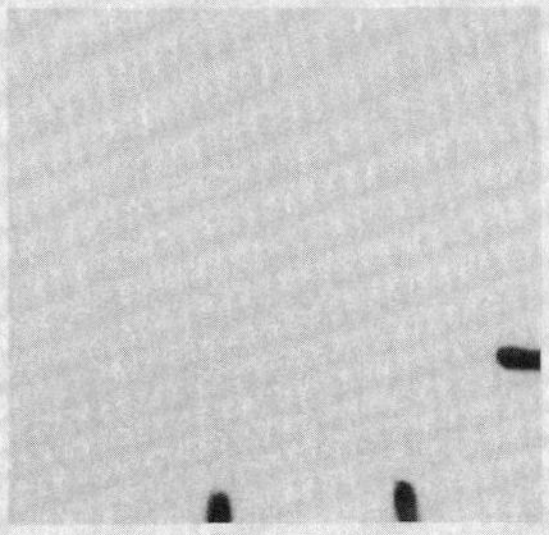

I
65-S-12, 1965
76×72 cm

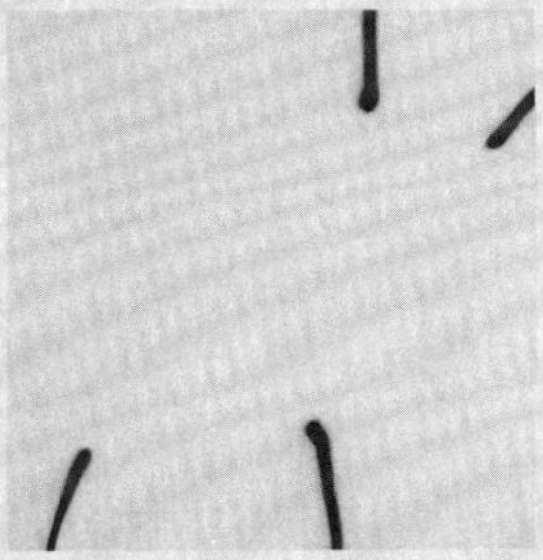

J
60-T-50, 1960
86×80 cm

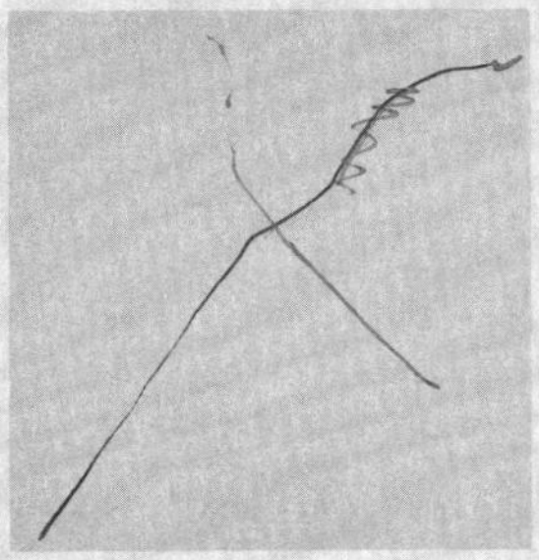

10
See on this subject the very rich study by Jean-Claude Lebensztejn, "Florilège de la nonchalance," in his book *Annexes—de l'œuvre d'art* (Brussels: La Part de l'Œil, 1999), 225–62. The remark concerning Giorgione, pp. 245–46, leads us straight to Barré: "Giorgione was perhaps the first master of modern mystery painting. Whereas in Bosch, or even in Piero di Cosimo, the enigma is conspicuous, insistent —a forest of locks without keys— the enigma of Giorgione, a little later that of Pontormo, is more curiously apparent and invisible, impalpable and unlocatable. It is not only the meaning that is hidden there, it is the enigma of meaning: it is the mystery itself."

11
Martin Barré, in Catherine Millet, "M. B. 'Elsewhere'" (1985), repr. in Yve-Alain Bois, *Martin Barré* (Cologne, New York, and Paris: Galerie Daniel Buchholz, Andrew Kreps Gallery, Galerie Nathalie Obadia, and Thea Westreich/Ethan Wagner, 2008), 273.

12
This is what the 2006 exhibition *Idées de la peinture. Hommage à Martin Barré* did, where, at the invitation of Nathalie Obadia, I proposed some similarities that could also be considered as contrasts. The artists presented at the same time as the paintings of Barré were Christian Bonnefoi, Raoul De Keyser, Peter Halley, On Kawara, Robert Mangold, Albert Oehlen, Bernard Piffaretti, Pascal Pinaud, and Christopher Wool (see the catalogue with the same title published on this occasion by the Galerie Nathalie Obadia).

13
Ibid., 275.

of a body of paintings?—is in itself exhilarating and reveals something of the thinking of the person engaged in it. Secondly, insofar as this is an artist to whom few people would immediately refer when thinking of Barré. Here again, nothing is self-evident. The largest painting we know of by Vermeer is *The Art of Painting*, K → p. 68 which measures 120 × 100 cm (not huge, by the way). In it, we see a painter at work, his tools, his work in progress, his model, a geographic map that has been proven to exist (and on which Vermeer signed his name),[14] the whitewashed wall on which it is spread out—a thousand clues of a profuse reflexivity that could not fail to capture Barré's attention, just as his oeuvre holds ours when, like him, we too agree to split into four.[15]

14

On *The Art of Painting*, examined in the light of developments in cartography in the Netherlands, and its role in the history of art, see Svetlana Alpers, *The Art of Describing: Dutch Art in the Seventeenth Century* (London: John Murray, 1983), chapter 4 ("The Mapping Impulse in Dutch Art").

15

[Translator's note] The title and final words employ versions of and wordplay around "se mettre en quatre" (literally: to put oneself into four [parts]), an expression which means to make a lot of effort or go to a lot of trouble and usually translates as "to bend over backwards."

1963
1967

“WHAT I WANTED TO SHOW, BY MEANS OF TRACES OF IMPACT IN A LIGHT SURFACE, WAS WHAT PAINTING WOULD BE LIKE WHEN ‘UNCLUTTERED’ BY OBJECTS, COLORS, AND FORMS, OFFERING ONLY FRAGMENTS OF A SPACE THAT EXISTED ELSEWHERE AS MUCH AS IN ITS *TANGIBLE* FRAGMENTS.”

Martin Barré, 1974

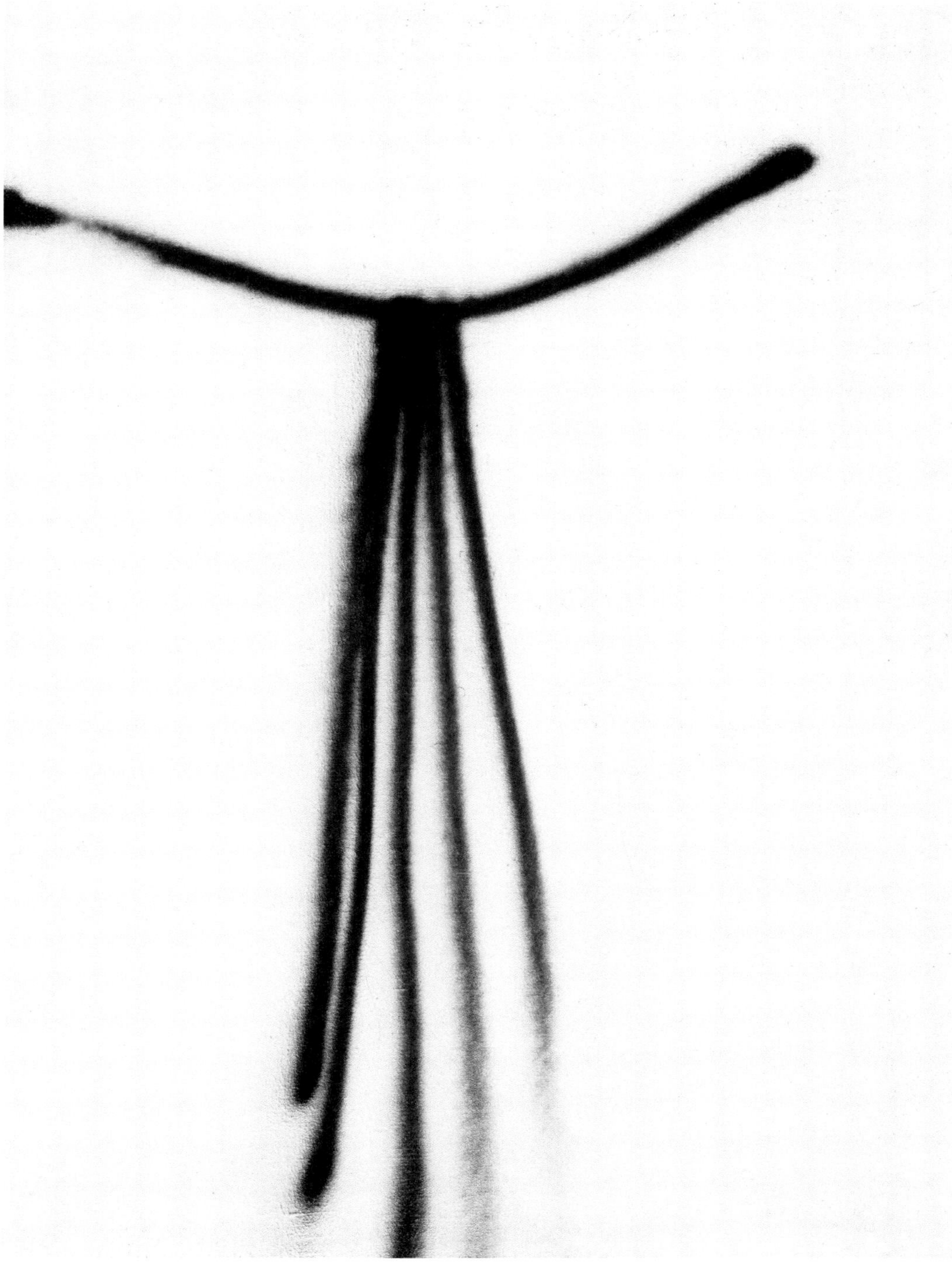

63-C, 1963
120 × 88 cm

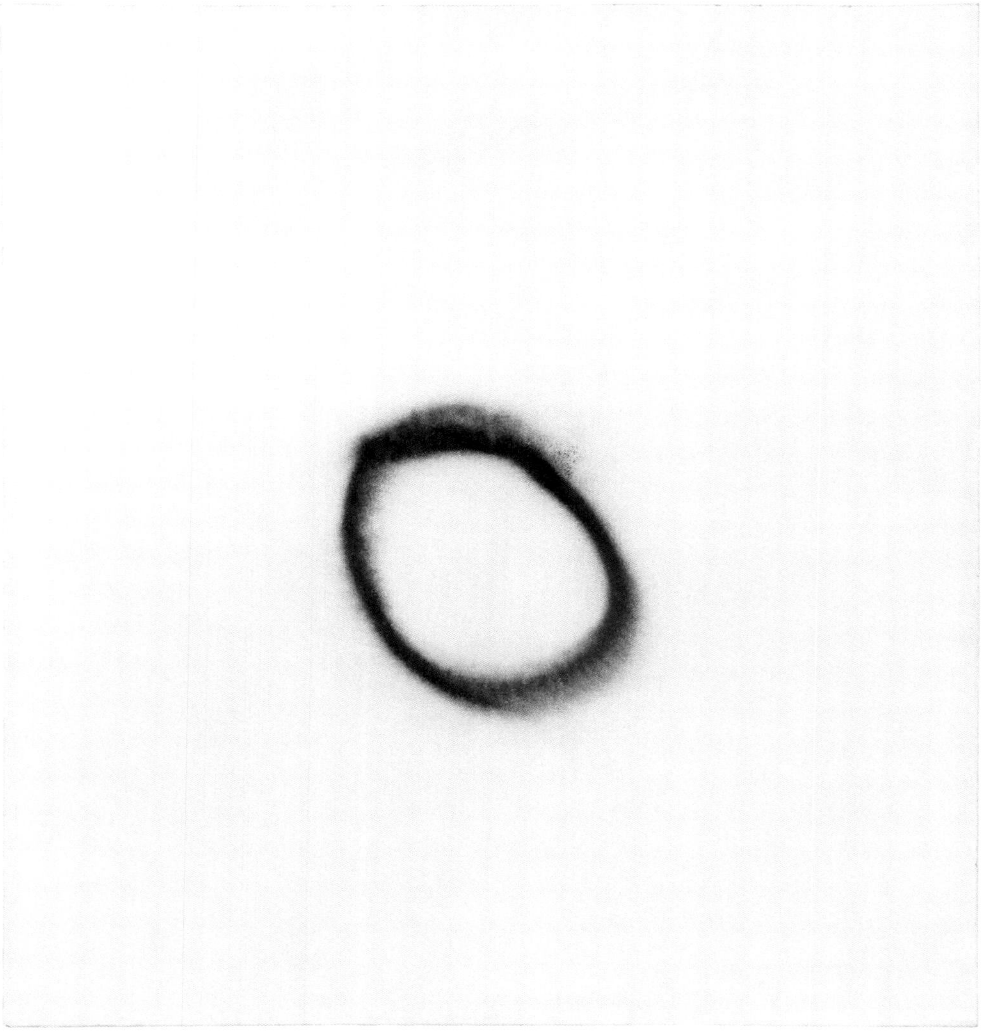

63-O, 1963
85 × 79 cm

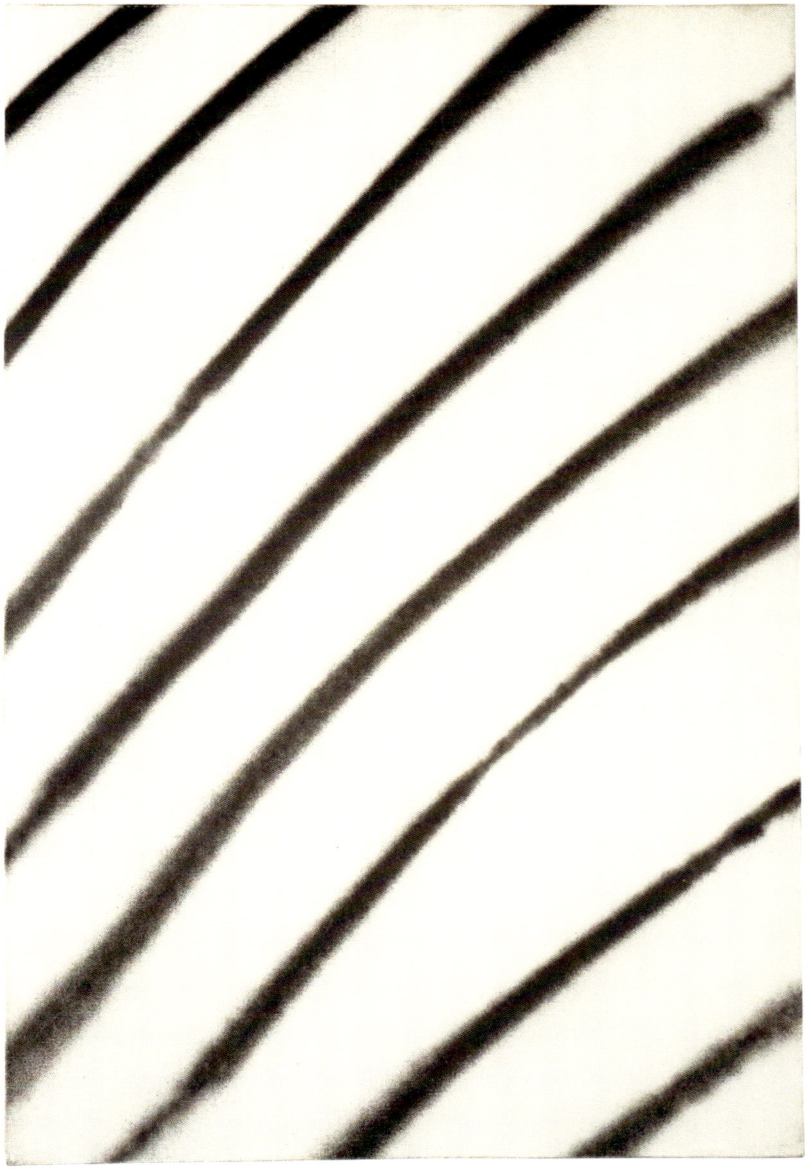

63-Z, 1963
81 × 54 cm

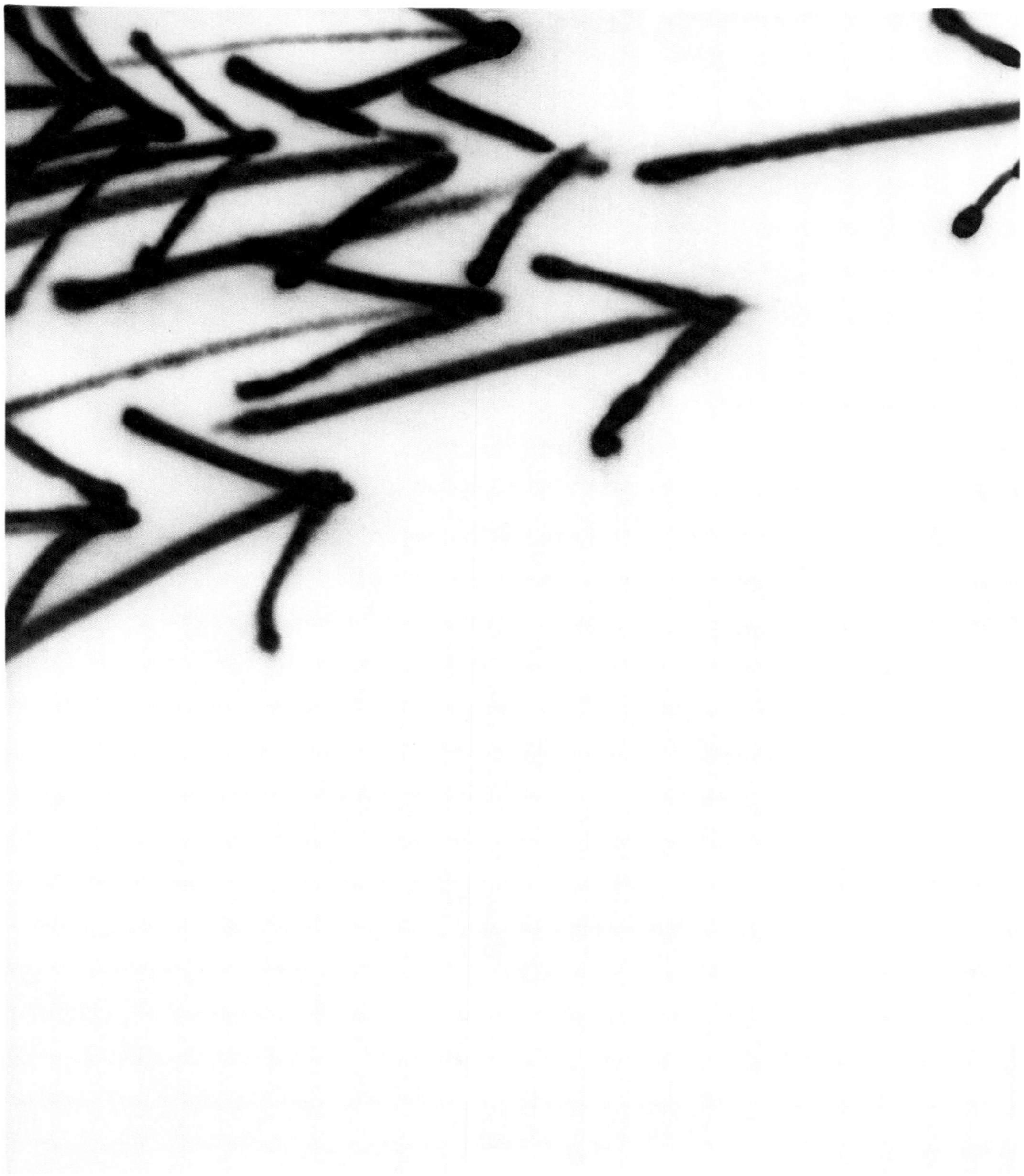

63-F-A, 1963
115 × 97 cm

65-A-50×50, 1965

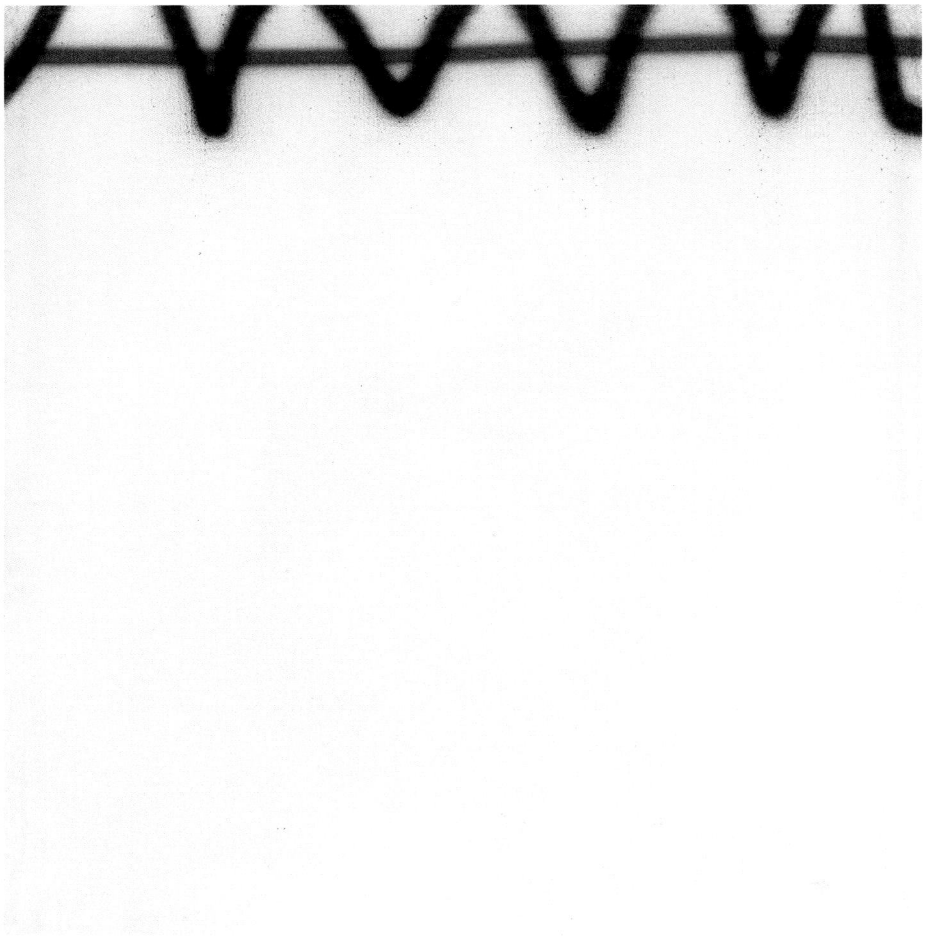

65-H-L-78×74, 1965

65-H-L-113×86, 1965

65-A-73×73, 1965

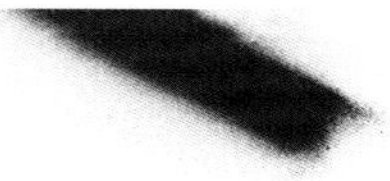

65-A-73×54, 1965

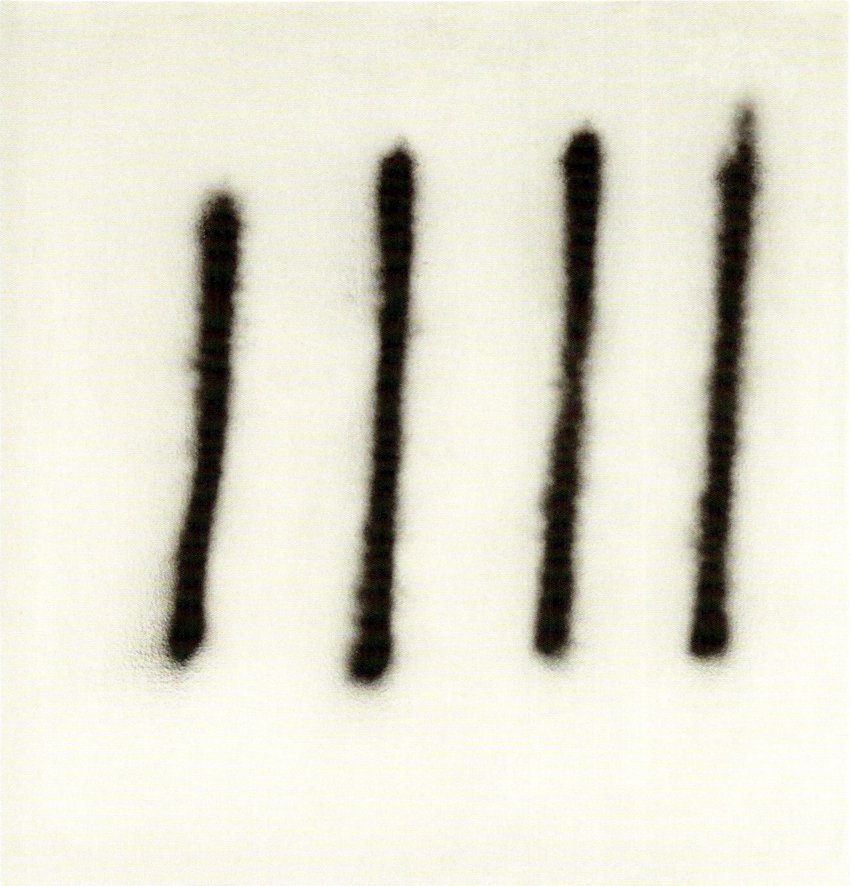

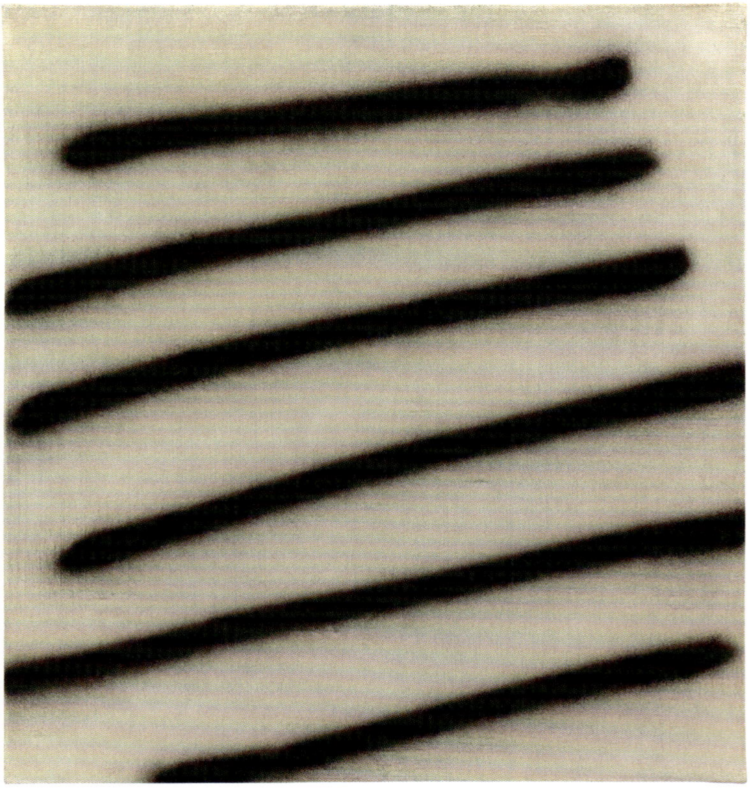

↑
67-Z-7-70×65, 1967

→
67-Z-18-43×40, 1967

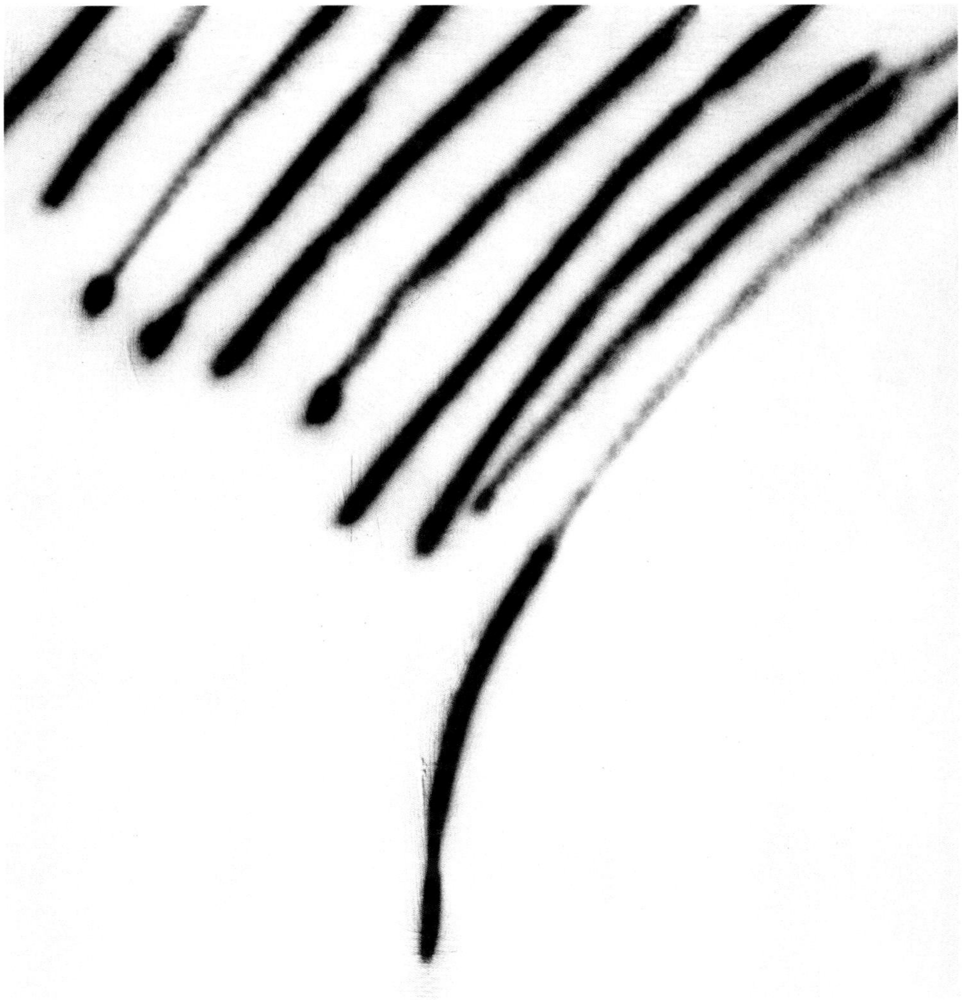

67-Z-1-86×80, 1967

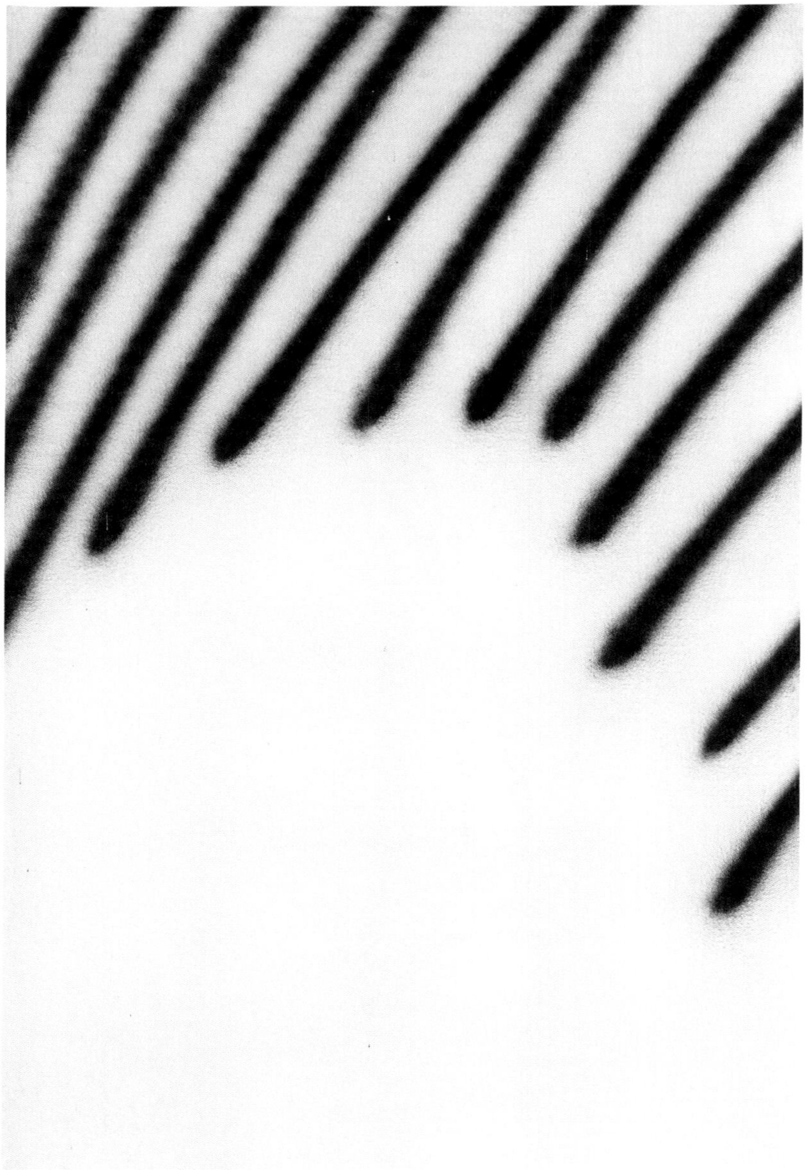

67-Z-3-81×54, 1967

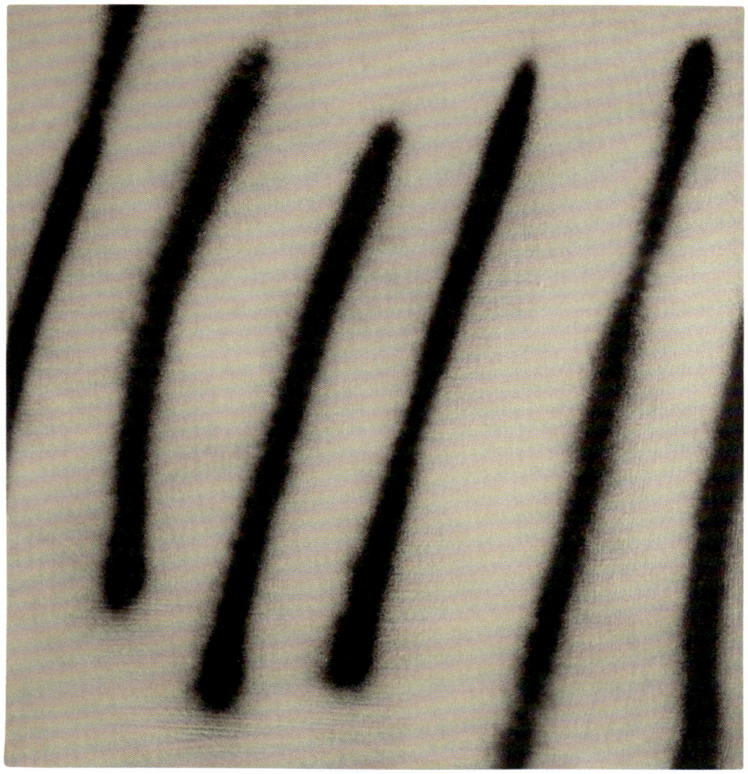

↑
67-Z-19-43×40, 1967

→
67-Z-26-70×53, 1967

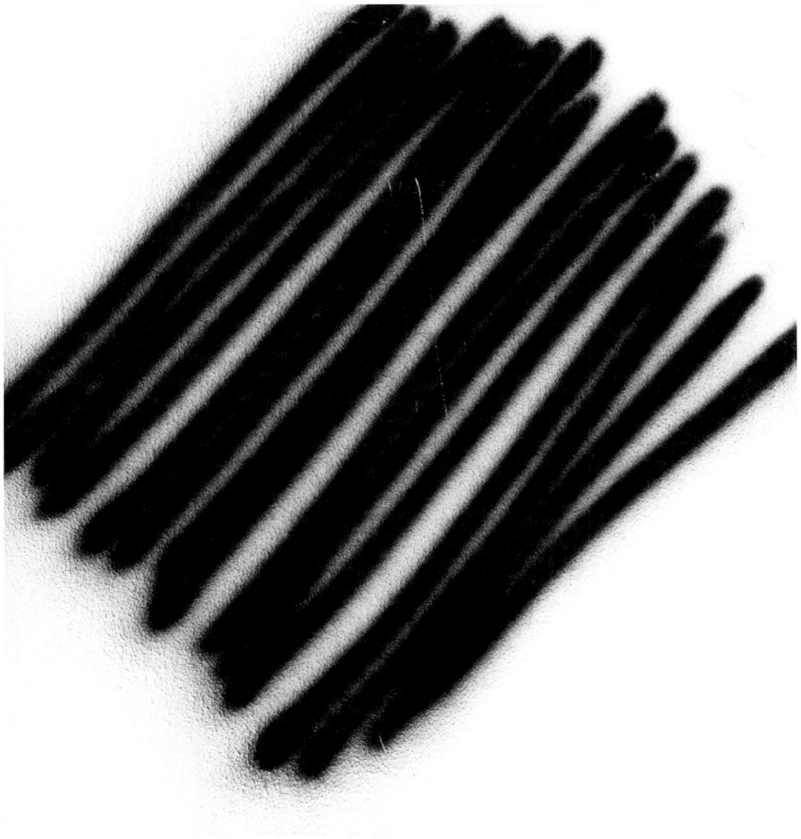

67-Z-4-53×49, 1967

67-A-Z-3, 1967
113 × 105 cm

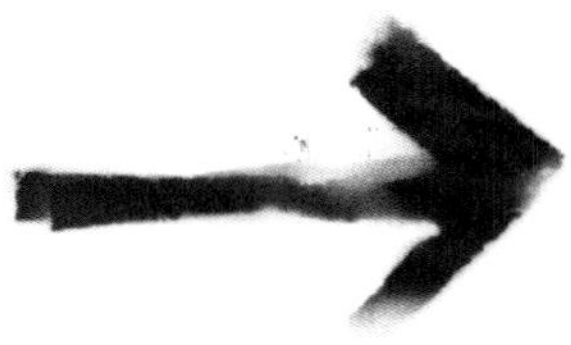

67-F-2-113×105, 1967

67-F-4-113×105, 1967

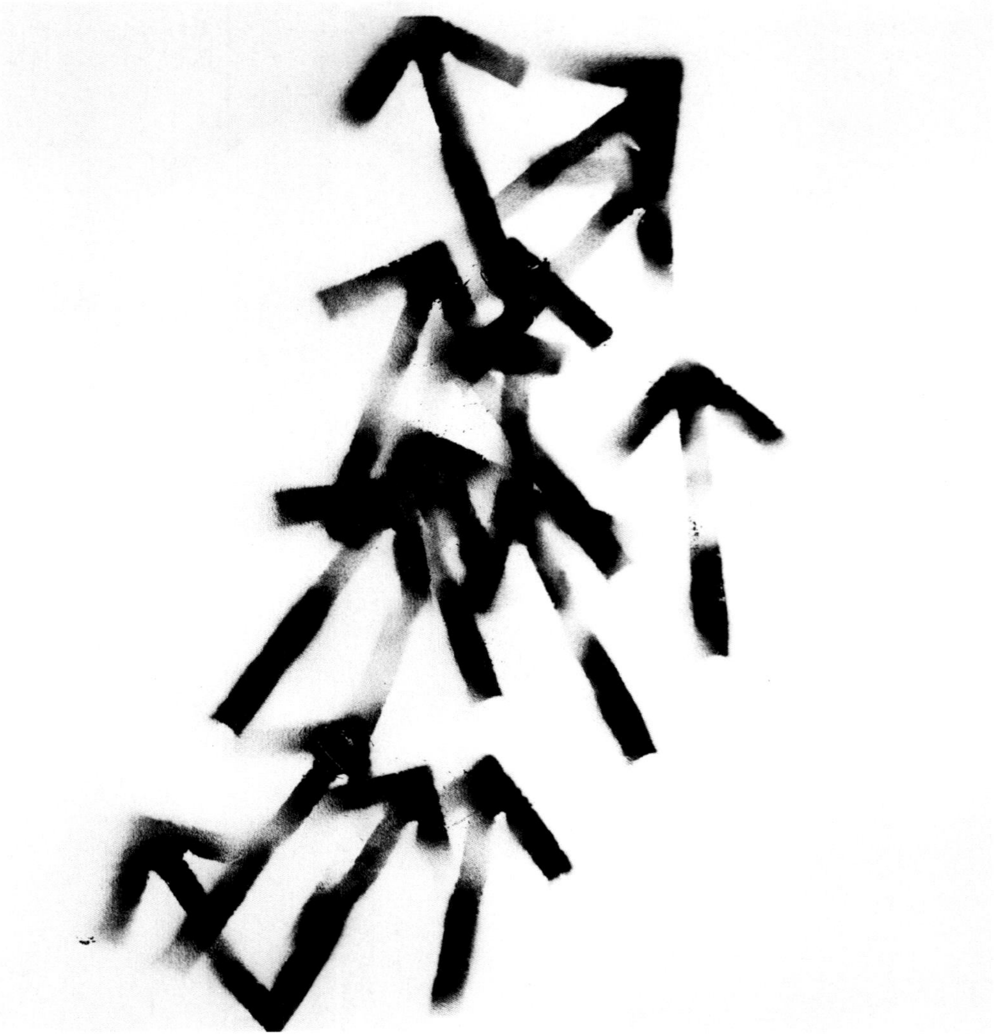

67-F-10-86×80, 1967

THE SPRAY PAINTINGS, 1963–1967: THE TEMPTATION OF DEGREE ZERO

Clément Dirié
Michel Gauthier

Between 1963 and 1967, Martin Barré created a resolutely innovative body of more than one hundred and fifty paintings and works on paper[1] using spray paint. Deepening and radicalizing the examination of pictorial parameters that he had been conducting since the mid-1950s,[2] the experiments of this period undoubtedly constitute a cardinal moment in the history of painting of the time. Indeed, the artist used the spray can for new purposes. In Hans Hartung's paintings of the mid-1960s, the spray can was used to achieve blurred effects and an undefined form, while Nicolas Schöffer's spray-gun paintings of the late 1940s were still very much linked to a surrealist desire for minimally mediatized expression. In Barré's work, the use of the spray can answer the desire to register the physicality and temporality of the pictorial process and to suppress direct contact between the painter's hand and the canvas. In 1968, proof if any were needed of the radicality of the spray paintings, Barré stopped painting —he did not return to it until 1972—as though he had reached a stage that, at the time, had no possibility of being extended.

In one of the first critical studies published about the paintings of these years in *Cimaise* in March 1964, Marc Albert-Levin returned to the origins of the use of spray: the graffiti in the corridors of the Parisian subway.[3] "[Barré] has recently been painting with these spray cans that sprayed O.A.S. on the walls of the Métro. His eye, particularly attentive to detail, was struck by the exceptional quality of these letters, these lines as though porous, of a foamy black."[4] For an artist who had constantly been experimenting since 1955 with ways of applying paint to the canvas—successively with a brush, knife, framing sticks, and paint tube—the fact of using a spray can as an instrument that was at once the pot, brush, and pigment could only be very promising. After a few unsatisfactory attempts with colored sprays, he decided to stick exclusively to black. The strict bichromy of the black and white and the perfect flatness of the pictorial marks favored a processual literalism: the curved lines want to be nothing but curved lines, going from one point

1
With that of the years 1957–60, this body of work is one of the few for which Martin Barré produced works on paper, mainly in 1964 and 1965 for exhibitions abroad. See Clément Dirié, "À fleur de feuilles. Les œuvres sur papier de Martin Barré," *Roven* 11 (2015): 32–37.

2
Through both solo and group exhibitions, notably at the Galerie Arnaud, presentations of tube paintings from 1960 through 1962 and spray paintings from 1963 through 1964 followed one another naturally. The appearance of the spray paintings was not, unlike their cessation, the result of a crisis—even if it is necessary to put into perspective the rupture that the transition from spray painting to photography would constitute. As early as 1967, the artist announced an exhibition of photographs in an article by Marc Albert-Levin (in *Les Lettres françaises*, June 1–7, 1967) and even envisaged producing his spray paintings via photography, according to the entry that Jean Clay devotes to the year 1967 in the catalogue of the exhibition at the ARC – Musée d'Art Moderne de la Ville de Paris in 1979.

3
In this respect, the painting *63-M-2* is probably the closest to Métro graffiti, since the letters R, O, and L can be made out.

4
Marc Albert-Levin, "Martin Barré ou les malheurs de la vertu," *Cimaise* 67 (January/February/March 1964): 42–52, here 47.

to another, and wanting to refer only to the process of their production. The canvas literally became a projection screen, and critics would liken it to Mallarméan poetry or the cinema of Michelangelo Antonioni.[5] The paintings would in any case be keenly discussed in artistic circles of the time, writers going as far as to speak of “anti-painting” and “painter-suicide of abstraction.” In a 1988 interview with Catherine Millet, Barré considered these works in retrospect as “less audacious than the tube paintings” —they are, it is true, much more popular critically and commercially than the latter—but confirmed that, with them, it was indeed a question of “approaching the limits of painting.”[6]

Two main moments can be distinguished in the corpus of spray paintings. First of all, there are the years 1963–66, which are those of an all-round exploration, revealed from January 1964 at the Galerie Arnaud. In these paintings, Barré simultaneously took up the “motifs,” configurations, and occupations of the pictorial space already experimented with via the paint tube in the years 1960–62 (the lasso, the crossed-out line,[A, B] the tie,[C] the line going around the canvas, the muddle of lines) and invented others (the circle,[D] the arrow, alone or in a group, and the stripe[E]). Then, at the end of the period, there was the output of 1967 during which Barré devoted himself to two specific series taking up a single “motif” honed in 1963: the “Zèbres” (“Zebras”) or “67-Z”; the “Flèches” (“Arrows”) or “67-F.” Each of them was presented during exhibitions at Galerie Arnaud, the first in May–June 1967, the second in January–February 1968—the latter being the artist’s final collaboration with this gallery. During these years, the paintings in question were also shown in solo exhibitions in Stockholm, Berlin, Hanover, Ibiza, and Rio de Janeiro. The few paintings in the “67-A-Z” subset were undoubtedly those which, throughout the entire period, displayed the pictorial process most forcefully—repetitions and erasures, superimpositions of layers which, in some of the paintings, allowed forms to appear by means of transparency.[F] All the works were in square or almost square format, with the exception of one painting, the tondo *63-CF*,[7] and the monumental stage curtain of the Maison de la Culture in Grenoble that Barré created in 1967 at the request of the architect André Wogenscky.

How should we ultimately view this now mythical corpus that occupied Barré for four years? We must certainly highlight its cinematic quality and its propensity to combine opposites. Indeed, these paintings seem to take place between the uncontrollable and the controlled, the freeze

5
Jean-Jacques Lévêque, “Martin Barré,” *Arts*, April 1964. According to the article’s author, it was Barré himself who suggested the reference to Michelangelo Antonioni. From the same author, in *Les Lettres françaises*, January–February 1964: “Martin Barré offers little to our imagination: an infinite space of a milky whiteness, too white, and those silently animated marks that run through it and never seem to want to stop. … It’s not so much painting, it’s more like cinema, but it’s still quite fascinating.”

6
Catherine Millet, “Martin Barré, 67-Z-7,” *Art press* 128 (September 1988): 88.

A → p. 52

B → p. 84
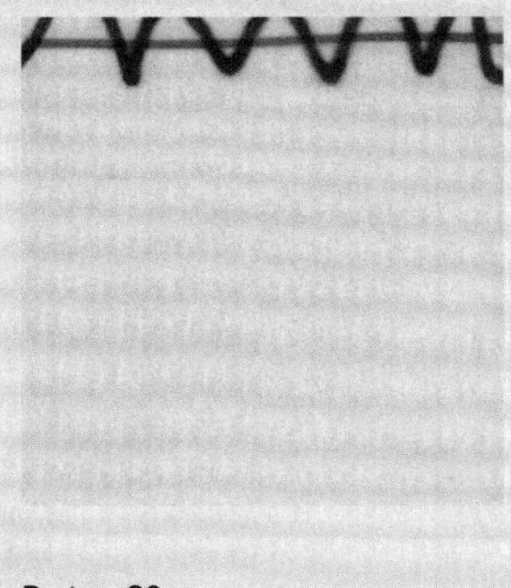

D → p. 80
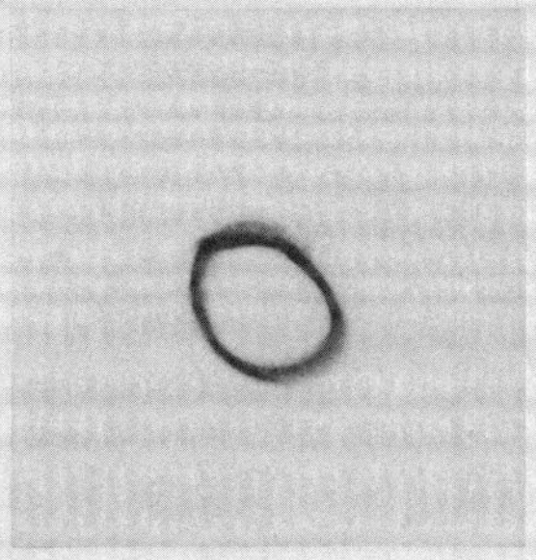

C → p. 79
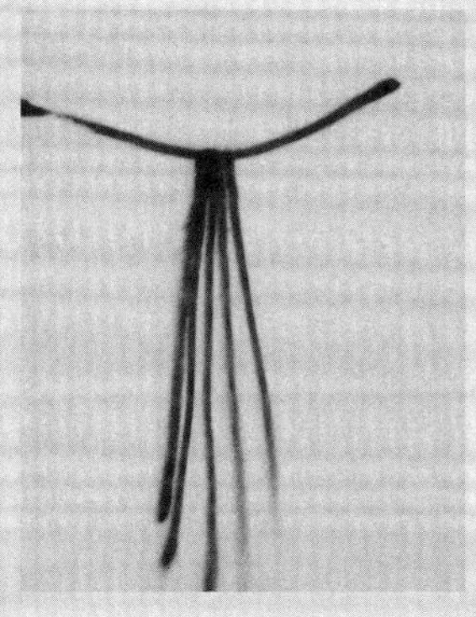

E → p. 81
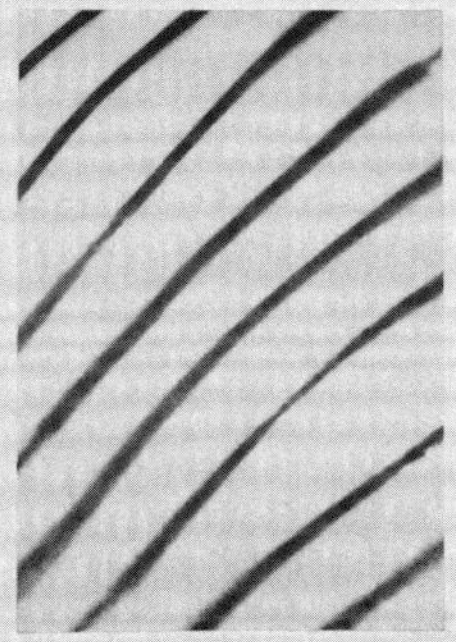

F → p. 93
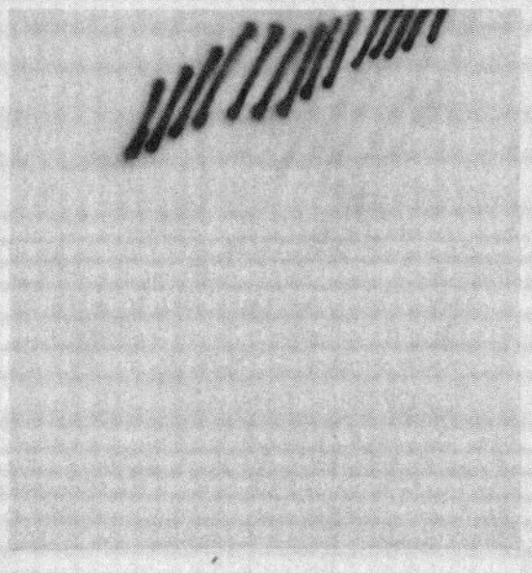

7
A one-off in Barré’s practice, this work was “commissioned” by the gallery owner Cérès Franco for an exhibition entitled *L’Œil de bœuf*, Paris, 1963, which brought together round and oval works by some one hundred artists. The exhibition then traveled to the VII Biennial of São Paulo, again curated by Cérès Franco.

frame and the suggestion of movement, the absence of direct physical contact between the artist and his work and the canvas as an almost photographic recording of the movement of the spray in front of it, the affirmation of an "open and perfectly designated space" (Catherine Millet), the simplicity of an elementary tool and the variety of shades it allows—the density of paint that blackens the canvas is a function of the distance between it and the spray can, the aerosol's spraying force depending on whether it is full or almost empty, the speed of execution, and the time it takes to place the canvas horizontally after having painted it vertically.

It should also be noted that the spray paintings are very diverse. As demonstrated particularly clearly by the "Zebras" series, Barré used this instrument —and the stripes it produced—to create paintings that were very different from one another. The marks do not all have the same thickness nor the same length, sometimes within the same painting; their density varies, sometimes in tight rows, sometimes widely spaced; they can cover the canvas in its entirety, from edge to edge,[G] or only fill a portion of it.[H] It should also be pointed out that the spray paintings were the first works by Barré to make the beyond-the-frame—that space where the majority of curved lines are initiated and continued—so active. This dimension is eminently noticeable when the paintings are exhibited together, as was the case with the retrospective at the ARC – Musée d'Art Moderne de la Ville de Paris in 1979.→ p. 222 Lastly, we should also add that, with the "Arrows" series, the spray paintings testify to a desire for passivity, for the painter's non-power, which echoes Simon Hantaï's paintings made using the folding technique. Indeed, the arrows were traced by means of a stencil larger than the painting itself so that Barré didn't know exactly where they would occur on the canvas→ p. 96 —the protocol thus created an indeterminacy in which the sensation of creative freedom that emanates from the 1963–67 works undoubtedly crystallized.

But it must also be said that these spray paintings, which are Barré's most famous works—those with which his oeuvre sometimes even tends to be confused —do not have a special place in his creative output. Admittedly, they distinguish themselves by the use of a new tool that Barré would not use afterwards. Admittedly, they precede an interruption of several years in his pictorial work that suggests a point of culmination, or crisis. However, they should be considered only as a waymark—essential, crucial, fascinating, but a waymark nevertheless—in Barré's practice. They are part of the continuity of a style of painting which, as early as 1960, gave primacy to line over form.

G → p. 91

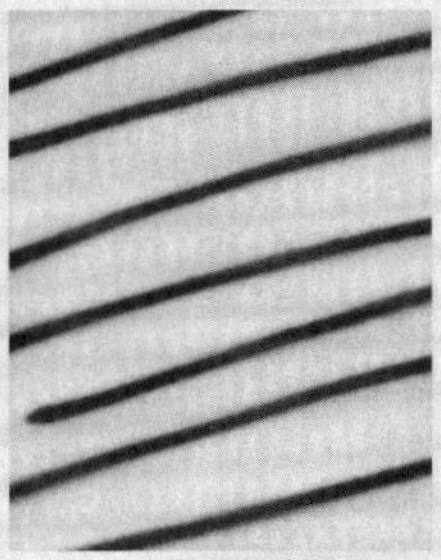

H → p. 88

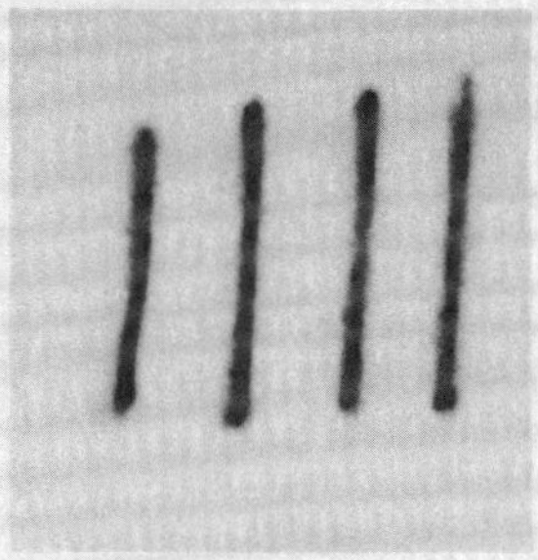

They adopt—especially in the case of the “Zebras”—a type of marking of the pictorial space present in the 1972–77 series, as radical in their processual excess as the spray paintings were in their quest for a degree zero. By suggesting a beyond-the-frame, they work towards a spatialization of the painting that will also be the concern of the late series.

Objectively, the spray paintings don’t occupy a singular place in Barré’s oeuvre. Subjectively, the same cannot be said: they have and will enduringly preserve in our aesthetic imagination something of a pictorial absolute that few other works—Frank Stella’s and Ad Reinhardt’s *Black Paintings*, Lucio Fontana’s *Tagli*, and Yves Klein’s monochromes, to stick to contemporary works—can lay claim to.

1972
1977

“I USE A RULE
(A ‘RULE OF THE GAME’);
I TRANSGRESS IT
WHEN THE PAINTING
***CALLS FOR IT.*”**

Martin Barré, 1977

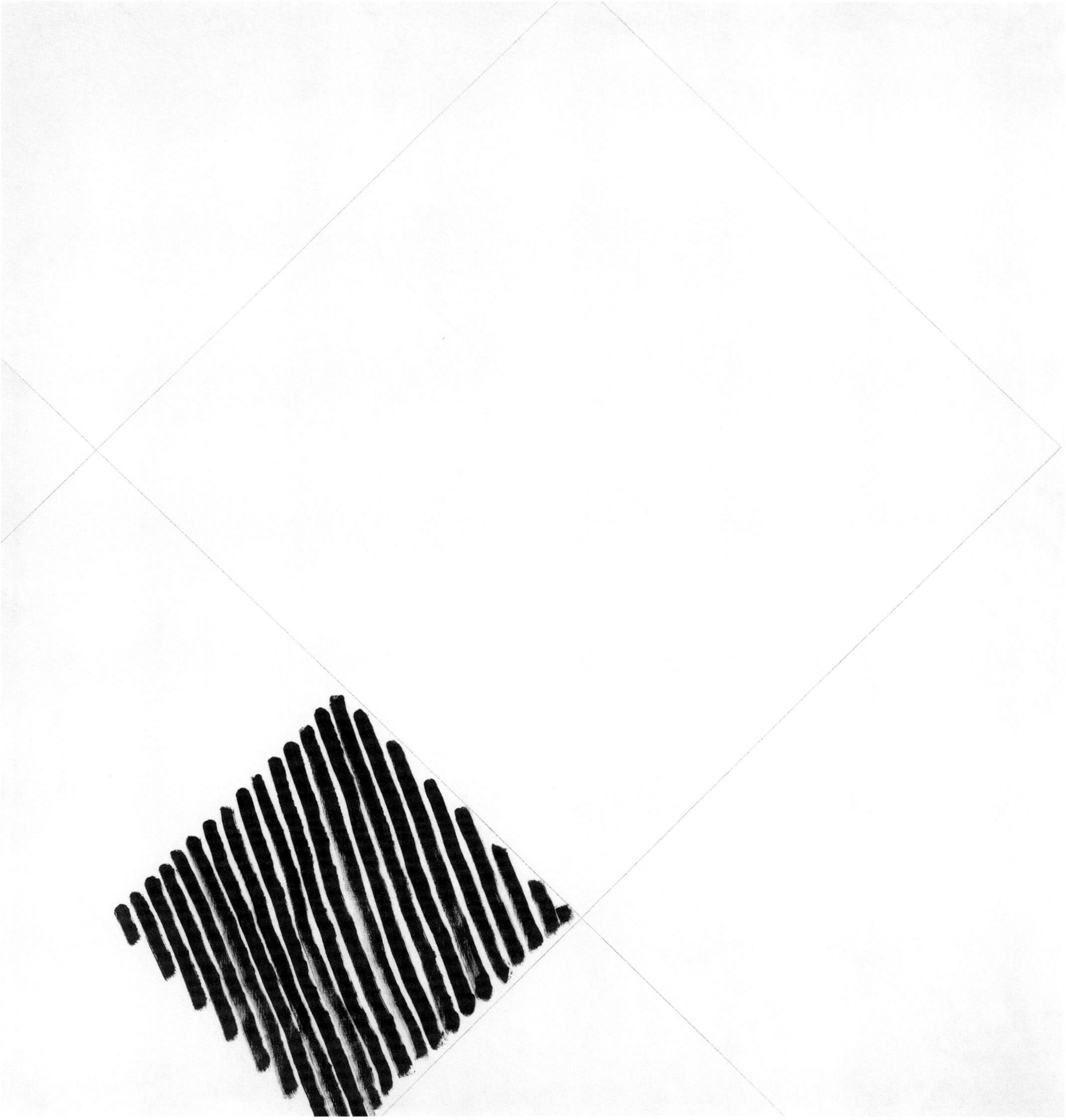

72-73-A-200×185, 1972–73

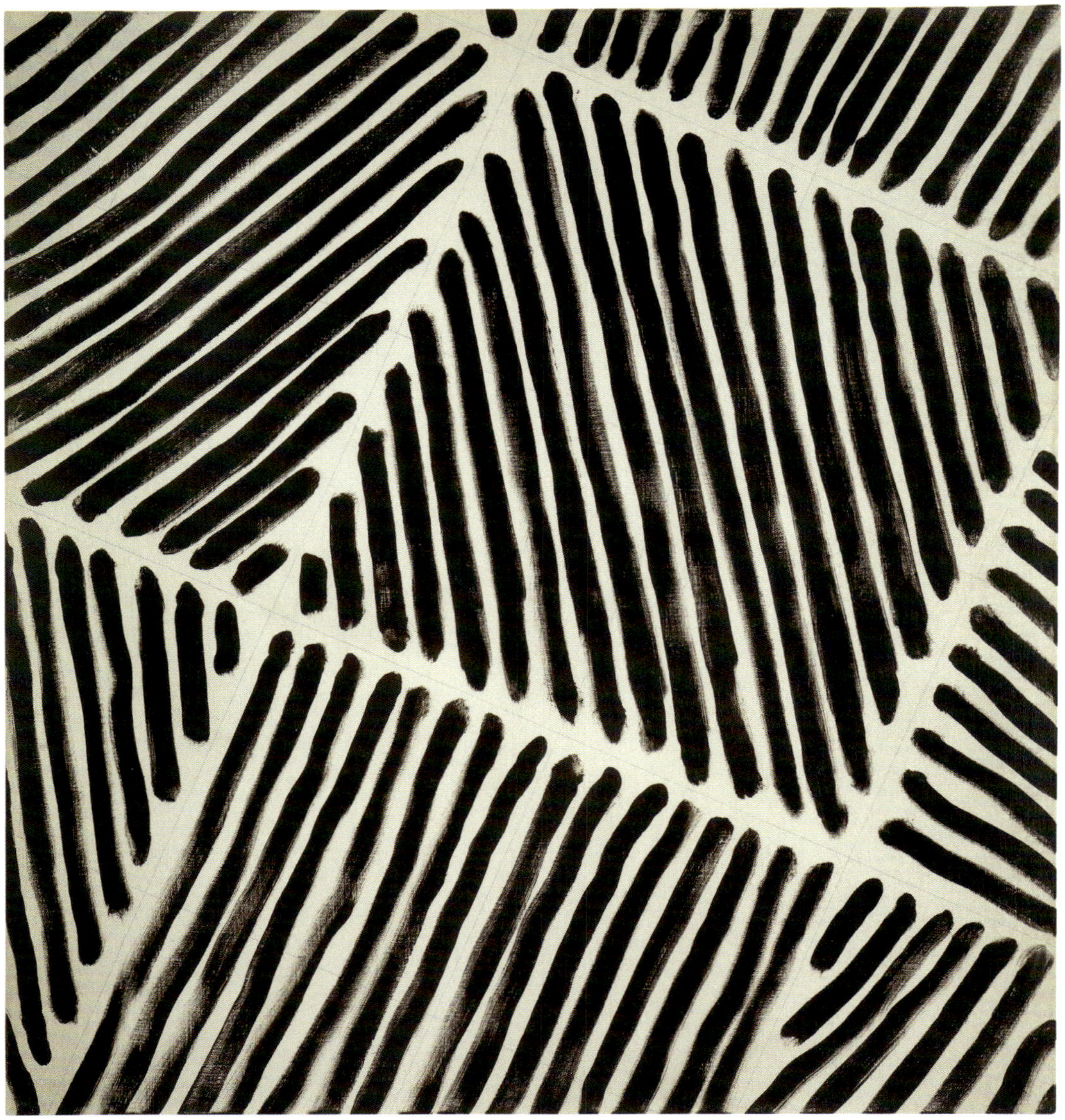

72-73-F-108×100, 1972–73

72-73-D-130×120, 1972–73

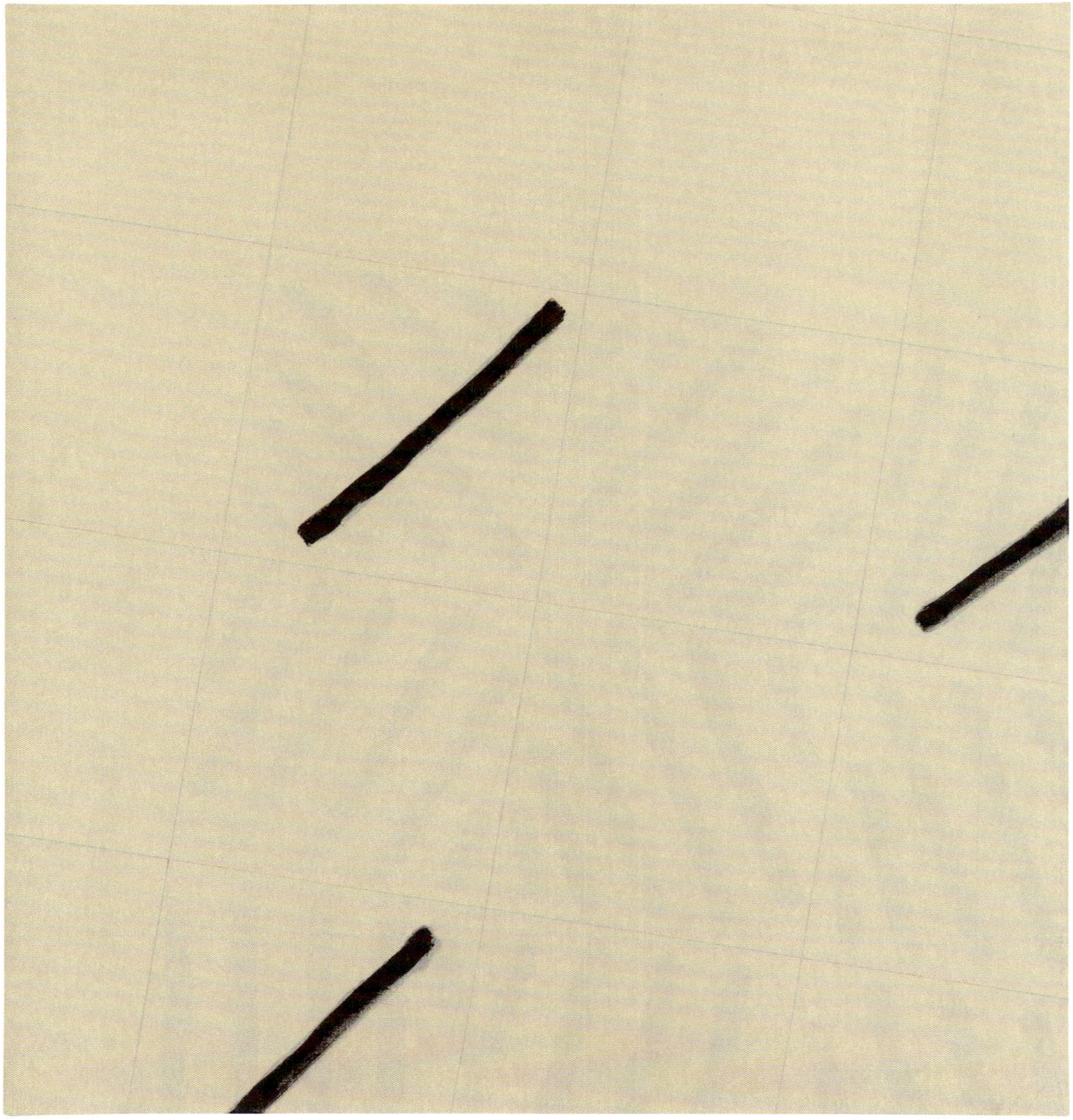

72-73-E-108×100, 1972–73

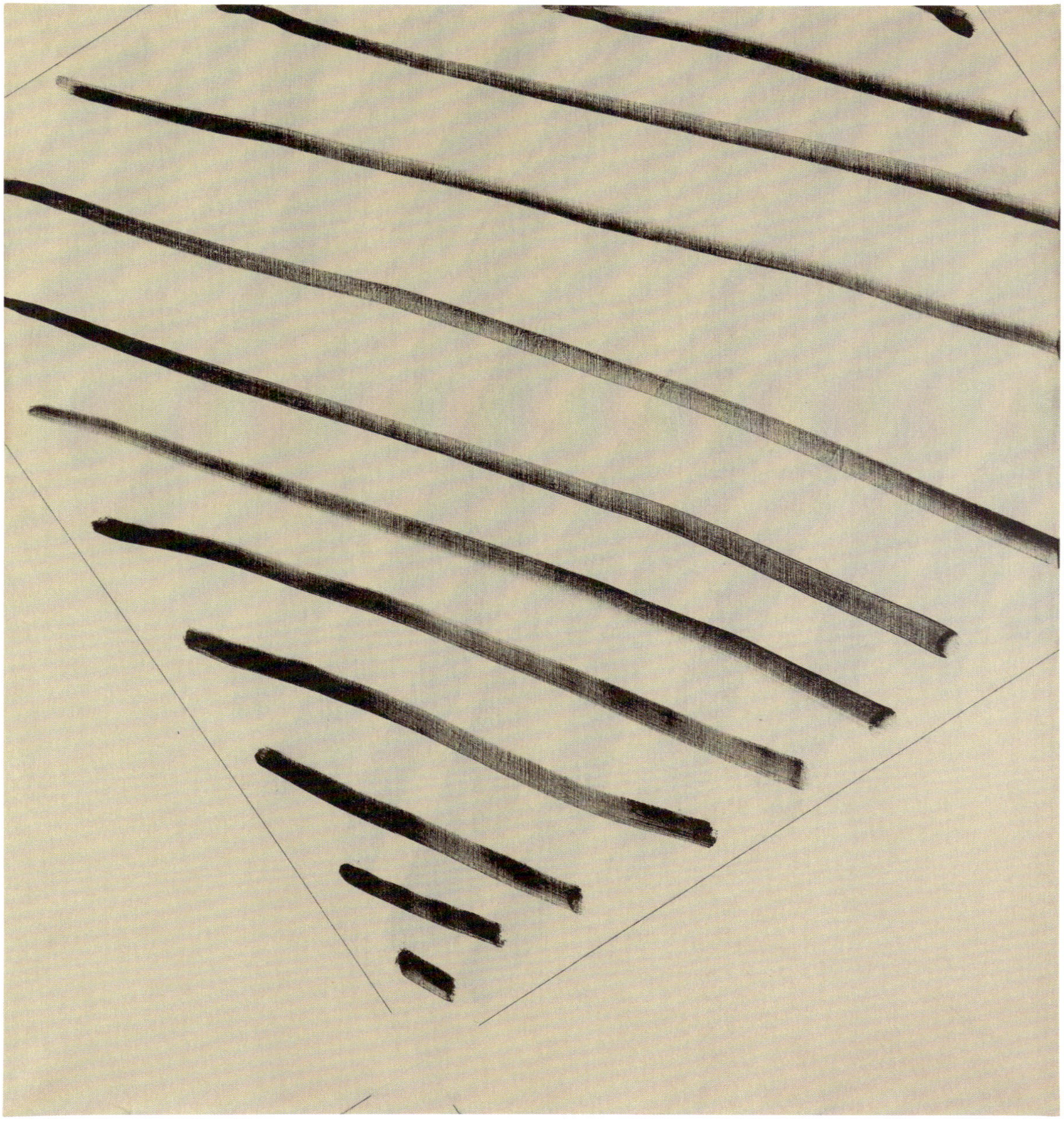

72-73-B-130×120, 1972–73

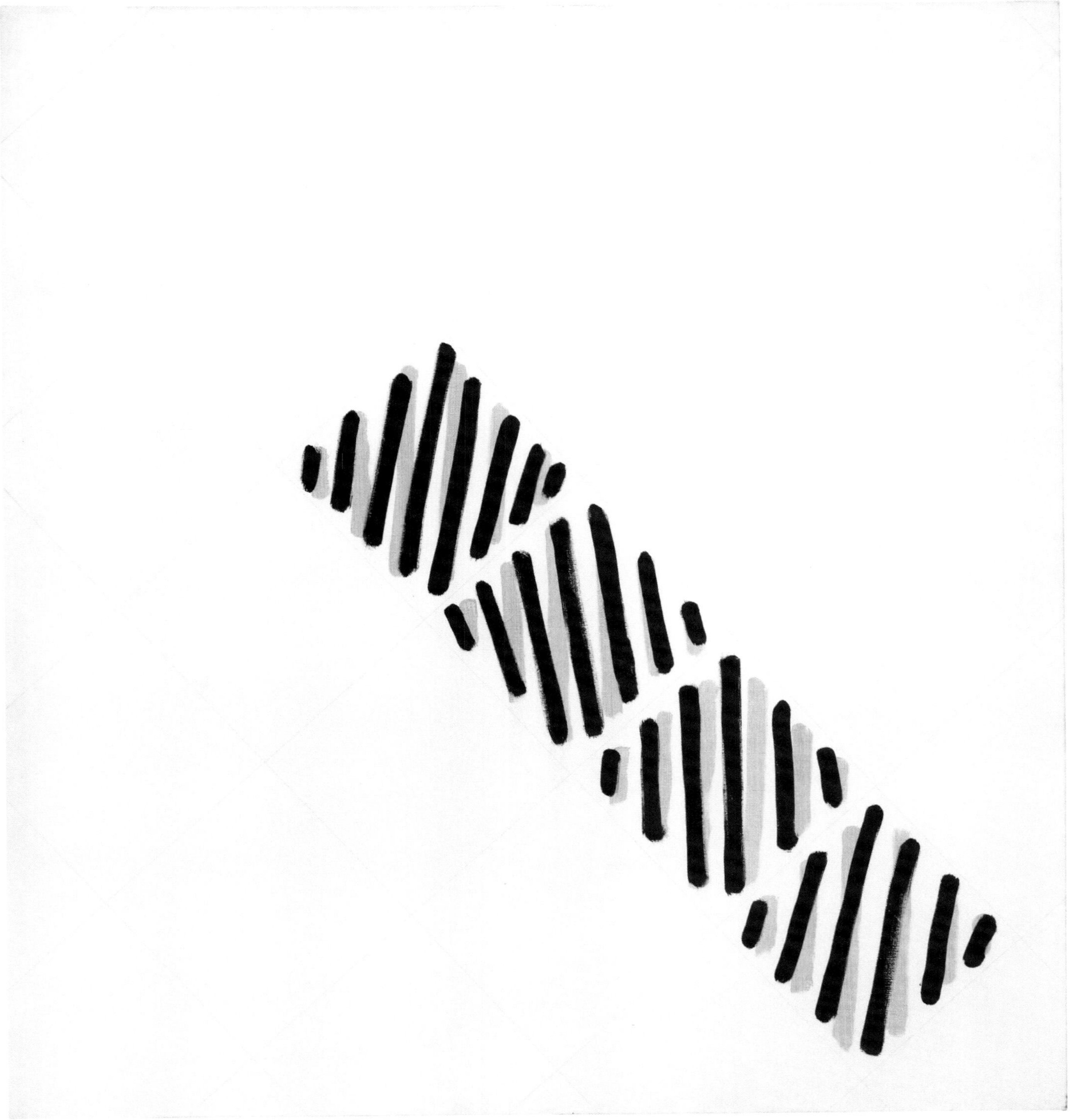

72-73-D-160×148, 1972–73

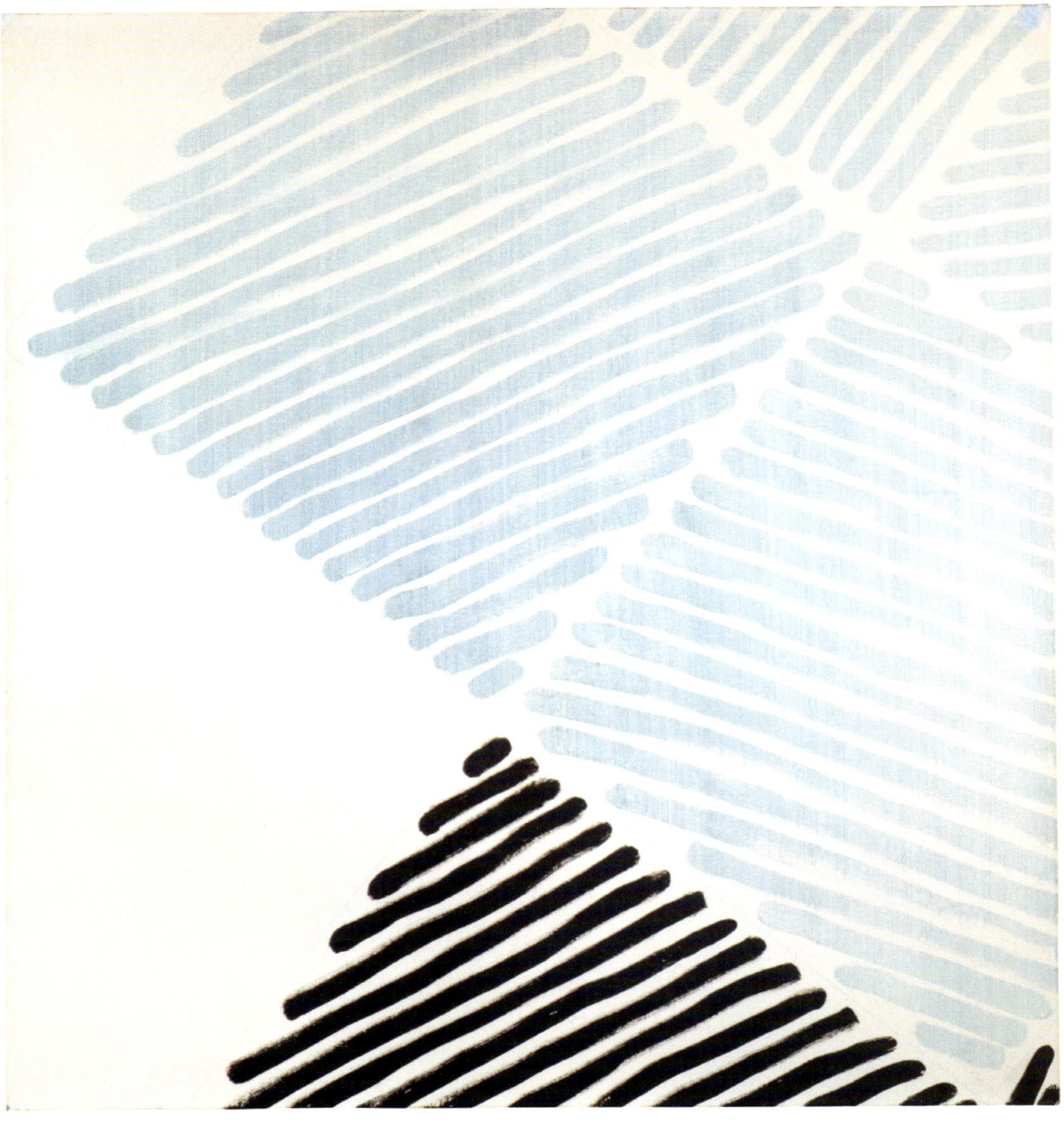

72-73-B-108×100, 1972–73

72-73-B-160×148, 1972–73

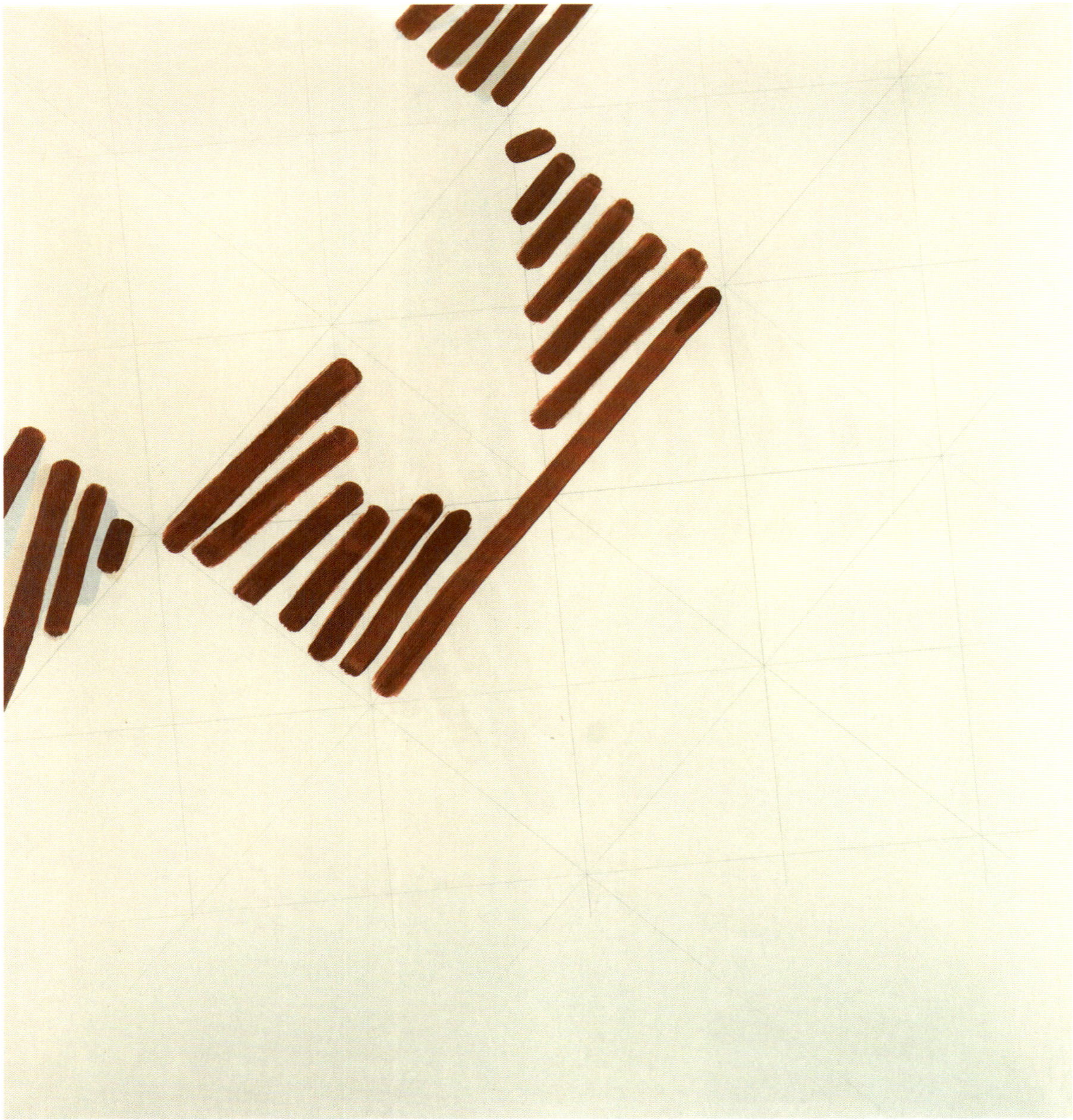

73-74-F-123×114, 1973–74

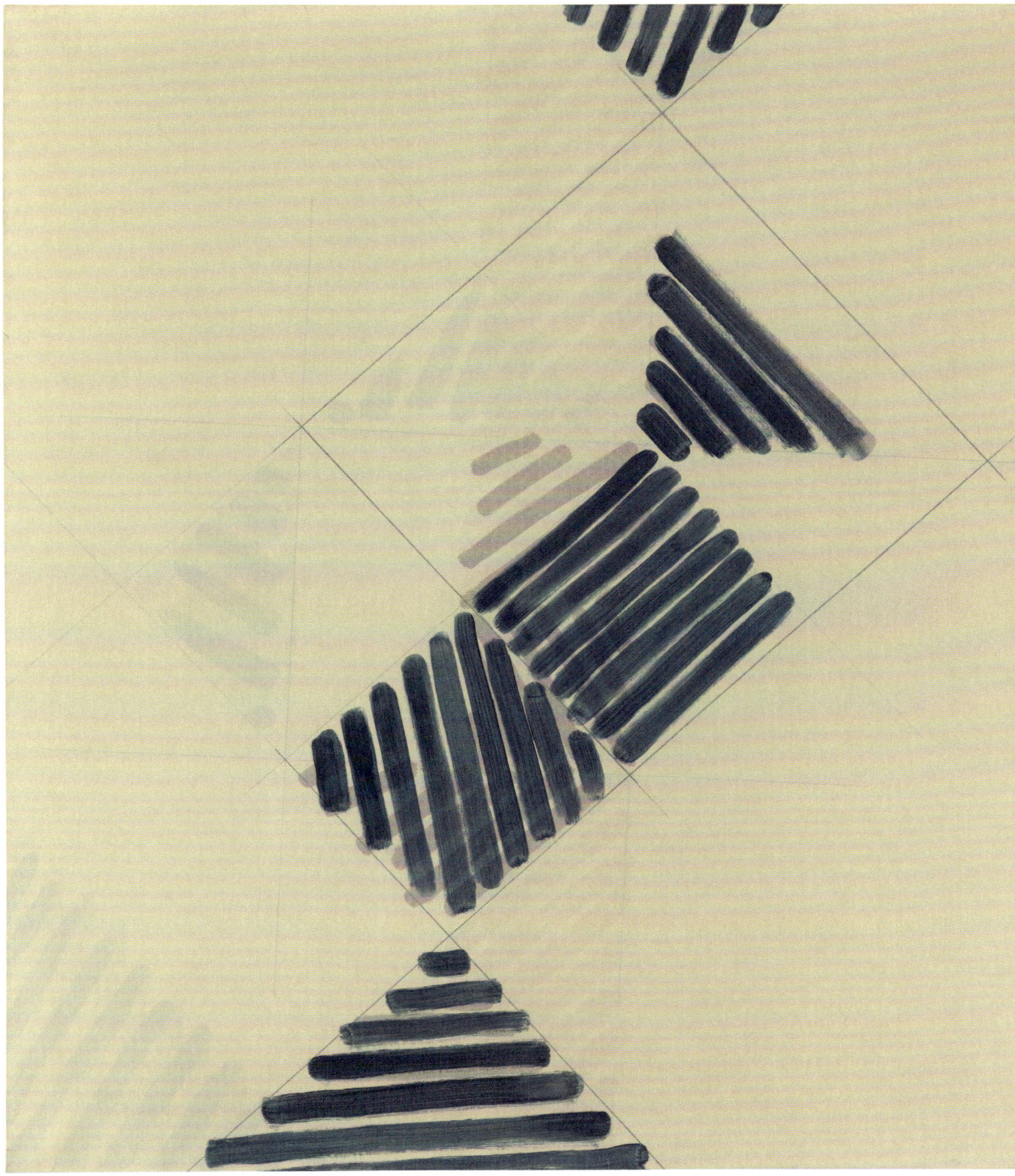

73-74-B-149×139, 1973–74

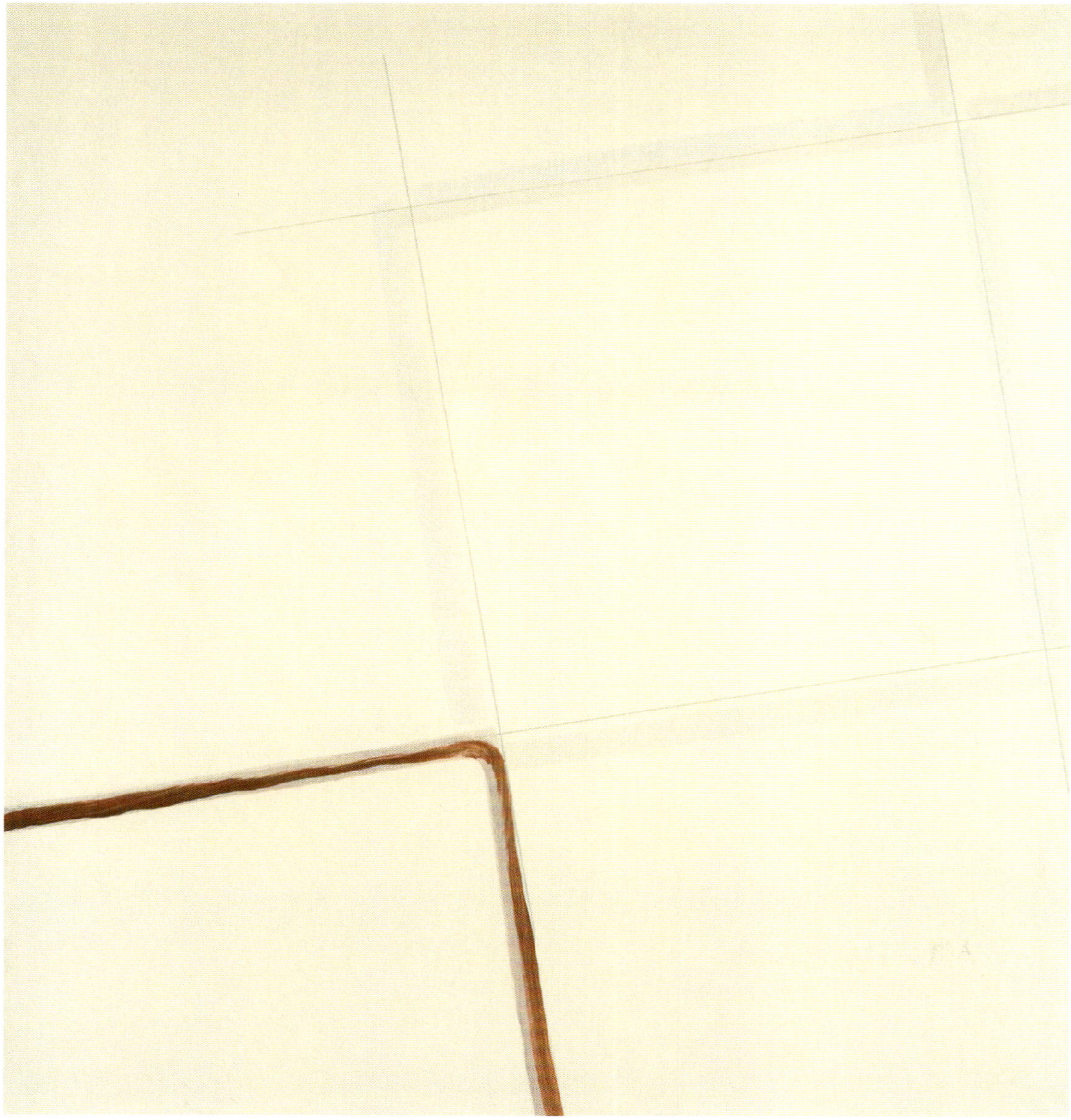

73-74-D-123×114, 1973–74

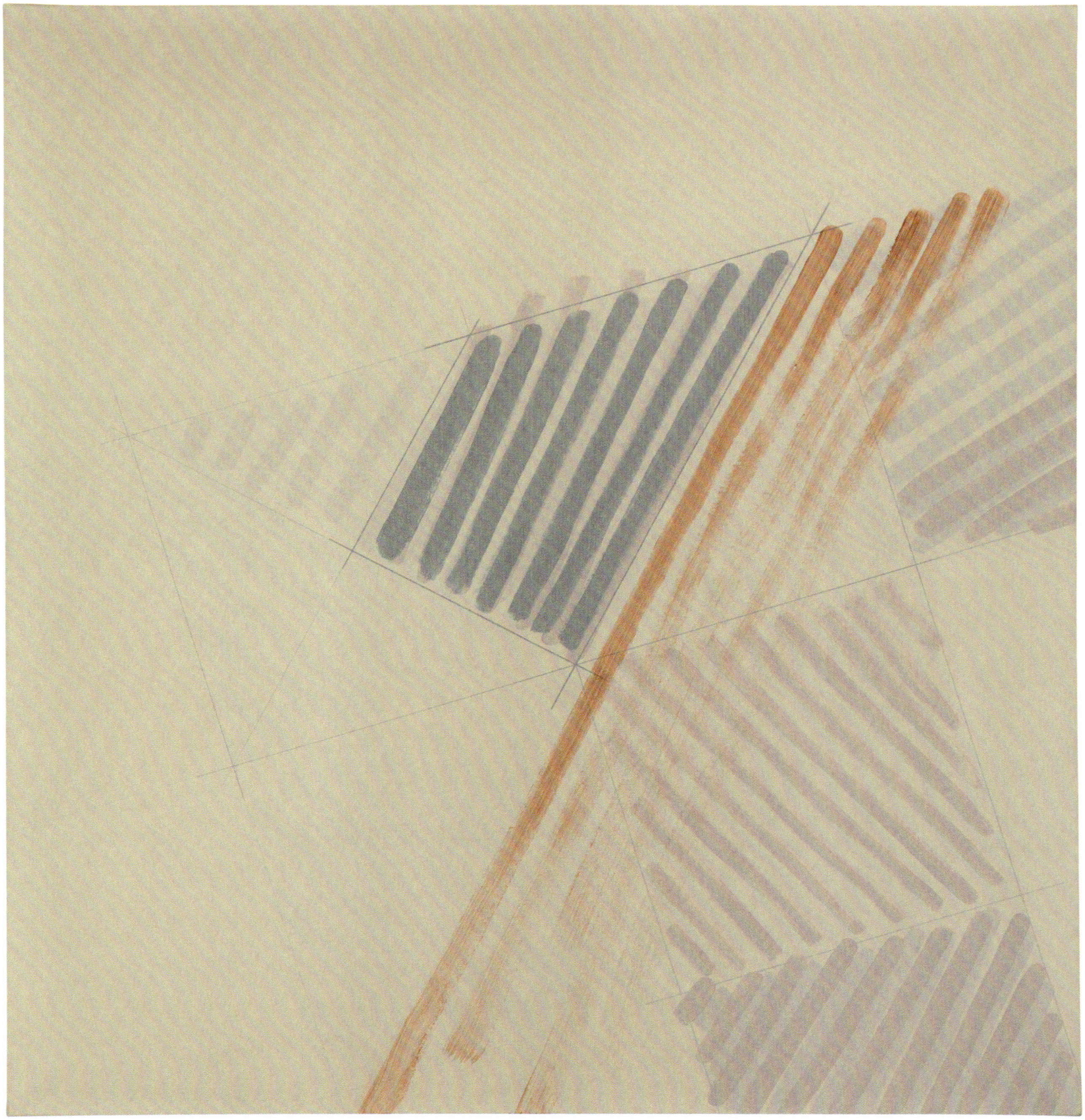

73-74-A-149×139, 1973–74

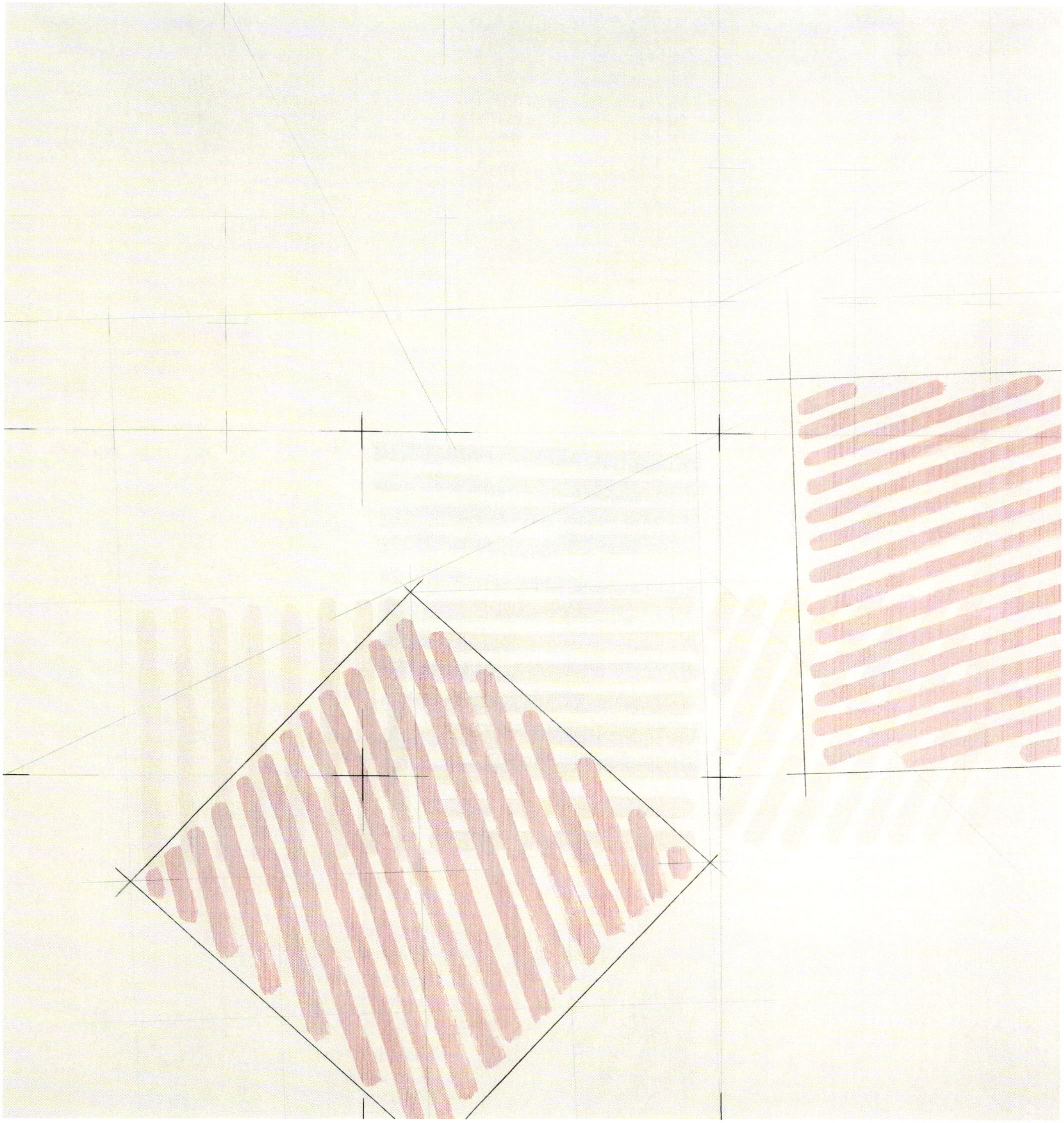

74-75-B-171×159, 1974–75

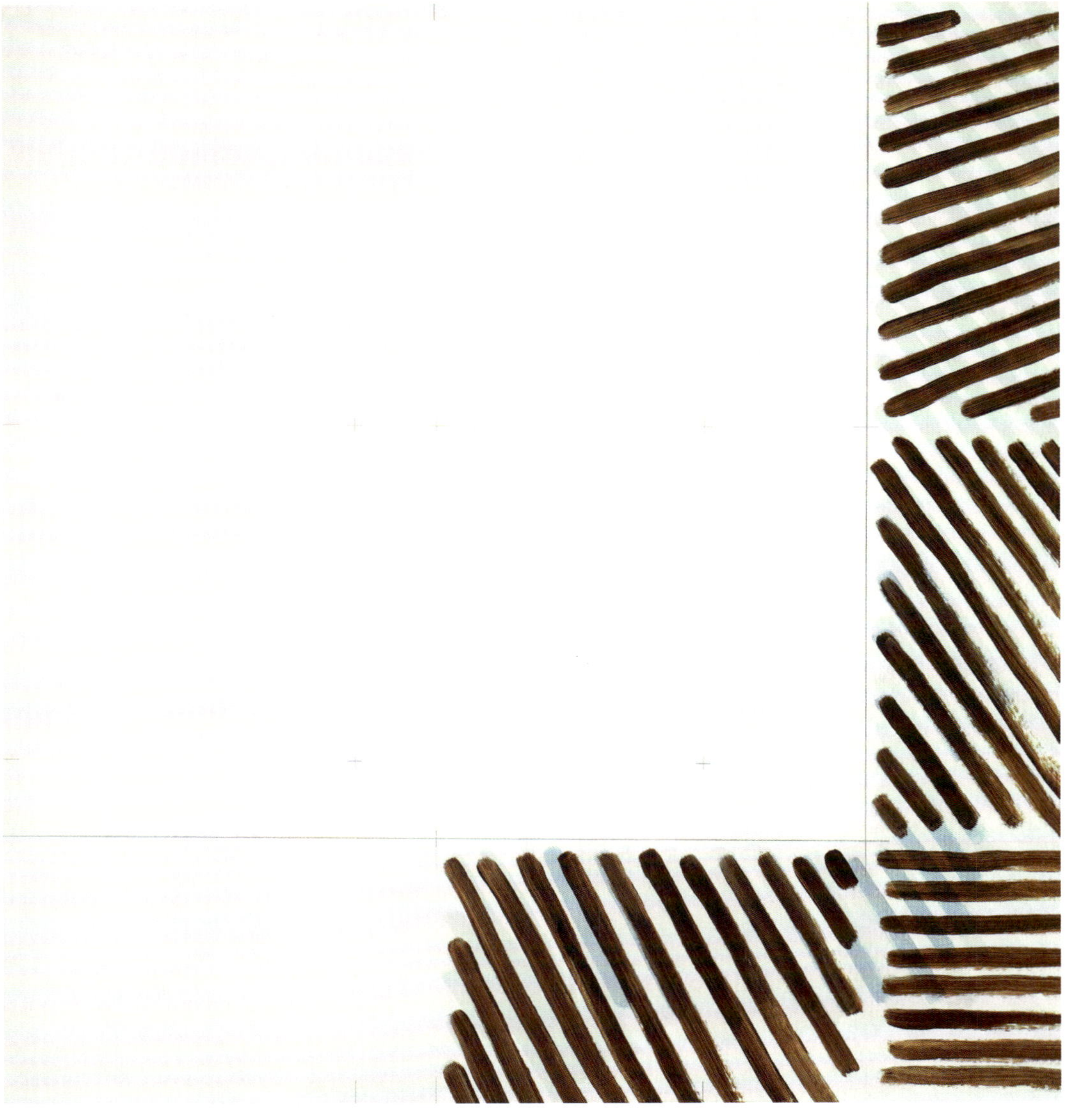

74-75-C-113×105, 1974–75

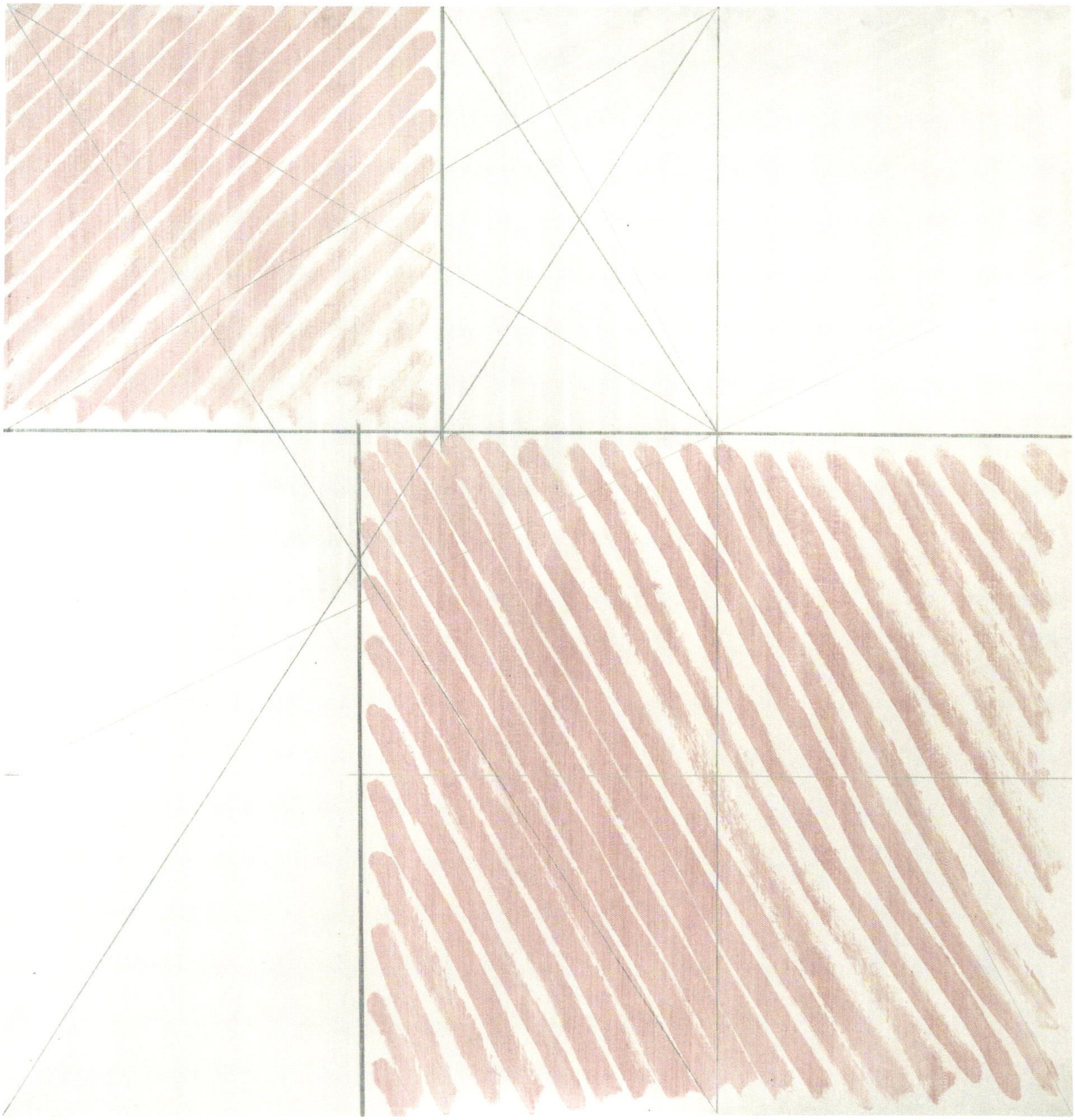

74-75-C-139×129, 1974–75

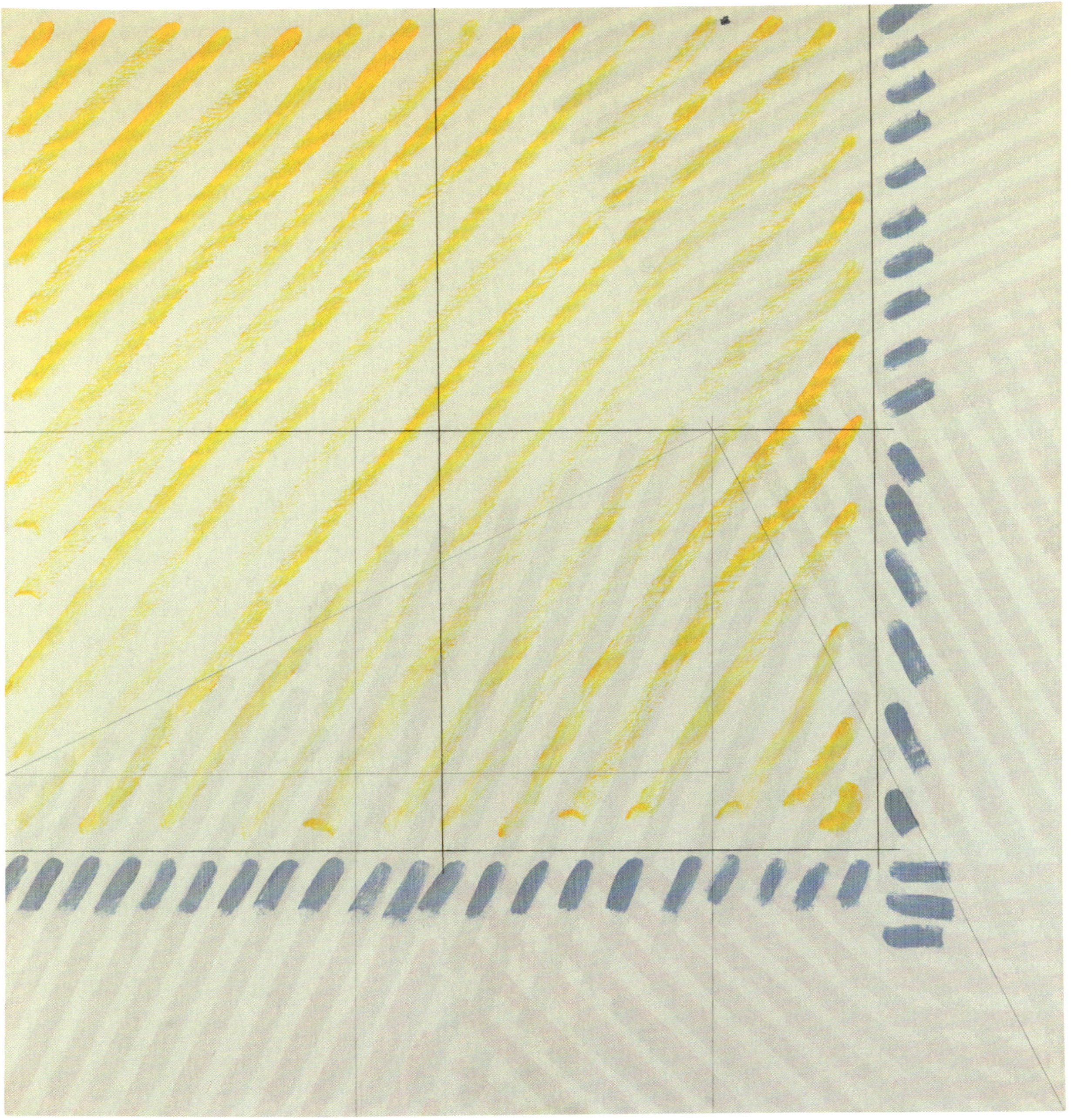

74-75-B-139×129, 1974–75

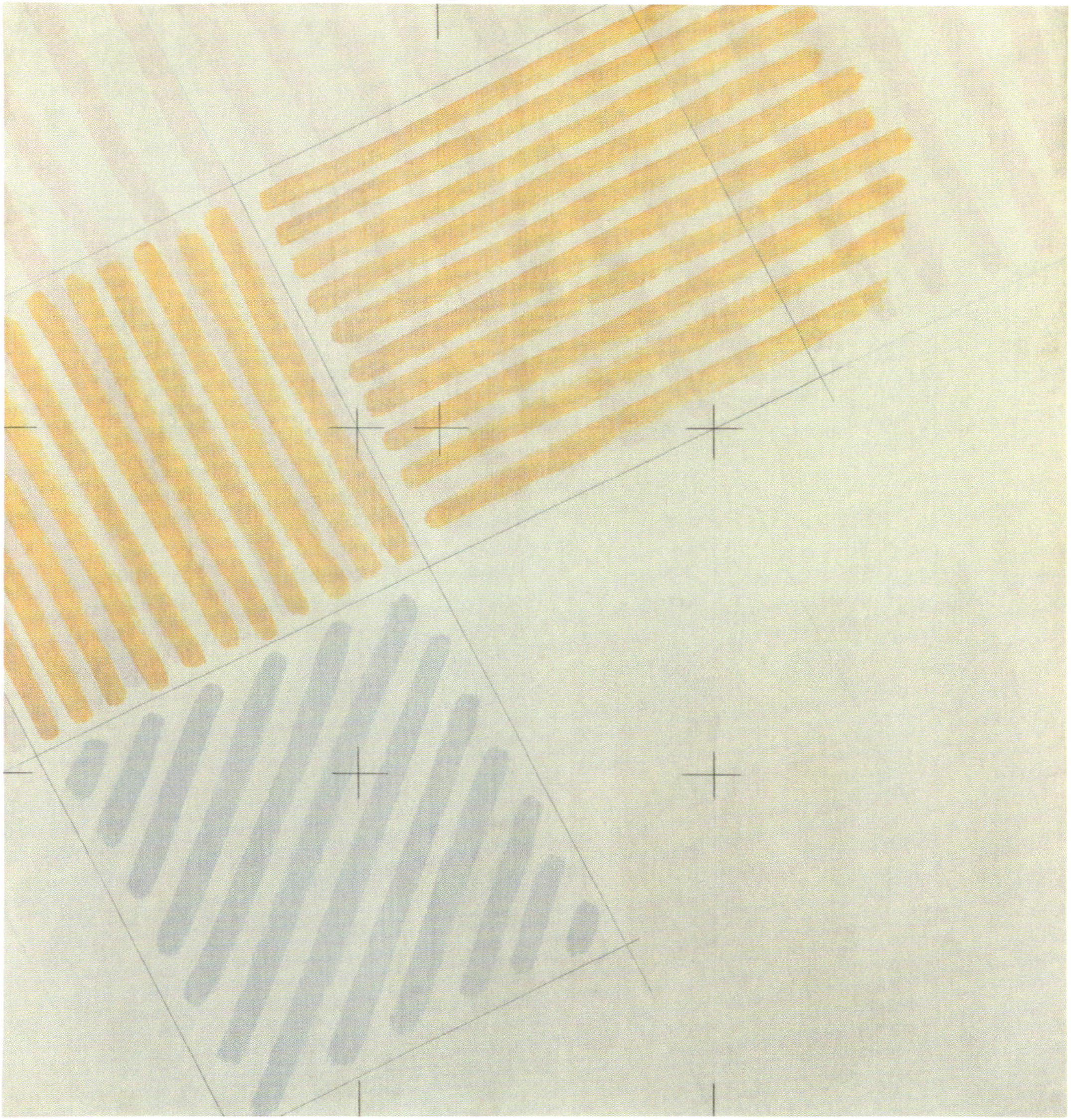

74-75-A-113×105, 1974–75

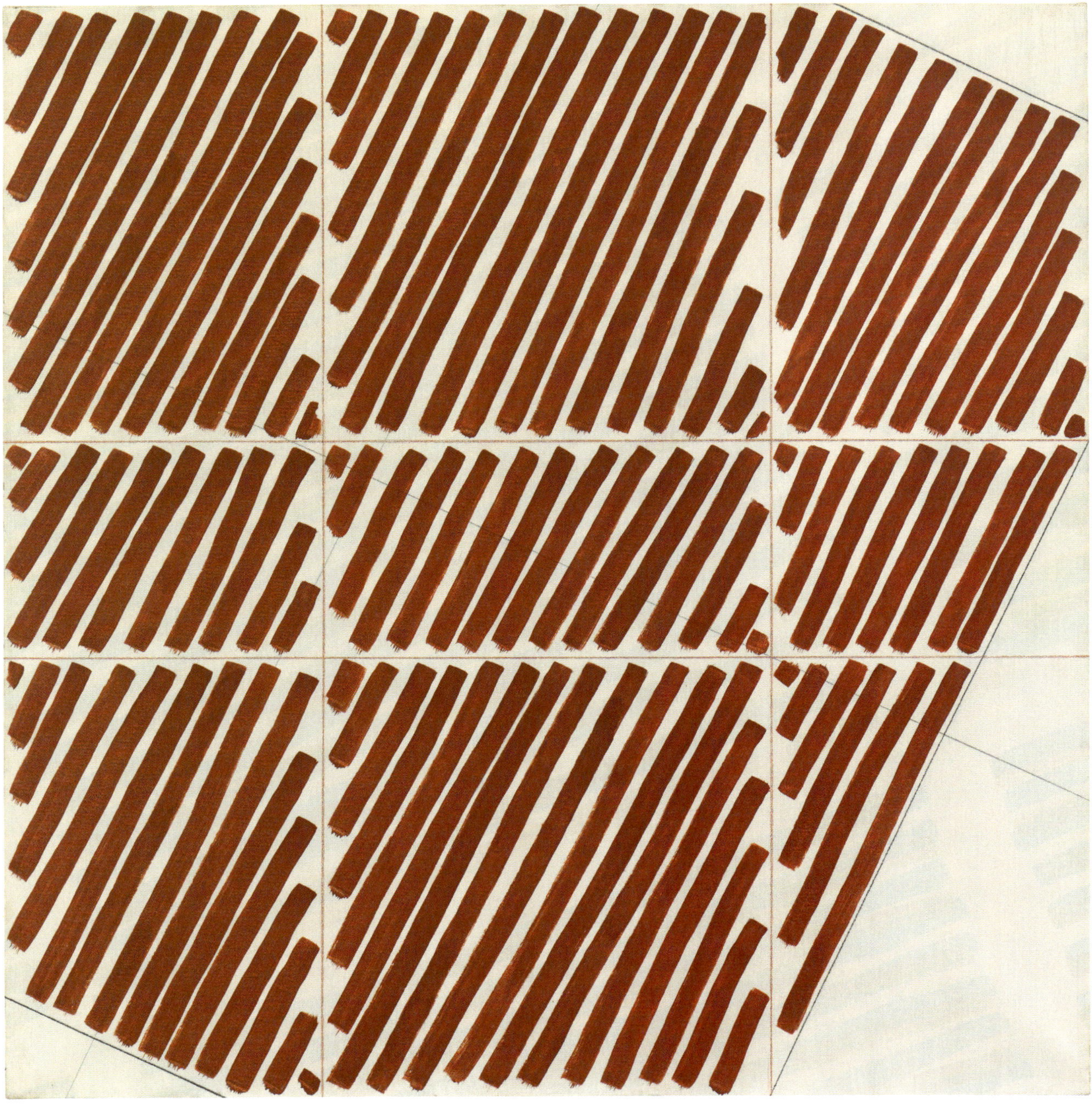

75-76-D-145×140, 1975–76

75-76-C-157×145, 1975–76

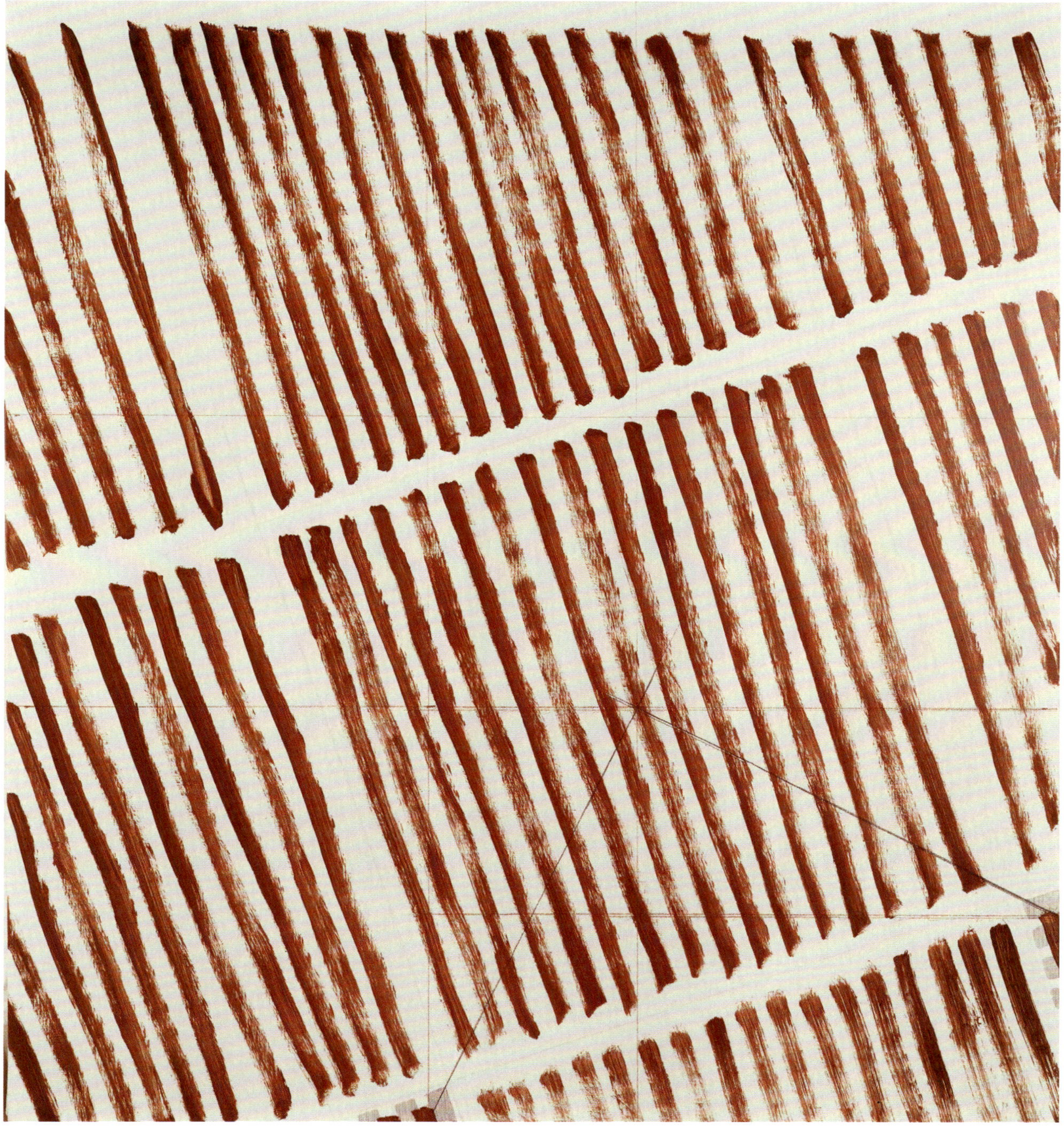

75-76-D-157×145, 1975–76

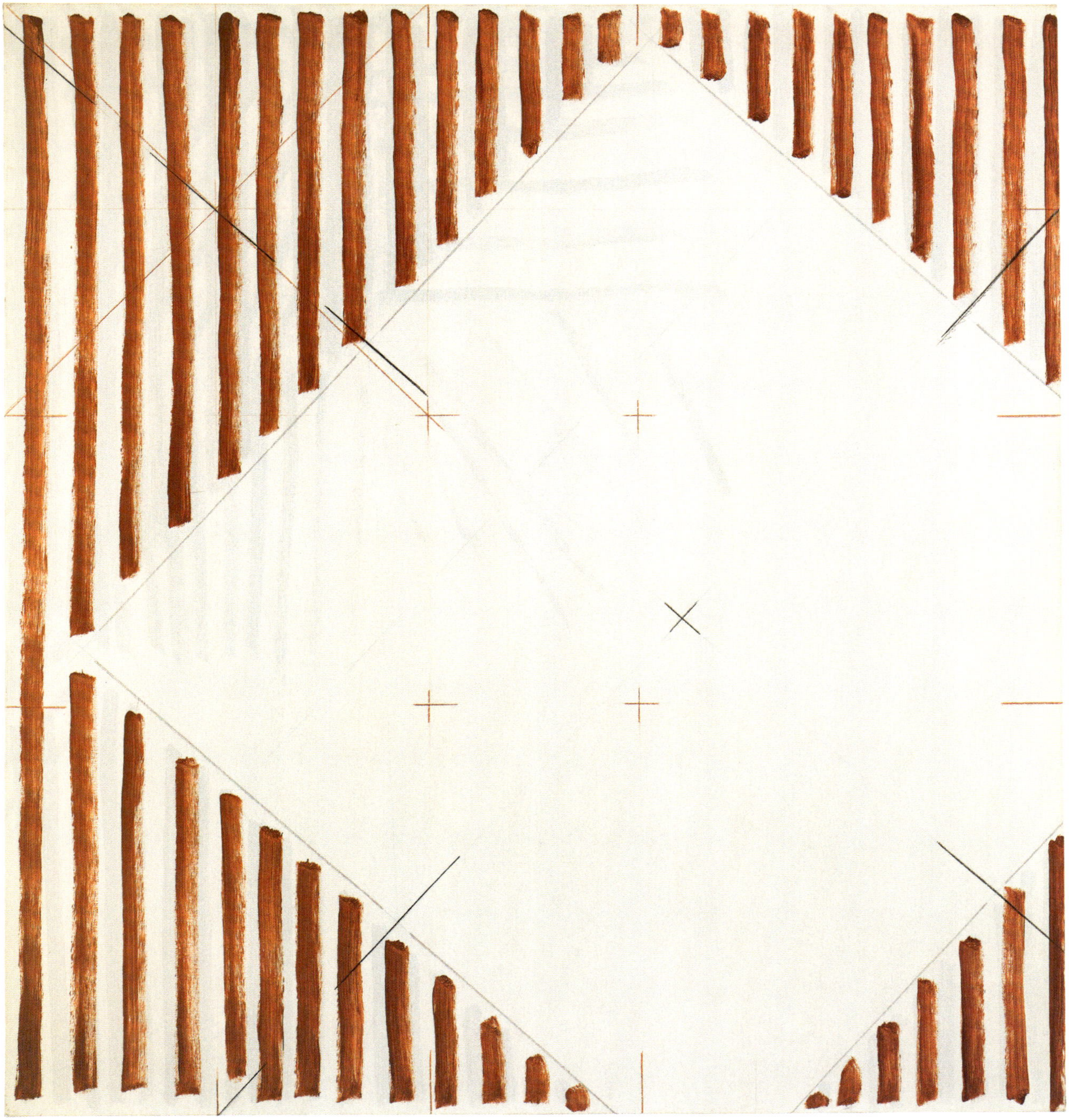

75-76-A-157×145, 1975–76

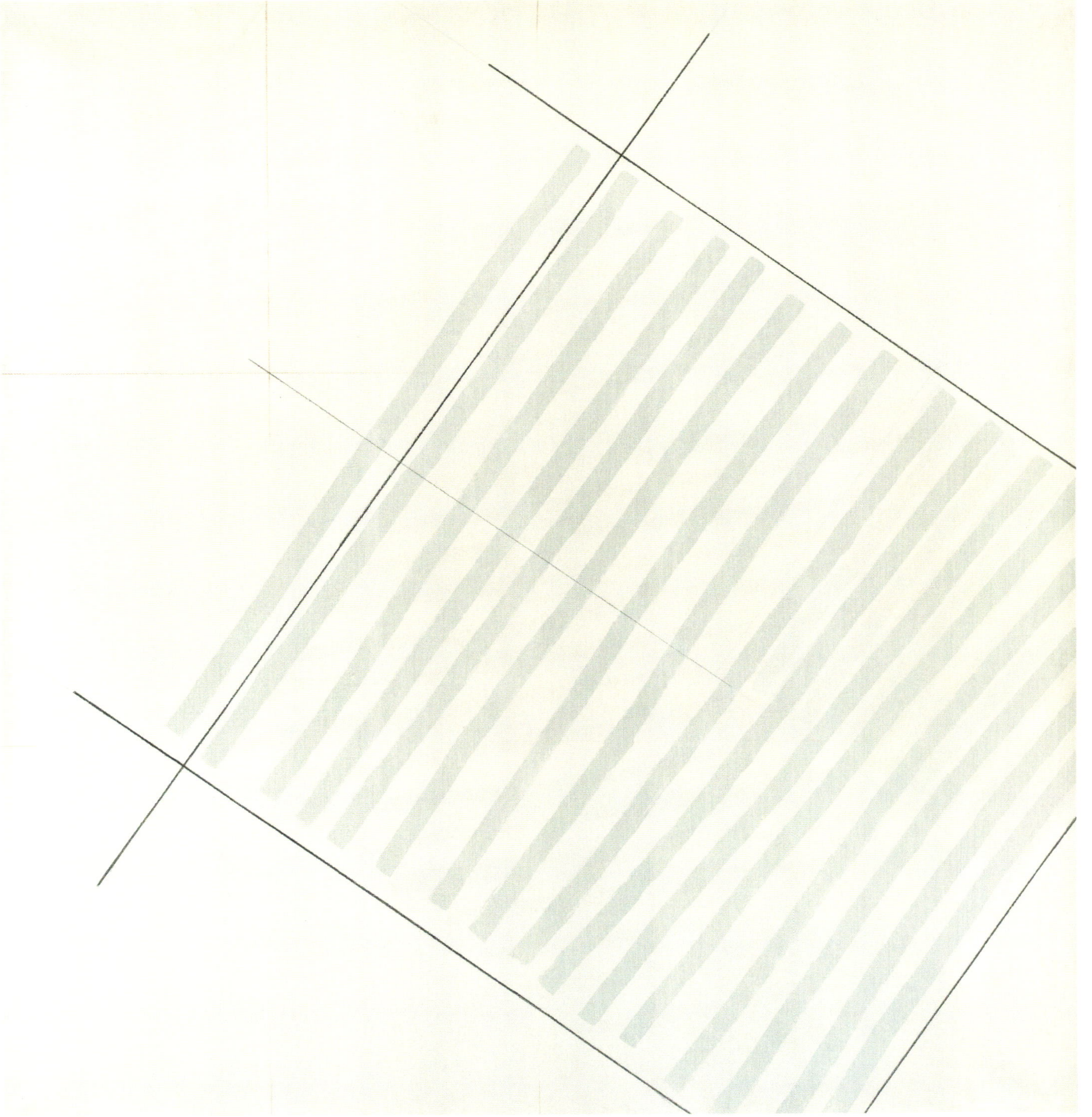

75-76-B-174×164, 1975–76

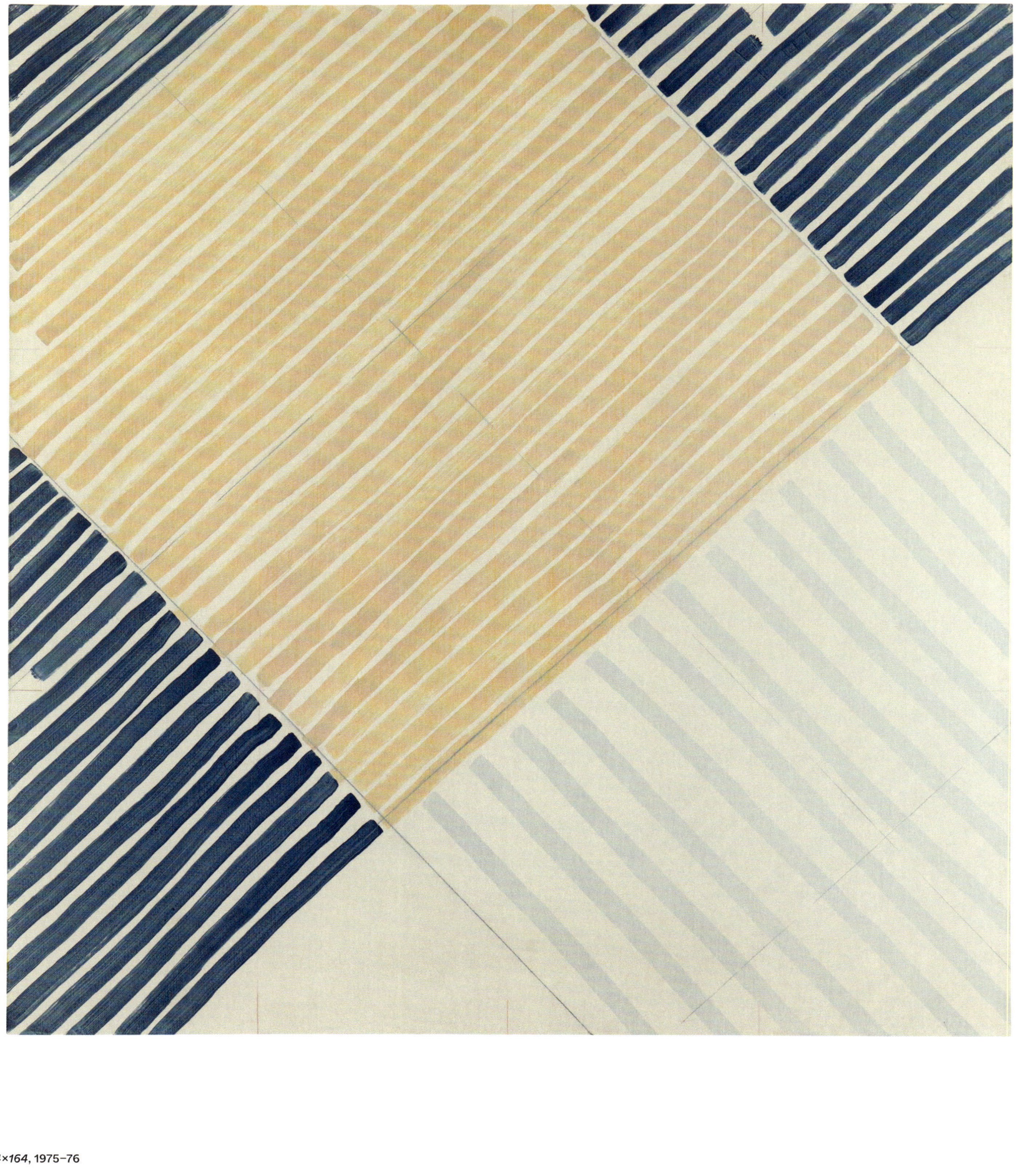

75-76-C-174×164, 1975–76

76-77-B-170×160, 1976–77

76-77-B-147,5×140, 1976–77

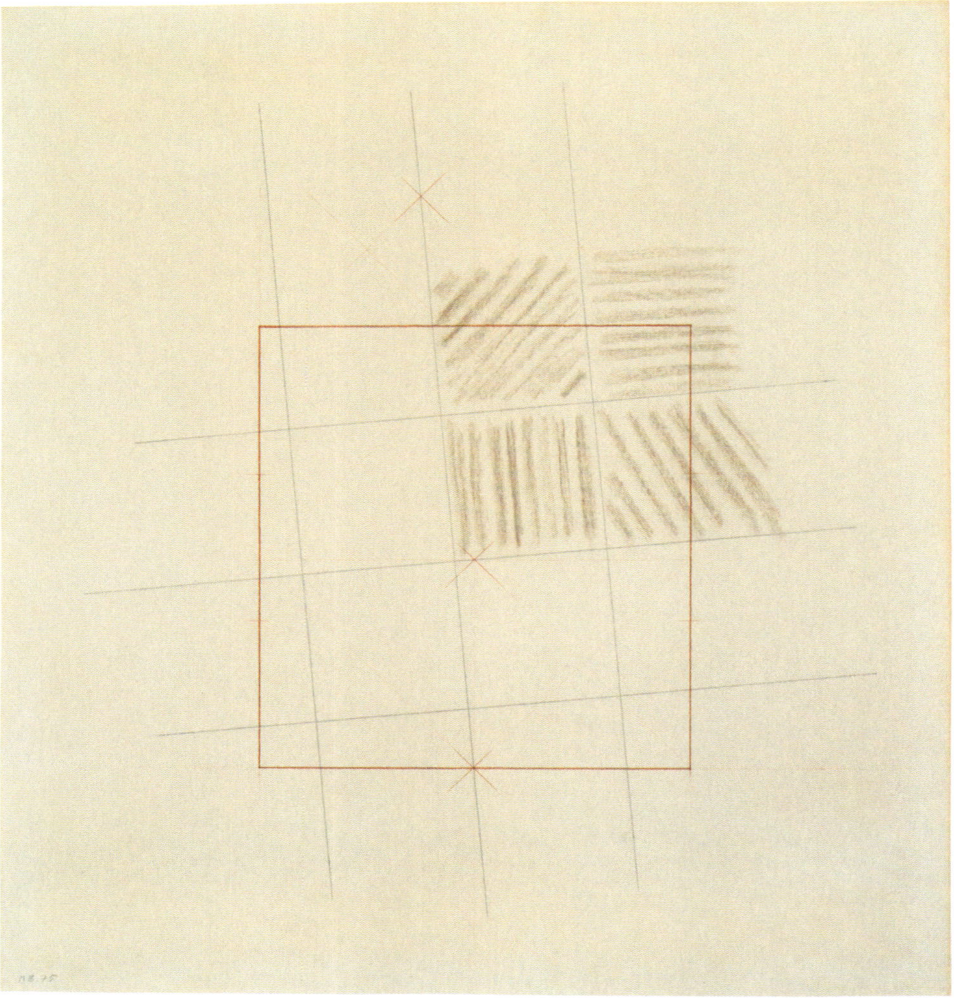

75-A-785×725, 1975

MARTIN BARRÉ RETURNS TO PAINTING, 1972–1977

Molly Warnock

In 1972, after a hiatus of roughly four years, Martin Barré returned to painting. Over the next five years, the artist would produce five series, each dated to a one-year interval. The inaugural painting group ("72-73") is the largest, numbering twenty-four canvases; the others, in chronological order, comprise eighteen ("73-74"), ten ("74-75"), eighteen again ("75-76"), and sixteen ("76-77"). All of the paintings reveal variously gridded and marked surfaces. Although the logic governing the dimensions of the formats and the grids varied from series to series, the broad outlines of the painting and marking process remained largely constant. Working exclusively with acrylic paints, Barré began by coating his canvases with red ochre. That preparatory ground he then covered in turn with as many laminas of thinned-out white paint as proved necessary to obscure it, thus yielding the already-layered entity that he called the support.[1] Additional work sessions, each devoted to a specific task, saw the artist inscribing the canvases with graphite grids; filling an area or areas of that lattice with painted hatch marks; or covering the grid and striations alike with a new, translucent wash of whitish paint. While the cycle repeated indefinitely, a canvas or canvases might be withdrawn from the otherwise ongoing labor at any point—"at a moment chosen and decided by the painter."[2]

The results have a paradoxical status in Barré's oeuvre. On the one hand, the paintings of the years 1972–77 stand among his best-known works. Individual series were exhibited shortly upon completion at major galleries in Paris and Cologne, and the corpus featured prominently in the artist's 1979 exhibition at the ARC – Musée d'Art Moderne de la Ville de Paris.[3] During that same decade, they also garnered strong critical essays by Tzvetan Todorov, Jean Louis Schefer, and especially Jean Clay, whose diagrams of the systems governing the different series remain integral to their reception.[4] On the other hand, these stratified surfaces, so recalcitrant to reproduction, remain exceedingly difficult to get in view. Where Barré's graphically striking, black-on-white sprayed paintings of the years leading up to the break increasingly privilege seemingly contingent, quickly produced marks and a certain form of procedural

1 Jean Clay, "Questions for Martin Barré" (1977), repr. in Yve-Alain Bois, *Martin Barré* (Cologne, New York, and Paris: Galerie Daniel Buchholz, Andrew Kreps Gallery, Galerie Nathalie Obadia, and Thea Westreich/Ethan Wagner, 2008), 270.

2 Ibid.

3 The galleries are Galerie Daniel Templon and Galerie Piltzer in Paris (in 1973 and 1974 and in 1976 and 1977 as Galerie Piltzer-Rheims, respectively), and Galerie Peccolo in Cologne (in 1975). Other exhibitions gathering together works from different series include those at Galerie Daniel Templon in Milan (1975), Galleria Lia Rumma in Naples (1975), Galleria Peccolo in Livorno (1976), and Galleria La Polena in Genoa (1976). For the 1979 exhibition, see Suzanne Pagé et al., *Martin Barré*, exh. cat. (Paris: ARC – Musée d'Art Moderne de la Ville de Paris, 1979).

4 See in particular Tzvetan Todorov, "Une peinture figurale," in *Martin Barré*, exh. cat (Paris: Galerie Daniel Templon, 1973), n.p.; Jean Clay, "Le dispositif Martin Barré. L'œil onglé," *Macula* 2 (1977): 67–83, and "La peinture en séton," in Pagé et al., *Martin Barré*, 6–17; and Jean Louis Schefer, "Ténèbre du blanc," in Pagé et al., *Martin Barré*, 4–7.

blindness, his canvases of the 1970s couple a concerted dilation of time with a newly deliberate mode of marking. Just as importantly, however, the revised procedure to which they bear witness gives way in turn to a newly rigorous avoidance of superimposition and accelerated visual delivery in the artist's work after 1977. Barré's canvases in the five years following the suspension of his painting practice remain importantly distinct both from the work that precedes them and from all that follows them.

In a 1985 interview with Catherine Millet, Barré refers to the late 1960s and early 1970s as a "period of questioning."[5] His abandonment of and subsequent return to painting conjure the similarly interrupted career of his younger colleague Michel Parmentier (1938–2000), who famously ceased to paint in 1968 only to resume activity in the 1980s.[6] Yet it is another painter of Barré's generation, the Hungarian-born Simon Hantaï (1922–2008), who offers the most instructive comparison. Over the course of a roughly one-year period stretching from the fall of 1958 to late 1959, Hantaï created a number of materially and temporally layered paintings that reorganized his practice as a whole. It is not a question of influence: indeed, the key canvas in this group, the extraordinary palimpsest *Peinture (Écriture rose)*, could not even have been known to Barré until at least 1976, when it made its public début in Hantaï's retrospective at the Musée National d'Art Moderne in Paris. Rather, this body of work appears a prior, no less deliberate attempt to refound painting on "systematic" bases. Born of Hantaï's complex reckoning with lyrical abstraction, these paintings substitute hand-copied script for gestural marking. Decisively relinquishing rapidity of execution as a means of outracing composition, they instead adopt a liturgical framework that conditions both the choice of texts to copy and—in the case of *Écriture rose*—the color of the ink used on any given day.[7] Standing before the completed canvases, however, one is above all struck by the thoroughgoing mediation of that would-be universality through a finally insuperable particularity, as manifest above all in the artist's immediately recognizable hand. Accumulating over time, the shifting webs of script undo themselves from within.

There are, to be sure, key differences between Barré and Hantaï. One concerns the nature of the time at issue in each body of work. Like Hantaï's written paintings of 1958–59, Barré's series are, as we have seen, all dated (and indeed, titled) to one-year intervals: "72-73," "73-74," and so on. But where Hantaï's interval is determined in advance by the liturgical calendar, Barré embraces an open-ended, non-developmental time from which

5 Catherine Millet, "M. B. 'Elsewhere'" (1985), repr. in Bois, *Martin Barré*, 271. This period without painting was not a period without work; rather, these years saw Barré turning to photographically based and markedly indexical conceptual investigations. For more on this period and the ensuing work, see Bois's valuable account in *Martin Barré*, especially 35–40. Bois, like Clay, attributes what I distinguish as agency to the sheer complexity of the structures Barré engages in the work of the 1970s.

6 For Parmentier's return to painting, see my "Peindre pour rien: Michel Parmentier," trans. Catherine Vasseur, *Les Cahiers du Musée national d'art moderne* 132 (Summer 2015): 18–39, repr. in English as "Painting for Nothing: Michel Parmentier," in Guy Massaux et al., *Michel Parmentier, December 1965–November 1999: A Retrospective* (New York: D.A.P./Distributed Art Publishers, 2019), 222–27.

7 More specifically, Hantaï followed the official ritual formulary of the pre-Vatican II Catholic Church, as transmitted in his bilingual French and Latin 1953 edition of the Daily Roman Missal. This liturgical book notes which texts should be read on any given day of the year, and also assigns a particular color to each day's Mass. For more on these paintings, see my *Penser la peinture: Simon Hantaï*, trans. Patrick Hersant (Paris: Gallimard, 2012), as well as my revised account in *Simon Hantaï and the Reserves of Painting* (University Park, PA: Pennsylvania State University Press, 2020).

paintings can be withdrawn at any point—a time, one might say, that can *only* be interrupted, never concluded. Interestingly, then, the latter's system in no way relieves him of determining when to cease working. On the contrary, precisely because it is not settled in advance, this choice now falls entirely to the painter once he is engaged in the act of painting.

A second distinction concerns the relation between the individual painting and the group. We might frame this roughly as a contrast between a painting that aspires to sum up—to *be*—a system within itself and paintings that are clearly determined by a system that precedes them. Hantaï's work on *Écriture rose* quickly overspills that canvas, generating a larger field of paintings. Those works are nonetheless subordinate to the master canvas, prolongations and displacements of the impetus put into play there. Barré's work, on the other hand, is conceived as serial from the first: individual paintings are as if cut out from a preexisting field of possibilities. This is the dynamic dramatized in Clay's famous diagrams, as in a rare drawing by Barré himself, in which a square slightly elongated along the vertical axis appears to punch itself out against an obliquely gridded and partially hatched ground.→ p. 132 The detachment is equally an individuation: as Barré emphasized, seriality as he construed it is not about producing many like paintings but about engendering works "as different from each other as possible."[8] That sense of individuation is further enhanced by the consistent verticality of Barré's formats, a feature that is particularly marked in the "76-77" paintings, in which bands of varied widths have been added to a square of constant size to produce the different formats.[9] Line or line segments separate the super-added section at the top or "head" from the rest of the canvas.

These differences, profoundly rooted in the two painters' distinct trajectories and temperaments, are not to be dismissed. Yet the force of my comparison is precisely to insist that the central issue each artist confronts in the course of these two bodies of work is not exclusive to any particular style, tendency, or movement but in fact lies deeper, having to do instead with what Stephen Melville, writing in another context, has termed "the inevitability of self."[10] For Barré as for Hantaï, this entails a new appropriation of painterly agency born precisely of the time work takes —the recognition, one might say, that all-over is not all-at-once. This discovery is not unique to these two individuals: rather, it seems to me the mostly untold story of so many "returns" to painting in the postwar period. That it remains untold testifies to the continued hold of largely undialectical conceptions of impersonality and neutrality—of the supposed *evacuation* of subjectivity—in writing about the art of the 1960s and 1970s (and indeed, beyond).[11]

8
Millet, "M. B. 'Elsewhere,'" 274.

9
As Barré noted, even slightly vertical formats inevitably read in the register of "the figure," a connotation he does not reject. See Catherine Millet, "Interview with Martin Barré" (1974), repr. in Bois, *Martin Barré*, 262.

10
Stephen Melville, "How Should Acconci Count for Us? Notes on a Retrospect," *October* 18 (Autumn 1981): 89.

11
I have addressed the limits of the critical emphasis on impersonal acts with specific reference to Hantaï and Barré, among others, in my review of one of several recent exhibitions to unite the two artists; see my "'Displace, Disclose, Discover: Acts of Painting 1960–1999,' Lille Métropole Musée d'Art Moderne, d'Art Contemporain, et d'Art Brut, Villeneuve-d'Ascq, France," *Artforum* 51, no. 2 (October 2012): 260–61.

The acceptance of artistic agency is nonetheless apparent in the works themselves, across the full array of features that define their surfaces. Take for example precisely that aspect detailed at length in Clay's diagrams and explanatory notes, the "grid of inscription" traced on each surface in graphite or, under certain conditions in the "75-76" series, in sanguine (red chalk).[12] Subject to changing calculations from one painting group to the next, and joined in 1975 by a second lattice used to determine the size of each pictorial support, the rectilinear armature visualizes the system underwriting the series as a whole. But precisely in becoming material, that system also proves both deformable and remarkable in its own right. It is not simply that Barré often appears highly selective about which part or parts of the grid to carry over from one session to the next, though this is increasingly true from the "73-74" series forward. The lines themselves are significant. Studying Barré's paintings at close range, one quickly notes that the redrawn segments are often thicker than the lines that visibly continue beneath the wash, thereby underscoring the independent impetus that produced them. At times, the line itself splits, as in two works from the "75-76" series, *75-76-A-157×145*[A] and *75-76-D-157×145*.[B] In each instance, Barré has reinforced and in fact redoubled a segment of the grid, producing two closely parallel or gradually converging traits rather than just one continuous line. A third line zigzags between the two or atop one in particular. The entire configuration recalls a similar event often found among the tube-squeezed traits of Barré's paintings of the early 1960s, including *61-T-2*[C] from 1961. Drawing, here, has ceased to function simply in the register of code, folding back into something more like painterly gesture.

Then there are the painted hatch marks. Produced with a round-headed brush, these allow no pretense of procedural blindness of the sort previously imposed, throughout the 1967 "Flèches" ("Arrows") immediately predating Barré's hiatus, by the use of spray paint and stencil. On the contrary, these striations often reveal a marked willfulness in terms of their placement relative both to the grid and to one another—idiosyncrasies that again bring us back to Barré's decision making before the canvas. Traces often pull back from one edge or corner of an otherwise filled-in quadrant, as in *72-73-B-160×148*;[D] alternately, they might exceed one bound of a module whose limits they otherwise respect, as in *74-75-A-113×105*.[E] In a work such as *73-74-F-123×114*,[F] the proximity of a relatively small number of traces only serves to highlight their heterogeneous nature. In the upper center, a short stroke at the apex of a triangular stack veers off from the group at an angle, like a grave accent.

12
According to Clay, for the "75-76" series, the grid of inscription is traced in sanguine when oriented orthogonally relative to the support's edges and in graphite when oriented obliquely. See Clay, "Le dispositif Martin Barré," 79.

A → p. 126

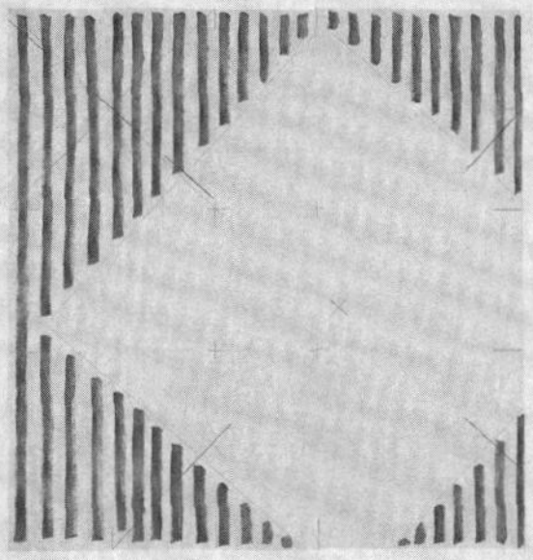

B → p. 125

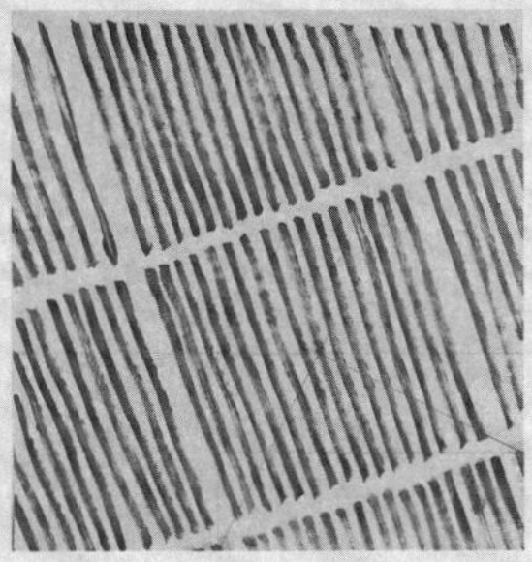

C → p. 52

D → p. 110

E → p. 121

F → p. 112

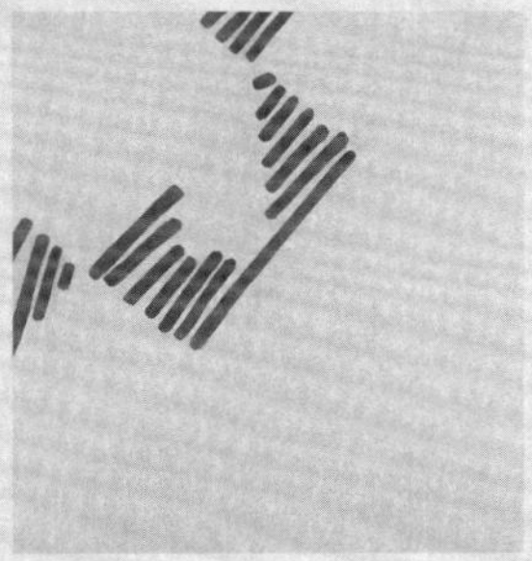

All of these deviations bring us back to something like the *fact* of subjectivity. Just as importantly, however, this is a subjectivity visibly constrained not only by the rules governing the system—the conceptual dimension, determined in advance—but also, and no less crucially, by materiality and process. Barré's return to the brush is part of the story: unlike the spray can, this implement necessarily encounters and indeed engages the resistance of the support. The difference is clear in a work such as *72-73-B-130×120*,[G] in which the irregularly spaced striations immediately recall the stripes in the 1967 "Zebras"—apart from the differential saturation that suggests the progressive depletion of an initially paint-laden brush, the thinning pigment highlighting as opposed to simply covering over the weave of the canvas. The effect is even more pronounced in *73-74-A-149×139*,[H] in which five strokes of orange-red paint descend from the upper right to the lower left. Two of the strokes are cropped by the painting's lower edge, while the other three vary in length. None are expressionistic in any conventional sense. They are nonetheless singular, as opposed to mechanically regular. As such, they invite the beholder to imaginatively reconstruct their making, even to identify kinesthetically with the body that enacted them.

G → p.107

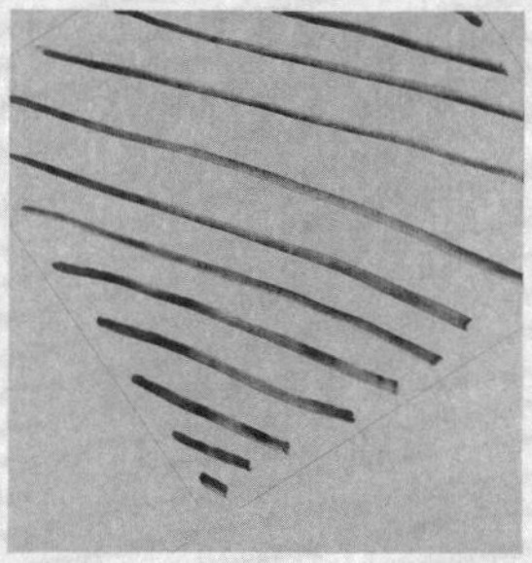

H → p.115

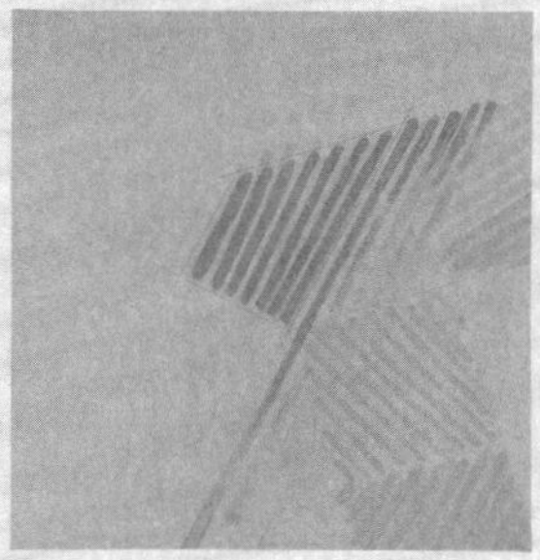

Barré's use of color introduces—or rather, reintroduces—another subjective dimension. Throughout the "72-73" paintings Barré uses dark brown paint for the hatch marks; later series deploy additional hues, prominently including a rich orange-red and deep blue. As the artist noted, these colors serve in part to mark different moments in the work's production: the brown, for example, appears pale blue once washed with white. At the same time, they strongly recall Barré's palette of the 1950s and early 1960s, effectively telescoping different stages in his practice. Returning with difference after the reduction to black and white in the late-1960s sprays, these choices are newly striking as decidedly *mixed* colors. As such, they bring us back yet again to authorial agency.[13]

In all of these ways, Barré's paintings appear allegorical of a fundamentally new conception of the painterly self, as at once conditioned but yet finally irreducible to laws that both precede and exceed it. Every painting is made up of a complicated interplay of contingency and intentionality, its autonomy always already heteronomy. One final example helps to sum up this understanding. *75-76-C-157×145*[I] reveals a relatively spare surface. Short lines in graphite and sanguine jut into the whitish-colored field from around the periphery, recalling certain sprayed canvases of the mid-1960s (for example, *65-S-12*,[J]). There is nonetheless an important difference from the earlier *bombes*:

I → p.124

J

65-S-12, 1965
76×72 cm

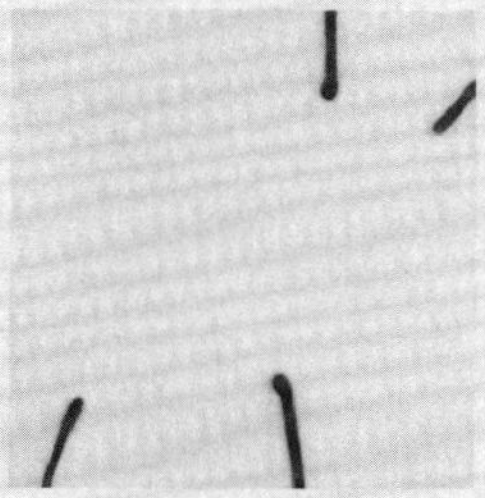

13

Significantly, in his 1974 interview with Millet, Barré rejects the notion that his earlier tube paintings derived from his desire to work with unmixed color, noting on the contrary that he filled the empty tubes "with the mixture of my choice" (Millet, "Interview," 263).

not one of these dash-like segments extends all the way to the nearest framing edge. Separated from the bounds of the support by slight but significant gaps, they frame the work as a discrete whole conscious of its edges —a figure in its own right.

Even from a distance, however, the beholder is aware of another, underlying layer or layers of marks. The grids of construction and inscription were at one point drawn in their entirety and remain more or less visible through at least one chronologically later wash of paint. In addition, two quadrants of the oblique grid have been filled with long hatch marks: those in the lower left, orthogonal within their compartment, descend toward the left, while those in the upper right, diagonally arranged relative to their module, descend toward the right. Unlike the graphite and sanguine lines, these painted stripes are cropped by the framing edges and register as continuing beyond those limits. In so doing, they recall the larger system on which this individual depends, the field to which it belongs. And they recall, too, the opacity at the heart of Barré's seeming simplicity: not one of these works delivers itself without remainder. Each comes to us both open and closed, a presence conditioned by absence.

1977
1978

“FROM THE START, I CONCEIVED OF THIS SERIES AS INDIVISIBLE. IN THE END IT BECAME A BIG POLYPTYCH.”

Martin Barré, 1985

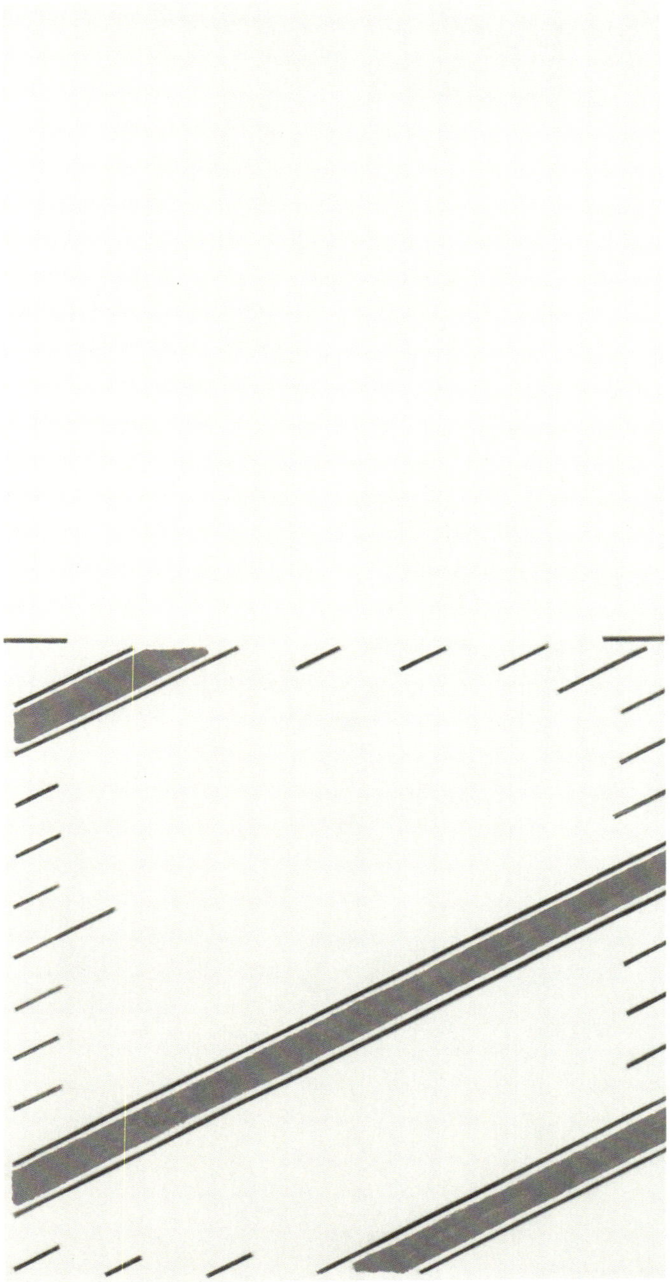

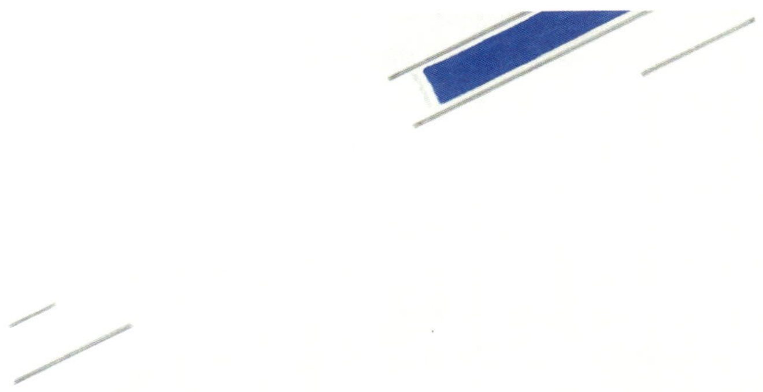

↑
77-78-1-162×81, 1977–78

↗
77-78-2-81×81, 1977–78

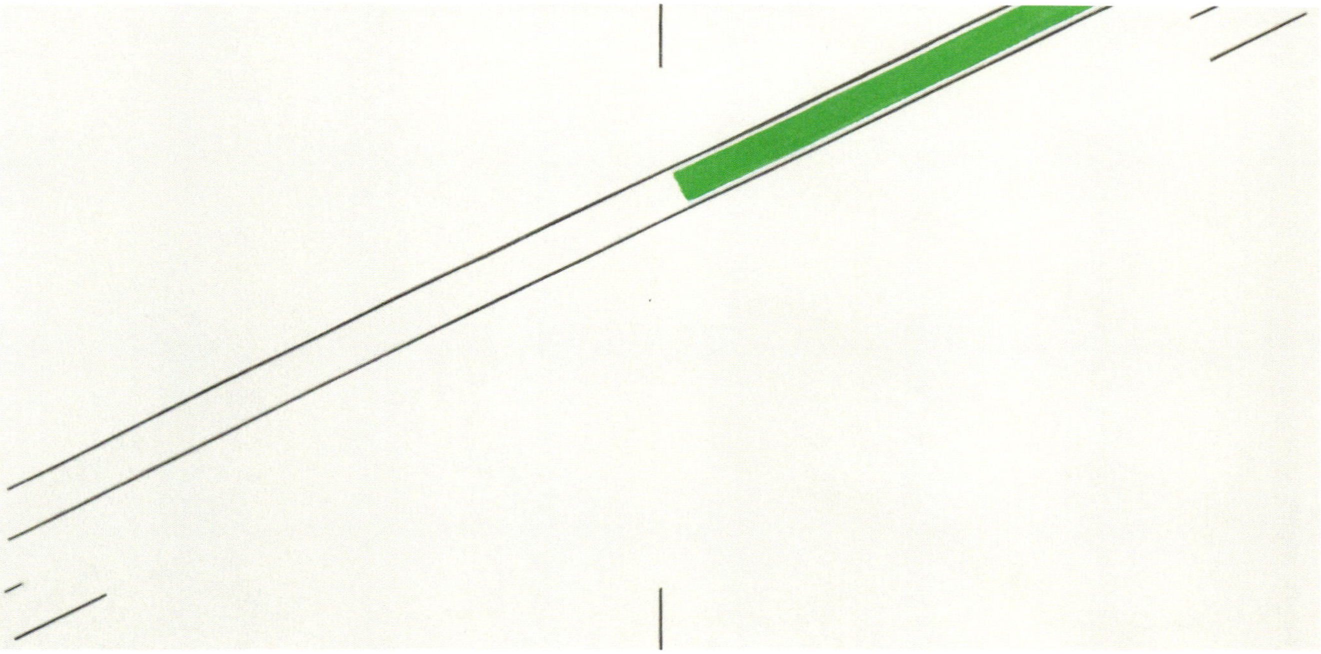

77-78-3-81×162, 1977–78

↑
77-78-4-100×62, 1977–78

↗
77-78-5-162×162, 1977–78

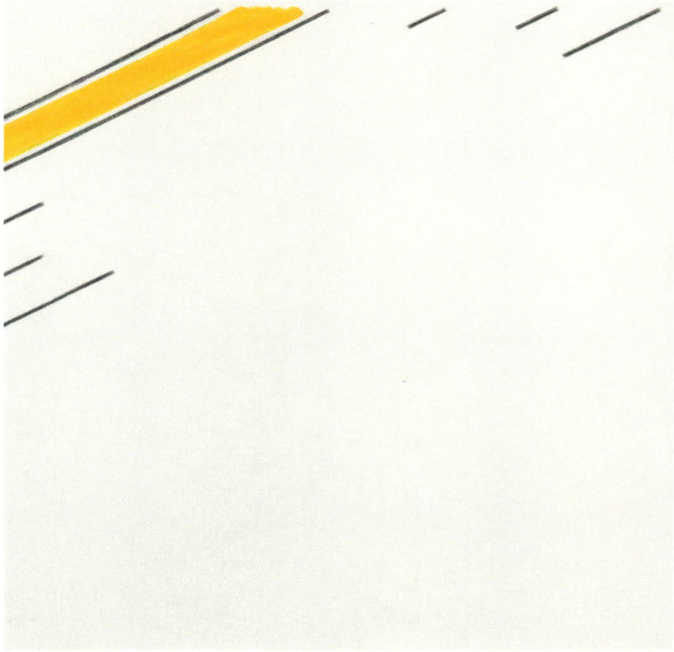

↗
77-78-6-81×81, 1977–78

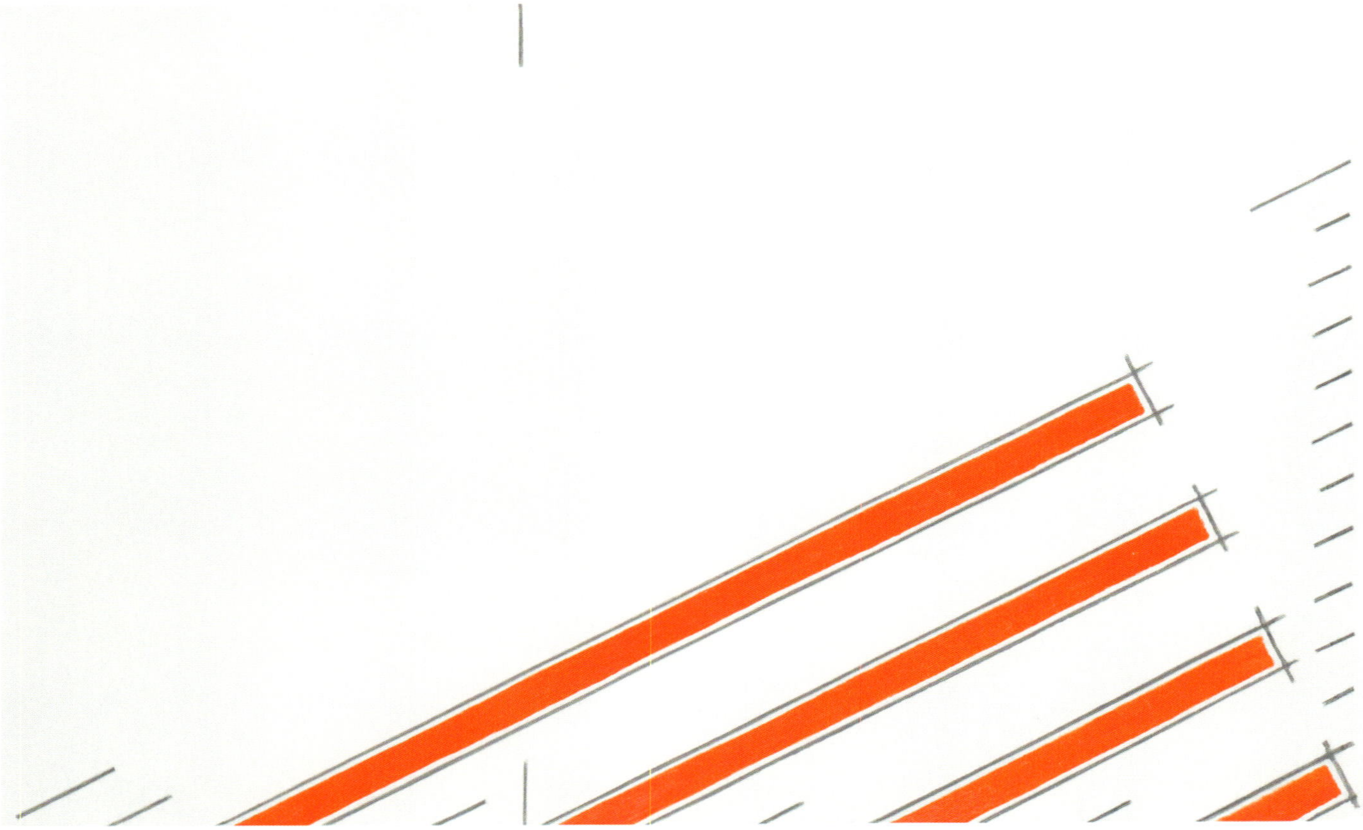

77-78-7-100×162, 1977–78

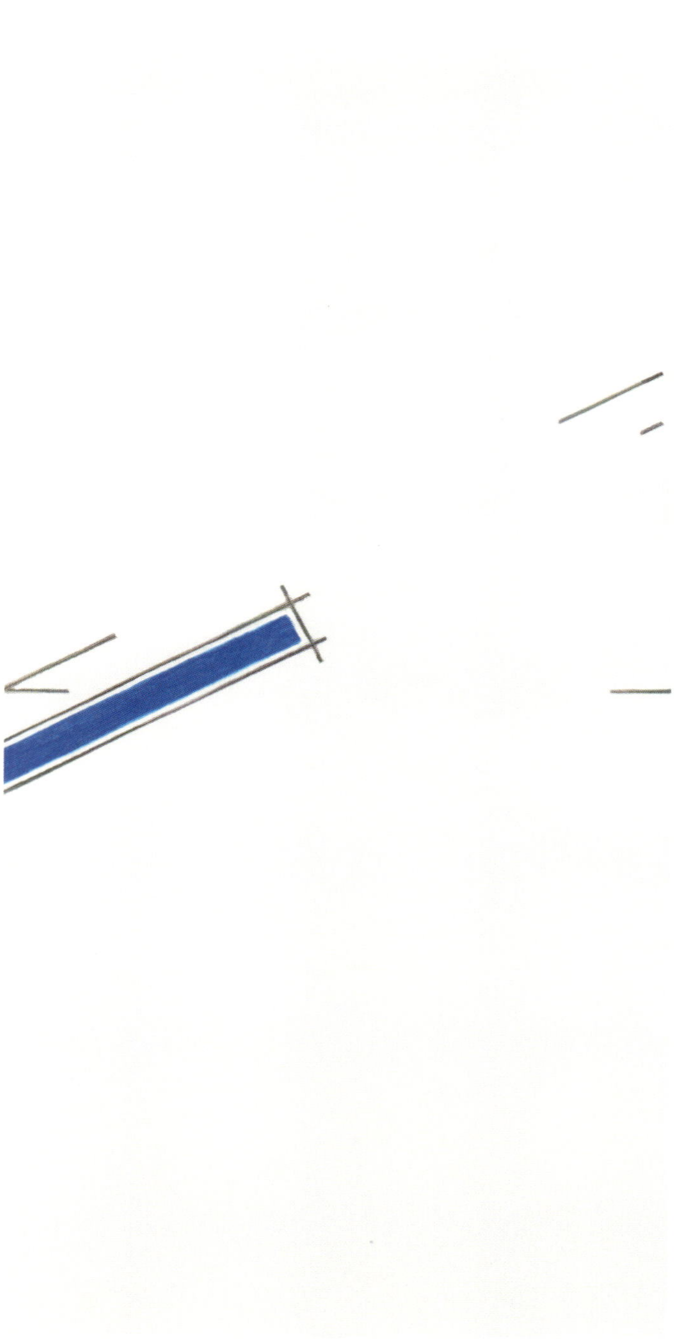

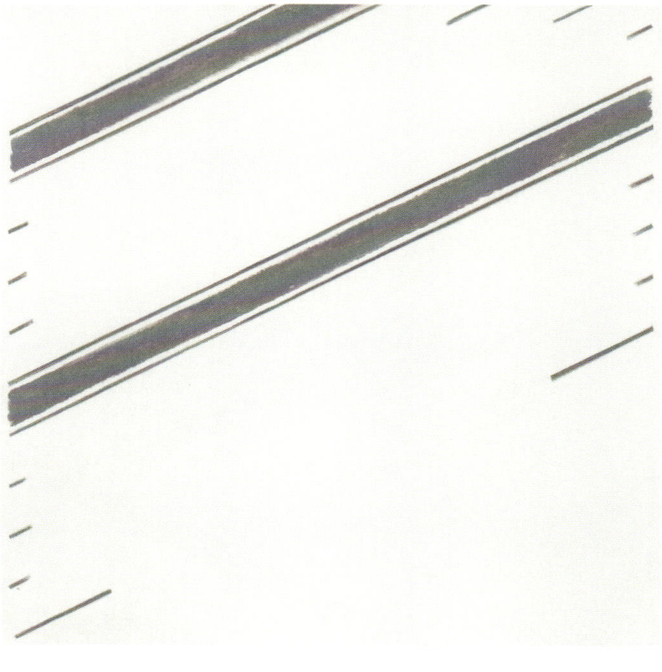

↑
77-78-8-162×81, 1977–78

↗
77-78-9-81×81, 1977–78

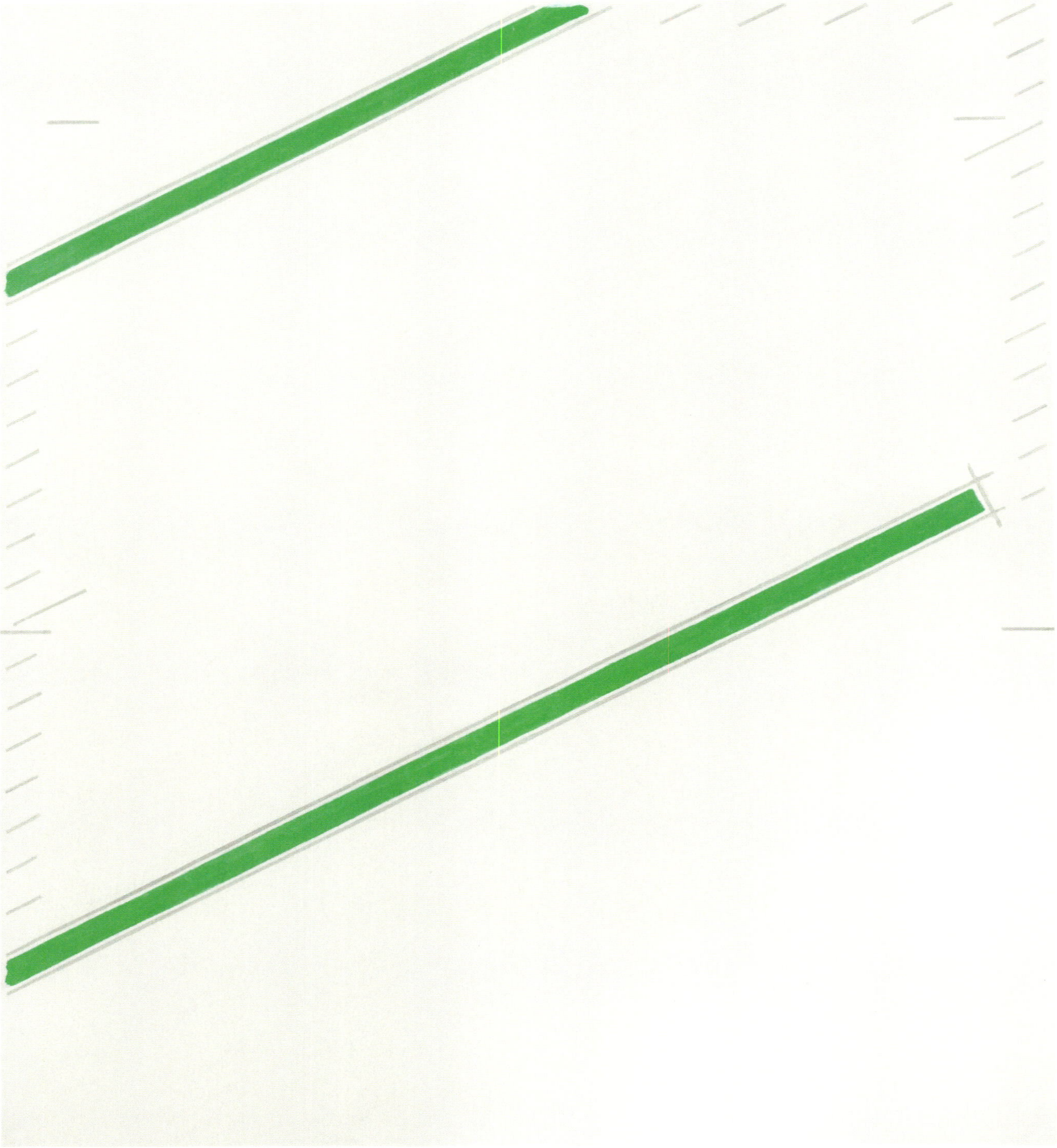

77-78-10-181×162, 1977–78

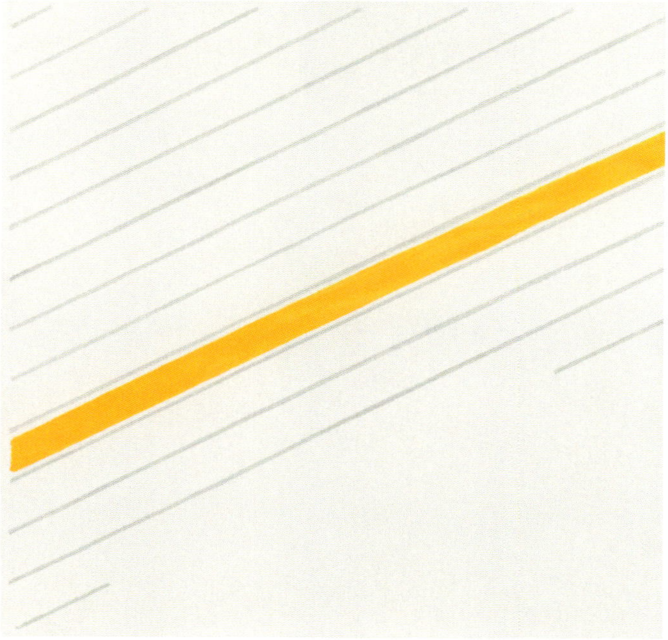

↑
77-78-11-81×81, 1977–78

↗
77-78-12-81×81, 1977–78

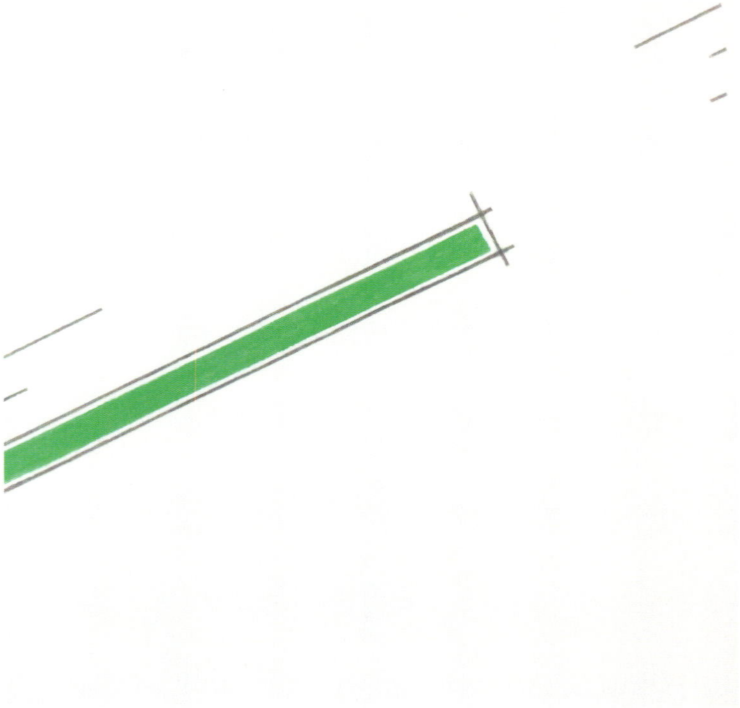

↑
77-78-13-81×81, 1977–78

↗
77-78-14-100×100, 1977–78

L'INDISSOCIABLE: A SCORE FOR THE OPUS

Ann Hindry

"The *plane* (flatness) is to painting what sound is to music."
Martin Barré, 1976[1]

Martin Barré's demanding pictorial approach led him, from very early on, to invalidate the usual hierarchies between a painting's various elements: a source of misunderstandings, of "mis-seeing," he would say. For the artist, the surface of the painting was never indeed a neutral place—a ground upon which autonomous signs were to be laid out—but remained instead part of a single plane where the inscriptions and the medium, whatever their particularity in terms of material or tint, whatever the stages of their creation might be, all pertained to the same surface and entered into play with each other, without chronology or hierarchy, leading to the "advent of the painting" as an entity.

In this regard, the great "suite" of *L'Indissociable* (*The Inseparable*, 1977–78) is a masterful, subtly arrhythmic demonstration that the painting-object can be both itself and an active part of a larger whole, made up of each painting in the series and the actual space of the wall the paintings occupy and reorganize. In this case, it is a series comprising fourteen paintings—eight squares, four rectangles in height and two rectangles in width—in six different formats, to which seven different dimensions[2] are added, with each one offering a variation on a single geometric theme. It should also be noted that the rectangles' dimensions systematically correspond to those formed by two squares placed side by side. The group thus plays numerically with the random distribution of only three measurement figures: 62, 81, and 100 centimeters. "I'm trying to make a two-dimensional painting," Barré liked to say. This remark, which may seem redundant, did not concern the various dimensions, but rather what these dimensions, generated together, would do to the whole! *L'Indissociable*, for such is its title—and Barré thus chose to make it resonate like an injunction to preserve its integrity—was naturally destined to unfold in space, on walls whose specific architecture would determine, not the immutable order as already devised by the artist, but the proposal for its implementation.

1 Martin Barré and Christian Bonnefoi, "Entretien avec Martin Barré," *Documents IV-V, Cahiers d'histoire de l'art contemporain* (1976), repr. in Suzanne Pagé et al., *Martin Barré*, exh. cat. (Paris: ARC – Musée d'Art Moderne de la Ville de Paris, 1979), 41.

2 [Editor's note] Six diverse formats: the square and five rectangular formats, one being used both vertically and horizontally; seven different dimensions: 81 × 81 cm, 81 × 162 cm and 162 × 81 cm, 100 × 100 cm, 100 × 62 cm, 100 × 162 cm, 162 × 162 cm, 181 × 162 cm. In 1979, Martin Barré installed *L'Indissociable* according to three different heights: 61, 71, and 90 cm for one, six, and seven paintings respectively.

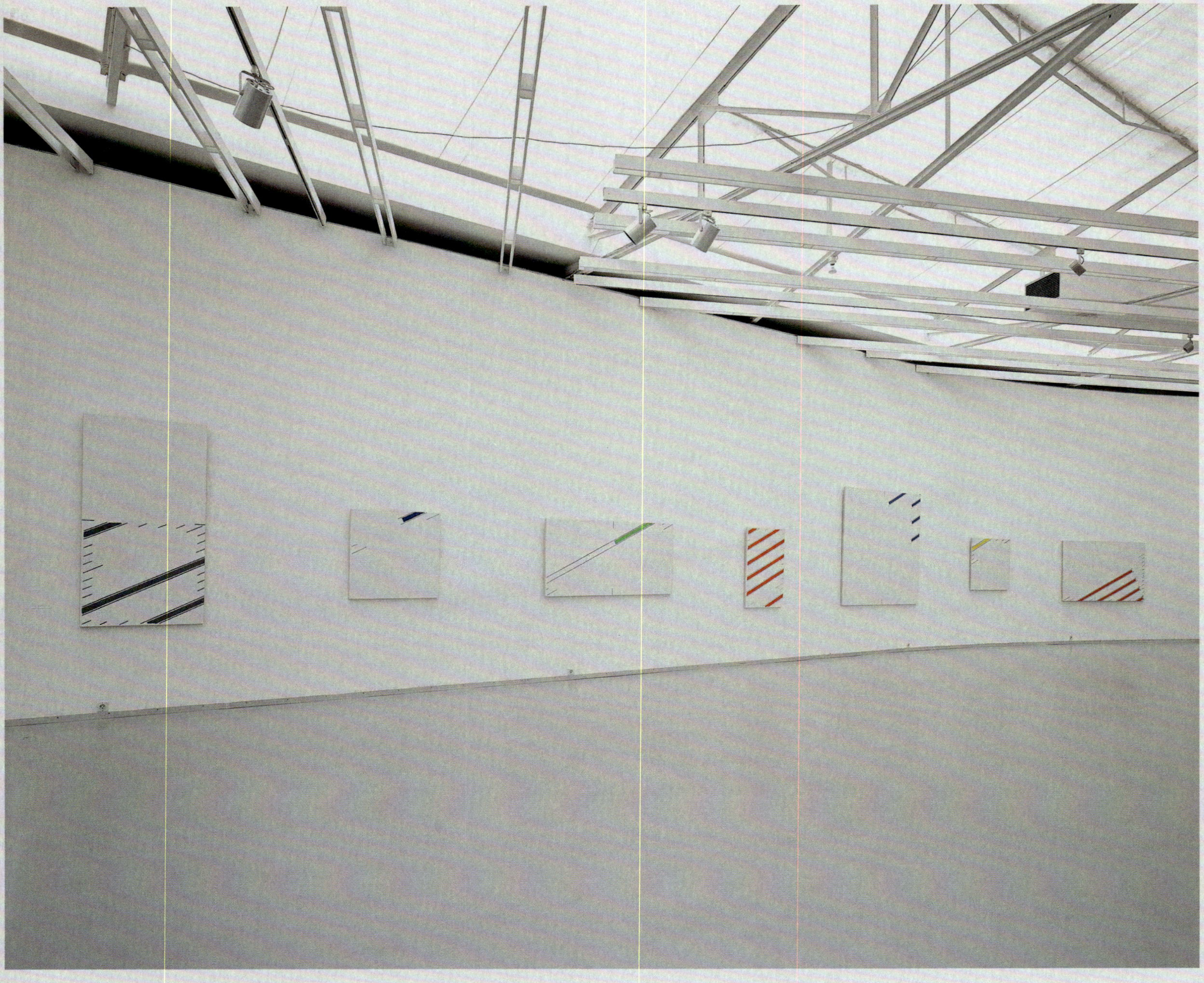

↑ ↗
L'Indissociable, 1977–78
Exhibition views, *Martin Barré*,
ARC – Musée d'Art Moderne
de la Ville de Paris, Paris, 1979

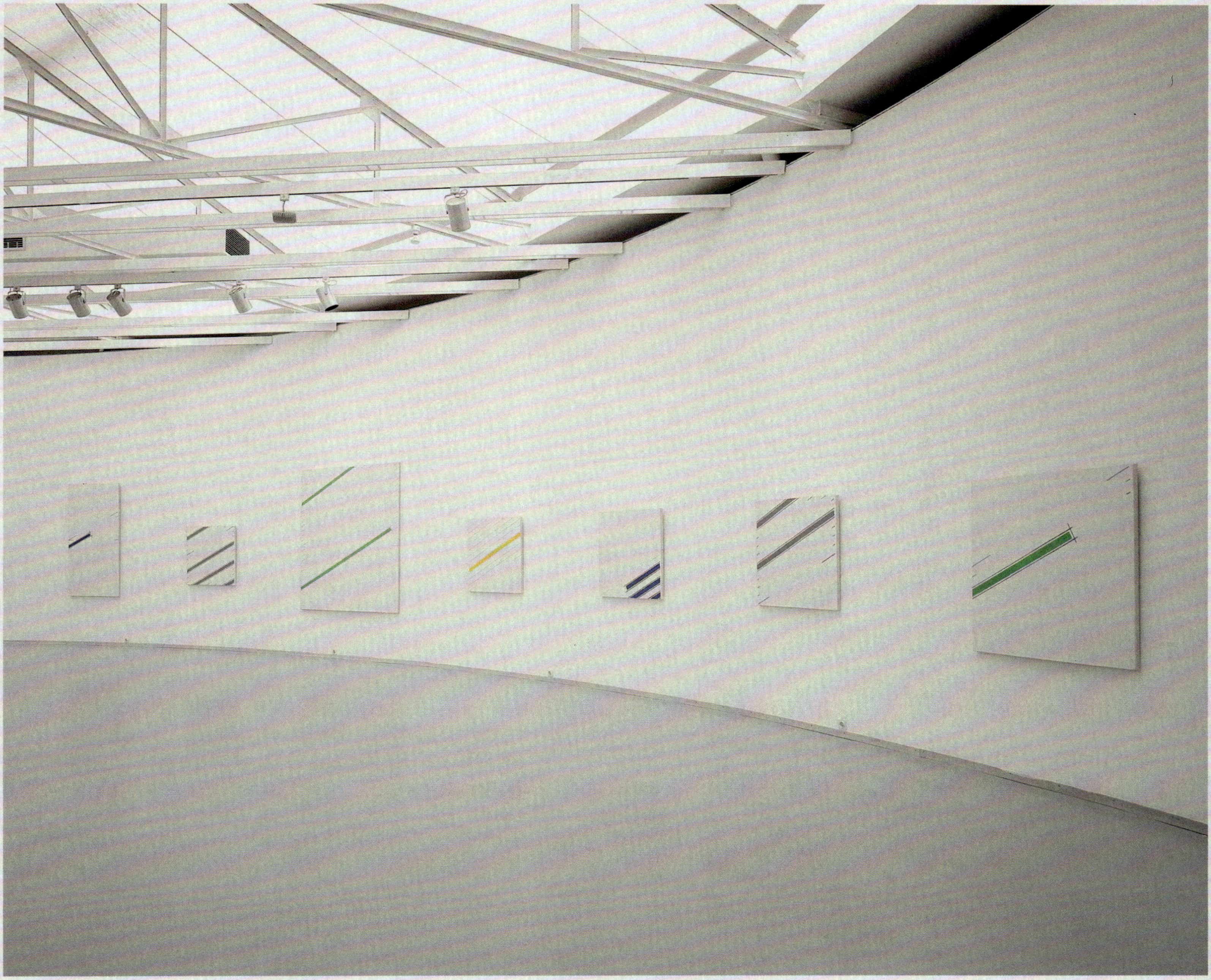

1977
1978

Ann Hindry

The work would thus assert the authority of its effective visual presence insofar as it activates and integrates its site of deployment rather than submitting to it. Like a great musical creation whose sound conditions won't change the score, *L'Indissociable* adapts to the architectural demands of the chosen site without changing its scenario. A scenario that stems from a subtle yet determined arbitrariness on the part of the artist, who thus adapted the vast suite to the spatial conditions imposed upon it while simultaneously continuing to propose—through the deliberately a-logical but imperative scansion of the placement of its various pictorial units in space—an unexpected comprehension for anyone who chose to take it into account. A subtle way of inviting the viewer to pay more attention to what painting can suggest as a wider area of perception?

The fourteen paintings that make up *L'Indissociable* —also entitled *Série Renault* because they were produced in collaboration with the then-named "Recherches Art et Industrie" department of the car firm at the end of last century—thus present a kind of oneness, a rhythm, an apparent declension of identifiable factors due to the chosen pictorial morphology: a white ground criss-crossed from side to side or partially, as if by surprise, by a "serried squadron" of several parallel, oblique bands of color which appear in formation, on all the paintings. The bands are delimited, not to say "contained," by fine gray lines that accentuate them and sometimes abruptly stop their momentum in the middle of the white of the canvas. In *sotto voce* of this dynamic score of the crossing of the pictorial space, the artist introduces a subtle reminder of the limits of the frame. The space of the painting is a finite space tolerating no illusion that would risk dissipating its foundation. These short lines, emerging discreetly from time to time from the contours of the canvas, are in a way a grand finale to the crossing of the space set in motion by the bars of color. They signal the limit of the inscribed field. They accentuate the real, "finished" identity of the image. The color "vectors" that could plow the white are neutralized on the surface and contained by them. The perception of what one is invited to experience—like an initiation to the journey, to coordinate its stages—is questioned by these short lines that subtly refer to the dialectic of the signs animating the inscribed surface. The colored diagonal stripes are either accentuated or impeded by these discreet but very present directional surges, these subtle markers that tend to quietly remind us of the concrete limits of the painting's space. The whole, as if captured by these contradictory dialectics, imposes from the outset a shared virtual setting in motion. Here, the subtlety of the artist's approach already lies in its essential consideration of the potential mobility of the active, deliberately unresolved space of each painting. The impeccable orchestration leads the ensemble into a virtual symphonic movement. The relationship to the walls—the stave—which defines the notes of this concert of forms, spontaneously refers spectators facing it to the virtual mobility of what they are experiencing.

The particularity of the curved space of the huge room offered to Barré in 1979 by the Musée d'Art Moderne de la Ville de Paris for an exhibition—which if not quite a retrospective was in any event on a large scale—and the perspective thereby provided by the choice of a semicircular layout, and thus a possible immediate overall perception of the entire series, definitely motivated the artist in his exhibition project. It was undoubtedly at this first experimentation stage that it became possible to understand that what would potentially be perceived as a single directional unit, a single work in several elements, was not really so. The extreme subtlety of Barré's pictorial approach lies in this discreet balance, this in-between experience between organized trace and perception. Each painting in the series remains absolutely distinct. What is articulated from the viewer's vision of the whole remains at the level of logical deduction. It is the onlooker's vision that can effectively trace a path.

Despite the dynamics instilled by the discreet suggestion of movement, also due to the almost automatic enumeration of each painting, each one of them remains clearly distinct, unique. The artist merely evokes the possibility of an overall movement while preserving the absolute, immutable integrity of each of the elements of the mise-en-scène, which is to say of each painting whose individuality must not be endangered even though the series undeniably exists as a whole.

Martin Barré's pictorial practice was made up of this: an almost mathematical rigor in the deployment by series of works that constituted so many pictorial parameters for what would continue to happen.

1979
1992

"ONE MIGHT WONDER
WHY SOMETHING
AS SIMPLE AS A TRIANGLE
COULD CAUSE SO MANY
DIFFICULTIES..."

"IT'S TRUE THAT
THE PAINTING MUST
MAKE THE WALL
'ACTIVE,' BUT ABOVE
ALL THE WALL
MUST ACTIVATE
THE PAINTING."

Martin Barré, 1985 and 1986

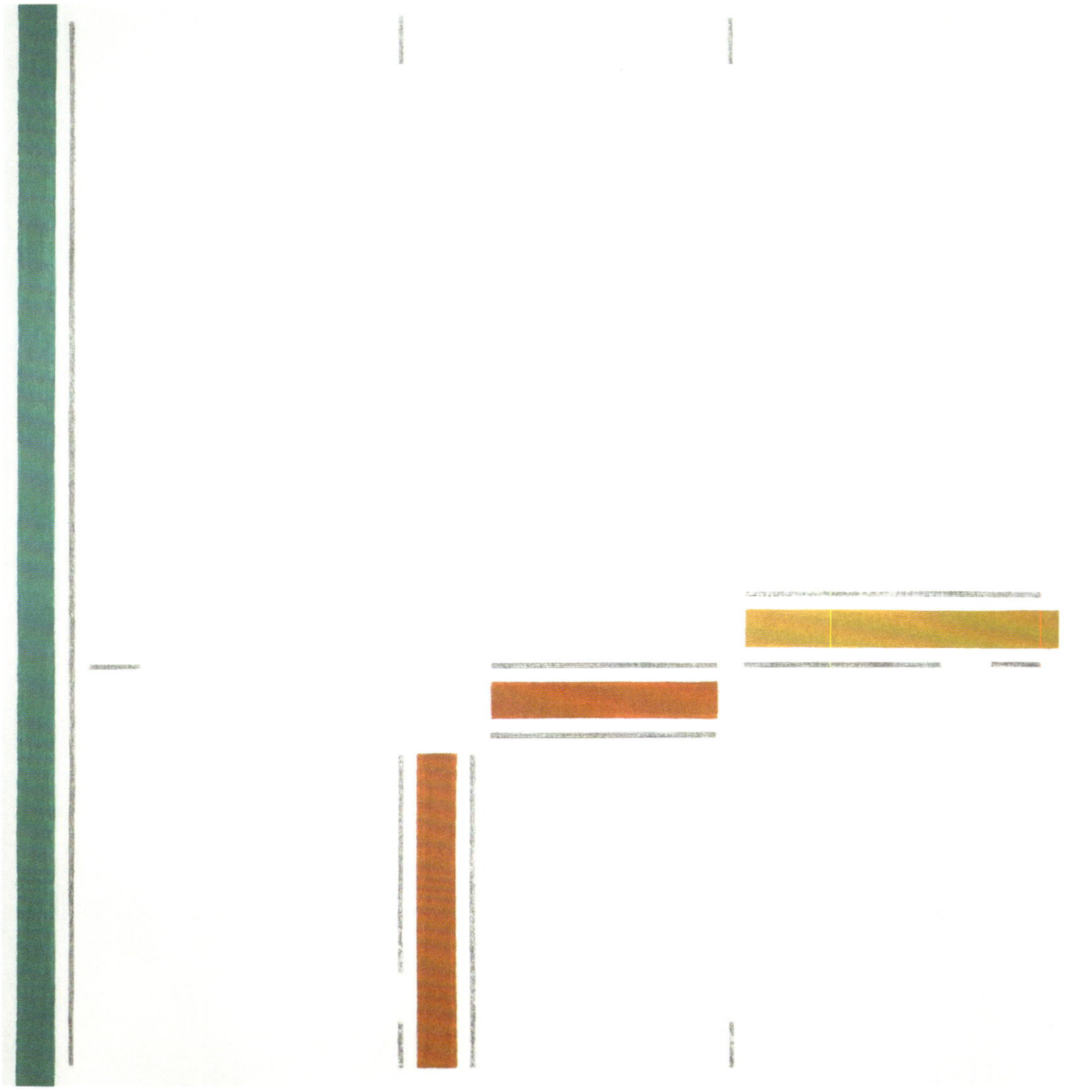

79-B-131×124, 1979

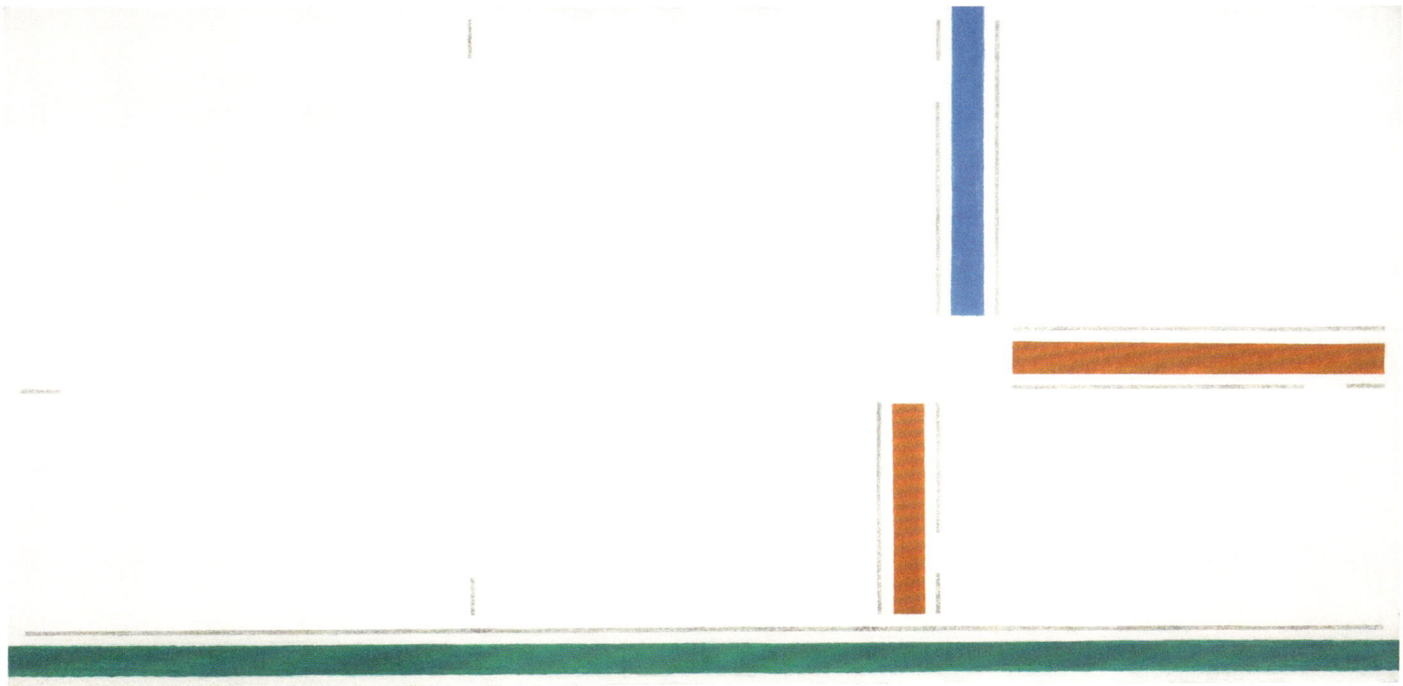

79-A-100×200, 1979

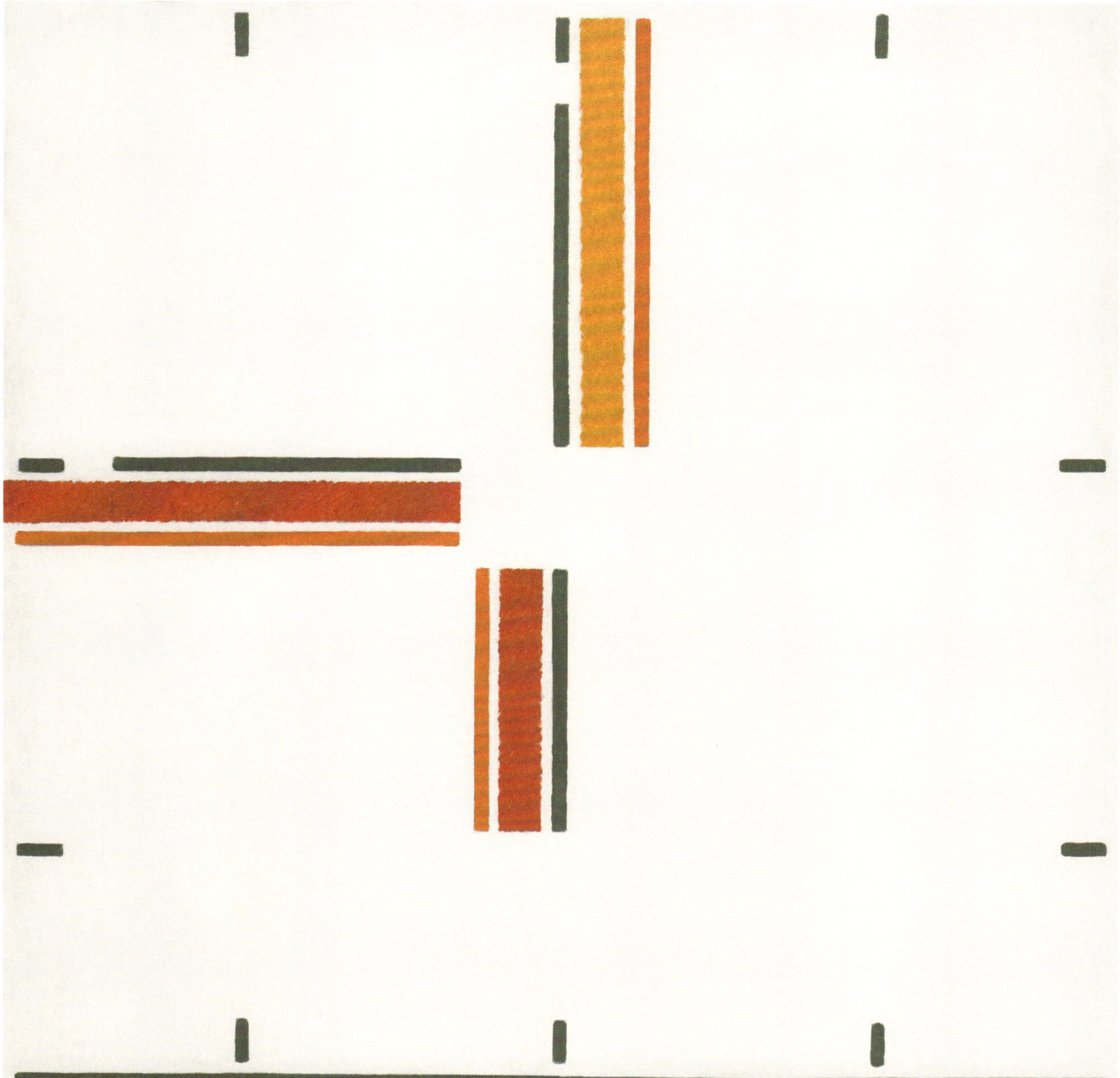

80B-150×140, 1980

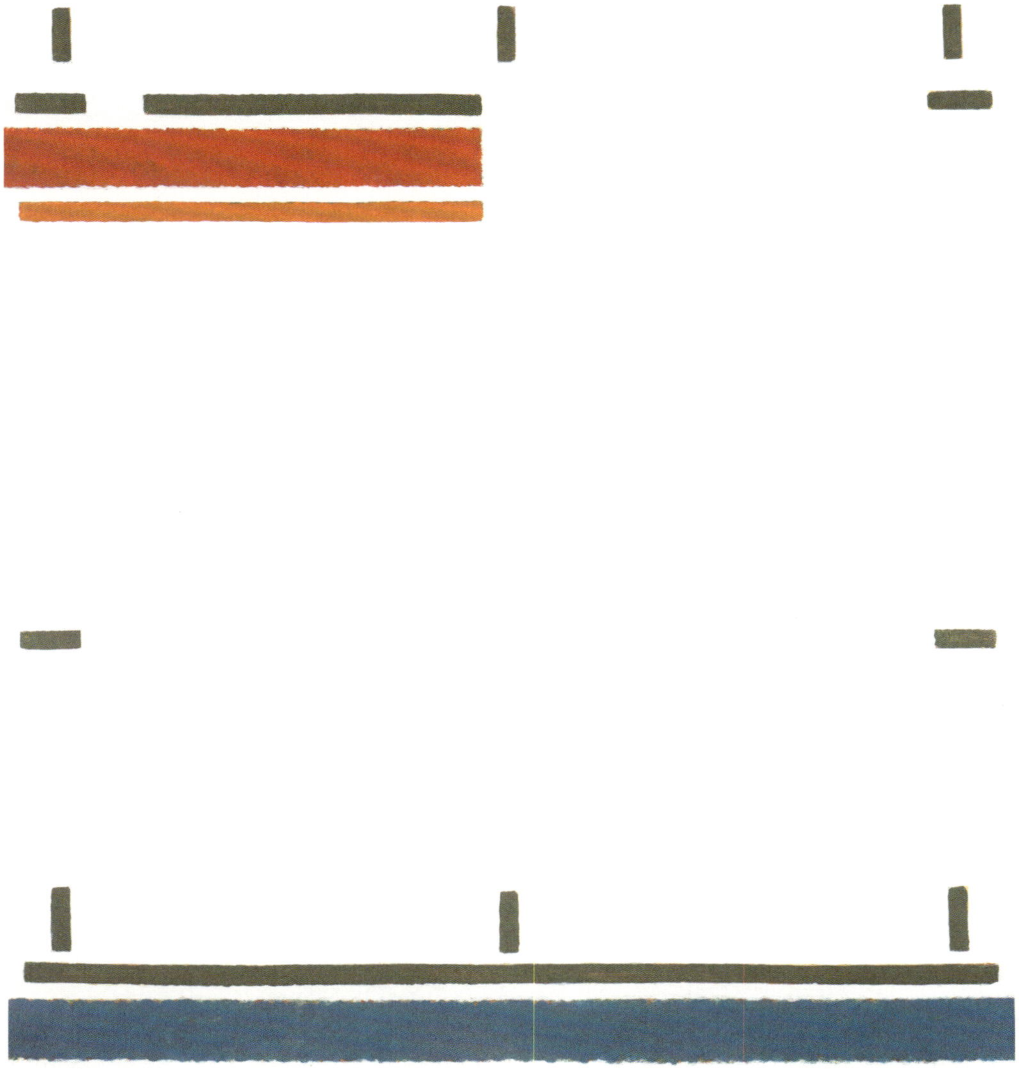

80B-100×90, 1980

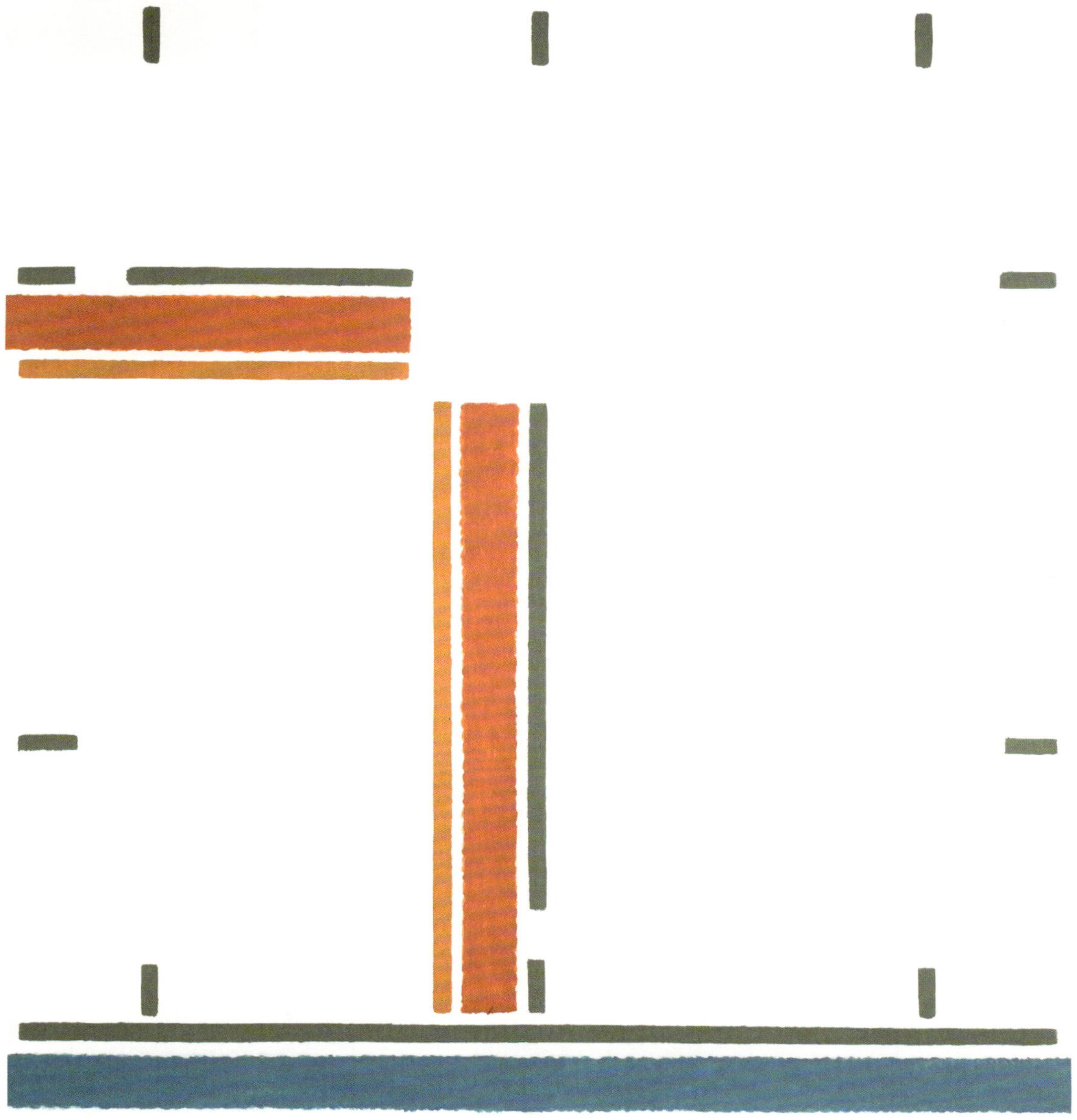

80B-120×110, 1980

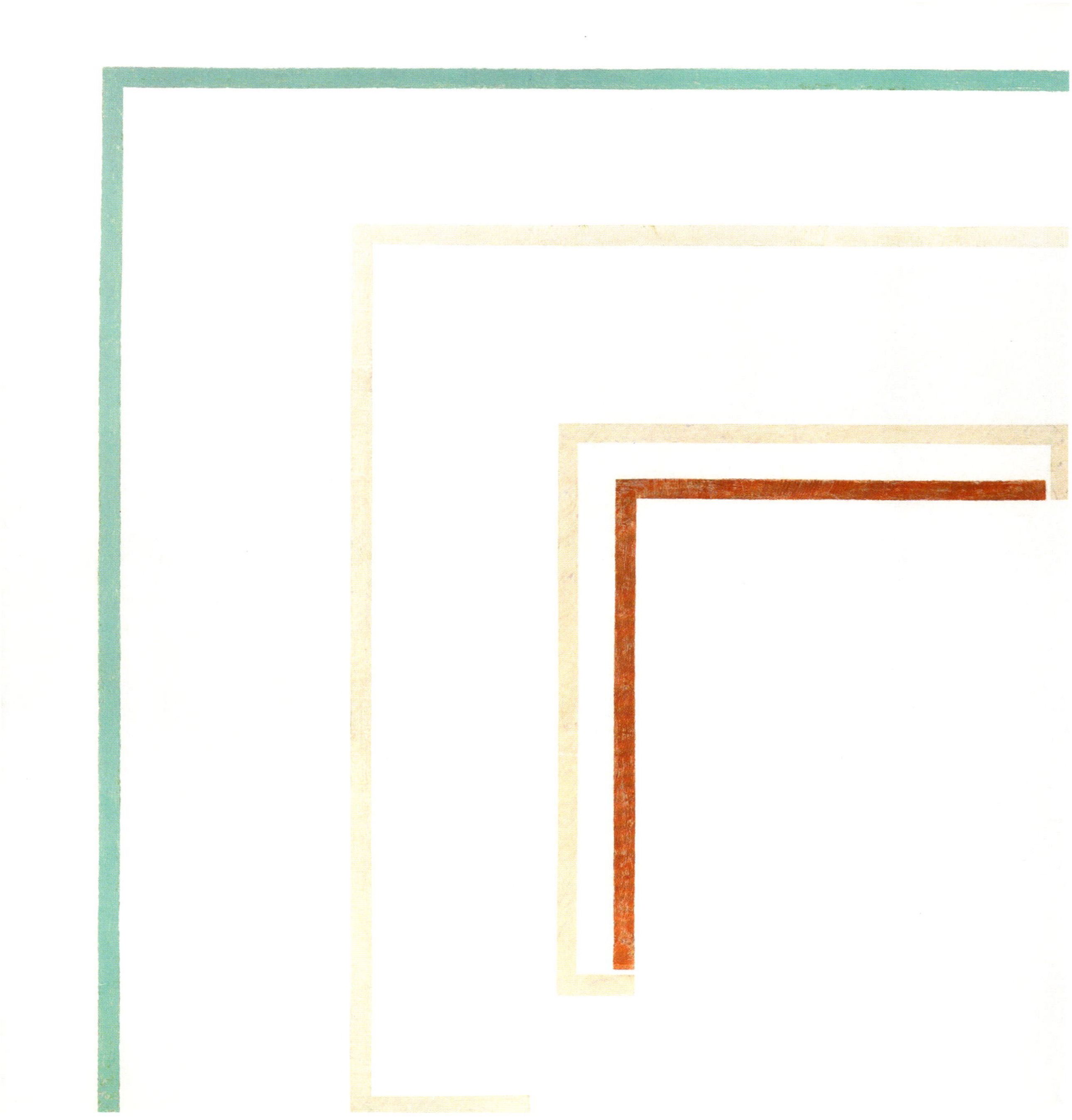

80-81-180×168, 1980–81

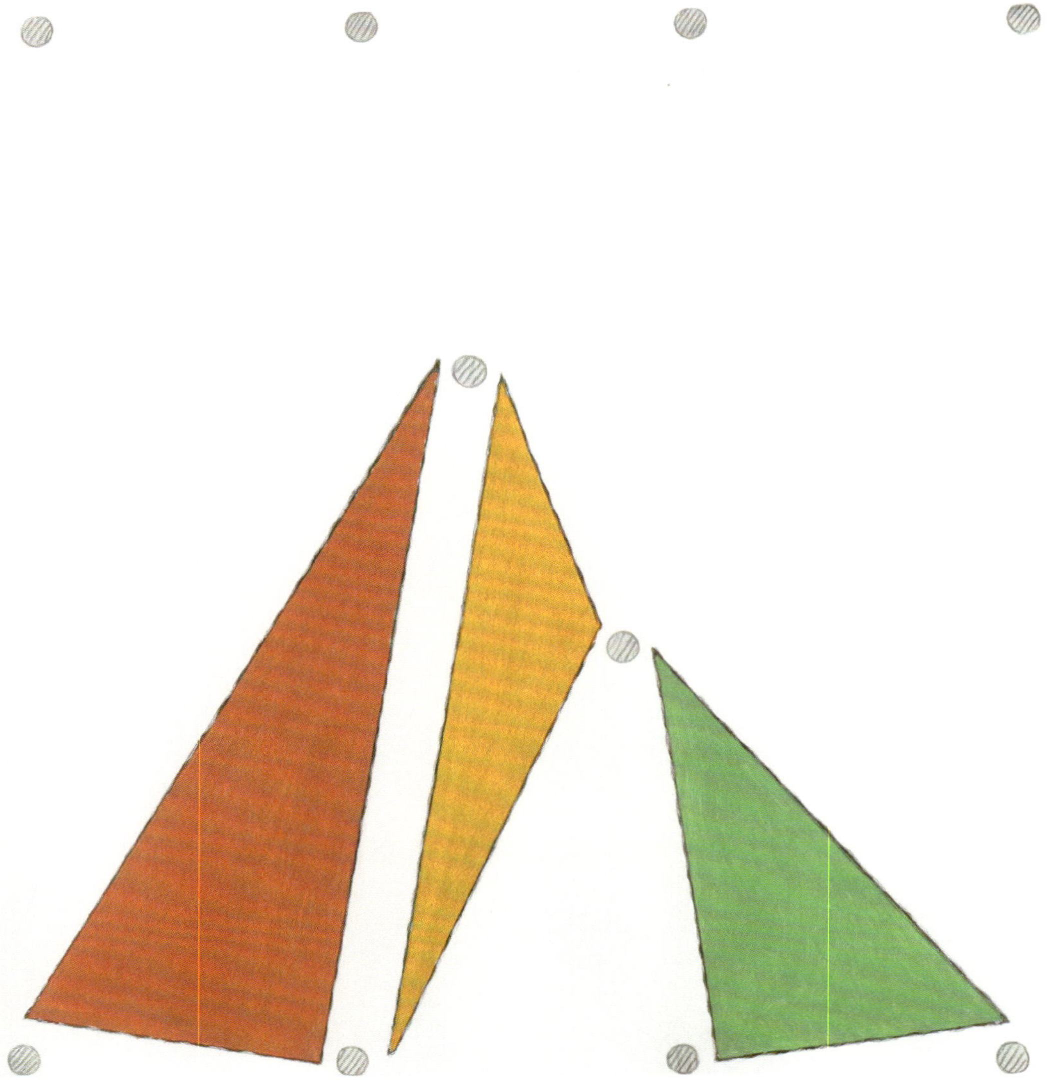

82-84-104×101, 1982–84

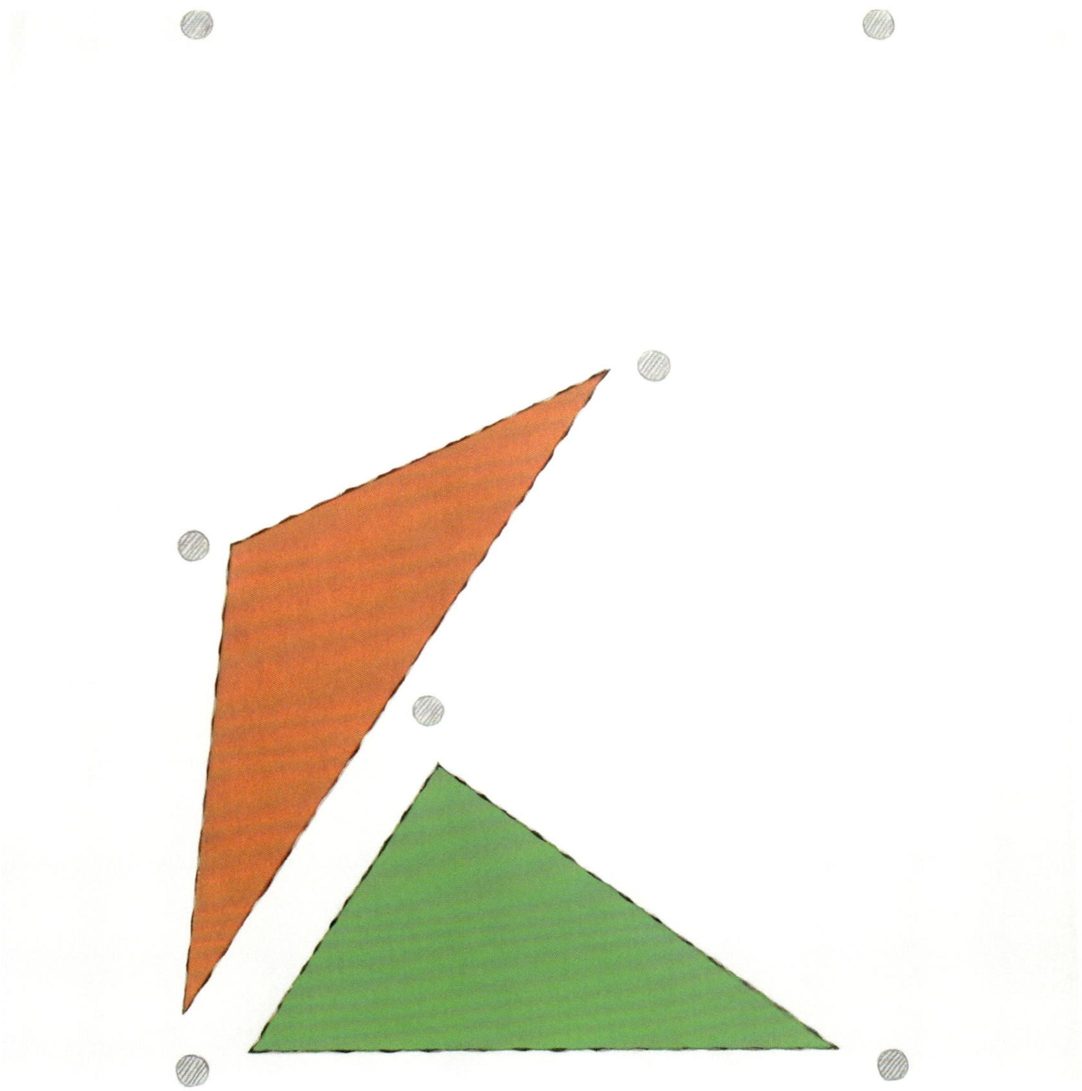

82-84-108×104, 1982–84

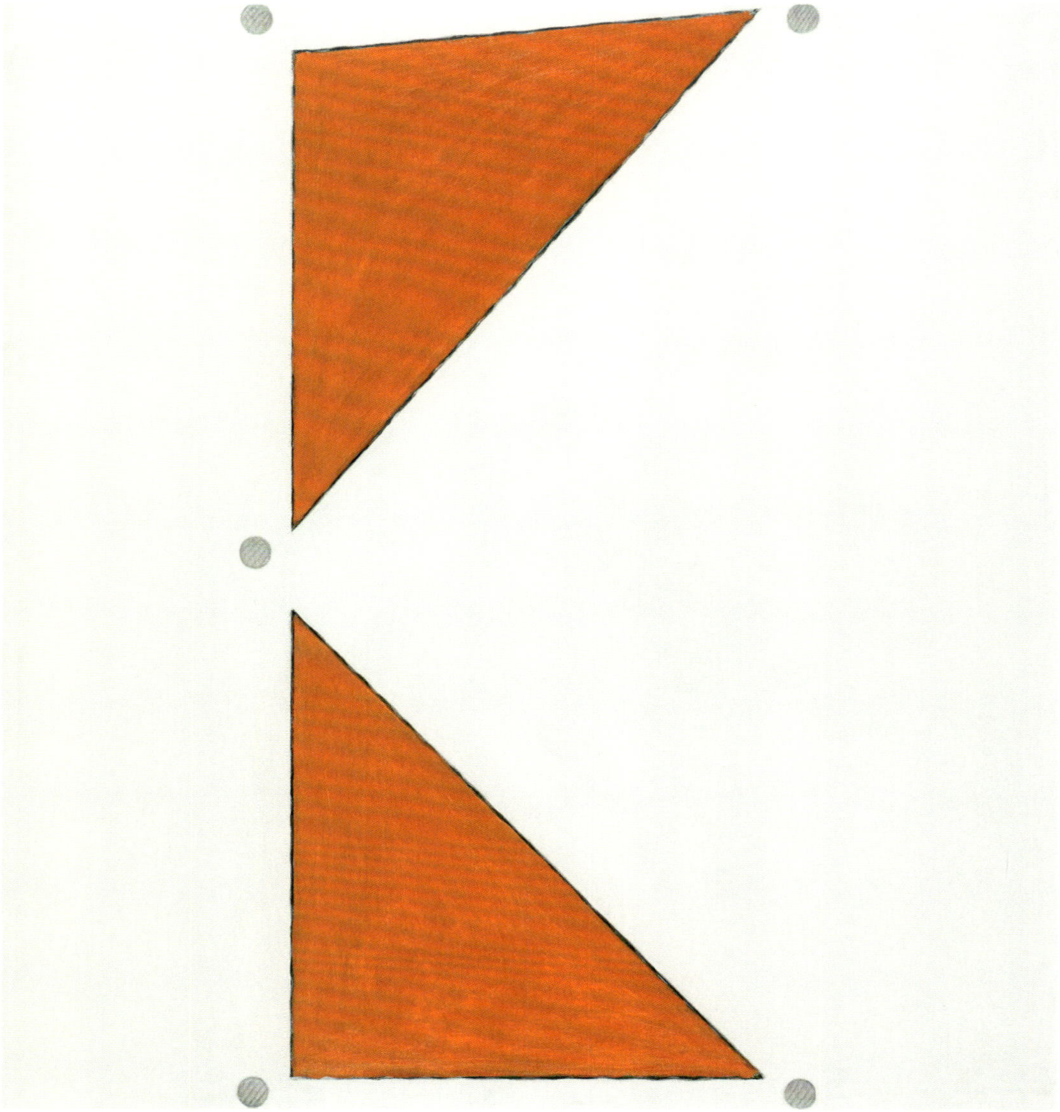

82-84-108×100, 1982–84

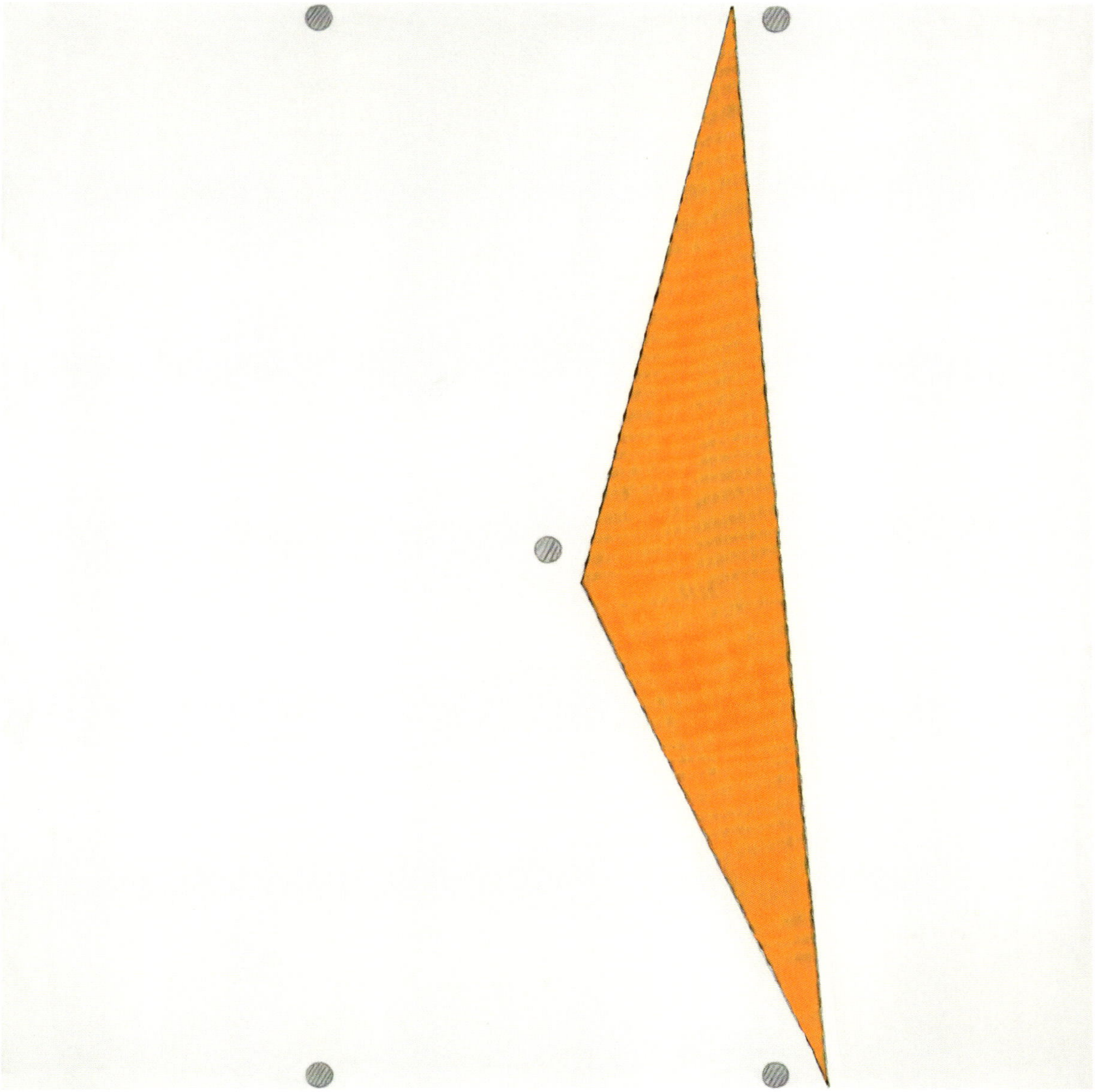

82-84-128×124, 1982–84

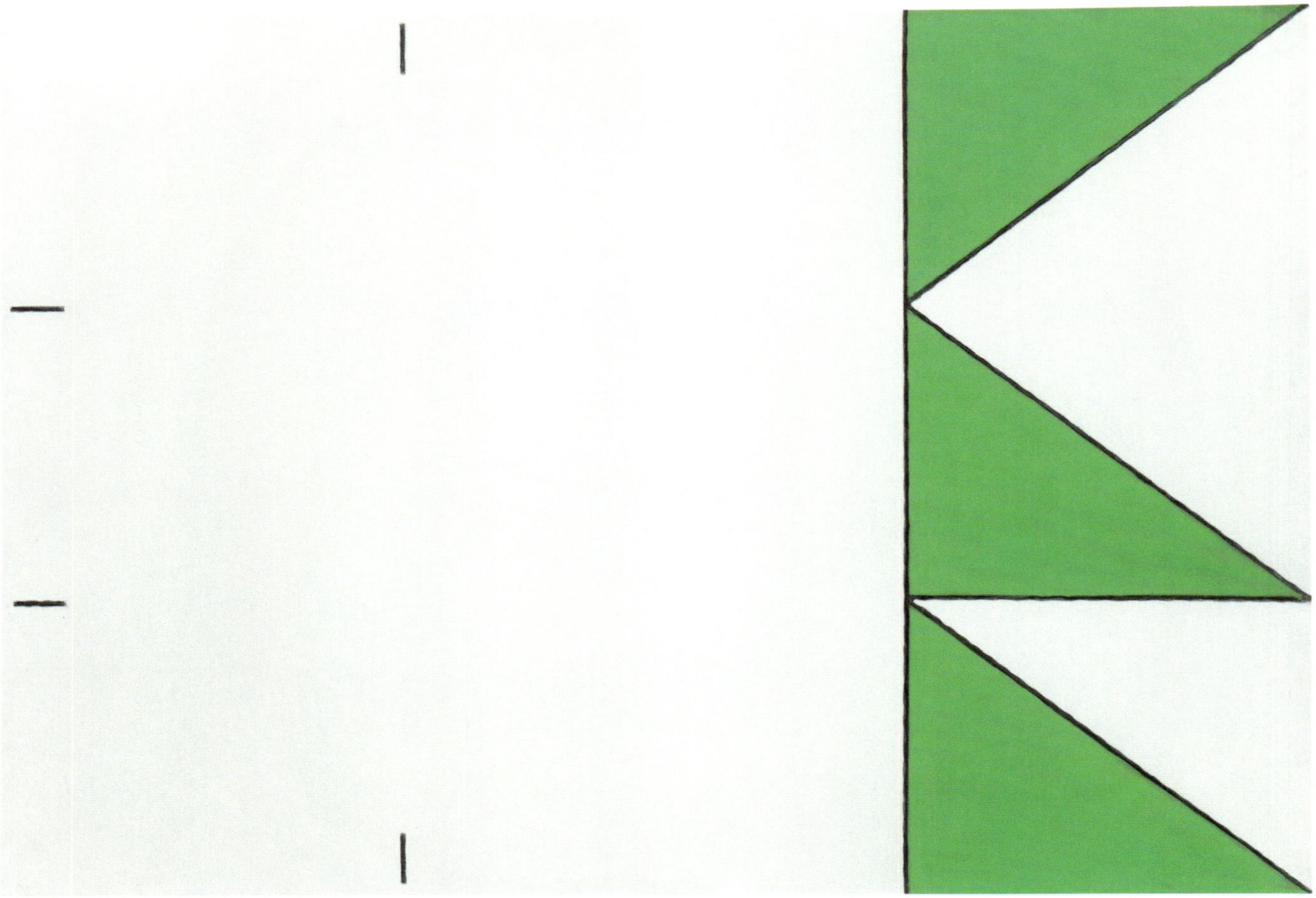

84-85-108×156-B, 1984–85

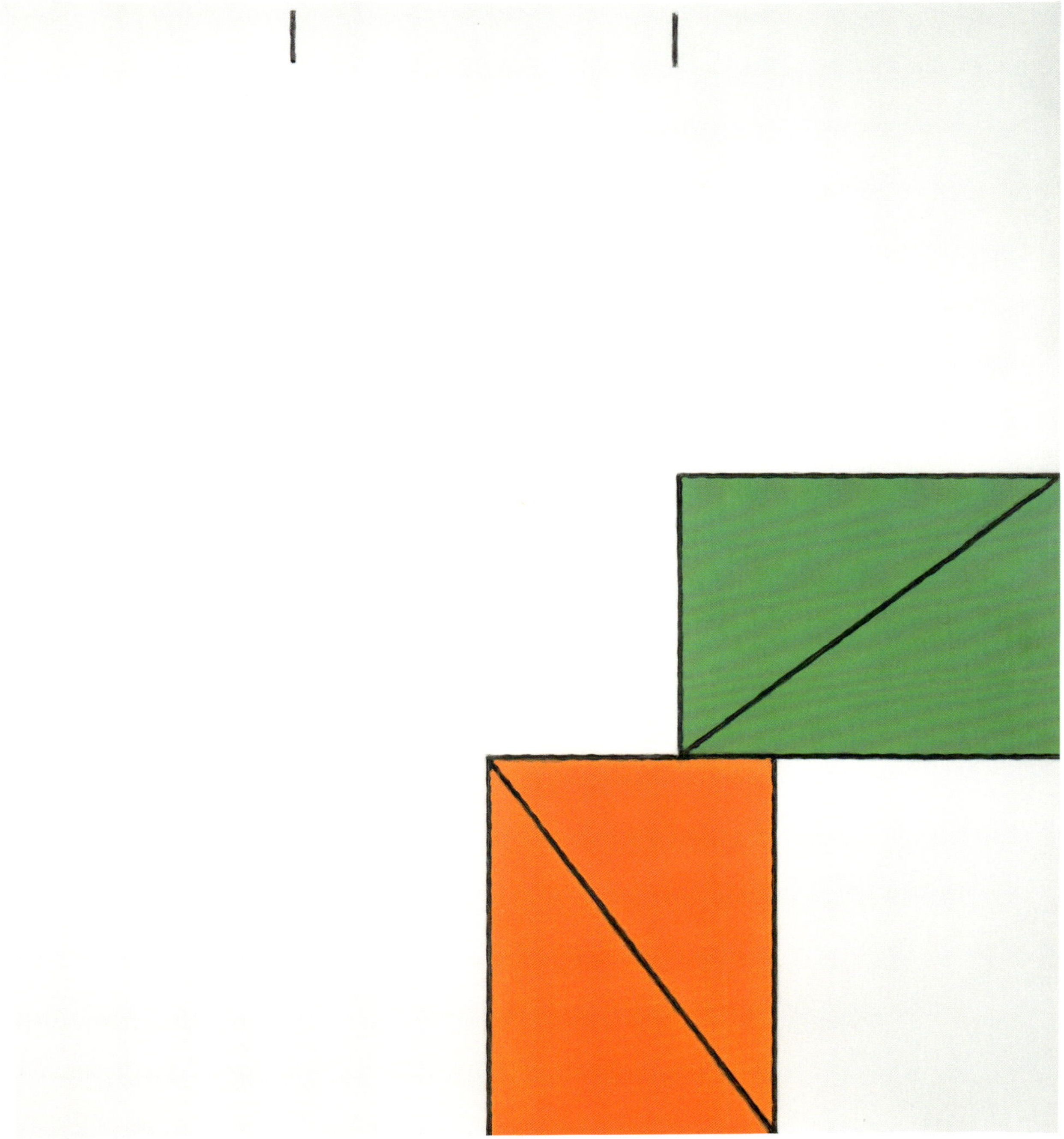

84-85-144×132-D, 1984–85

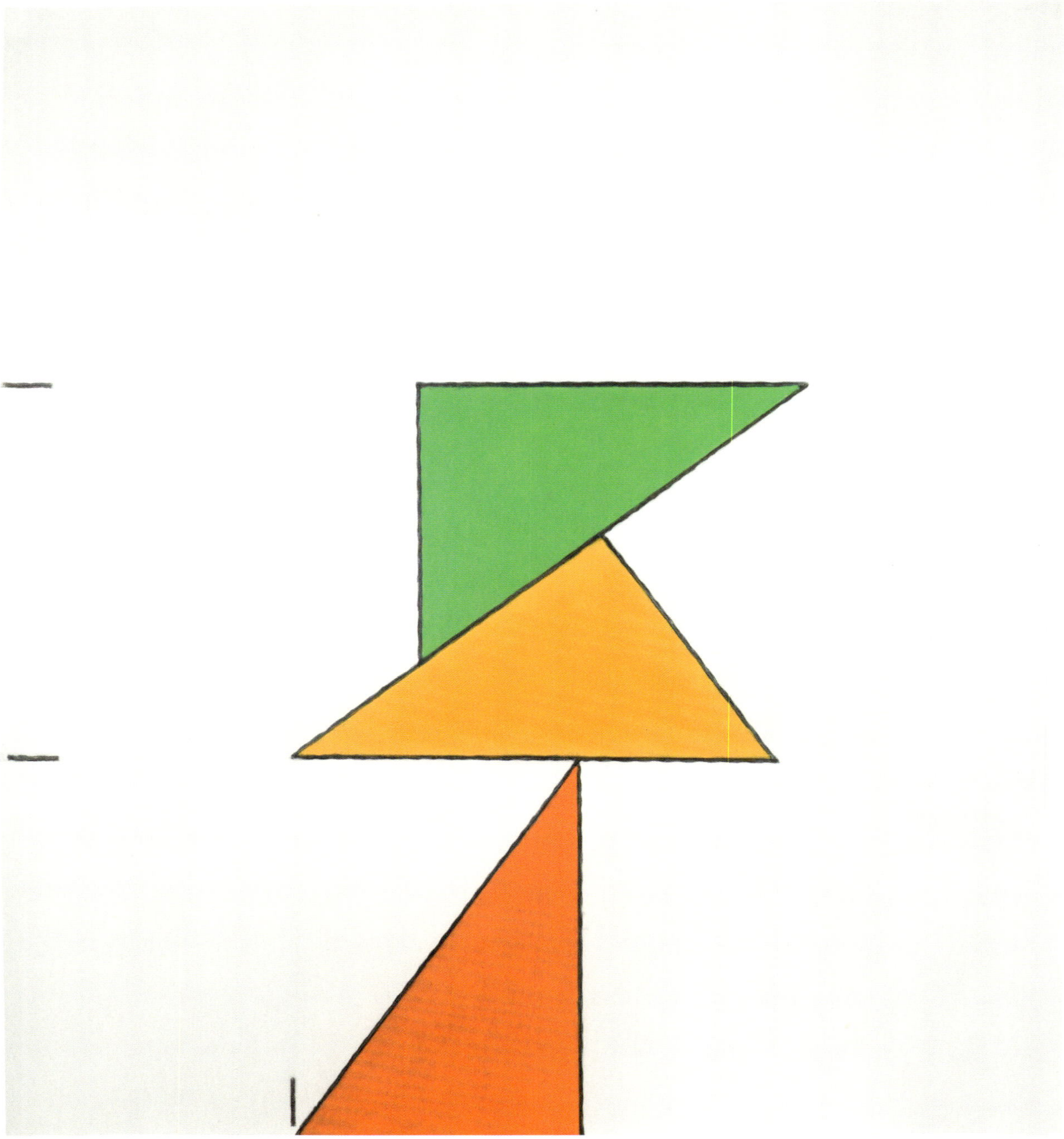

84-85-144×132-A, 1984–85

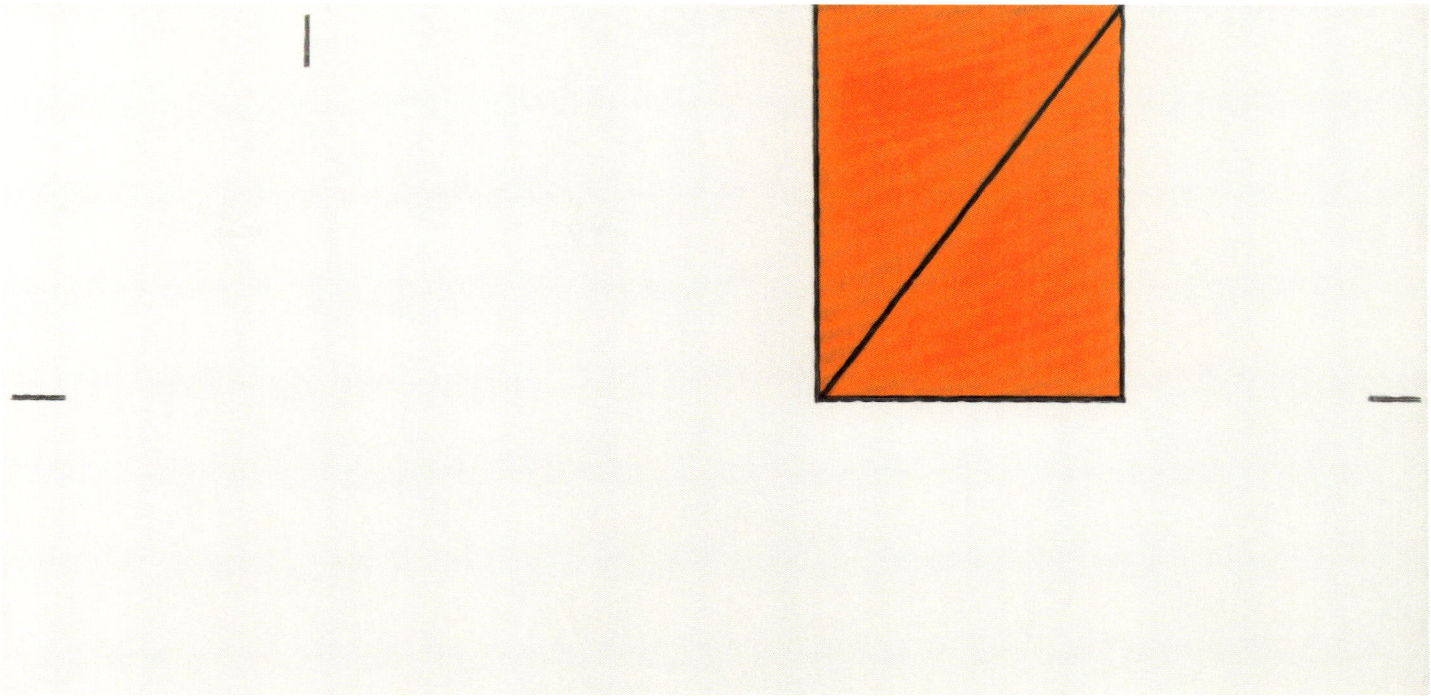

84-85-84×168-B, 1984–85

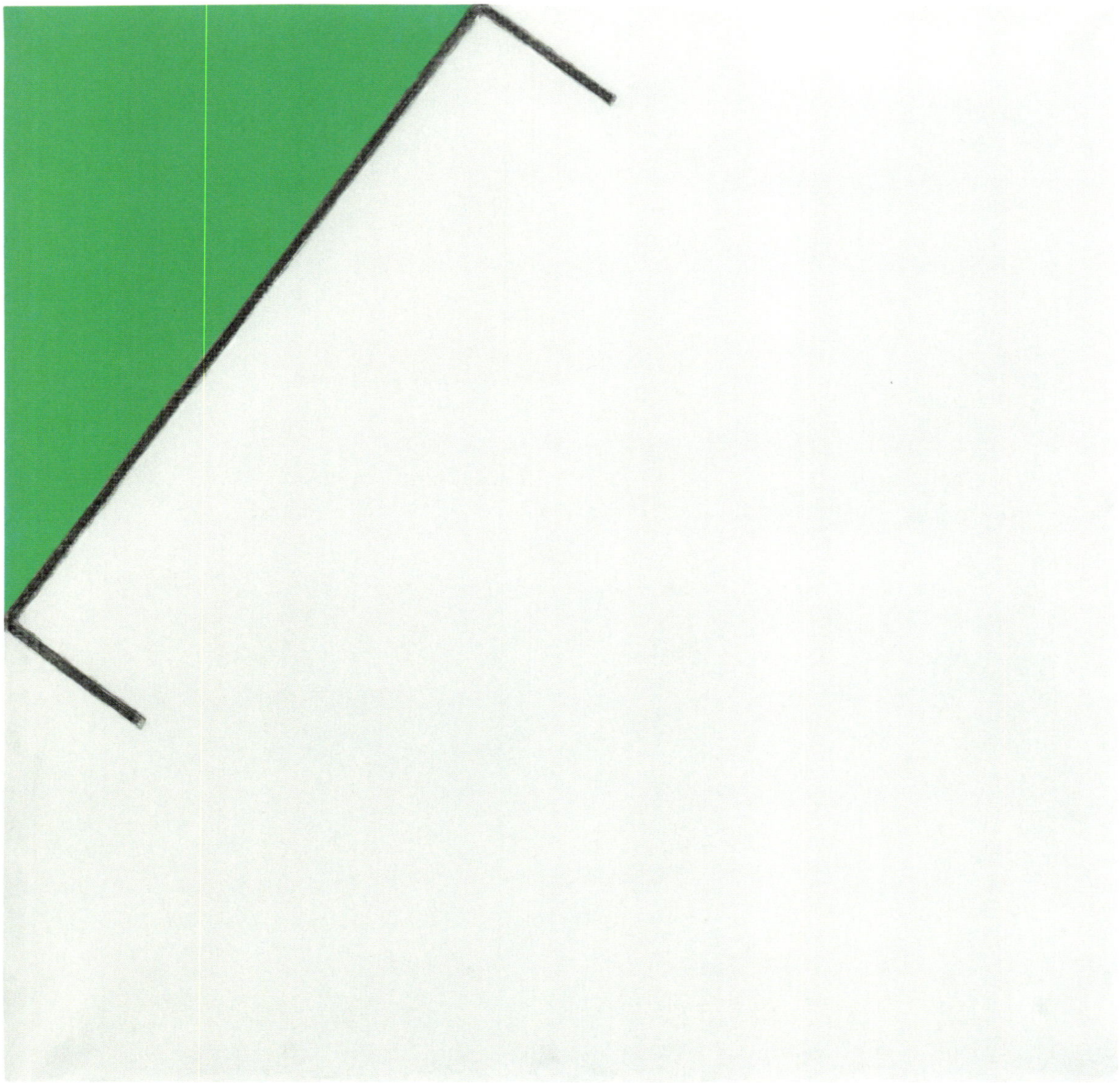

86-87-120×120-A, 1986–87

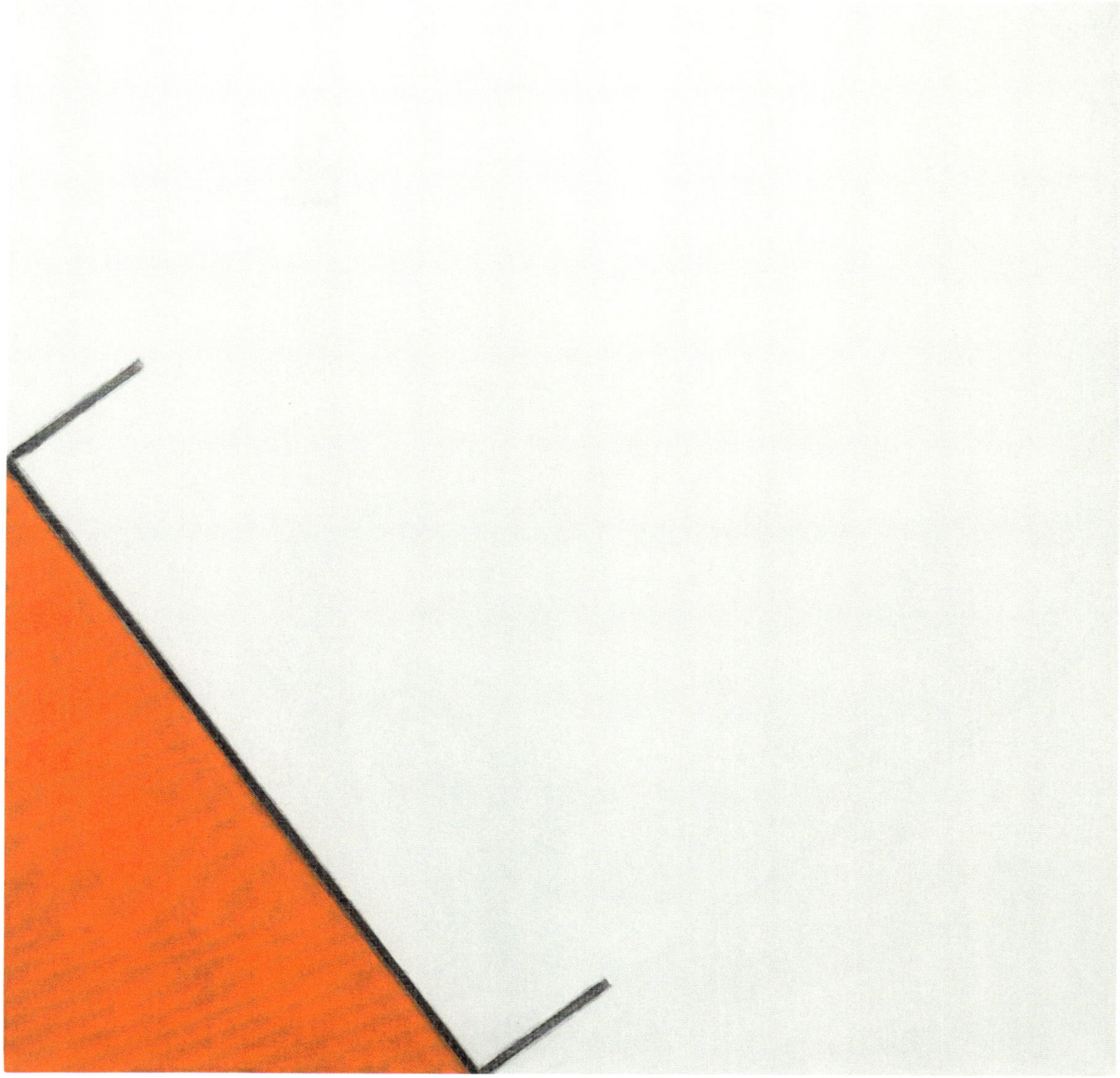

86-87-120×120-B, 1986–87

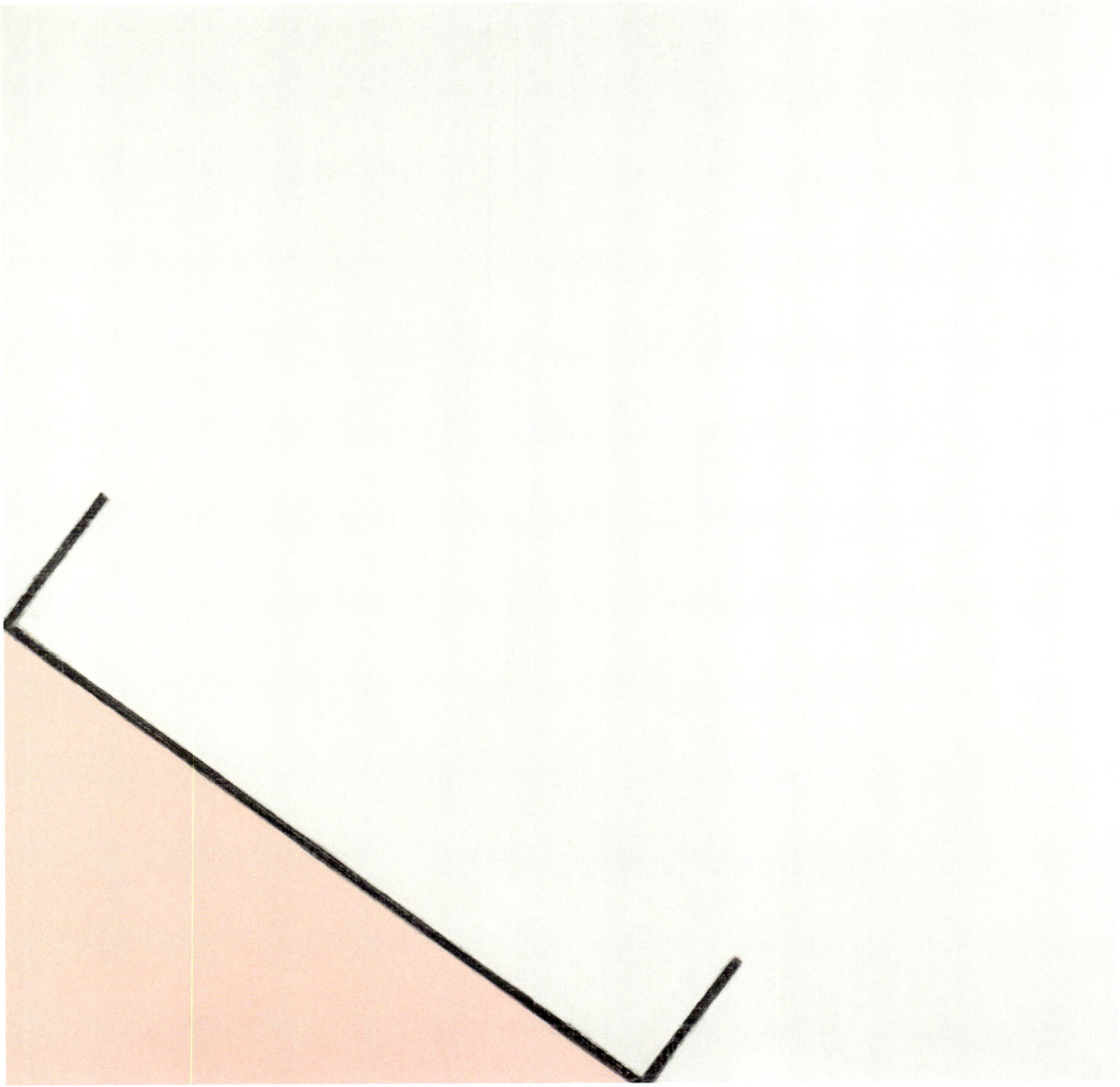

86-87-120×120-C, 1986–87

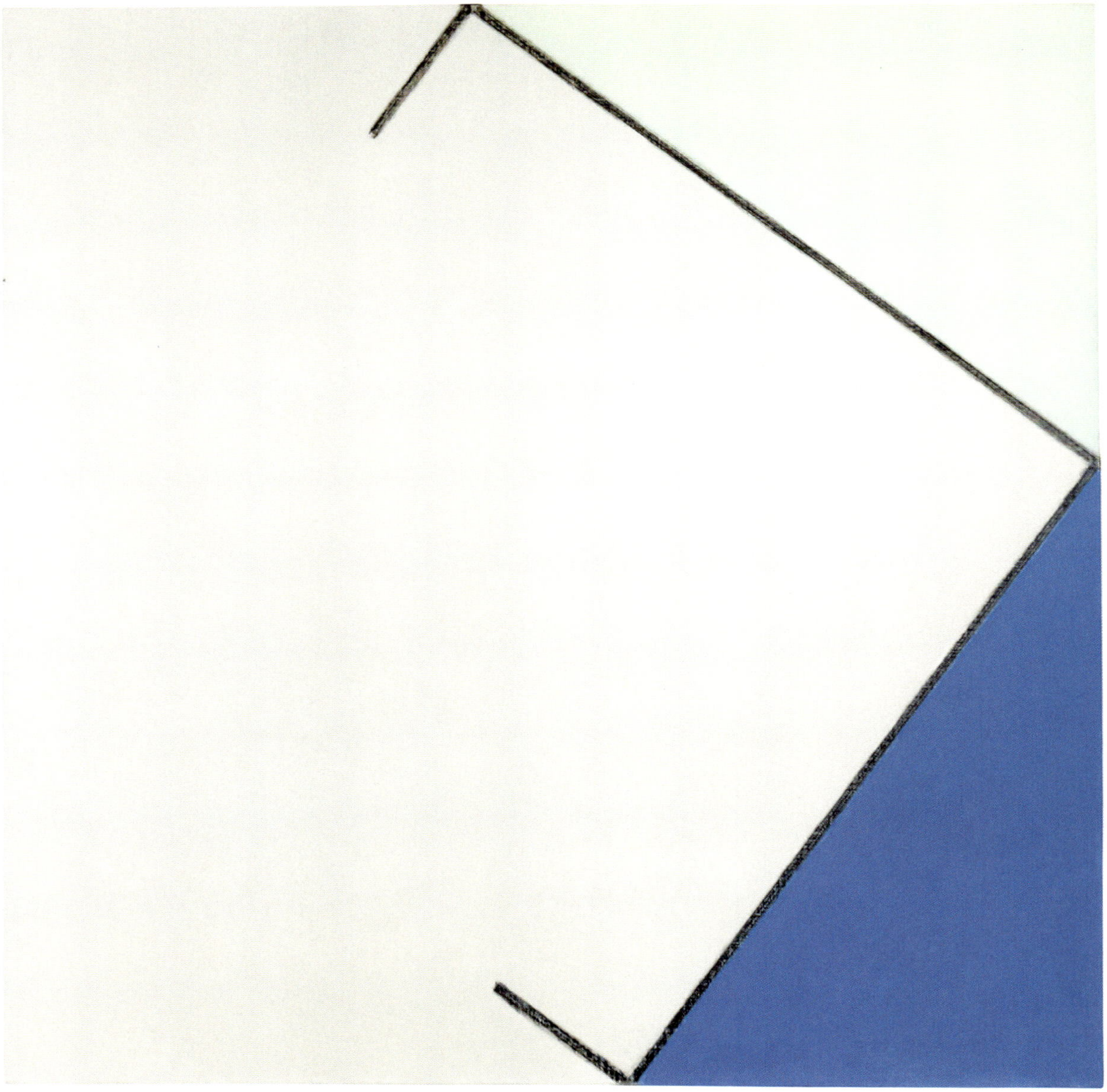

86-87-120×120-D, 1986–87

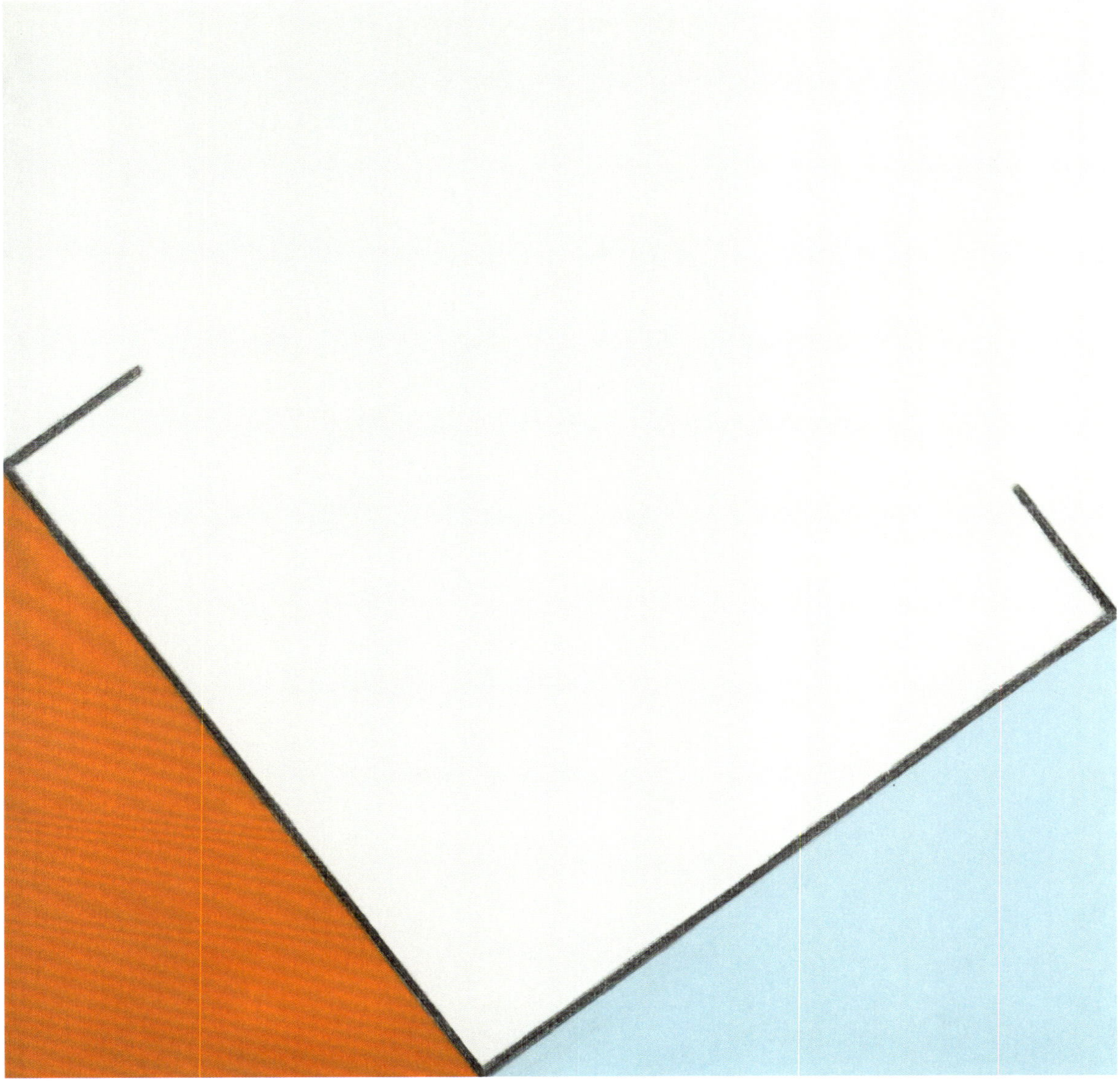

86-87-120×120-E, 1986–87

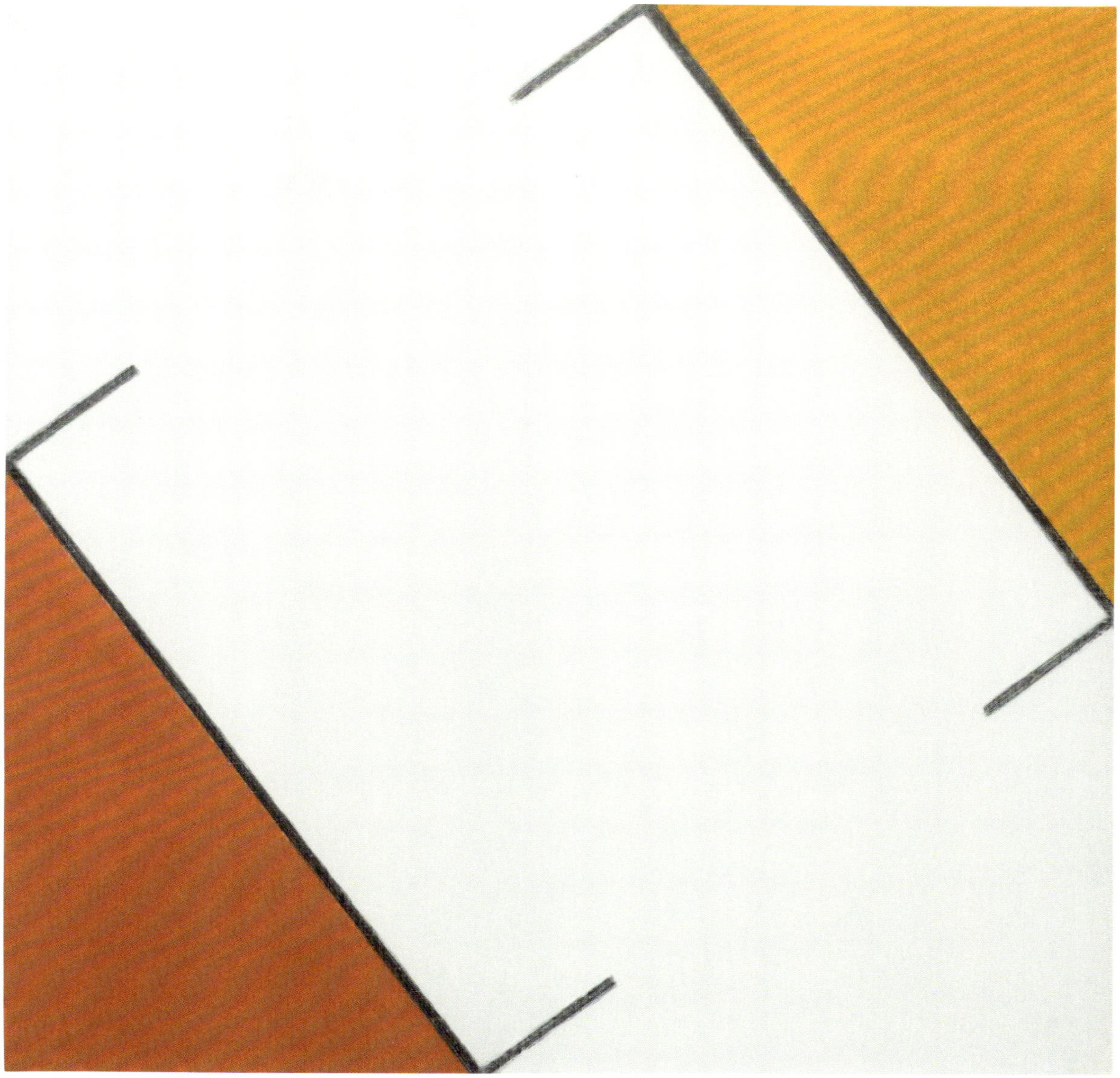

86-87-120×120-I, 1986–87

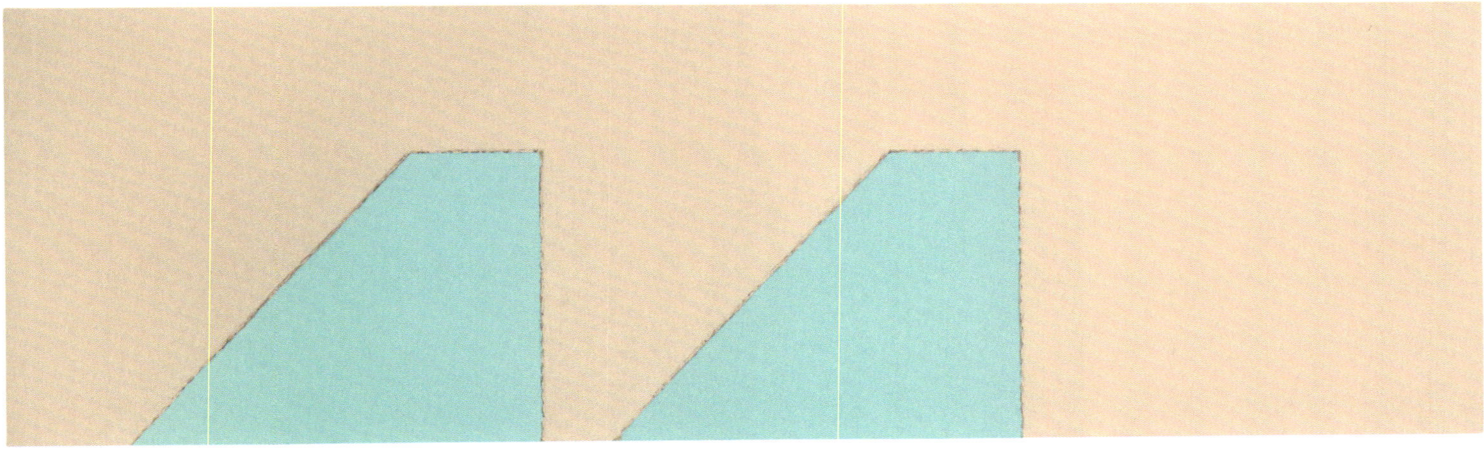

90-91-54×180-A, 1990–91

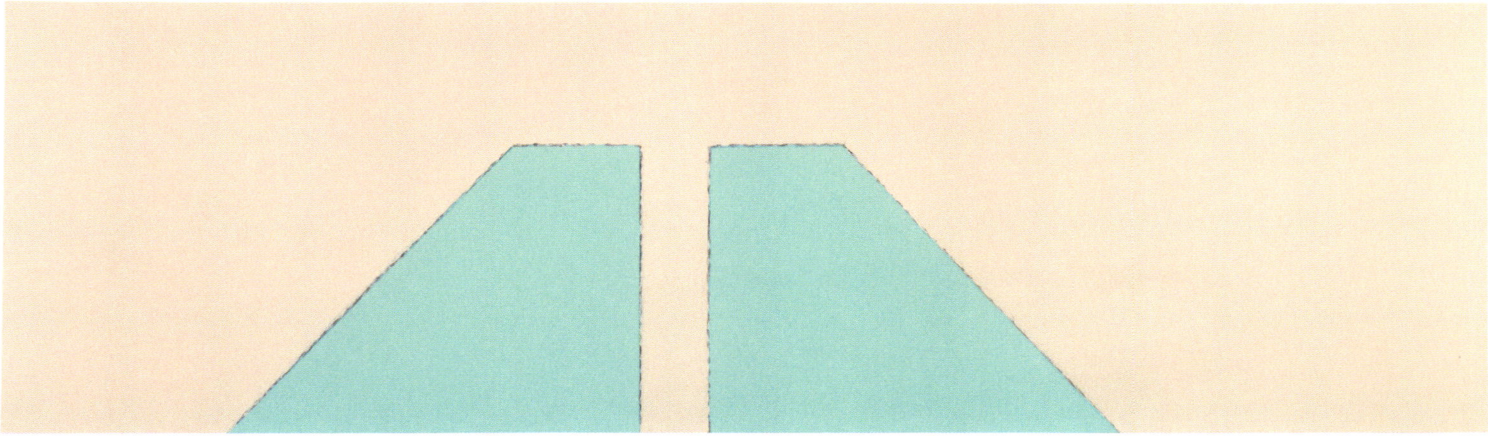

90-91-54×180-B, 1990–91

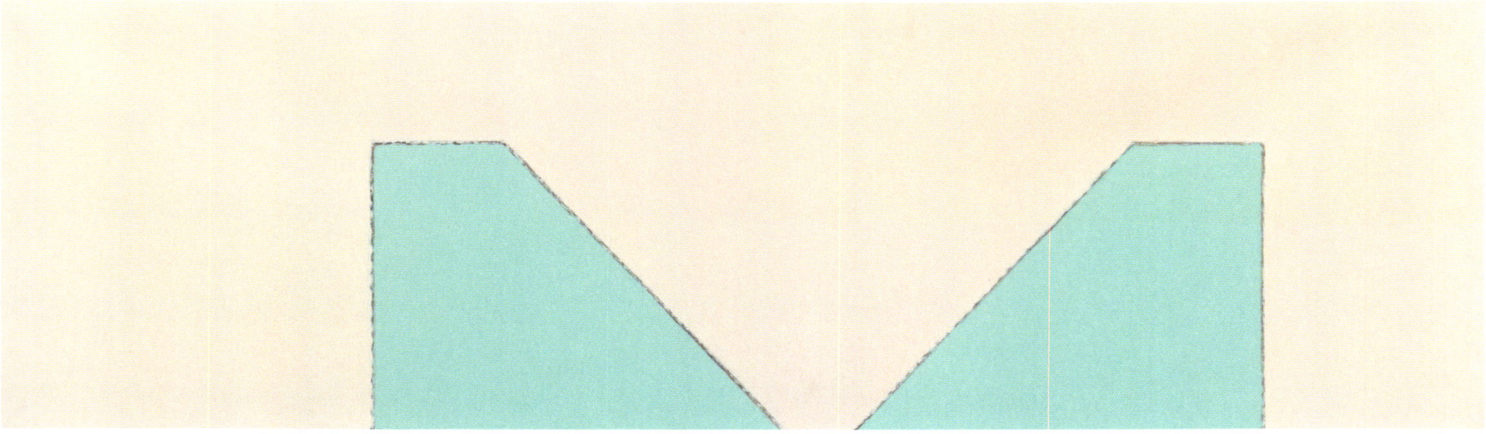

90-91-72×144-A, 1990–91

90-91-54×180-C, 1990–91

90-91-72×144-B, 1990–91

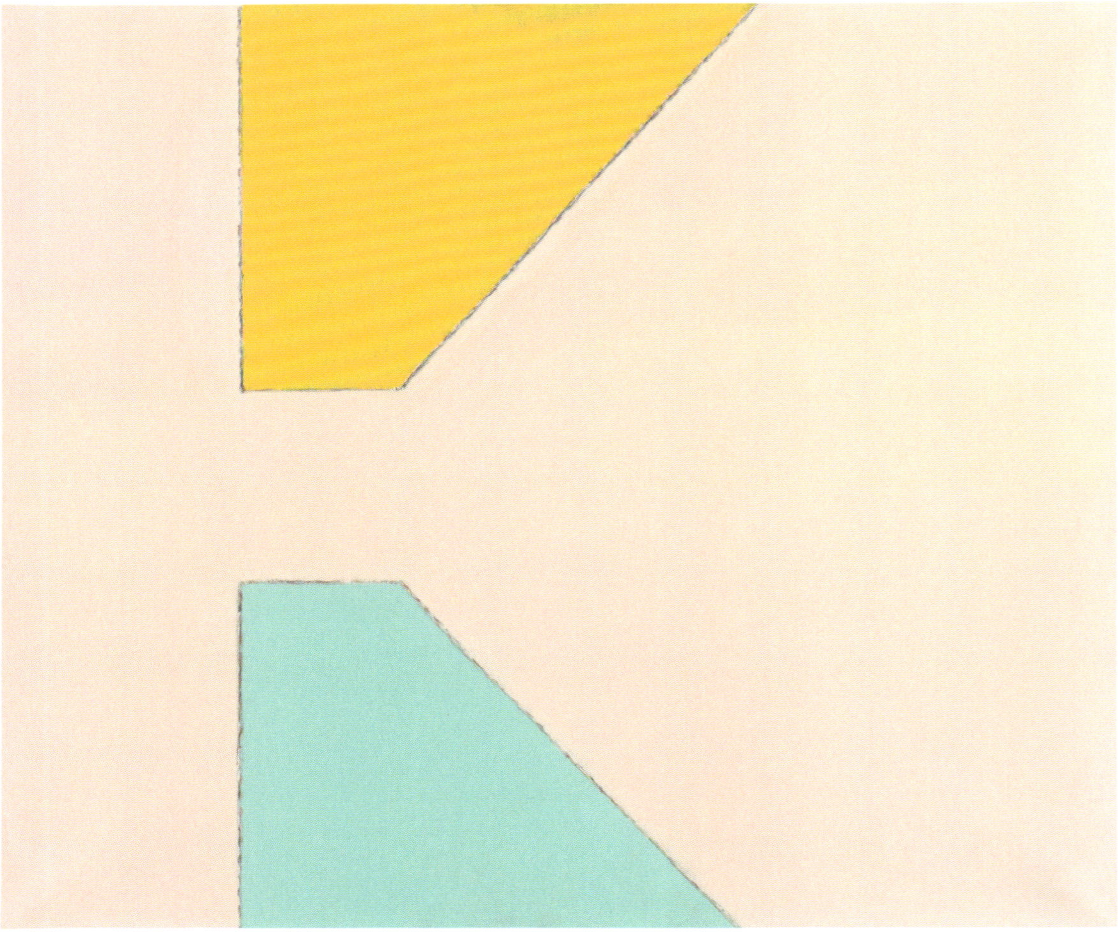

90-91-96×112-A, 1990–91

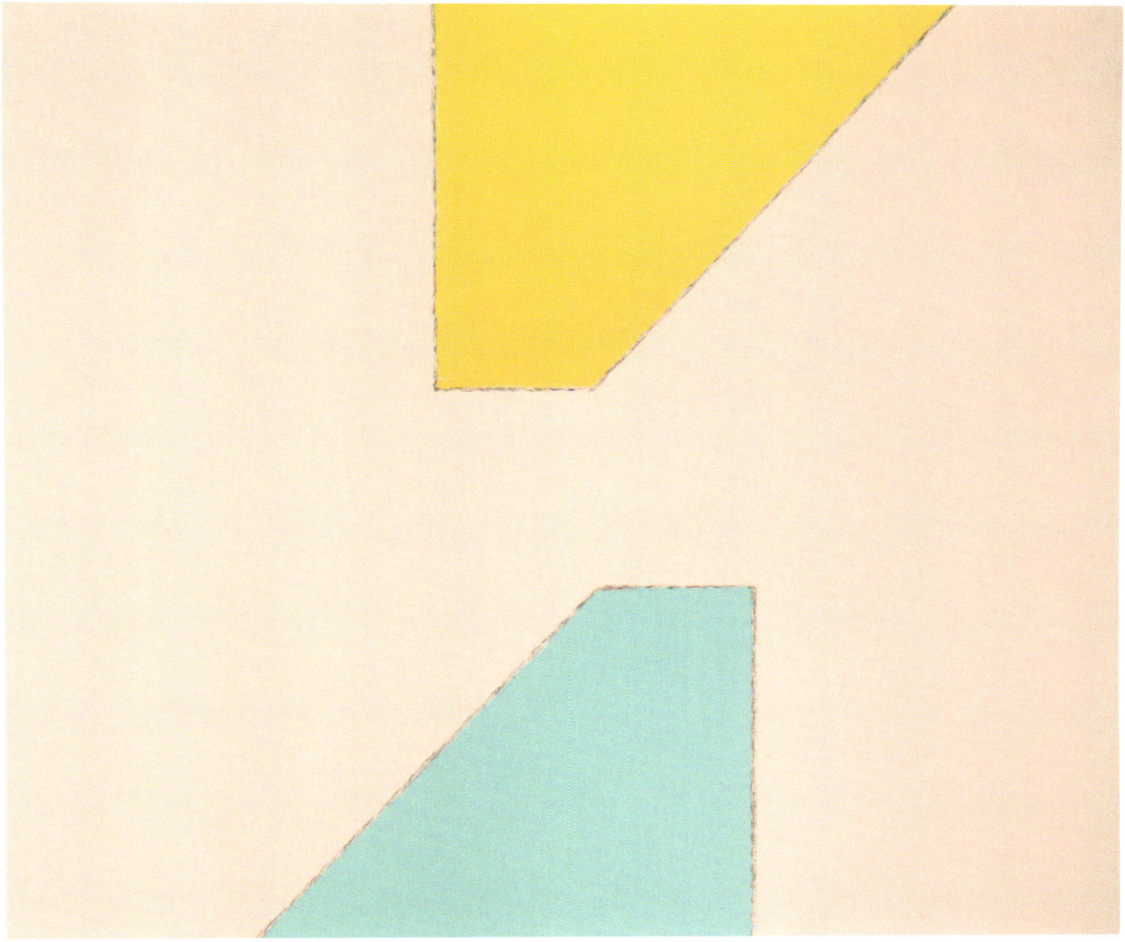

90-91-96×112-C, 1990–91

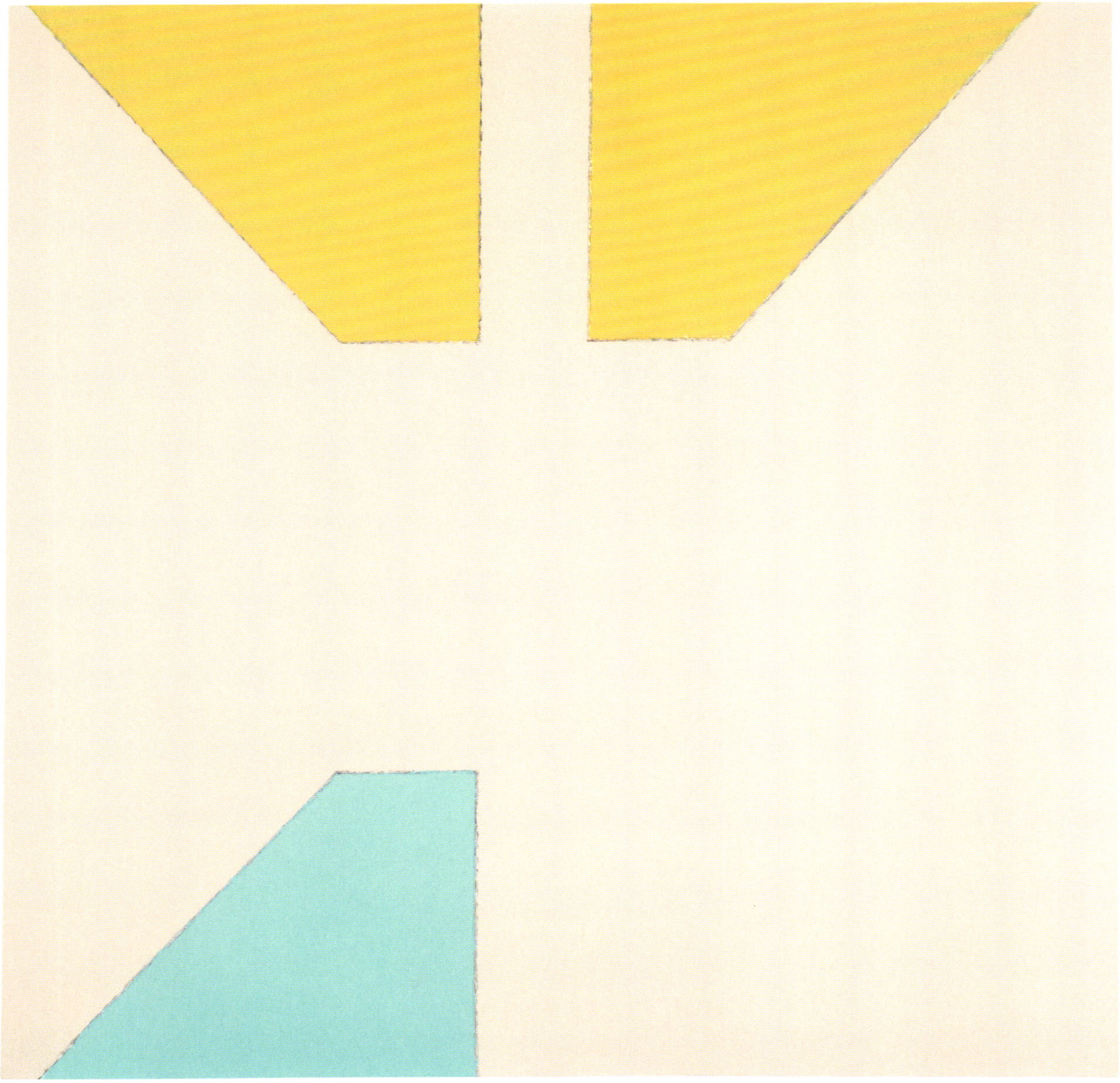

90-91-126×126-A, 1990–91

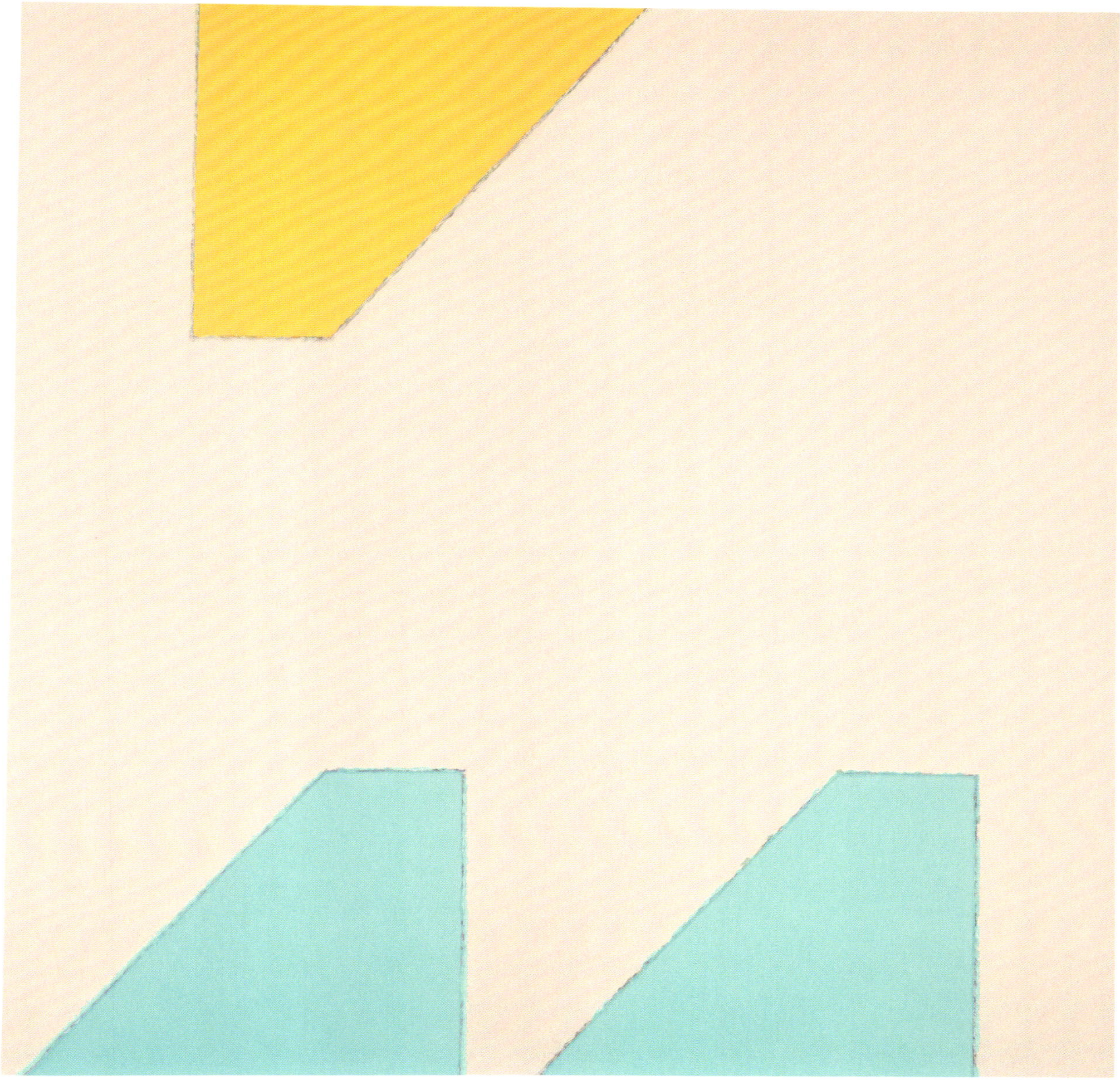

90-91-126×126-B, 1990–91

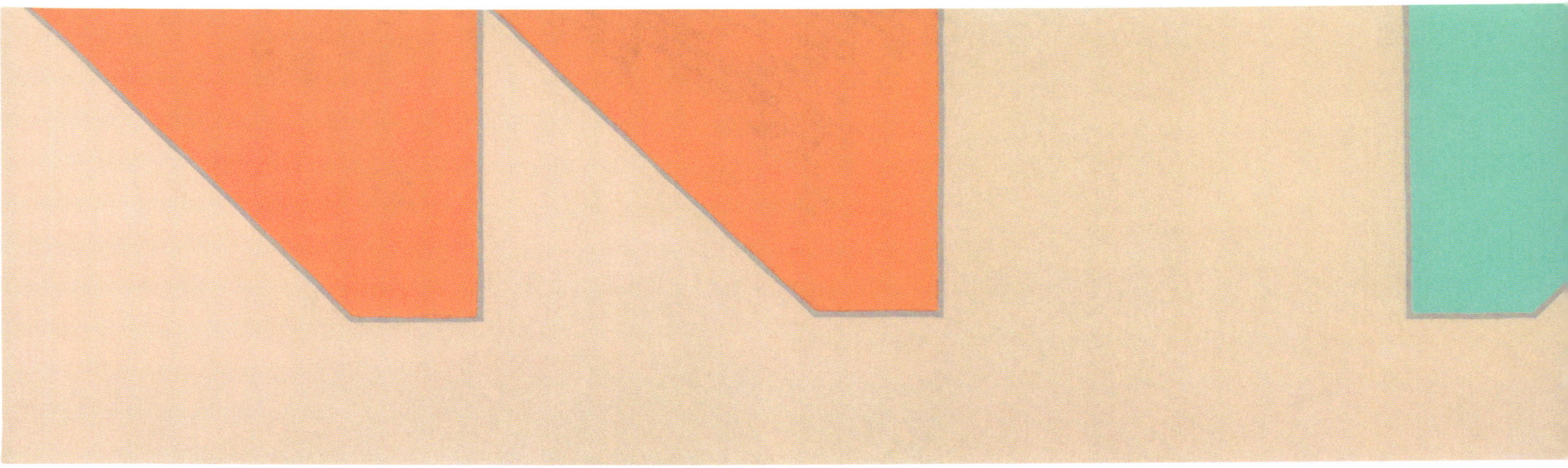

91-72×288-A, 1991

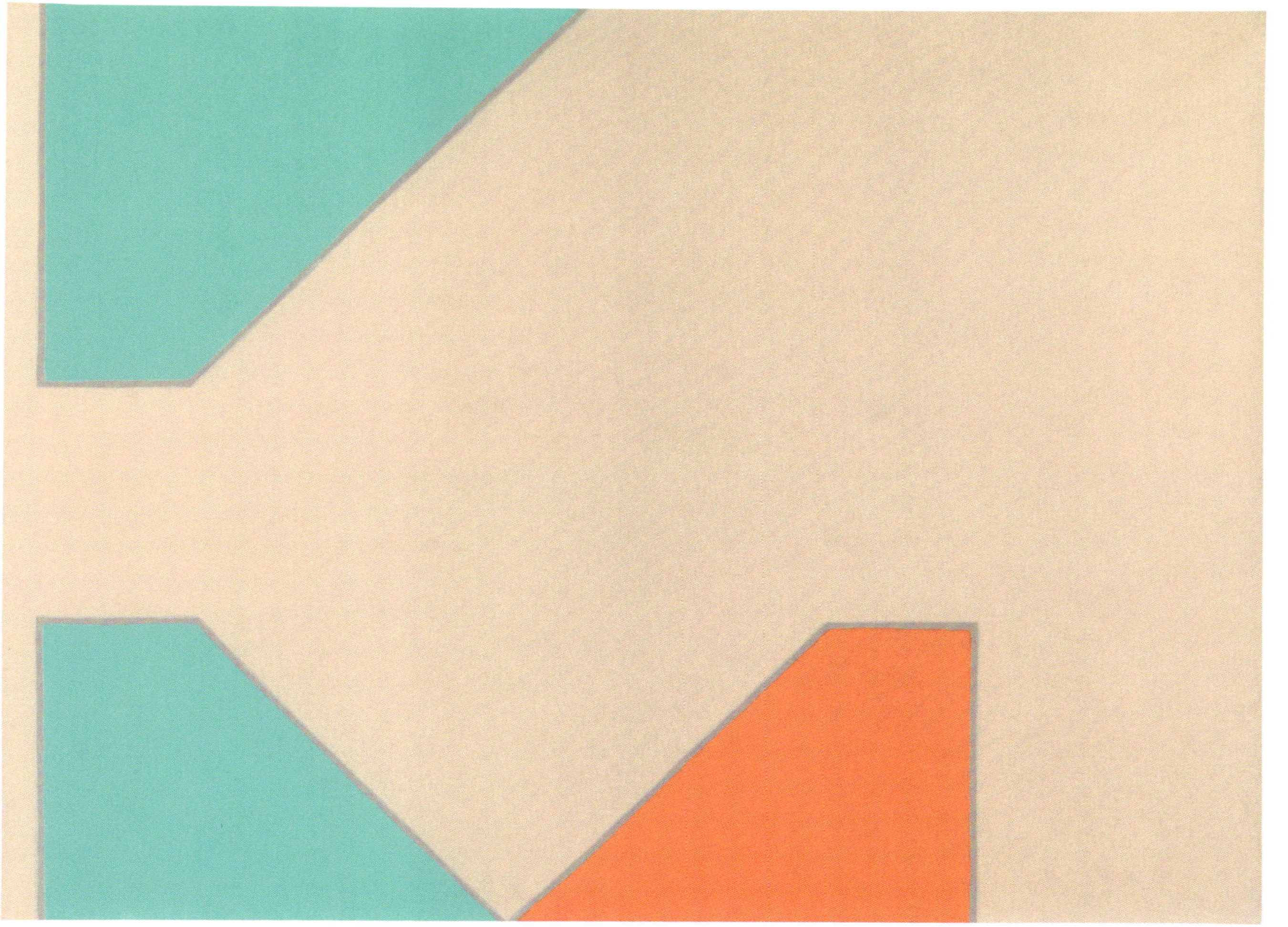

91-120×160-A, 1991

91-92-42×168-C, 1991–92

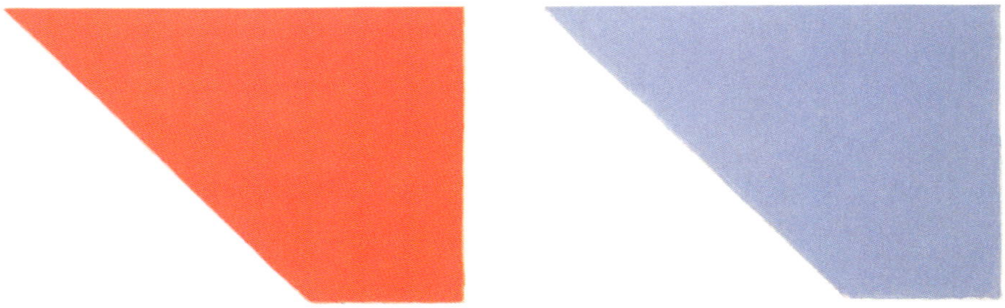

91-92-42×168-D, 1991–92

91-92-42×168-B, 1991–92

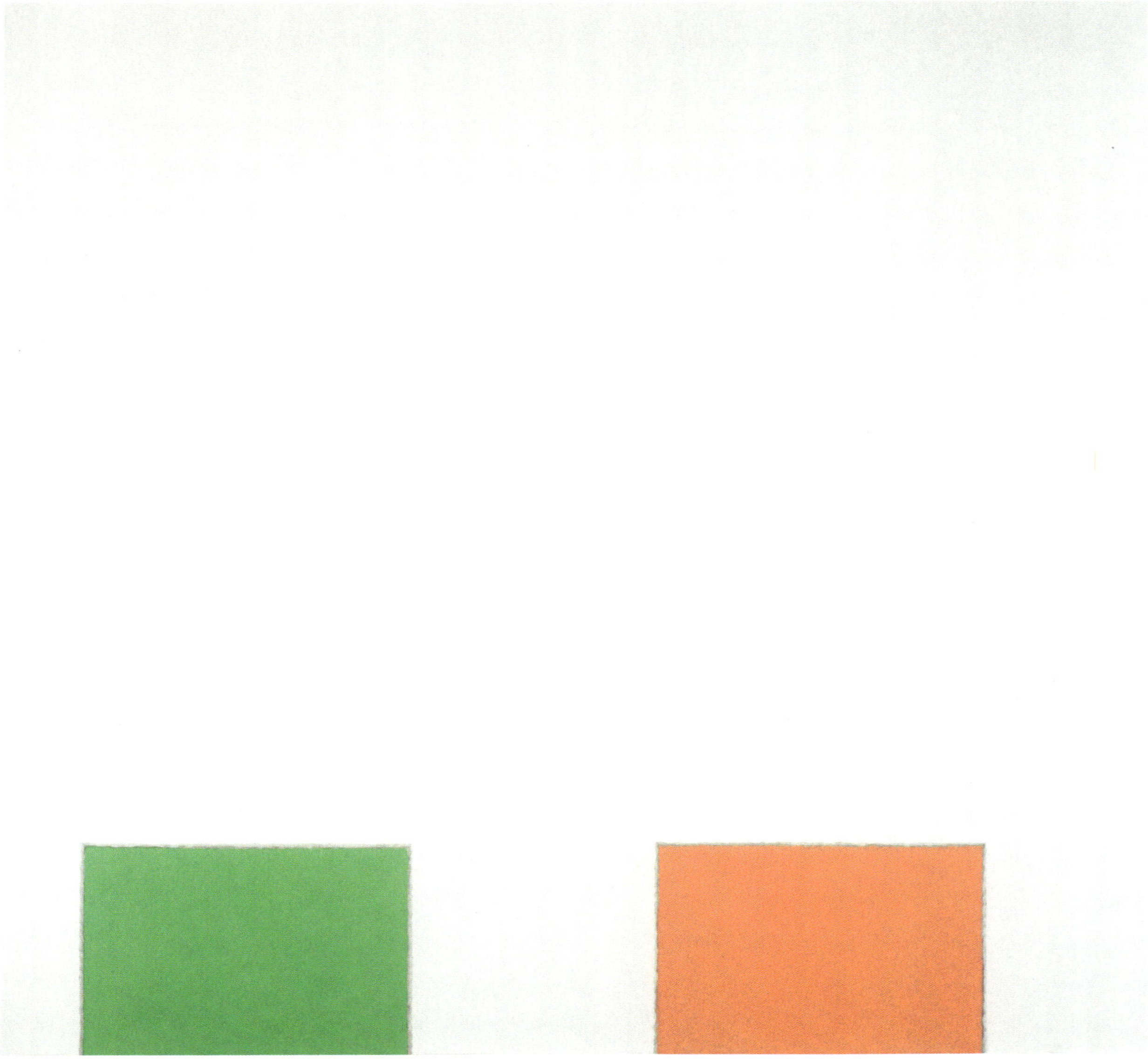

92A-120×126-C, 1992

92B-124×128-D, 1992

92B-124×128-E, 1992

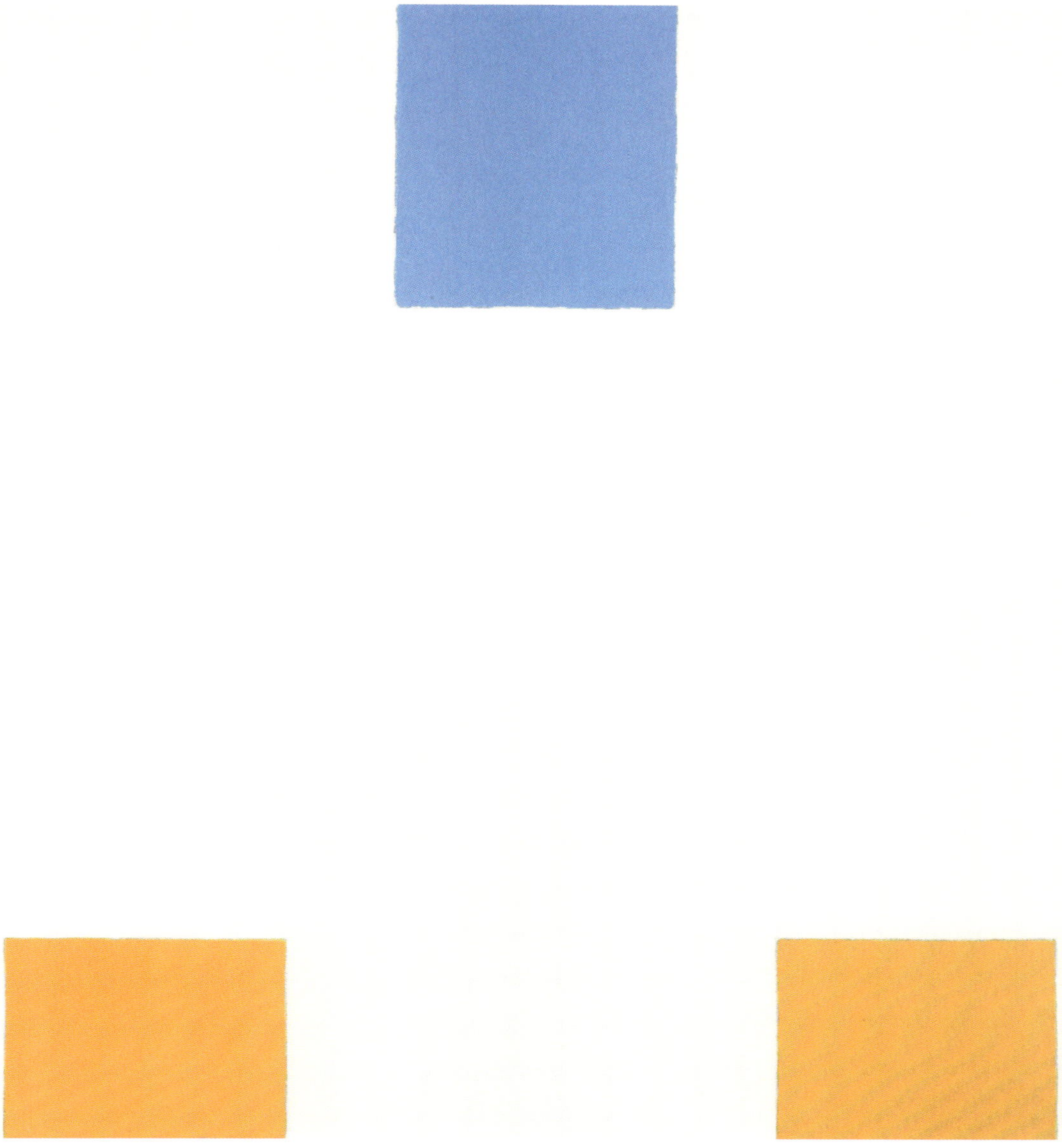

92B-124×128-A, 1992

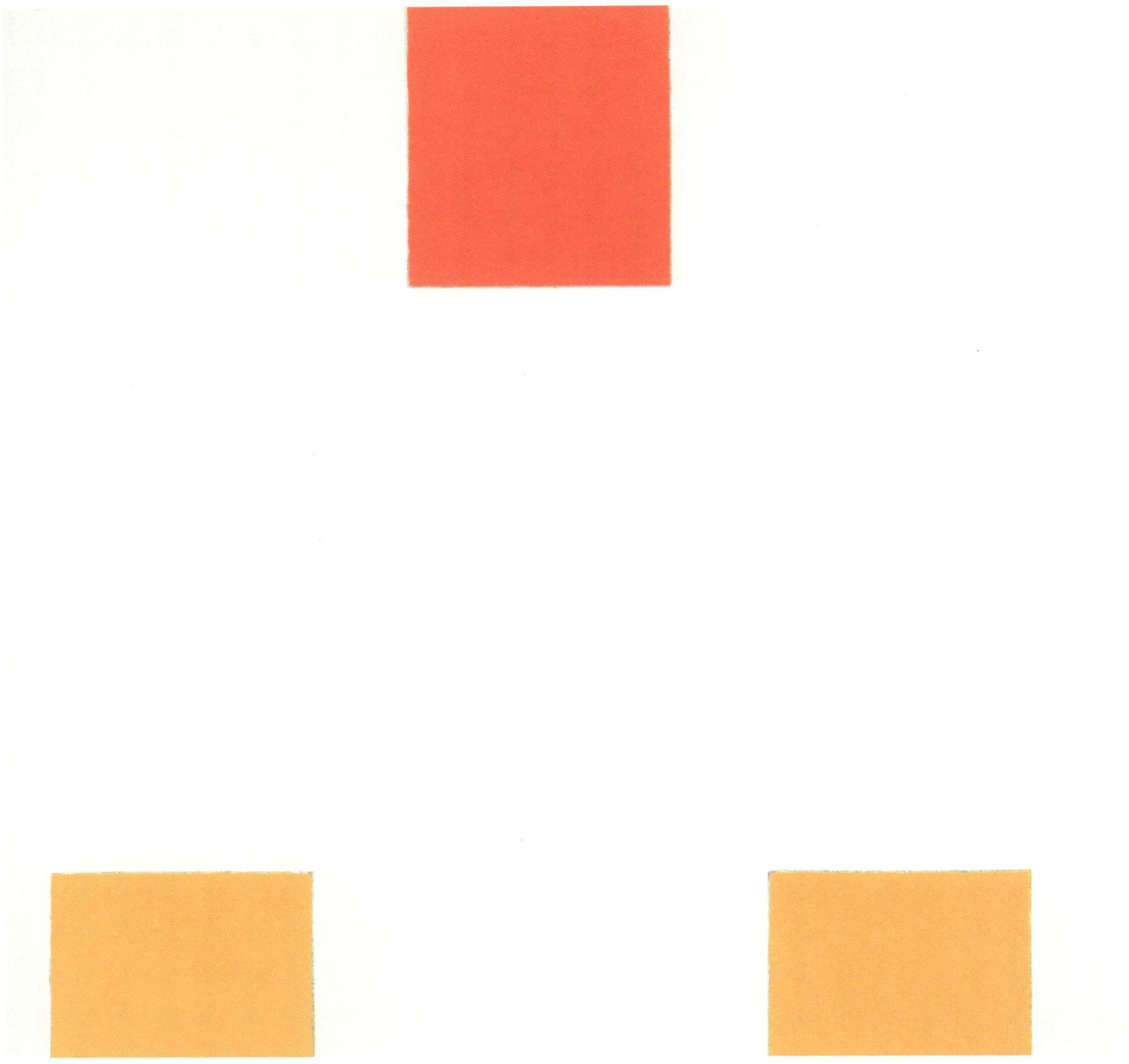

92B-124×128-B, 1992

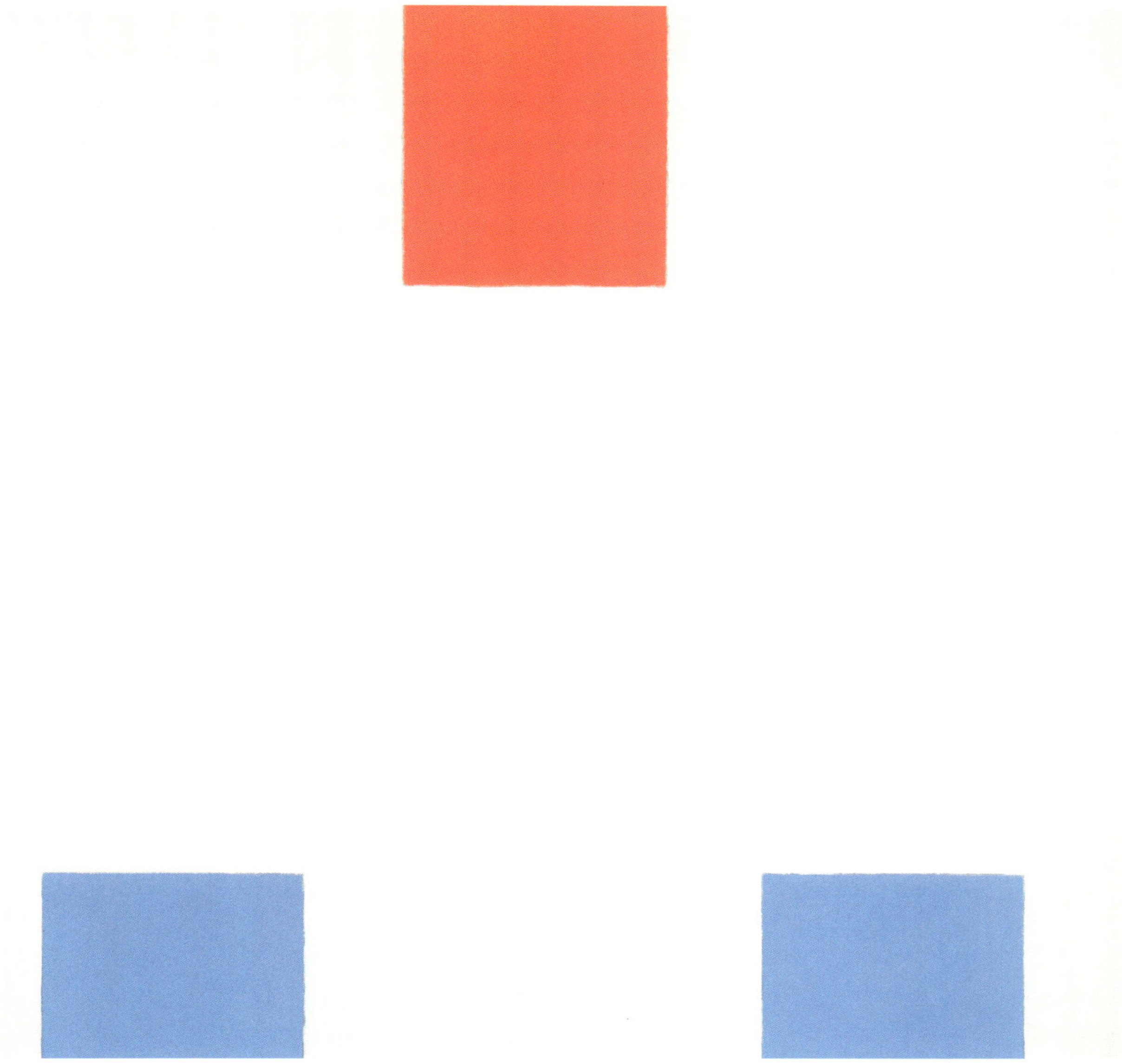

92B-124×128-C, 1992

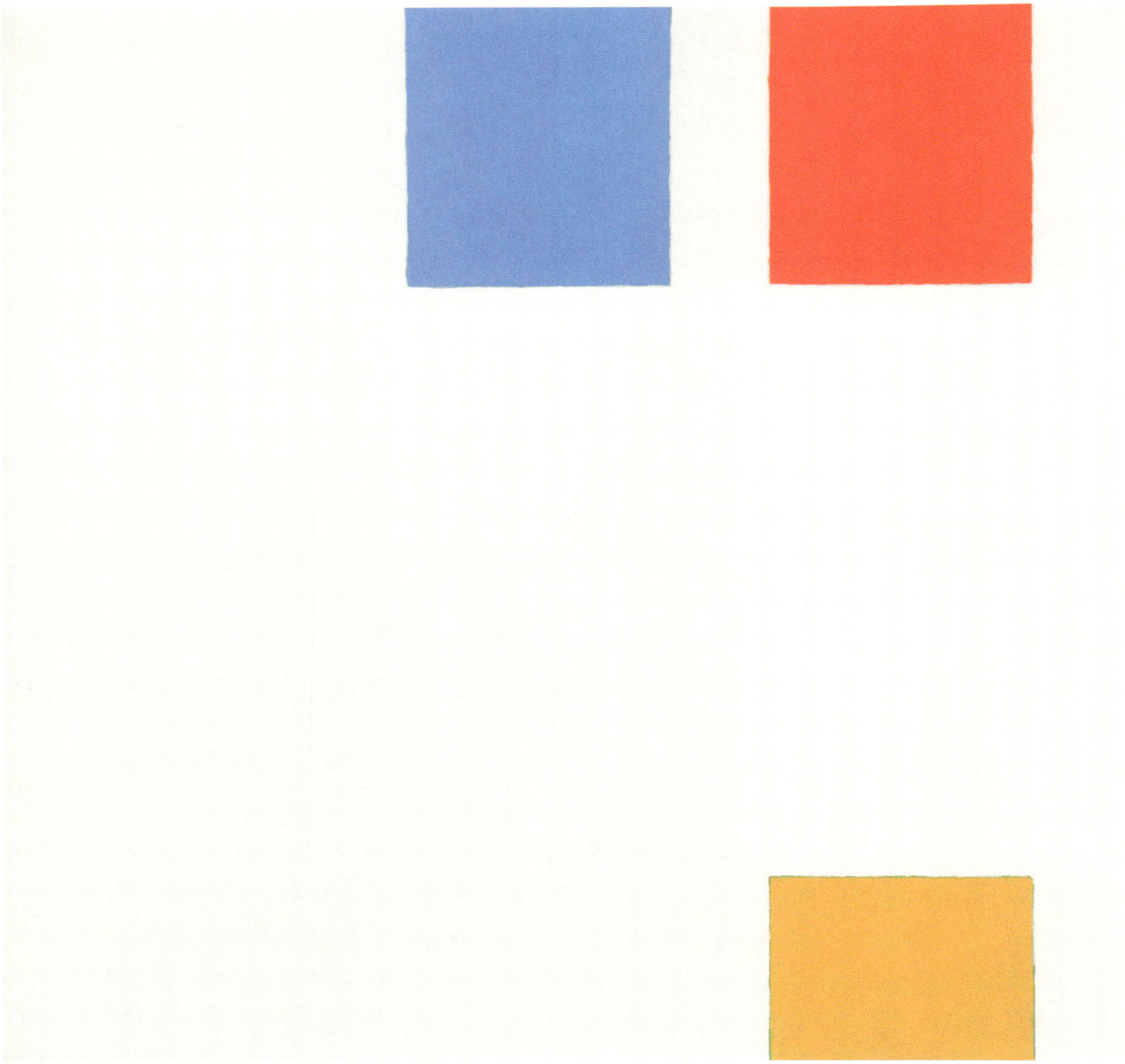

92B-124×128-G, 1992

AUDACITY, CONFIDENCE, AND MAYHEM

MARTIN BARRÉ'S PICTORIAL RESEARCH IN THE 1980s AND 1990s

Clément Dirié

—You have always remained faithful to geometric shapes. What do they bring you?
—What do you want them to take away from me? [Laughs]
Martin Barré, in response to Henri-François Debailleux, *Libération*, 1993[1]

When looking at length at the paintings of the "92A" and "92B" series, both separately and in relation to each other, it is blindingly obvious: white. What we call white, for want of a better word. It weaves between the quadrangles of color, rubs against their quivering edges, reveals its own existence by interlacing with the figures of which it is neither the negative nor the positive, but a reliable companion with changing morphologies. This white, we could it call space, expanse, biotope, laboratory, or even time, to take up the epiphanic expression of the pioneering filmmaker Jean Epstein: "If we vary time, an object becomes an event."[2] Or sky, since its bluish tonality gradually imposes itself on us and ends up making it conspicuous. This white, which should no longer be described as a background, an underside, a support; this white which is precisely no longer a backdrop, but rather a worked, freed form, emblematic of the irremediable autonomy of the painting of Martin Barré, the artist who set his own pictorial system and held to it. This "solid-white"—an expression that underscores its concrete, immanent value and the fact that it is neither ancillary nor a hollow reserve—which jumps out at the eye and paces the surface of the painting, we already came across it *mutatis mutandis* thirty-five years earlier. In a work such as *57-100×100-A* [A] (1957), it made itself square within the square, a matrix image of an oeuvre that achieved the tremendous feat, over four decades, of remaining radical and coherent.[3] In all of the series from the 1980s and 1990s, this solid-white is everywhere, with a chromatic hue modulated on each occasion.[4]

In the "92A" and "92B" series, which share a common general composition, this solid-white is twelve times distinct, either because its total area never fills the surface of the painting in the same way, or because its chromatic articulation with the colored figures produces, each time,

1
Martin Barré in an interview with Henri-François Debailleux, "La géométrie, c'est mon geste," *Libération*, March 18, 1993.

2
Jean Epstein, 1928, mentioned in James June Schneider, *Jean Epstein: Young Oceans of Cinema*, film, 68 mins, 2011.

3
For an analysis of the "white" in Martin Barré's work, carried out in reference to works prior to 1979, see Jean Louis Schefer, "Ténèbre du blanc," in Suzanne Pagé et al., *Martin Barré*, exh. cat. (Paris: ARC – Musée d'Art Moderne de la Ville de Paris, 1979), 4–7. See also his article "L'espace écarte les figures," *Art press* 96 (October 1985): 11–12.

4
Thus, the white of the "86-87," "91," and "91-92" series is perceived as tinged with green, pink, and pale brown, respectively. "My white is what is called off-white, as house painters say. Off-white [*blanc cassé*] is a nice expression." In "Casser le blanc," Martin Barré interviewed by Henri-François Debailleux, *Libération*, July 9, 1993.

A → p. 33

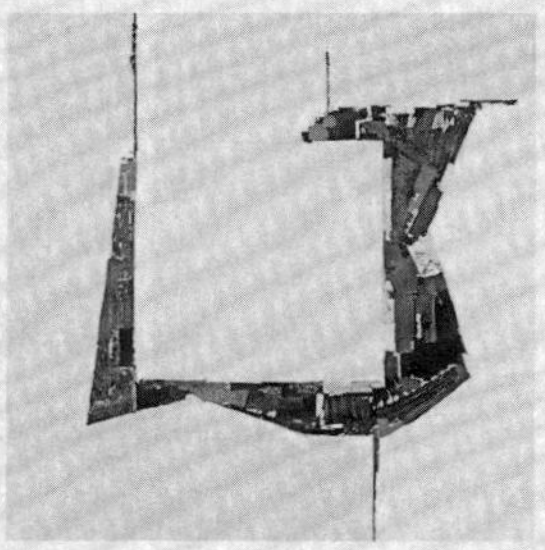

B → p.194

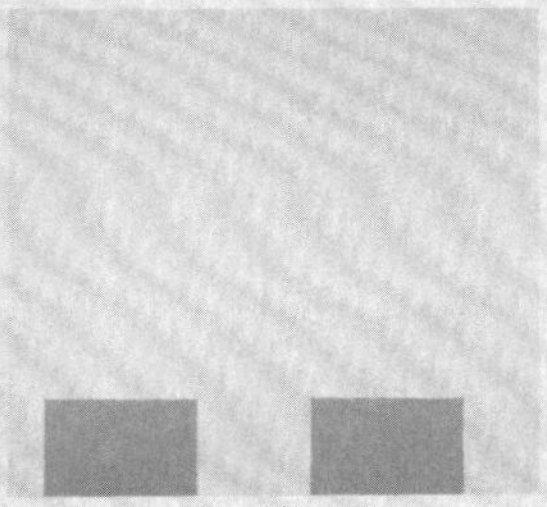

C → p.197

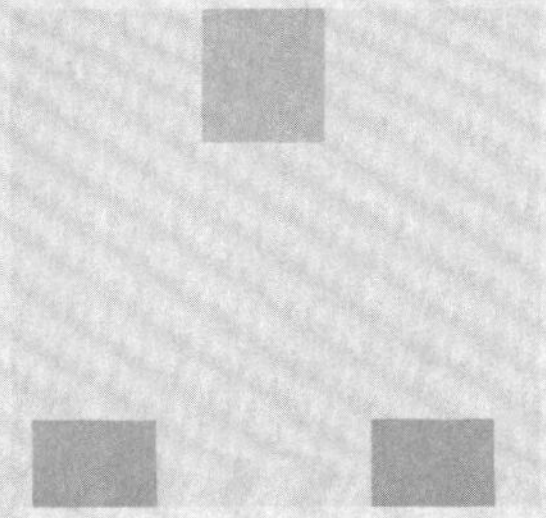

D → p.196

a particular retinal synthesis, even when the distribution of the figures is identical. The last series conceived by Martin Barré (1924–1993) for two exhibitions—the first, a group exhibition, at the Westfälisches Landesmuseum in Münster in 1992 ("92A"[B]); the second, monographic, at the Galerie Nationale du Jeu de Paume in Paris in 1993 ("92B"[C, D])—were in no way testamentary. They were effectively the artist's final series, but not by his doing. On the contrary, examined in relation to the immediately preceding series of 1989–91, they testify to a new perspective that his pictorial approach wished to take up. No one can say what the content of subsequent series would have been. But speculating on the possible beyond-the-frame of an oeuvre, for which the beyond of the painting was always a fundamental given, delights the mind. These series from 1992 thus constitute a freeze-frame of the artist's practice at a specific moment. There was a future. There is no doubt, moreover, that the conception of "92B," developed precisely with a view to the Jeu de Paume exhibition, where it completed a show only dedicated to the 1980s and 1990s paintings, was part of a chosen pictorial design: it concluded and opened the exhibition, just as *L'Indissociable* (*The Inseparable*, 1977–78) did for the retrospective organized at the ARC – Musée d'Art Moderne de la Ville de Paris in 1979.[5]

After the truncated rectangular (or trapezoid) triangles of the four previous series, in "92A" and "92B" Barré experimented with a rectangular shape, new in his oeuvre. Of course, some of the principles used throughout the 1980s were summoned here, but what stands out is the powerfully dynamic impression—almost cinematographic, vertical like a film strip—of these paintings, whose figures seem to rise, fall, and animate the pictorial "sky," especially when they are looked at together, linked by our eye moving across them, by our bodies shifting about. This global view then redoubles the vertical axis of the figures' emergence from a horizontal axis of movement, completing the sensation of enormous energy offered by painting as paradoxically "steady" as that of Martin Barré.

Let us look at them more closely. The series "92A" and "92B" are composed of four and eight paintings in almost square format—120 × 126 cm for the first one; 124 × 128 cm for the second. One of Barré's preferred shapes, this format and ratio—extended in height or width according to each series—give the illusion of a square while allowing it to be freed from an overly strict geometry. Both series share a similar organization whose chromatic differences—three colors each time—and painted forms—two modules

5
Another parallel, no doubt desired by the artist, who was always involved in the publications concerning him: the painting *92B-124×128-D* features all alone on the cover of the Jeu de Paume catalogue, just as *77-78-7-100×162*, from *L'Indissociable*, features on that of the ARC catalogue.

E → p.195

F → p.200

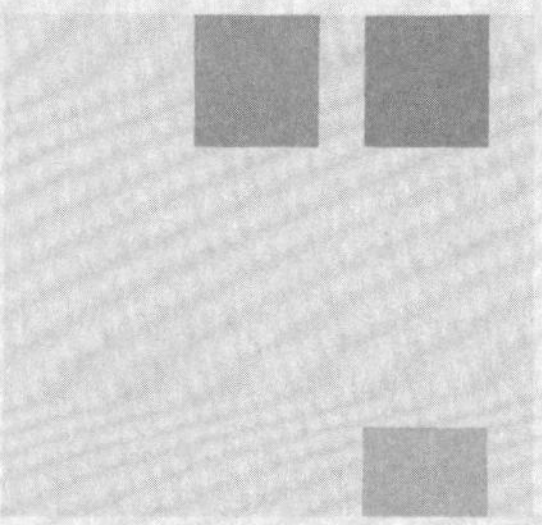

with different dimensions for each series—offer formal and visual compositions to each painting. Descending from the upper edge of the canvas or ascending from its lower side, monochrome rectangles, with paint evenly applied, are placed on the edge, surrounded by a charcoal border drawn on the three sides in contact with the solid-white. The fourth, outer side is not separated from the beyond-the-frame, connecting the figures directly to the beyond of the painting. Is it therefore still a side? One or more colors correspond exclusively to the upper and lower parts of the paintings—each color being thereby linked to precise dimensions. Only one color, the blue of the "92B" series, is granted the privilege of being inscribed both at the top and bottom of the canvas and of filling two types of quadrangles, injecting an extra visual dynamic that defies the feeling of déjà vu. This "thorn in the painting"—Martin Barré's favorite process, because at the moment when we understand, when we think we have mastered something, that very something escapes us—also applies to the positioning of the figures in the painting. The latter is not structured according to a symmetrical principle: the solid-white gutter on the left is always narrower than the one on the right. From these principles of distribution, the rules of the game unfold, making each painting an existing solution chosen—since it is painted by the artist—from among the countless possible outcomes. The rules of the game and not the golden ratio, or, to put it another way, the surpassing of a program, in principle through the freedom of the favored formal resolution. This formal resolution per painting is coupled, at the moment when the works are hung, with a solution of proximity: choosing to exhibit *92B-124×128-D*,[E] *92B-124×128-E*, and *92B-124×128-G*[F] according to such and such a sequence infuses a dynamic specific to the experience of their joint perception.

The effects of the hanging on the paintings and how they are perceived by viewers, a programmatic and audacious reflection on the composition of the canvas, the constant tension between the pictorial space within it and with its surroundings: these parameters, constantly renegotiated, with which Martin Barré had been painting since the mid-1950s, remain present in his last series. But something, characteristic of the works of the 1980s and 1990s, is also present here: the assurance of a plenitude and the serene "reductionism" that succeeded the centrifugal power of the palimpsests of 1972–77; the implementation of a steady pictorial gesture after the performativity of the spray paintings of 1963–67 and the layering-over of the 1970s; a celebration of the all-visible after the geological stratifications of 1955–60 and the 1970s;

the development of a frank chromatic palette after the complex hues of 1955–60 and the darkly humorous colors of 1960–62.

Between 1979 and 1992, Martin Barré developed a new phase in his investigation of painting, which he had always considered a visual and conceptual playground. At the beginning of this period, a first retrospective at the ARC – Musée d'Art Moderne de la Ville de Paris presented his career from 1960 through 1978—also an opportunity for the artist to take stock of his practice.[6] At its conclusion, an exhibition devoted to paintings from the 1980s and 1990s was the exact continuation of this, while allowing him to show series that had not been included in the retrospective organized by the museums of Nantes, Tourcoing, and Nice in 1989. Between these two dates: sixteen series of paintings, each comprising between six and eighteen canvases, with different gestation periods. "82-84" comprises eighteen paintings painted over three years. Between 1990 and 1992, forty-eight paintings, belonging to five series, were produced. These sixteen series were presented in solo exhibitions in Cologne (Galerie Ricke: "79" in 1980), Nice (Galerie Anne-Marie Rey: "82-84" in 1985), Nîmes (Galerie Interface: "90-91" in 1991), and Paris (Galerie Jean Chauvelin: "79," "79-80," "80A" in 1981, jointly with the Galerie Gillespie-Laage-Salomon: "80B," "80-81"; Galerie Gillespie-Laage-Salomon: "84-85" in 1985; Galerie Laage-Salomon: "86-87" in 1987, "87-89" in 1989, "91-92" in 1992; Jeu de Paume[G, H]: all the series up to "92B" in 1993).[7] Why this enumeration?

To indicate, firstly, that the exhibitions organized in 2019 and 2020 by MAMCO in Geneva and the Musée National d'Art Moderne/Centre Pompidou in Paris are indeed the first complete retrospectives of the oeuvre, making it possible (at last) to embrace the artist's whole career and to hinge together successive periods, beyond interpretations that were sometimes too segmented chronologically.

Secondly, to recall that, with very few exceptions, each series was first presented only in its entirety. Since, during the 1980s–1990s, each painting by Barré "contained" all the others in the series, in the manner of a synecdoche or the key to a map, an overall vision was necessary to get the full measure of the work from the outset. However, care must be taken not to overdetermine the "form-series." What mattered most for the artist, it seems, was the work *in series*, which was more a means than an end. "The point of seriality is not to produce canvases that are almost identical but to produce paintings that are as different from each other as possible.

6
This retrospective exhibition was then shown at the Henie-Onstad Kunstsenter in Høvikodden (Oslo), testifying to the important critical and institutional reception of Martin Barré's work in Scandinavian countries throughout the 1960s and '70s.

7
To this list of solo exhibitions should be added the group exhibition *L'Amour de l'art*, the first Lyon Contemporary Art Biennale, in 1991, at which Barré exhibited the "91" series for the first time. During the 1980s, several exhibitions devoted to works from the 1950s and 1960s were also organized, notably by the Galerie Daniel Templon and the Galerie Jacques Barbier —further opportunities to look back on the painter's career as he continued to pursue it.

G → p. 227

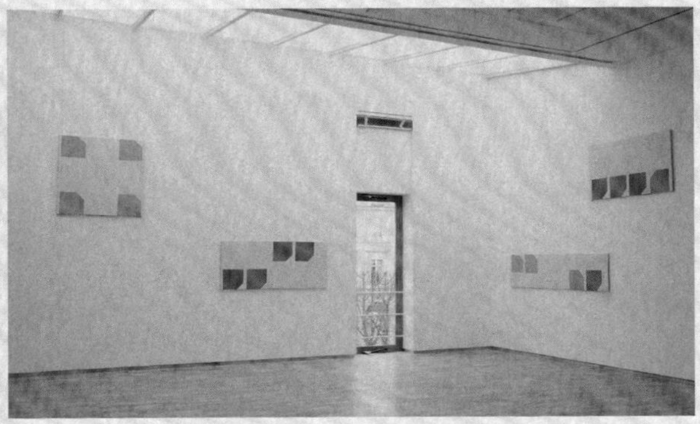

H → p. 227

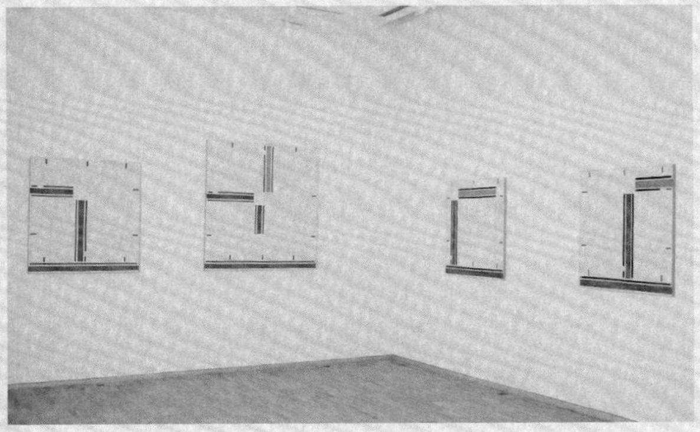

What counts is the picture object. Seriality is the means of producing them. It is not so much the paintings that make the series as the series that produces the paintings,"[8] he pointed out in 1985. Undoubtedly, this desire to reveal each new stage of his pictorial research in one go favored the shock of rediscovery and the examination of its evolution —which Ann Hindry expressed when she discovered the new "87-89" series in 1989: "I do not know of another contemporary work that succeeds so well in keeping intact to such a degree the ever-repeated magic of the first contact."[9]

And, lastly, to emphasize the importance of the "form-exhibition" in Barré's pictorial thinking during the 1980s–1990s period. This consideration of the exhibition, like the work in series, was not to the detriment of the "form-painting" but, on the contrary, at its service. Nevertheless, it did not in any way imply an affirmation of the presentation mechanism as belonging to the category of installation, in the immersive sense that this term assumed from the 1990s onwards. "It's true that the painting must make the wall 'active,' but above all the wall must activate the painting. I always insist on deciding where each painting should be placed. But this isn't a part of my work's development. When I paint, I don't think about the hanging, even though I know where the paintings will be exhibited. On the other hand, when the paintings arrive at the 'recipient,' I absolutely want to direct this work, which can be described as an 'installation.'"[10] Of course, in the 1960s–1970s—with the peak represented by the presentation of *L'Indissociable* at the ARC in 1979.→ pp. 158–59 —Martin Barré was already giving clear importance to the hanging of some of his exhibitions, but not systematically.[11] Most often, in the years 1972–77, the paintings were "simply" aligned by their middle; from time to time, two paintings were aligned on the same wall from the bottom or the top.[12]

In the 1980s–1990s, however, this "curatorial parameter" took on an unprecedented importance, as the contemporary critical fortunes of the exhibitions reveal, particularly at the Jeu de Paume. Often defined by the rigor and absoluteness of his abstract vocabulary in the exhibition reviews and articles devoted to him, Barré was also analyzed through the prism of his hangings, which the artist himself described as "tossed."[13]

As of the exhibition of the "79" series in Cologne in 1980,[I] the singularity of the hanging became fertile terrain. In his review, Yve-Alain Bois immediately noted: "In this case, the first difference that strikes you, the capital exception, in Martin Barré's most recent exhibition, is perpetrated by the hanging, which goes far beyond its role as wrapping

8

Martin Barré, in Catherine Millet, "M. B. 'Elsewhere'" (1985), repr. in Yve-Alain Bois, *Martin Barré* (Cologne, New York, and Paris: Galerie Daniel Buchholz, Andrew Kreps Gallery, Galerie Nathalie Obadia, and Thea Westreich/Ethan Wagner, 2008), 274.

9

Ann Hindry, *Martin Barré 87-89*, exh. cat. (Paris: Galerie Laage-Salomon, 1989), n.p.

10

Martin Barré in Bernard Lamarche-Vadel, *Qu'est-ce que l'art français?*, exh. cat. (Labège-Innopole and Paris: Centre Régional d'Art Contemporain Midi-Pyrénées and La Différence, 1986), 30.

11

Undoubtedly, the experience of the conceptual episode of 1968–71 played a pivotal role in this consideration of the exhibition space—a period to be seen as a means of pursuing, in new ways, his examination of the pictorial medium and its conditions of presentation.

12

For the solo exhibitions of the 1950s, it is more difficult to measure the freedom with which Martin Barré was able to hang his works and the leeway granted by gallery owners. It is worth noting that the thinking around exhibitions as manifested during his solo exhibition at the Galerie Arnaud in 1960 was concomitant with the appearance of polyptychs involving the principles of combinatorics and permutation (*60-T-43*, *60-T-45*, and *60-T47* from 1960).

13

Mentioned by Hindry in *Martin Barré 87-89*. A few titles of articles published in 1993: Raoul-Jean Moulin, "L'ordre radical de Martin Barré met l'œil au défi," *L'Humanité*, February 27, 1993; Michel Nuridsany, "Les chahuts harmonieux de Martin Barré," *Le Figaro*, March 6, 1993; Philippe Piguet, "Abstrait: le code Barré," *La Croix*, March 16, 1993.

I → p. 223

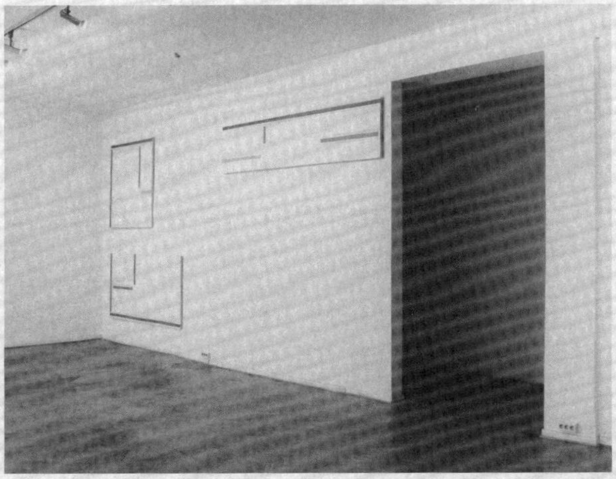

to inform and transform each painting by linking it to the others." He continued: "The power and autonomy of each painting is abolished by the ligature of their layout on the wall."[14] This "ligature," drawing an invisible but mentally perceptible line, is fruitful because it emphasizes the fact that, although the hanging "transforms" each painting, this potentiality resides precisely within the painting. The autonomy of each work is henceforth subsumed by the autonomous relationship unfolding between them —in a way, there is not so much a loss of autonomy as an increase in its visibility thanks to the combined action of the form-series and the hanging.[15] The paintings, put together, imply a common hanging, regardless of the space that hosts them and the size of the walls that carry them. Several series from the 1980s and 1990s bear witness to this principle. For the "80A" and "80B" series,[H] a strip running along the lower edge of the painting indicates the height of the hanging: whatever their formats, these eight paintings are "hooked" at the bottom. For the fourteen paintings in the "90-91" series, their position in relation to each other is based on the mental "ligature" of two parallel "lines": those of the yellow figures at the top, those of the blue figures at the bottom.[16]

In other series, the principle of the hanging did not depend on the distribution of the forms in the painting. This time it was the space that determined the hanging, especially when the artist's familiarity with a particular space (the Galerie Laage-Salomon, in this case) favored experimentation —for example, hanging just below the ceiling. For the "86-87" series presented in 1987,[J] Barré developed a fragmented hanging, made up of gaps and staircase effects, which in a way shattered the series' legibility—perhaps one of the most didactic he ever painted—and the systematicity of the place of the figures in the pictorial space, a completely new systematicity compared to the paintings of previous years. Two years later, the exhibition devoted to the "87-89"[17] series in the same space[K] gave way to more mayhem, as though he were applying the principles of distribution of the triangles of the "82-84" series to the paintings, drawing a clear parallel between the plane-painting and the space-wall.

Lastly, the Jeu de Paume exhibition offered a record, a sort of recapitulation, of the hangings of the decade, linking the series together, while also differentiating them, particularly in the room presenting "82-84," "86-87," and "87-89."[G] Having necessitated in places a reconfiguration of the museum space, in particular the mounting of partitions designed to accommodate panoramic works—a "predella" format recurring from 1987 through 1992, the largest of which measured 82 × 312 cm—the exhibition revealed

14

Yve-Alain Bois, "Martin Barré, Gal. Ricke, Cologne," *Artistes* 4 (April–May 1980): 41. The article attempts to precisely describe the "79" series, constituting a model of its kind for the analysis of Barré's series from the 1980s–1990s. All the elements of the article are taken up again in Bois, 2008, p. 53–56.

15

It should be pointed out here that this hanging was temporary, linked to the first showing of the series. Each painting subsequently remained independent, at the time of its acquisition or a new exhibition. With *L'Indissociable*, only the "79-80" series, known as *L'Indissociée*, formed an indivisible whole with an imposed hanging. This series, like "80-81," was also atypical in Barré's work, since they functioned on the principle of the fragment: either the ten details of a square with monochrome edges painted according to variable focus ("79-80"), or more or less close zooms on an overall composition made up of successive incomplete frames that is not shown in its entirety ("80-81").

16

The fact that two sets of different sizes (126 × 126 cm and 96 × 112 cm) both have yellow and blue figures causes a "thorn in the painting" (the equivalent of Claire Stoullig's "lure of geometry"?): on which line should the three paintings measuring 96 × 112 cm be hung? On the top one or the bottom one? In either case, the ligature would break (see illustration 4, p. 232). Let us note that the next two series, "91" and "91-92," prohibit a hanging governed by a similar principle. Although apparently structured by two parallel lines, the ten paintings in "91" and the twelve paintings in "91-92" have colors distributed both above and below. In "91," for example, the truncated figures on the right are blue, those truncated on the left are red, regardless of their position on the canvas.

17

For an in-depth analysis of this series, see Hindry, "Série 89," in *Martin Barré 87-89*. I note this passage: "But who would here speak of facility? Or difficulty. The core is simplicity, that luminous archaic simplicity that we have progressively allowed to be buried under layers of time and culture," this "luminous simplicity" echoing the serene plenitude that I detect in the works from 1986 through 1992.

J → p. 225

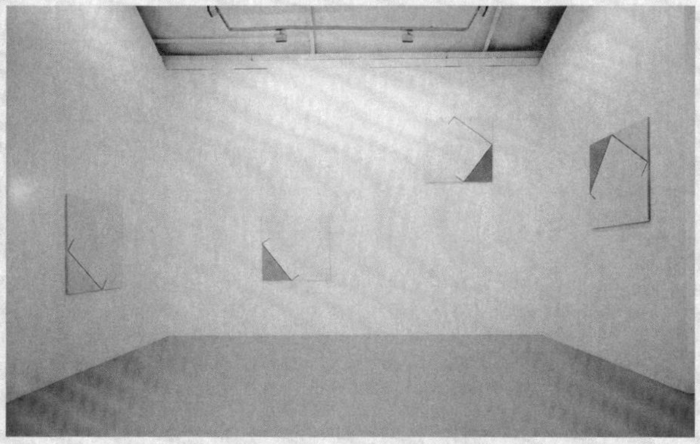

K → p. 226

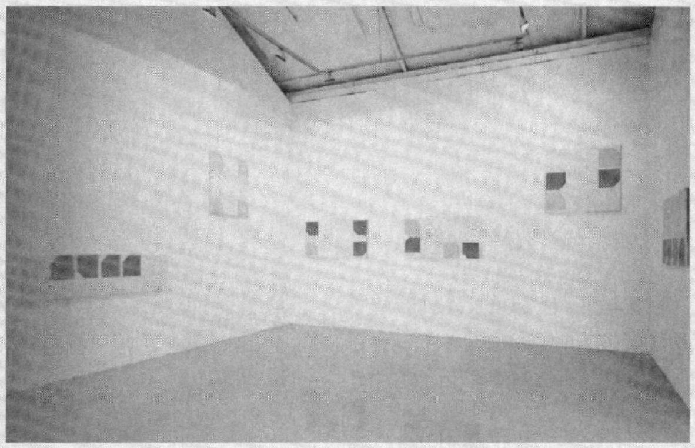

the artist's overall thinking, offering a display of rhythms and developments. Some series were aligned from below, when a colored rail required it; [H] others were tossed about when they allowed it; [G] still others were aligned by the middle, such as the "92B" series. To take stock of the singularity of Martin Barré's work in the 1980s–1990s is therefore to grasp the extent to which the exhibition had become an essential component of his approach.

Let us take a closer look at a few selected series[18] by this "painter of the end of the 2nd millennium A.D.," to borrow the phrase used by the *Art press* in 1985. This expression did not arise by chance. It enabled things to be said about Martin Barré's genealogies and artistic relatives. A few names regularly recur in the studies devoted to him: for his contemporaries, and with regard to the years from 1970 through 1990, James Bishop, Alan Charlton, Helmut Federle, Ellsworth Kelly, Robert Mangold, Brice Marden, Agnes Martin, and Robert Ryman;[19] for the modern masters and the 1950s, Piet Mondrian and Kazimir Malevich were favored by critics. Here is what the artist said in 1987: "Although Mondrian and Malevich meant a great deal to me, Picasso, Léger, and Matisse did not lose their importance, for all that, and they didn't prevent me from looking further than the impressionists who preceded them and from finding in them Vermeer, Hals, and many others, and subsequently a new interest in Egyptian and Greco-Roman antiquity. For, if a distant era has already been a source of new possibilities, why not look again for what perhaps had not yet been properly seen there?"[20] The series from the turn of the 1980s answer, in a way, this rhetorical question in the affirmative. With their ochre colors and textured treatment, similar to that of the Italian fresco, their entablature compositions and—dare we say it—their "auratic *je-ne-sais-quoi*," they evoke ancient Roman wall painting, especially "80-81," nicknamed the "Pompeii series"[21] by the artist himself. These series from 1979 through 1981 also complete the pictorial evolution begun by *L'Indissociable* at the end of the 1970s.

The 1980s–1990s series, including "79," show an undeniable process of simplification, often described as "reductionism," compared with the works of the previous period. The geometric shapes (line, frieze, triangle, square, trapezoid, quadrangle) emerge legibly: they are now filled monochromatically with specifically chosen shades, in a more or less textured way depending on the series—some colors returning from one series to another. Their perimeters are highlighted either by rails that accompany them in a continuous or discontinuous manner ("79," "79-80," "80A," "80B"), or by borders of varying design, chromatism,

18

For more detailed analyses of certain series from the 1980s–1990s, see, in addition to those already mentioned by Yve-Alain Bois ("79") and Ann Hindry ("87-89"), the studies by Marcel-André Stalter, "Martin Barré: tableaux '90-91' et '91,'" *Revue du Nord* LXXIV, no. 295 (April–June 1992): 355–70, and those by Bois in his 2008 monograph and Gauthier about the "84-85" series in this volume, 21–22.

19

On the subject of American painters, one of their rare mentions in Martin Barré's interviews: "I knew their work through exhibitions and catalogues, but I never met them personally. And without being marked by them, I've seen some interesting works. I think in particular of those by Franz Kline," in "Casser le blanc." See also on this subject the catalogue of the *Idées de la Peinture. Hommage à Martin Barré* exhibition organized by Jean-Pierre Criqui at the Galerie Nathalie Obadia in 2006, which brought together works by On Kawara, Peter Halley, Robert Mangold, Albert Oehlen, Bernard Piffaretti, Pascal Pinaud, Christopher Wool, Christian Bonnefoi, and Raoul De Keyser. A close study of the relationships and differences between Martin Barré and the artists mentioned here would be welcome in order to see their kinship more clearly.

20

Martin Barré in *Peindre en 1987*, Supplément au Calendrier des expositions d'art contemporain en Bretagne et Pays de la Loire, no. 8 (Nantes: Artelier-Cas d'urgence, 1987), n.p. On the subject of Vermeer, it is delightful to read Barré's deconstruction of the "little patch of yellow wall," cherished by Marcel Proust, in an interview with Jacques Henric: "Martin Barré, peintre de la fin du 2ᵉ millénaire après J.-C.," *Art press* 96 (October 1985): 8–10, here 10. According to him, it doesn't exist: "Too bad for Vermeer, good for Proust, because his pretty little sentence will still be very successful for a long time to come, even if there is no little patch of yellow wall in the *View of Delft*, but in fact a plane inclined at forty-five degrees which *verticalizes*, one almost feels like saying *Cézannizes*, the edge of the left-hand tower."

21

The Pompeii site is one of Martin Barré's favorite references. In his interview with Catherine Millet, he draws a parallel between "abstract paintings made of stripes," seen in a villa whose excavations began in 1964, and his "Zèbres" ("Zebras"), initiated in 1963, concluding "Maybe the history of abstract painting needs to be rewritten." See Bois, 2008, p. 273.

and intensity. The grid line is suppressed in favor of markers alone—thick colored lines, round markers, thin dashes perpendicular to the edges—before disappearing altogether from 1987 onwards. The diagonal, omnipresent in the works of the 1970s, gives way to a mesh of horizontal and vertical lines that cross the pictorial space before also fading away, from 1982 onwards, in favor of geometric figures. The latter, alone, then animate the painting, a veritable space for formal in-vitro experiments: first according to complex juxtaposition effects ("82-84," "84-85"), then according to a more quiet distribution of forms systematically attached to one of the four sides of the painting.[22] As such, "86-87"[L, M, N, O] constitutes a pivotal moment, taking up the colored triangles of the two previous series but fitting them into the right-angles of the paintings. The ten canvases thus form a tribute to the square, mentally present but visually absent, always fleeing—like a musical fugue—or ghostly. Within a single square format (120 × 120 cm) are triangles in red, green, blue, and yellow, painted in varying intensities (from pale pink to orange-red and magenta-red, for example) and bordered by a thick charcoal perimeter. Each color is assigned to a corner. No more than two triangles are ever presented together. Viewed in relation to each other, these paintings provoke the mobile variable appearance and disappearance of a central square, this movement redoubling the almost syntactic formation of Barré's works —how elements (figure, color, outline, arrangement, etc.) articulate with each other—with a choreographic dimension. In "86-87," the "song of colors" gives form to a score of great clarity for which the expression "the rules of the game," in its compositional and playful sense, has never seemed so appropriate.

Above all, in the 1980s–1990s period, the guiding principle of distribution is what governed the paintings' composition, according to computational modalities modified for each series. The fact that, for "87-89," the surface area of each painting remained the same, despite the use of four different formats based on a standard surface area of 108 × 108 cm, and that the color and white areas were identical, confirms this "painting by distribution" approach. In this respect, "82-84"[P, Q] constitutes a case study with its powerfully structured works in which the triangle, subjected to multiple magnetizing effects, is the exclusive figure, playing with the diffraction of time and space through movements of extension and approximation. "One might wonder why something as simple as a triangle could cause so many difficulties,"[23] the painter recalled when mentioning this series in an interview with Catherine Millet. "Difficulties," another way of saying possibilities for a series of paintings based on a layout by zones—a color corresponds to each zone,

22
"I'm passionate about space. ... There is the space of the painting, the one that constructs the painting but also the space that is around it. Besides, I can't stand it when someone puts a frame around one of my paintings: it's enclosed. It has to be open. That's why my figures are often in the corners." Martin Barré interviewed by Henri-François Debailleux: Debailleux, "La géométrie." On Barré's aversion to the frame, see "À propos du Salon de mars: l'art à la maison," *Art press* 167 (March 1992): 30.

L → p.174

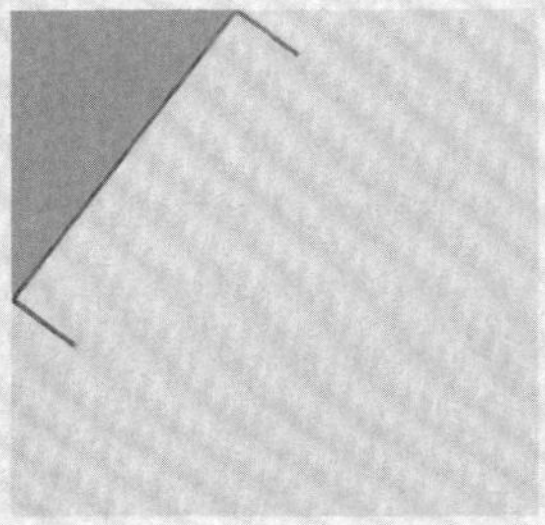

M → p.175

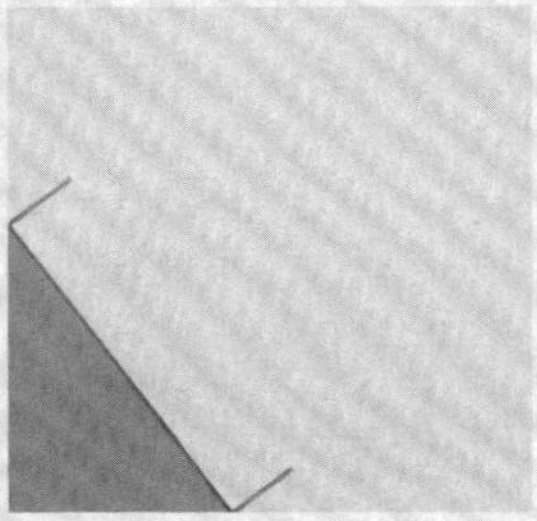

N → p.177

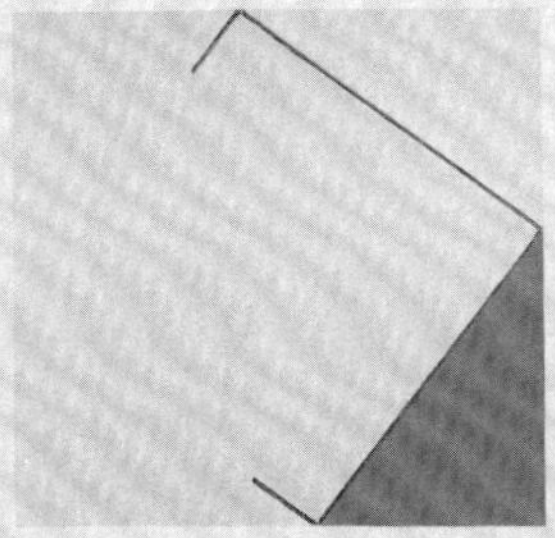

O → p.179

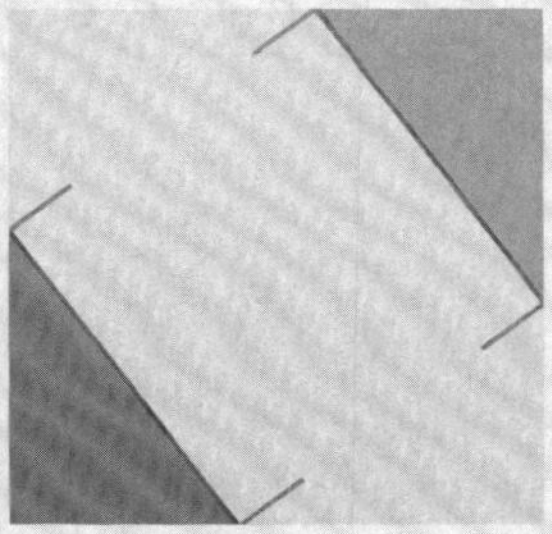

P → p.166

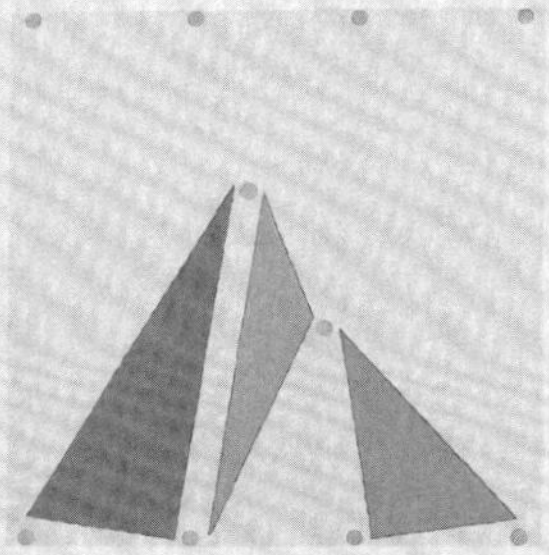

Q → p.168

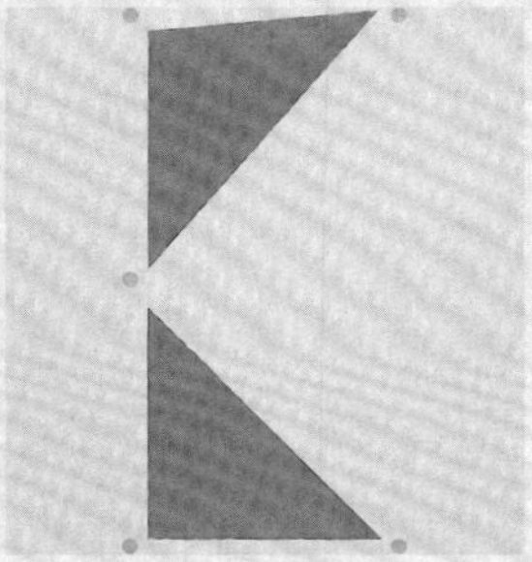

23
Martin Barré in Bois, 2008, p. 274.

from which a triangle flourishes—and crossed triangulations, generated by markers spaced at three different intervals. This complex distribution gives rise to a statistical infinity of singular triangles, of which only a few interact with the solid-white. Some of them, it should be noted, already continue beyond the frame but, unlike the rectangles of "92A" and "92B," we can still reconstruct their borders. They have not yet sailed away.

·

To consider Martin Barré's artistic research between 1979 and 1992 is both to look back on the profoundly autonomous way in which he constantly renewed his pictorial language, drawing on his own previous experiments, and to understand the visual plastic solutions specific to the series produced in the 1980s and 1990s. It is also, in my opinion, to take stock of the active confidence that Barré placed in painting, in its possibilities of appearance and analysis, in the "exemplarity of its mode of permanent questioning."[24]

24 Martin Barré and Christian Bonnefoi, "Entretien avec Martin Barré," *Documents IV-V, Cahiers d'histoire de l'art contemporain* (1976), repr. in Pagé et al., *Martin Barré*, 41.

1924
2020

CHRONOLOGY

Rita Cusimano

1924

- Birth in Nantes of Lucien Michel, known as Martin Barré. His father is an architect and his two grandfathers are carpenters.

Architecture had some influence on my work. I am often tempted to say that I see painting as less a means of expression than as a means of construction.[1]

1939–43

- Studies at the École des Beaux-Arts (School of Fine Arts) in Nantes. First takes architecture courses, soon afterwards painting courses. Thanks to Paul Deltombe, teacher and director of the school, discovers modern painting (Gauguin, Renoir, Cézanne).
- First trip to Paris in 1943. For eight months, works in free studios including La Grande Chaumière.
- Post-cubist paintings.

1945

- Befriends Michel Ragon who will introduce him, during the 1950s, to the Parisian art world. Ragon would later recall Barré's admiration for Le Corbusier, Mies van der Rohe, Schlemmer, and Loos as well as his taste for music (New Orleans jazz, Ravel, de Falla, flamenco, and Varèse).

1946

- First solo exhibition, Galerie Michel Columb, Nantes.
- First theater sets for plays by Sartre, Giraudoux, and Anouilh, Théâtre d'Essai, Nantes.

1947

- First participation in a Parisian exhibition organized by Ragon, Galerie L'Arc-en-Ciel.
- First attempts at non-figurative paintings.

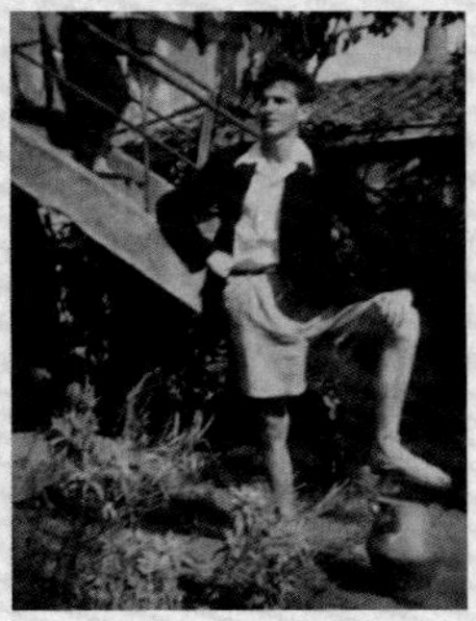

Martin Barré, Nantes, c. 1945

1948

- Weds Martine Delalande. Two children: Josquin born in 1949 and Brigitte in 1951. They part at the end of the 1950s.
- Settles permanently in Paris where he lives in difficult conditions. Spends several years in hotels.

1949–50

- First solo exhibition in Paris in 1949, Galerie du Vert-Galant: figurative works influenced by Miró and some non-figurative paintings.
- Afterwards, devotes himself to abstract painting. Works with a bookseller friend's, Josquin Huteau, whose cellar he uses for painting.

It wasn't so much this "passage" from the figurative to abstraction that was important, it was when I decided to paint without a "motif," without the model in front of my eyes and, while the object was still there, I really felt a great liberation; . . . afterwards, the object was eliminated and it became embarrassing and useless.[2]

- Stays in Bayonne for health reasons. Under the influence of Mondrian and Malevich, encountered in the magazine *Art d'aujourd'hui*, makes abstract geometric collages, as he lacks material means to paint.
- Paints lyrical abstract gouaches. Palette limited to different shades of umber-brown on white.

1951

- Brief incursion into Art Informel, then return to form: gouaches made with the handle of the brush.
- A photograph by Hans Namuth showing Jackson Pollock painting, published in *Art d'aujourd'hui*, impresses him.
- Works as a house painter with Ragon, an activity he pursues for many years.

1952

- Makes orange gouaches using Plaka, a new casein paint. Due to a lack of canvases, paints on wood and rounds the edges of the support to try non-rectangular formats.
- Sees Malevich's paintings for the first time, including *Suprematist Composition: White on White* (1918), in the exhibition *L'Œuvre du xx*[e] *siècle* at the Musée National d'Art Moderne, Paris.

1953

- Abandons the brush for a "tachist" episode (splashes and drips from bottles and cans). Also works with a putty knife. Destroys several paintings to recover the supports.
- Ragon gives him his room on Rue des Saints-Pères.

1954

- First canvases preserved. Up until 1958 paintings are characterized by the structured aspect of the compositions and the balance of rectilinear and colored forms. The background, white or light, is homogeneous. Efforts to destabilize the figure/ground relationship. First paintings with lines going from the shapes to the edges.

> *I have always tried to greatly reduce my artistic means in order to obtain greater* concentration. *That's why in 1954 I was using only three colors: white, Prussian blue, and Venetian red, with which I obtained grays, browns, and blacks.*[3]

- Participates for the first time in the Salon des Réalités Nouvelles, Paris. Also participates in 1956, 1957, and 1958.

> *In 1954, my paintings had structures "in spite of everything," but already not against the background but "in" or rather with it. . . .*[4]

1955

- First solo exhibition of abstract paintings, *Qui est Martin Barré?*, presented by Ragon, Galerie La Roue, Paris. Critics reproach him for his "white background" and his "poor colors."

> *Regarding the color of the ground-spaces, I can tell you that in 1954–55, the date of the first exhibited canvases, the "spaces" were really white. . . . It wasn't long before I started "breaking" my whites.*[5]

- *Divergences 3* at the Galerie Arnaud, Paris, with which he collaborates until 1968 —the gallery owner, Jean-Robert Arnaud, is co-founder, in 1953, of the magazine *Cimaise*; *17 peintres de la génération nouvelle*, Galerie Kléber, Paris; *Junge Malerei in Frankreich*, Werkkunstschule, Offenbach am Main; *Éloge du petit format*, Galerie La Roue, Paris.

1956

- Uses small varnish brushes. The palette is enriched with yellow ochre and black. Flat surfaces scraped with a knife in the dark areas; portions of unpainted canvas are sometimes visible.

> *Venetian red dominated for longer than [1954], and it was starting to become a bit of a "trademark." . . . I gradually started introducing other colors.*[6]

- Solo exhibition, Galerie La Roue.

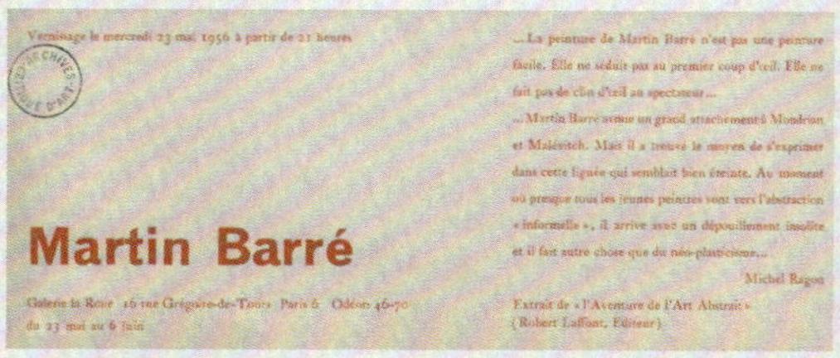
Vernissage le mercredi 23 mai 1956 à partir de 21 heures

Martin Barré

Galerie la Roue 16 rue Grégoire-de-Tours Paris 6 Odéon 46-70
du 23 mai au 6 juin

…La peinture de Martin Barré n'est pas une peinture facile. Elle ne séduit pas au premier coup d'œil. Elle ne fait pas de clin d'œil au spectateur…

…Martin Barré avoue un grand attachement à Mondrian et Malévitch. Mais il a trouvé le moyen de s'exprimer dans cette lignée qui semblait bien éteinte. Au moment où presque tous les jeunes peintres vont vers l'abstraction « informelle », il arrive avec un dépouillement insolite et il fait autre chose que du néo-plasticisme…

Michel Ragon

Extrait de « l'Aventure de l'Art Abstrait »
(Robert Laffont, Éditeur)

Invitation card, Galerie La Roue, Paris, 1956

- *Jeunes peintres* (Barré, James Guitet, Guy Resse) and *Éloge du petit format II*, Galerie La Roue, Paris; *Divergences 4*, Galerie Arnaud, Paris (touring to the Stedelijk Museum, Amsterdam and Schiedam); 1st Festival of Avant-Garde Art, Unité d'Habitation de Marseille (Le Corbusier, 1952), curated by Ragon; *Das Kleinbild. Dialogue en couleurs franco-allemand*, Galerie Inge-Ahlers, Mannheim; *Pentagone*, Galerie Arnaud, Paris, curated by editors of *Cimaise*.
- In *L'Aventure de l'art abstrait*, Ragon concludes the chapter devoted to the new generation with a text on Barré.[7] An eponymous exhibition takes place at the Galerie Arnaud. Ragon also writes a text about Barré in *Seize peintres de la Jeune École de Paris*—a book introduced by Hubert Juin.[8] The artist rejects Ragon's interpretation of his painting as "abstract landscape art."

1957

- The palette knife replaces the brush, even for the ground. Also uses framing sticks to accentuate the vibration of the shapes. White areas are becoming increasingly important.

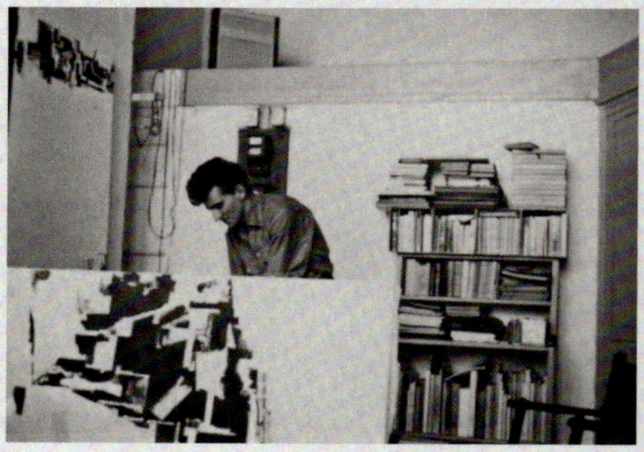
Martin Barré in his studio, Paris, c. 1957

- After a few titles such as *Greenwich*, *Gulf Stream*, *Grenam*, and *Bélouga*, adopts more factual titles, now noted on the reverse side of the canvases: date, format, and distinctive capital letter—a formula retained until 1959. On the back also, an arrow now systematically indicates the top of the painting. The signature remains on the front and not always at the same angle. In publications, the *Peinture* and *Composition* titles remain.
- First solo exhibition at Galerie Arnaud, noticed by French and foreign critics. In *Art Digest*, Annette Michelson points out "the possibilities of dynamic relations between active and residual space."[9]

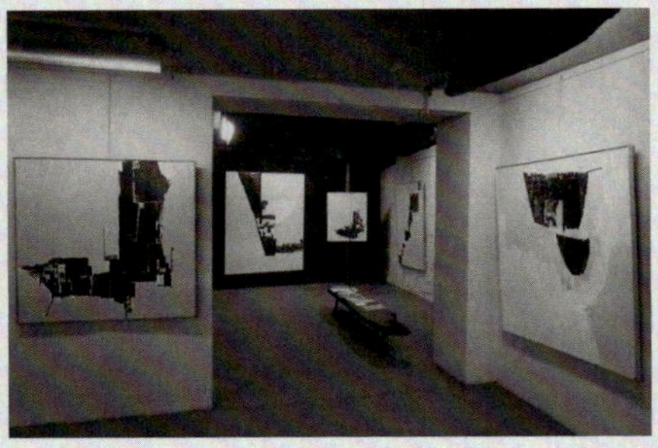
Exhibition view, Galerie Arnaud, Paris, 1957

- Salon Comparaisons, Paris (also in 1958, 1959, 1964, and 1966); *Biennale 57. Jeune peinture, jeune sculpture*, Musée des Arts Décoratifs, Paris; *50 ans de peinture abstraite*, Galerie Creuze, Paris, organized on the occasion of the publication of Michel Seuphor's *Dictionnaire de la peinture abstraite* in which a painting by Barré is reproduced;[10] *Expression et non-figuration* and *Gouaches et collages*, Galerie H. Le Gendre, Paris; *Divergences 5*, Galerie Arnaud, Paris; Festival of Avant-Garde Art, Cité Radieuse, Rezé-lès-Nantes; Milan Triennial XI; *Six from Paris*, Howard Wise Gallery, Cleveland.
- First Parisian exhibition devoted to Mondrian and *Précurseurs de l'art abstrait en Pologne* at the Galerie Denise René, Paris. The Iris Clert and Colette Allendy galleries, Paris, jointly organize *Yves Klein. Propositions monochromes* featuring works in blue pigment and an empty room, Klein's first "immaterial."

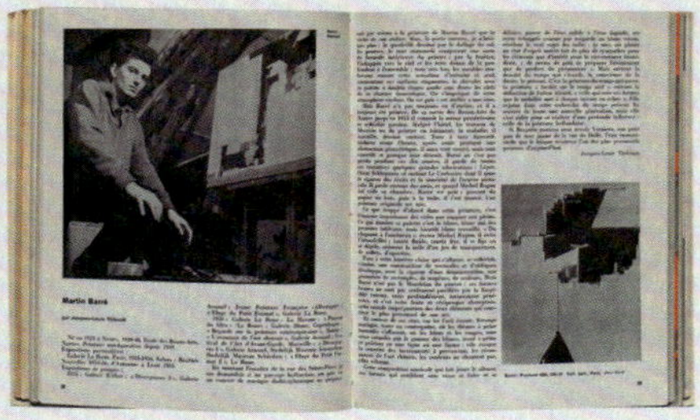
Spread from the magazine *Cimaise*, no. 3, January–February 1957, one of the first articles published on Martin Barré by Jacques-Louis Thibault alias Jacques-Louis Binet

1958

- Trip to the Netherlands: Franz Hals, Rembrandt, Johannes Vermeer, Malevich.
- Trip to Spain: El Greco, Diego Velázquez, Francisco de Zurbarán.

> *In around 1957–58, I moved gradually away from painting in flat swatches of color: the touch became freer. . . . This was due more to the influence of Frans Hals than to that of the gestural painting of those days.*[11]

- Gradually frees himself from standard formats and reduces the gap between the height and width of the canvas while maintaining its verticality. Growing search for dynamism and instability.
- Some paintings dated across two years (1957–58), a practice that is regularly repeated in the 1970s, 1980s, and 1990s.
- *4 Maler aus Paris*, Galerie Parnass-Jährling, Wuppertal; *Divergences 6*, Galerie Arnaud, Paris, and Galerie Grange, Lyon; *Rencontres d'octobre*, Musée des Beaux-Arts, Nantes.
- Acquisition of *Greenwich* (1957) by the Solomon R. Guggenheim Museum, New York, and of *57-58-30F3* (1957–58) by the National Gallery in Oslo; publication of Ole Henrik Moe's article "Corneille og Martin Barré, en ny generasjon" in the Norwegian art magazine *Kunsten Idag*.[12]

1959

- Colors and shapes are reduced. The structured and orthogonal compositions disappear, and the edges of the canvas no longer act as anchors but as interruptions.

> *From 1959–60 and 1961 onwards, many people had the impression that there was not much left on the canvas, that a fairly "good painter" . . . only offered canvases with almost nothing on them (many painters painted very thickly).*[13]

- Solo exhibition, Galerie Arnaud, Paris: twenty works, including predominantly white paintings made with Plaka, paintings with areas of unprepared canvas, and two large canvases of a rectangular format hung from one of its corners.
- *La Peinture actuelle*, Galerie Arnaud, Paris; *La Escuela de Paris*, Museo de Bellas Artes, Caracas; 1st Biennale de Paris, Musée d'Art Moderne de la Ville de Paris; *Inaugural Selection*, Guggenheim Museum, New York; *Divergences 7*, exhibition touring to the Musée Renier, Verviers, APIAW, Liège, and Galerie Arnaud, Paris.
- Interviewed by Jean Grenier for RTF.

My white period (1959) . . . is, for me, an advent of color; for color takes precedence over form, over substance. Color becomes space.[14]

1960

- Return to oil paint. Starts painting directly with the tube. Ready-made colors are quickly replaced by mixtures introduced in tubes whose opening is filed away to obtain wider strokes. The prepared white ground of the canvas remains visible, the artist thinking "that the white would go off naturally over time."[15] Curved lines, hatching, scratches, and pentimenti (pictorial traces half erased with turpentine and often covered with a light whitewash leaving them visible by transparency). A group of paintings with the same aigrette motif announces the serial work of the 1970s. First polyptychs. Removal of the frame to create a better relationship between the painting and the wall.

It was with the canvases I made in 1960 that I started getting a sense of the use I could make of traces of corrections . . . , that is to say, not hiding the process of the painting's emergence. Matisse, Picasso, and Rembrandt in his engravings, opened the way here.[16]

- The actual titles of the paintings (year/capital letter/number or size) begin to appear in the publications.
- Solo exhibition, Galerie Arnaud, Paris, with tube paintings. In *Cimaise* Pierre Restany hails Barré's evolution towards a sign that "in its absolute simplicity takes full possession of the space it creates through its cursive inscription on the blank canvas" and claims to find in these paintings "the irresistible call of the ecstatic void"[17] that Klein expresses differently in his blue monochromes.

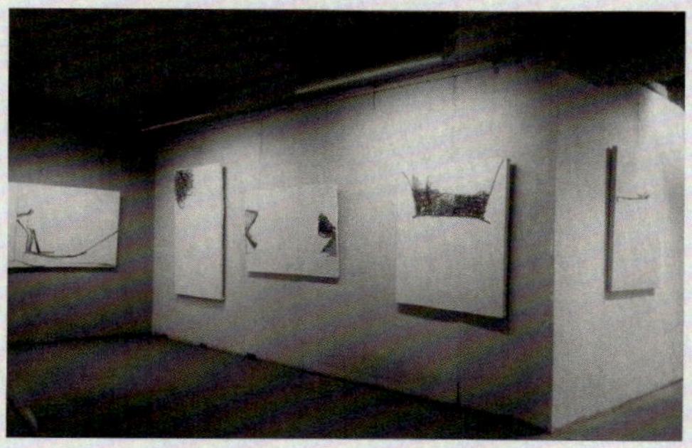

Exhibition view, Galerie Arnaud, Paris, 1960 (see pp. 63, 67)

When I painted directly with the tube, it wasn't the tube that interested me, but the fact of getting rid of the brush and palette knife that I had used before, all this towards a greater reduction-concentration.[18]

- *Fransk konst av i dag. Akvareller, gouacher och pasteller*, Göteborgs Konstmuseum; *Quatre peintres de l'École de Paris. Barré, Corneille, Gillet, Maryan*, Galleri Kaare Berntsen, Oslo; *Young French Painters*, The Art Club of Chicago (touring to Cincinnati, Denver, Minneapolis); *La Peinture française d'aujourd'hui*, Tel Aviv Museum (touring to Jerusalem, Haifa).
- Visits the Malevich retrospective, Louisiana Museum of Modern Art, Humlebæk.
- Ragon writes *Martin Barré et la poétique de l'espace* (publisher: Galerie Arnaud), the first monograph devoted to the painter: "Barré isn't only one of the major painters of his generation—by far—but one of the major painters in contemporary art"[19]

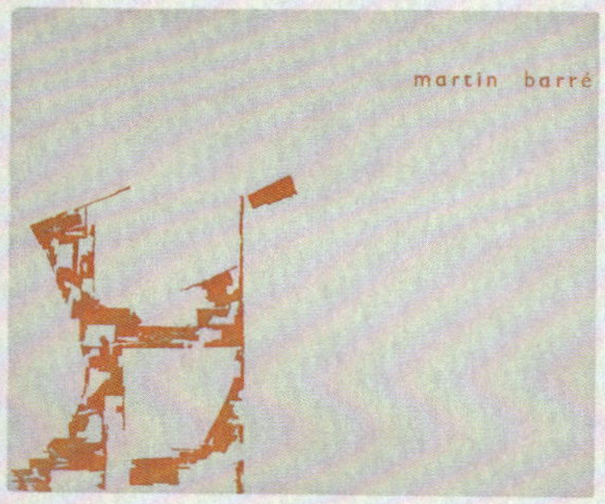

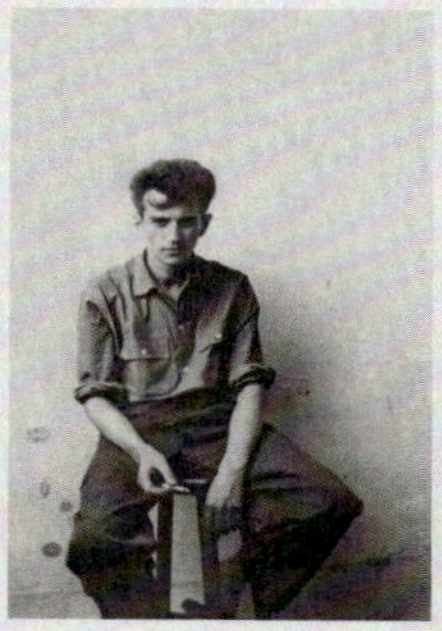

Cover of Michel Ragon, *Martin Barré et la poétique de l'espace*, Galerie Arnaud, Paris, 1960. Shot by Michel Ragon, this portrait is featured in his book.

1961

- The tube marks become more concise, often reduced to a single line, crossing the white, homogeneous surface of the canvas from one edge to another, or being limited to a shorter path. Often monochrome, it is sometimes tinged with colored accents. For Yve-Alain Bois, "the inscription of time had become an essential component of Barré's approach. . . . Now it was paramount: how to declare time in painting without making a spectacle of it?"[20]

I refused the illusion of depth, which meant that my painting had to be situated on a single plane. . . . The fact of wanting to show the succession of interventions, the time of production, does not create a "perspective"—well, perhaps a "time-perspective" but not a "space-perspective." . . . There is no "vanishing point."[21]

- Solo exhibitions, Lefebre Gallery, New York, first solo exhibition in the United States (1960 works alongside older paintings); Kunstnernes Kunsthandel, Copenhagen.

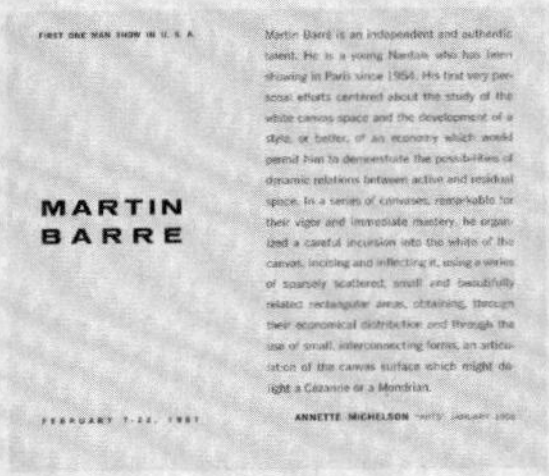
FIRST ONE MAN SHOW IN U. S. A.

MARTIN
BARRE

Martin Barré is an independent and authentic talent. He is a young Nantais who has been showing in Paris since 1954. His first very personal efforts centered about the study of the white canvas space and the development of a style, or better, of an economy which would permit him to demonstrate the possibilities of dynamic relations between active and residual space. In a series of canvases, remarkable for their vigor and immediate mastery, he organized a careful incursion into the white of the canvas, inciting and inflecting it, using a series of sparsely scattered, small and beautifully related rectangular areas, obtaining, through their economical distribution and through the use of small, interconnecting forms, an articulation of the canvas surface which might delight a Cézanne or a Mondrian.

FEBRUARY 7-22, 1961

ANNETTE MICHELSON

Invitation card, Lefebre Gallery, New York, 1961

- Salon de Mai, Paris; *École de Paris*, Galerie Charpentier, Paris; *Exhibition of International Twentieth Century Paintings*, Finch College Art Gallery and Museum, New York; *The 1961 Pittsburgh International Exhibition of Contemporary Painting and Sculpture*, Carnegie Institute, Pittsburgh; *Explorers of Space*, Akron Art Institute (touring to Louisville, Winter Park, Stanford, Houston).
- Acquisition of *60-T-48* by The Museum of Fine Arts, Houston.

1962

- Solo exhibition, Galerie Arnaud, Paris: recent tube paintings.

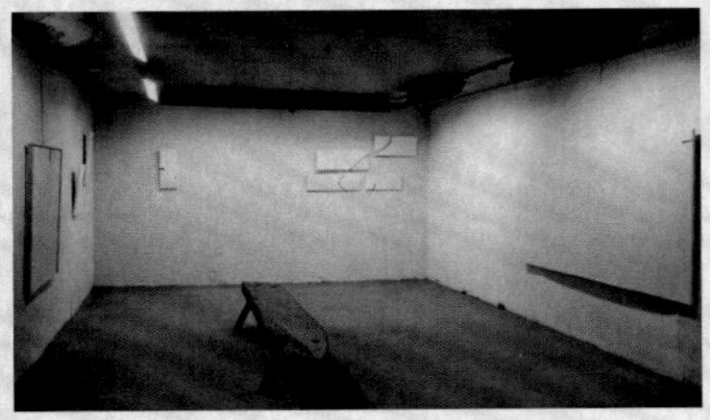

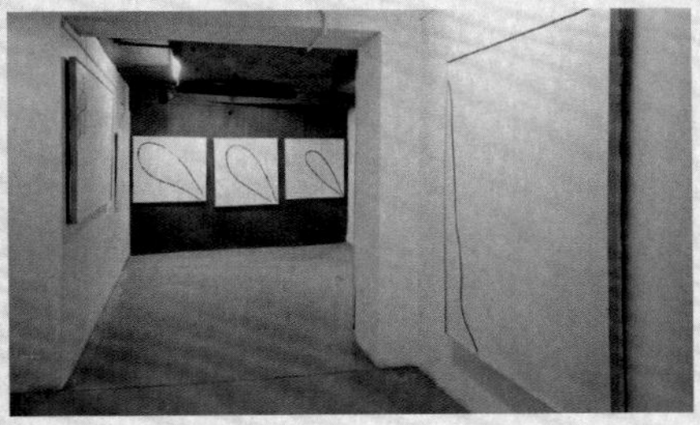

Exhibition views, Galerie Arnaud, Paris, 1962

- New polyptychs. To obtain wider strokes, reuses knives and framing sticks. Returns to polychromy and sometimes even to simplified figures, obtained by bringing together large dots. Gérard Gassiot-Talabot in *Aujourd'hui. Art et Architecture*: "This painter enjoyed such esteem that the radical simplicity he adopted two years ago left critics perplexed, but not reproving.... The most recent canvases ... herald a happy return to pictorial plasticity."[22]

1963

- Beginning of the spray paintings period. Graffiti seen on the walls of the Paris subway is the origin of the use of the spray can that would replace the pot, the brush, and the pigment. Thanks to the spray can, any physical contact with the canvas is eliminated. Barré renounces color because of the glow and holds on to matt black. Initially, the white prepared canvas is left visible; subsequently, to varying degrees depending on the occurrences, a final re-whitening with a roller or brush is often performed to erase the projections of paint droplets. Canvases are painted vertically and then laid flat to prevent dripping. First paintings with parallel stripes, arrows, and even a circle. Various formats. The signature leaves the front of the painting for good.

> [*Using only the black and white contrast*] *shouldn't be seen see as abandoning the "problem" of color. It would be more accurate to say that I stopped using the color element in order to introduce a new presence into my painting, that of the total absence of color.*[23]

- VII Biennial of São Paulo, on the initiative of Céres Franco; Salon des Surindépendants, Paris.

1964

- *Peintures récentes de Martin Barré*, Galerie Arnaud, Paris: about thirty spray paintings from 1963. Annette Michelson writes a positive review in *Art International* about the show. Marc Albert-Levin in *Cimaise*: "[Barré] welcomes with equal indifference all the titles that can be given to his paintings: the blank, the zebra, the ties, the bottle, sometimes using them himself for convenience. No single title, however, can reduce all the aspects of a painting conceived in total indifference to the subject."[24]

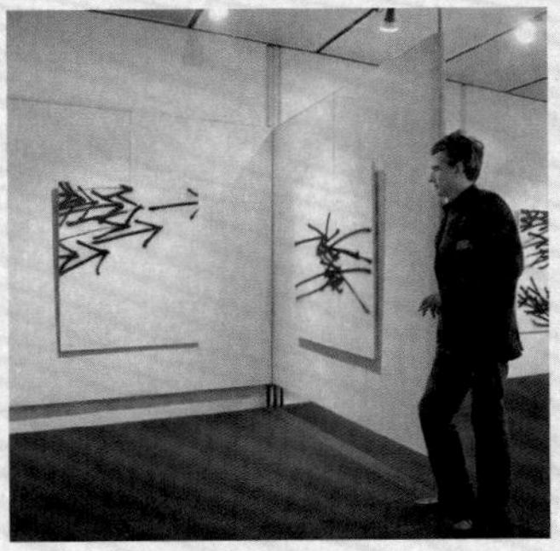

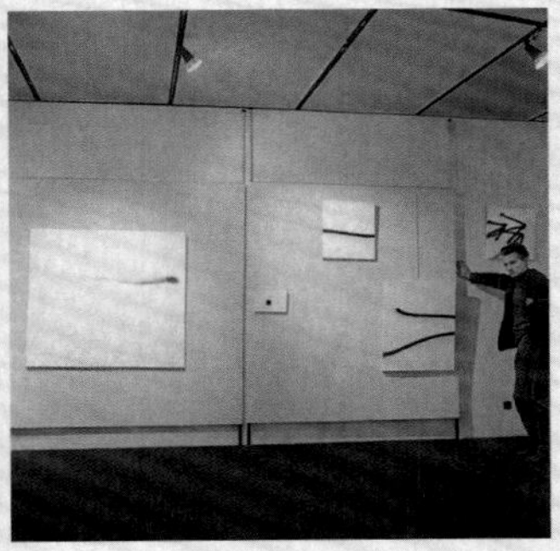

Exhibition views, Galerie Arnaud, Paris, 1964

> *At the first exhibition of these paintings that one could see through a window, I remember two walkers stopped. The first one says: "Here, look, these are photos," and the other one dragging him away: "Hey, come on! They aren't even photos."*[25]

- Solo exhibition, Ivan Spence Gallery, Ibiza: canvases and works on paper, also made with the spray can, from 1963 and 1964.
- *Eight Artists Working in France*, The Stone Gallery, Newcastle; XXXII Venice Biennale: in the section "Arte d'oggi nei musei," the Guggenheim Museum presents *60-T-44*, a painting acquired in 1963.

1965

- Solo exhibitions (spray paintings), Museu de Arte Moderna, Rio de Janeiro (acquisition of *63-M-2* by the museum, painting now destroyed); Galleri Hedenius, Stockholm; Haus am Lützowplatz, Berlin (works from 1964–65 for these last two exhibitions).
- Selected by Pontus Hultén for a tribute exhibition to Malevich, Naum Gabo, and Klein, Moderna Museet, Stockholm; acquisition of *65-S-12* by the museum.

Perhaps I was doing work that would have been better received in the 1970s, but that was not likely to interest the public and the critics at that time.[26]

1967

- Realization of two specific series of spray paintings: about thirty "Zebras" and about twenty "Arrows"—two series that, according to the artist, are better able to affirm the flatness of the surface. The "Arrows" are made using a kraft paper stencil which is the same for all the canvases and larger than them. This stencil is blindly placed on the canvas lying flat on the ground. By sliding the stencil over the surface, the number of arrows on the canvas can be multiplied. As for the formats of this series, the golden section is used, and the width of the canvas is then increased by half. The new ratio, fixing a slight increase in the height of the square, will then be used for the series made between 1972 and 1975.

The idea of using a stencil came to me from photography. . . . For me every trace is the result of a gesture except in photography where it was due —and this too is marvelous—to the trace of light, or in printing, to a trace of pressure. The projection from a spray gun through a stencil (which is a negative) produces a trace and not a gesture. The gesture lay in moving the stencil over the canvas.[27]

In 1967 the series that people couldn't help calling "Zebras" was more an attempt to annex the space provided by the simplest gesture.[28]

- Solo exhibitions, Galerie H, Hanover (works from 1963–65); *Les Zèbres de Martin Barré*, Galerie Arnaud, Paris: very dense hanging at various heights.

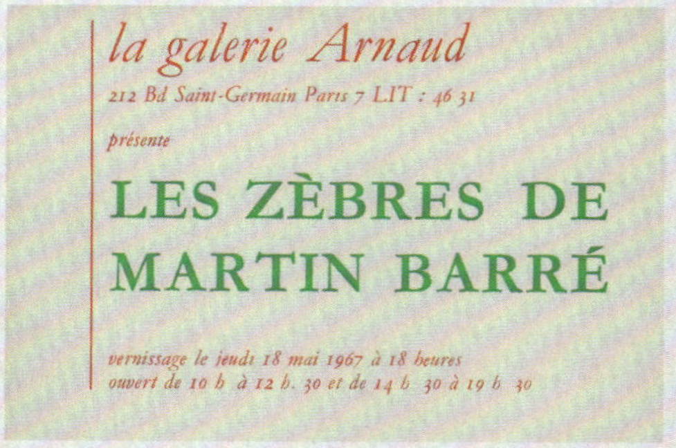

Invitation card, Galerie Arnaud, Paris, 1967

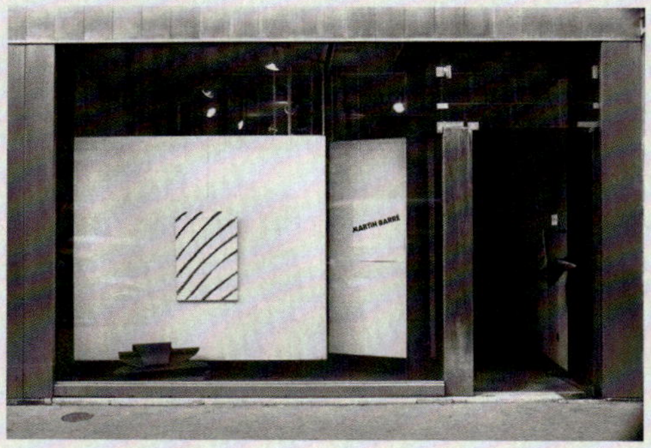

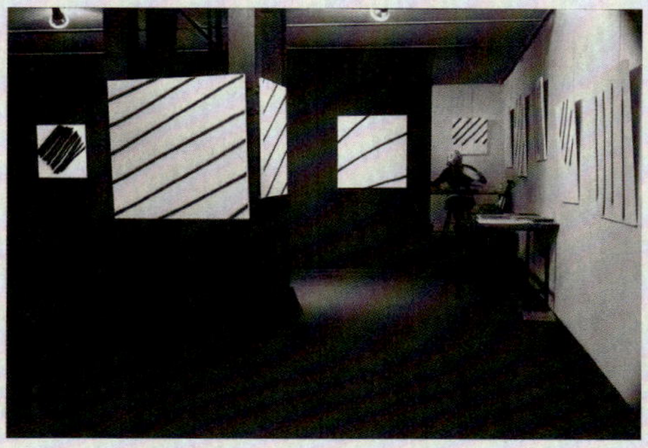
Exhibition views, Galerie Arnaud, Paris, 1967

- *50-57. Une aventure de l'art abstrait*, curated by Ragon, Musée Galliera, Paris.
- Commissioned by the architect André Wogenscky to paint the stage curtain of the large hall of the Maison de la Culture in Grenoble (inaugurated in 1968): a bundle of large black arrows pointing to the free space of the huge white canvas.

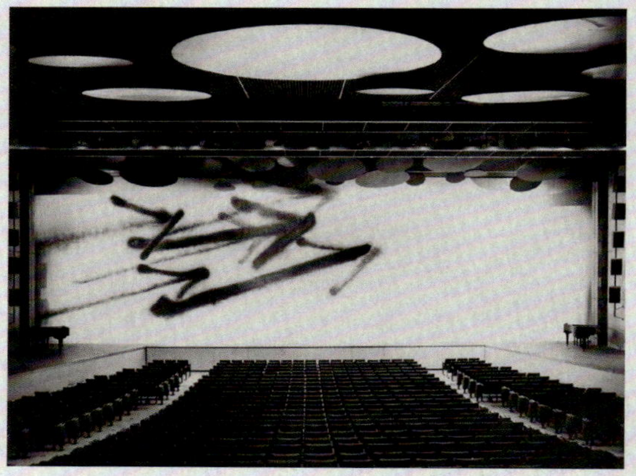
Stage curtain, Maison de la Culture, Grenoble, 1968

1968

- *Les Flèches de Martin Barré*, Galerie Arnaud, Paris: twenty paintings of the series and model of the Grenoble stage curtain. Last exhibition of Barré's work in this gallery.

Invitation card, Galerie Arnaud, Paris, 1968

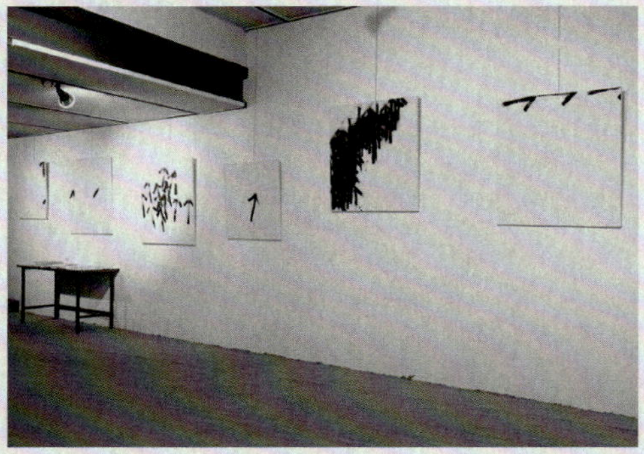

Exhibition view, Galerie Arnaud, Paris, 1968

- Between 1968 and 1971, abandons painting for a "conceptual episode" during which he practices a form of photo-conceptualism.

I thought that painting was finished . . . as a technique; I wanted to use only photographic material. . . . Photography still embodied the idea of reducing the means of painting to zero.[29]

- Meets Michèle Gozland who will share his life to the end.

In 1965, when I was twenty years old, I planned to open a gallery on Rue Bonaparte to exhibit young artists. Through Georges Boudaille, in charge of the Arts section of Les Lettres françaises, *I met Marc Albert-Levin, a young critic who also wrote for* Cimaise, *an art monthly published by the Galerie Arnaud. It was he who, at the beginning of 1966, introduced me to Martin Barré. Standing out among the nondescript abstract artists of the École de Paris, his spray paintings immediately fascinated me. I experienced them both as a provocation and an absolute of painting. It was ascetic and sensual.*

My interest was heightened when I saw his exhibitions of "Zèbres" (1967) and then of "Flèches" (1968). Martin came regularly to my openings. I wanted to know more and visited him shortly afterwards in his apartment, which served as his studio. Modest, every square centimeter was used. Martin welcomed me in his usual way, charming and nonchalant. Not very talkative, as one could tell from his painting, his answers to questions were brief. He gave no explanation of what he was doing. He smiled mischievously and mysteriously, puffing continuously on his Gitanes cigarettes. Yet he knew exactly what he was doing.

Martin was no longer satisfied with the Galerie Arnaud and this forced cohabitation with painters with whom he had no affinity. He quickly made me understand that he would be ready to come to my gallery, whose program he appreciated. He wanted to meet up with younger artists. We soon came to an agreement. He said, "Give me a date." That was his method. He would only "get to work" when he had a date for the opening of an exhibition.

The exhibition of the "Objets décrochés" in May 1969 was quite the event. A painter abandoning painting to embark on a conceptual approach as yet unknown in France that went beyond the appropriation of objects as per the Nouveaux Réalistes and entered the field of photography! The small Parisian artistic world was deeply intrigued. Martin was proud of his "coup." The Calendrier *exhibition in 1970 was even more radical. This installation shocked visitors who were not used to this type of work. This time, "he made fun of us." There were many questions, but Martin was still not very talkative when it came to explaining what was expected of him concerning his approach. An enigmatic smile was the only answer. In the end, this was his way of being, whether in private or in public. There was no snobbery or intellectual arrogance involved. Shyness, fear, anxiety, refuge? His way of living in a good mood and a state of permanent relaxation —or at any rate this is the way it appeared—has left me with the memory of a man as sensitive as he was profound, a man of unfailing determination in his artistic approach.*

—Daniel Templon, spring 2020

1969

- First solo exhibition, known as "Les objets décrochés," at the Galerie Daniel Templon, Paris, for a collaboration that will last until 1975. It is one of the first conceptual art events in France. In the empty space of the gallery, eight black-and-white photographic panels exhibited close to the objects they represent at scale 1 (electric socket, basement piping, fragment of wall, projector, guest book, etc.). In the catalogue, Tzvetan Todorov writes: "The objects seen on these canvases [*sic*] have only one common property: that of not being chosen. They are depicted . . . because they were already there."[30]

He emphasizes the tautological dimension of this proposition, which "calls into question the very principle of representation (by showing nothing other than what is already there)."[31]

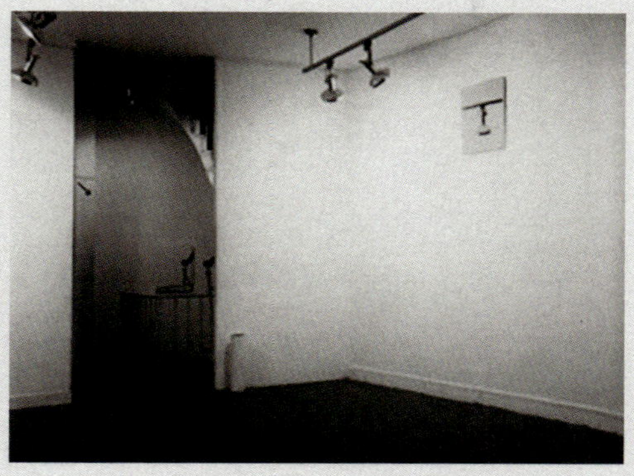

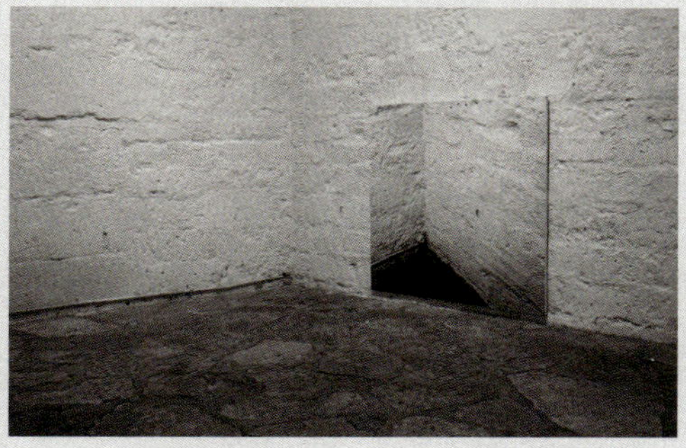

Exhibition views with *La Rampe*, *Le Projecteur*, *Le Coin*, Galerie Daniel Templon, Paris, 1969; photographs by Martin Barré

- *50 Years of Living Art*, Henie-Onstad Kunstsenter, Høvikodden (Oslo).
- Through Lygia Clark, meets art historian Jean Clay, founder of the magazine *Robho* (1967–71). Beginning of a long friendship solidified by their collaboration for the ARC – Musée d'Art Moderne de la Ville de Paris exhibition in 1979.
- First acquisition of a work by the French State: *65-S-3*, now in the Centre Pompidou collection.

In the 1950s or early 1960s, it was rather foreign museums that bought French artists; I haven't been the only one to have works abroad and nothing in France for a long time.[32]

1970

- Solo exhibition, known as "Le Calendrier," Galerie Daniel Templon, Paris. On the walls of the gallery, photographic enlargements of twenty pages of an ephemeris, retracing the days of the exhibition from April 7 to 25, offer the visitor the experience of a spatial environment of time.

I did two very anti-painting exhibitions (using photography) in what was a very anti-painting era, which was not very original. But this period enabled me to get a bit of a perspective on my pictorial work.[33]

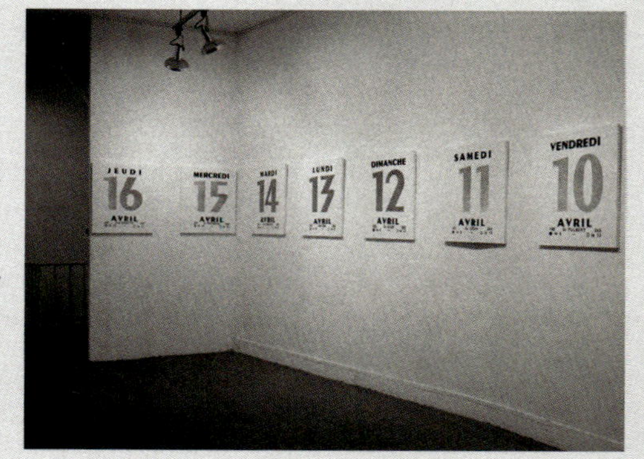

Exhibition view, Galerie Daniel Templon, Paris, 1970

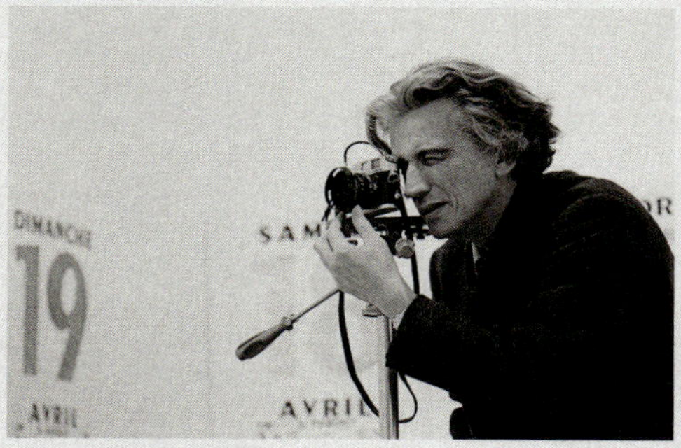

Martin Barré, Galerie Daniel Templon, Paris, 1970; photograph by Patrick Maurisson

- *Art Concepts from Europe*, curated by Restany, Galeria Bonino, New York. Among the artists in this project exhibition are Christian Boltanski, Marcel Broodthaers, Hanne Darboven, David Lamelas, Tania Mouraud, and Alina Szapocznikow. Exhibits *Projet nº 70-B-1* without realizing it.
- *Umwelt-Akzente. Die Expansion der Kunst*, curated by Klaus Honnef, Kunstkreis, Monschau. Carries out *Projet nº 70-B-1*: a metal rod starting from the ground is tilted so as to be parallel to an imaginary line rising vertically on another point of the globe, in this case the Europa Center in Berlin. This symbolic monument of the city "twinned" with the project is present in the exhibition space in the form of a photograph. Another conceptual project not realized: *Projet nº 70-B-2*, similar to the first one.
- Barré's conceptual work is analyzed by Catherine Millet in the magazines *Opus International* and *VH 101*.[34]

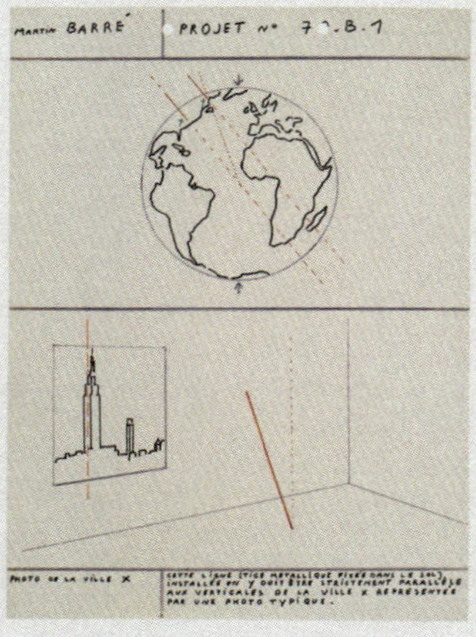

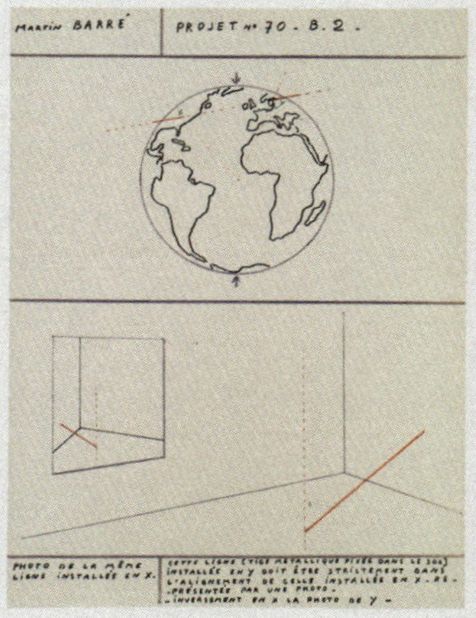

Projet nº 70-B-1 and *Projet nº 70-B-2*, 1970

Martin was very handsome, with dark eyes staring out from under his tousled white hair; I'm certainly not the only one who thought he looked like his emblematic paintings. Perhaps because he lived in Montparnasse when I knew him, I always thought he had kept a "montparno" side to him—the kind of guy who hangs out on café terraces as if he had nothing better to do. Nonchalance, which is a form of modesty and which I feel nostalgic for when I'm dealing with certain busy artists today. From Montparnasse to Saint-Germain-des-Prés and the Marais, it's as if he carried those terraces with him. Martin had a very slow hand gesture when he was fetching a cigarette from his lips. It makes me think that his painter's gesture, contrary to those of the lyrical, hysterical, and, worse, industrious, was the suspended gesture. Suspended from what? From that light and penetrating thought that attaches itself to the passerby, who, when he or she turns the corner, abandons it to its vaporous destiny?

—Catherine Millet, spring 2020

1971

- *Peintures et objets*, Musée Galliera, Paris: exhibition organized by the Société des Amis du Musée National d'Art Moderne. Exhibits a photographic enlargement of a wall paper detail.
- Moves to a larger studio in Rue Dauphine.
- Abandons his conceptual work.

1972

- Definitive return to paint, brush, and color. Use of acrylic, which favors transparency effects. Five series between 1972 and 1977 share the same system of elaboration, reiterated several times and simultaneously for all the paintings in a series, but interrupted at different stages depending on the canvases: inscription of a grid (specific to each series and of which each canvas occupies a fragment), hatching of all or part of the grid's cells, covering the grids with a translucent wash of whitish paint. Formats always in a square with a raised height.

The point of seriality is not to produce canvases that are almost identical but to produce paintings that are as different from each other as possible. What counts is the picture object. Seriality is the means of producing them. It is not so much the paintings that make the series as the series that produces the paintings.[35]

- *Aspects de l'avant-garde en France*, Théâtre de Nice (artists selected by Millet); *Museum Pieces of the Post-War Era*, Guggenheim Museum, New York.

1973

- Exhibition of the twenty-four paintings of the "72-73" series, Galerie Daniel Templon, Paris. Text by Todorov who states "here, the pictorial is always already metapictorial; the painting, necessarily, a theory of the painting."[36]

[In the 1970s] we talked about "murality," "parietality," etc., when the big "novelty" of the day, especially in France, was the freestanding canvas, without a stretcher. From that point of view, I was going pretty much in the opposite direction. Still, non-figuration was allowed once more, which meant that my work became viewable again, was much more acceptable than in the 1960s.[37]

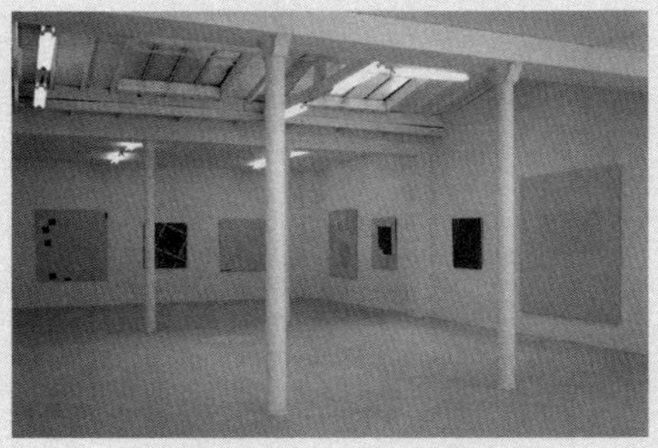

Exhibition view, Galerie Daniel Templon, Paris, 1973

The first time I heard of Martin Barré was through Jean Clay, shortly after my return from the US where I had spent a year after my baccalaureate, in 1969–70, as an exchange student. Jean had no doubt asked me to collect for him as many photographs as possible of what were then the most interesting practices in contemporary art, and I brought him back my booty, gleaned from New York galleries (Virginia Dwan, Leo Castelli, John Gibson, Paula Cooper, O.K. Harris, etc.) and sometimes from the artists themselves. He was delighted with my collection because he was already working on his great provocative text, "Quelques aspects de l'art bourgeois: la non-intervention," published in 1971 in the last issue of the journal Robho, *which he had co-edited since 1967. It was during a discussion about the approach he wanted to take in this article—I didn't always agree with the all-round criticism he was making of recent American art—that he showed me photographs of Martin's two "conceptual" exhibitions. To tell the truth, I was not too impressed: I had seen quite similar things in New York, and I couldn't understand his enthusiasm for these works, which contrasted so sharply with his skepticism about what artists across the Atlantic were doing at the time.*

It wasn't until three years later that I "met" Martin again—and then I was smitten forever. It was Lygia Clark, with whom I was very close at the time, who encouraged me to go and see his 1973 exhibition at Daniel Templon's, the one where he officially acknowledged his return to painting. (I believe it was she who had already pointed out to Jean his conceptual exhibitions).

Jean had also advised me to go and see Martin's recent paintings. I may have been a little reluctant—in any case, Lygia dragged me along to this exhibition, which we spent a long time going round together. It was always a pleasure to see an exhibition with her: I regret not having kept a diary to record her always absolutely unexpected remarks.
The exhibition fascinated me. Shortly afterwards, Lygia invited me to dinner at her place with Martin and Michèle: second love at first sight. I remember it as if it were yesterday. We were all sitting on the floor in Lygia's studio on Boulevard Brune, talking until late at night. At one point, I don't know why, we were talking about Jacques Derrida, and when I said that I, like him, was born in Algeria, specifically in Constantine, Michèle was flabbergasted, shouting: "me too!" That was the beginning of a long friendship between the three of us.

—Yve-Alain Bois, spring 2020

1974

- Exhibition of the eighteen paintings of the "73-74" series, Galerie Daniel Templon, Paris.

*The grid (*receptacle grid*), which is a progressive grid, fragments the given surface. It is inscribed in this space, which is already a choice, with its height-width ratio and which ... is divided into squares because that is the most* non-figuring *figure, and because it multiplies or divides as simply as possible.*[38]

- Solo exhibition, Galerie Daniel Templon, Milan.
- *L'Art au présent*, curated by Templon, Palais Galliera, Paris.
- Interview with Millet, followed by her article "Le geste et la règle," *Art press*.[39]

I met Martin Barré and discovered his work in the early 1970s at the Galerie Daniel Templon, where he was one of the gallery's artists and where I was training as an assistant. With his wife Michèle, we gradually became a trio of friends. I remember our regular lunches together at the modest corner bistro near his home in the Saint-Germain-des-Prés neighborhood of the time. Hard-boiled eggs with French mayonnaise for him, salad for me, two glasses of bad wine. Few words. Painting, art. The serenity of being there, friends, together. Good.

In the 1980s, almost a ritual. The series is completed... We are invited to go and view it. After the hugs and exchanges on arrival at Martin and Michèle's home, we sit down and, in a silence that is both imperative and joyful, we look at the new paintings that Martin shows us, slowly, one by one, in silence, without a single comment, but with joy in our eyes. Privileged, unforgettable moments. What's next? Let the party begin!

—Ann Hindry, spring 2020

1975

- Solo exhibition, Lia Rumma/Studio d'Arte, Naples then Rome (works from the "72-73" and "73-74" series). On the occasion of these Italian exhibitions, visits archaeological sites near Naples.

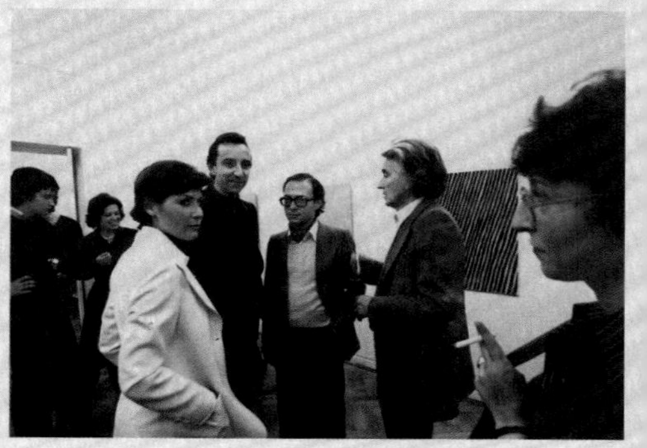

Exhibition opening, Lia Rumma/Studio d'Arte, Naples, 1975. Left to right: Lia Rumma, Lucio Amelio, Daniel Templon, Martin and Michèle Barré

- Exhibition of nine paintings out of the ten forming the "74-75" series, Galerie Peccolo, Cologne.
- *Analytische Malerei*, curated by Honnef and Millet, Galerie La Bertesca, Düsseldorf, with, among other artists, Marc Devade, Raimund Girke, Giorgio Griffa, Carmengloria Morales, Claudio Verna, and Claude Viallat (touring to Nordjyllands Kunstmuseum, Aalborg, and Fyns Stifts Kunstmuseum, Odense).

I paint paintings, proposals in paint, questions about/to painting.[40]

- Following his encounter with Barré, painter Christian Bonnefoi publishes "L'espace, pratique du temps," which analyses Barré's serial painting process, in *Peinture, Cahiers théoriques*, followed the next year by the publication of an interview in *Documents IV-V, Cahiers d'histoire de l'art contemporain*.[41]

1976

- Exhibition of the eighteen paintings from the "75-76" series, Galerie Gérald Piltzer, Paris. Thicker marks than in the previous series, using sanguine and pencil.
- Solo exhibition, Galleria Peccolo, Livorno.
- Acquisition of a first painting, *74-75-B-171×159*, by the Musée d'Art Moderne de la Ville de Paris.

I use a means of "assembly" (the golden section or another) to build the surface best suited to a certain painting process (I always prefer to say painting rather than my painting). Means that the standard formats could not provide me with.[42]

1977

Solo exhibition, Galleria La Polena, Genoa.
Exhibition of the sixteen paintings (eight are on plywood) from the "76-77" series, Galerie Piltzer-Rheims, Paris. New procedure for erasing the paint surface with an electric sander to make the layers smooth and flat before each new application. Color marks are more controlled, sometimes doubling the grid lines.

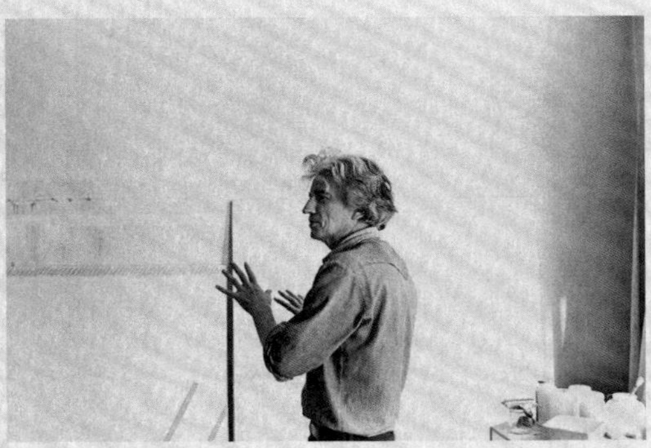

Martin Barré in his studio, Rue Dauphine, Paris, 1977; photograph by Hans Namuth

Aspects historiques du constructivisme et de l'art concret, Musée d'Art Moderne de la Ville de Paris; *Rosc'77. The Poetry of Vision, An International Exhibition of Modern Art and Early Animal Art*, curated by Dominique Fourcade, Hugh Lane Municipal Gallery of Modern Art and National Museum of Ireland, Dublin; XIV International Biennial of São Paulo; *Bilder ohne Bilder*, Rheinisches Landesmuseum, Bonn (interview in the catalogue).
Develops a close relationship with the *Macula* magazine team (published 1976–79). He designs the cover of the second issue (1977) in which Jean Clay publishes "Le dispositif Martin Barré. L'œil onglé," accompanied by an interview with the artist.[43]

> *For me, neither the* constructive, *nor the* useful, *nor the* functional *are in any way opposed to the* poetic, *to the* sensory; *on the contrary, one* engenders *the other.*[44]

1978

The fourteen canvases of the "77-78" series, called *L'Indissociable*, are characterized by more frank and contrasting colors and a clearly marked line. Square, faux-square, and rectangular formats, five bright colors (one per canvas), dashes, diagonal marks. It is from this series that the system of visible repentance disappears definitively.

> *I and Claude Renard, the head of the department (Art and Industry Research department at Renault), agreed that this was an opportunity to keep an ensemble together. From the start, I conceived of this series ["77-78"] as indivisible. In the end it became a big polyptych.*[45]

- *Aspects de l'Art en France. Art 9'78*, Basel Art Fair; XXXVIII Venice Biennale; *Daniel Templon. Dix ans*, Galerie Templon, Paris.
- *Peinture* (1956) enters the Musée des Beaux-Arts de Nantes collection.

1979

- First museum retrospective, at ARC – Musée d'Art Moderne de la Ville de Paris, under the title *Martin Barré*, curated by Suzanne Pagé and Annie Mérie: some fifty works from the 1960s–1970s (tube paintings, spray paintings, canvases from the 1972–77 series and *L'Indissociable*). In the catalogue, Pagé states: "Ignored by art historians and major official events in France, little known by critics and the public, such is Martin Barré, a 55-year-old Parisian painter whose work arouses the loyal enthusiasm of some major international collectors and the demanding attention of young artists attracted by the austere ambition of his work."[46] Texts by Clay and Jean Louis Schefer in the catalogue. Touring to the Henie-Onstad Kunstsenter, Høvikodden (introduction by Moe).

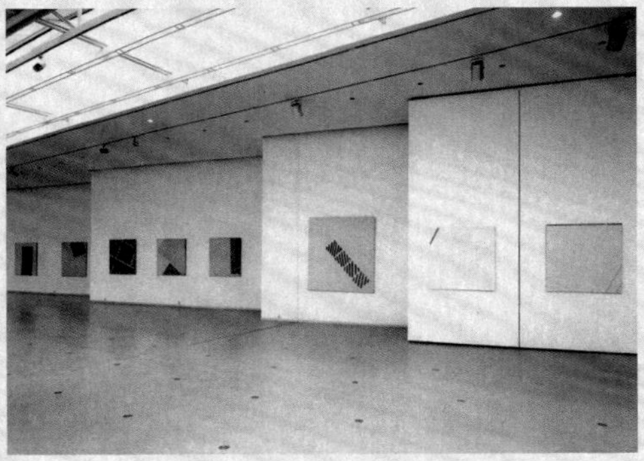

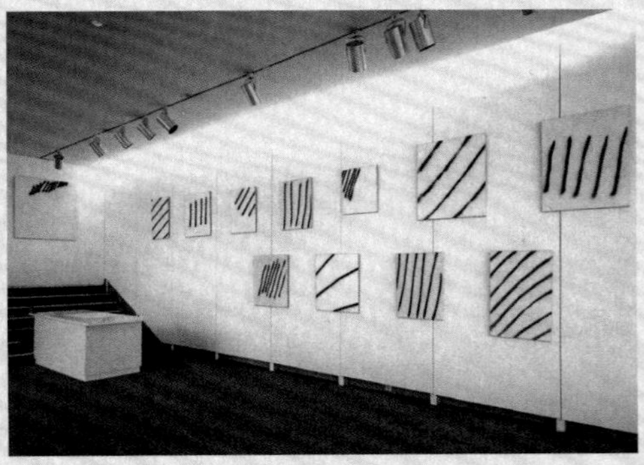

Exhibition views, ARC – Musée d'Art Moderne de la Ville de Paris, Paris, 1979 (see pp. 152–53)

Martin Barré was for me a friend and a master. The urgent preparation of the catalogue for his 1979 exhibition at the Musée d'Art Moderne de la Ville de Paris sealed our friendship. The introduction I wrote then owed much to our discussions and his explanations, full of rigor and elegance. I am singling out the following passage, on page 15, as a contribution to this current book: "In Martin Barré's work ... production is always synchronic*.... The canvases are painted together. The network that ensures the series' coherence is not additional, but a component of it. Each painting owes its morphology and the weaving of its surface to it. These works are fragments in the instant that they emerge as works. Barré's task is precisely to declare, to bring to the level of a system the correlation of the canvases between themselves and to give shape to what was still vague, implicit, potential, or denied in the constructivist generation. Immaterial correlations which, when intertwined, constitute the latticework, the wall* in absentia *where the paintings stand out."*

—Jean Clay, spring 2020

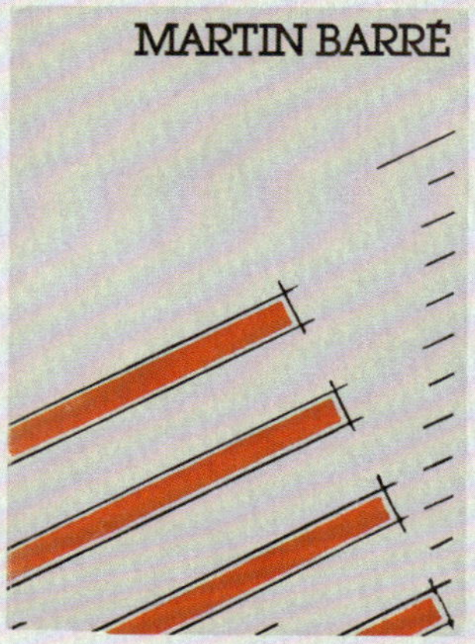

Cover of the exhibition catalogue, ARC – Musée d'Art Moderne de la Ville de Paris, Paris, 1979

Looking back, four decades later, on the experience of organizing Martin Barré's first retrospective at the ARC, many of the analyses I shared in my introduction to the catalogue remain the reasons why his painting continues to convince me, resolutely. I wrote: "What makes it singular is the very special balance it strikes between the economy of vocabulary and the control of syntax (mathematical determination of formats, very precise diagrams of grids, marks, a limited range of colors...), and, if not improvisation, a certain 'play' of the sensory and the unexpected: the line is never hard, the gesture impersonal, the line regular, or systematic, the white uniform." Another quality of this unclassifiable oeuvre, and which undoubtedly explains the reasons for its slow but sure recognition, is its uncompromising character, irreducible to any ease of discourse or approach—which, in my opinion, gives it more than ever today its incisive power.

—Suzanne Pagé, spring 2020

The part of my work that people know best is the period that begins (or begins again) after this "flirtation" [with conceptual art]. There were several exhibitions including the one at the ARC that put the emphasis on what was in fact my newest work at that time, accompanied by some older canvases that Suzanne Pagé wanted.[47]

- *Tendances de l'art en France 1968–1978/9.1: Les partis-pris de Marcelin Pleynet*, ARC – Musée d'Art Moderne de la Ville de Paris.
- Makes the "79" series: eight canvases in faux-square and rectangular formats, one of which is very stretched. It is the first of an ensemble of four successive series (finishing in 1981) based on an orthogonal distribution of rectilinear colored stripes. Dashes and lines bordering the colored stripes in several of these series.

1980

- Solo exhibition, Galerie Ricke, Cologne. Presentation of the "79" series: paintings hung very high and very low, interdependence of the canvases, and integration of the wall in the presentation idea. Bois analyses the series in a review published in *Artistes*.[48]

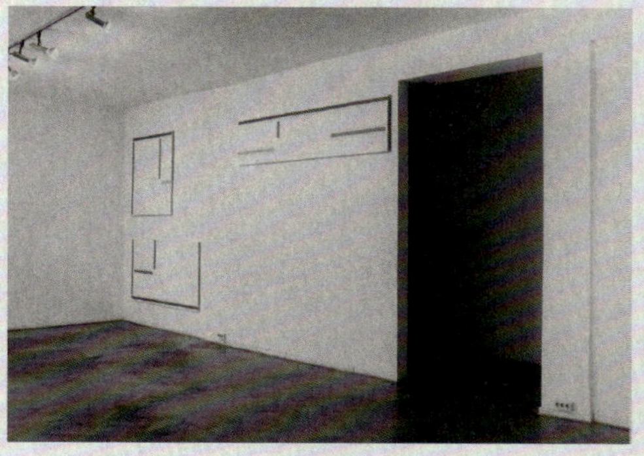
Exhibition view, Galerie Ricke, Cologne, 1980

- Completes the series "79-80," named *L'Indissociée*, because the artist decides not to separate the ten paintings forming it. Paintings arranged in three irregularly spaced rows; small elongated rectangular formats gathered into five pairs. Visual elements reduced to a few colored stripes arranged at right angles and bordered by thin red lines.
- Makes the series "80A" and "80B": four paintings each. All the canvases are faux-squares stretched in height. Wider, vibrant stripes of color.

1981

Joint solo exhibitions: *Martin Barré "79," "79-80," "80A,"* Galerie Jean Chauvelin, and *Martin Barré "80B," "80-81,"* Galerie Gillespie-Laage-Salomon, Paris (first exhibition of Barré with this gallery). The series "80-81" (six paintings in faux-square format) is the last of the ensemble with orthogonal bands. Each painting presents a different framing of a linear figure that never appears in its entirety and opens onto the wall space. The chromatic tones and the evocation of architectural motifs of Roman wall painting have earned this group of paintings the name "Pompeii" series.

Although Mondrian and Malevich meant a great deal to me, Picasso, Léger, and Matisse did not lose their importance, for all that, and they didn't prevent me from looking further than the impressionists who preceded them and from finding in them Vermeer, Hals, and many others, and subsequently a new interest in Egyptian and Greco-Roman antiquity. For, if a distant era has already been a source of new possibilities, why not look again for what perhaps had not yet been properly seen there?[49]

37 Aktuella Konstnärer från Frankrike, Liljevalchs Konsthall, Stockholm; *Paris-Paris. Créations en France 1937–1957*, Centre Pompidou, Paris (*57-100×100-A*). Publication of Bois, "Les énigmes de Martin Barré," *Libération*.[50]

1982

Solo exhibition, Galerie Artline, The Hague: works from 1979–81. *Choix pour aujourd'hui. Regard sur 4 ans d'acquisitions d'art contemporain*, Musée National d'Art Moderne, Centre Pompidou, Paris; *Collection Bernard Lamarche-Vadel*, Musée Sainte-Croix, Poitiers. Publication of Bois, "Martin Barré, Strategies of Concealment," *Art in America*.[51]

1984

- Completes the "82-84" series: eighteen canvases in faux-square format. Arrival of flat colored geometric figures. This series has the triangle, painted in different configurations, as its basic figure. Three colors (red, yellow, green) present in different shades. Appearance of hatched dots to mark the pictorial field.

Behind these canvases [the "82-84" series] there is a whole lot of hidden work that went on for a very long time and that I was never really satisfied with, which is why several series were piled up together. . . . Yes, the result was that the average amount of time spent on each painting was very great, so the output in that period wasn't very big.[52]

- *Carte blanche à Denise René. L'Aventure géométrique et cinétique*, Paris Art Center, Paris; *Autour de Michel Ragon*, Musée des Beaux-Arts, Nantes.

1985

- Exhibition of the "82-84" series organized by Serge Aboukrat, Galerie Anne-Marie Rey, Nice.
- Exhibition of the ten paintings from the "84-85" series, Galerie Gillespie-Laage-Salomon, Paris. Rectangular or square formats often larger than the previous ones, three colors. The only figure is a right-angled triangle of constant dimensions. The spatial marking is entrusted to black dashes as thick as the borders of the triangles. In the presentation at the Galerie Gillespie-Laage-Salomon, the hanging height is higher than usual.

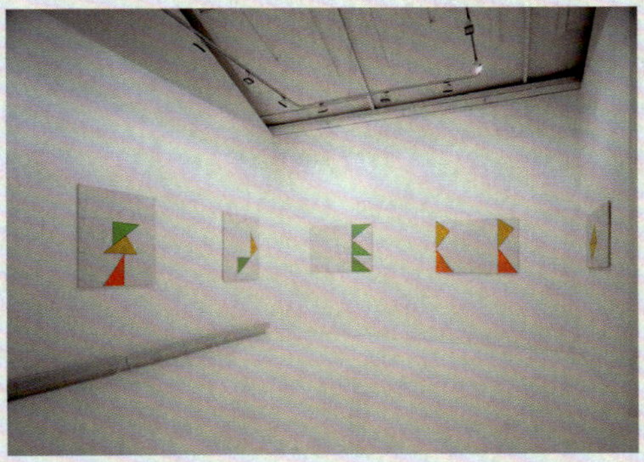

Exhibition view, Galerie Gillespie-Laage-Salomon, Paris, 1985

Martin Barré, a "radical abstract": these are the first words that come to mind when I think of him. I met him in 1980. His solitary and reserved personality was not always predisposed to speeches. This was a major trait of his personality, which corresponded to his "meditative painting." His working method was very specific to him. I remember the way he conceived his exhibitions, especially the six we hosted with Nancy Gillespie and Elisabeth de Laage in our gallery between 1981 and 1992. He loved to hang his paintings. He always defined his exhibitions according to the site, just as he determined the precise number of paintings for each of his series. His hangings transformed the space and sometimes raised a lot of questions, as when he hung the "86-87" series in 1987, playing with different heights. During the 1980s, which saw the reawakening of figurative painting, his successive "series" separated him from the art world of his time. His stubbornness in pursuing this radical abstraction is today recognized for its true worth.

—Gabrielle Salomon, spring 2020

- *6 Peintres français d'aujourd'hui*, Seoul Gallery, Seoul.
- "Barré" section in *Art press*. Jacques Henric: "I consider Martin Barré to be one of the most important contemporary painters. Few works have such rigor, such cogency";[53] text by Schefer and interview with Millet.[54] For Ann Hindry, Barré is "one of the great artists, and the great discreet ones, of abstraction and French painting. . . . Unclassifiable and always ahead of the history of painting of his time."[55]

1986

- *Qu'est-ce que l'art français?*, curated by Lamarche-Vadel, Centre Régional d'Art Contemporain Midi-Pyrénées, Labège-Innopole (Toulouse), interview published in the accompanying catalogue; *Hors tendances. Martin Barré, Jean-Pierre Bertrand, Christian Bonnefoi, Daniel Buren, François Rouan*, curated by Millet, Galleria Vivita, Florence (touring to the Fundacão Calouste Gulbenkian, Lisbon); *Trends in Geometric Abstract Art. Gift from the Riklis Collection of McCrory Corporation and Works from the Tel Aviv Museum Collection*, The Tel Aviv Museum.
- Article by Claire Stoullig in *Artstudio*.[56]

When I paint, I paint. I don't tell myself I'm doing French painting. Perhaps what can make me think of myself as very French now is that I haven't really looked at America—except as a spectator.[57]

1987

- Exhibition of the ten paintings from the "86-87" series, Galerie Laage-Salomon, Paris. Square canvases in a unique format. A "ghost square" in the center and colored right-angled triangles in the corners. Four colors (blue, red, green, yellow) in different shades on each canvas but always assigned to the same angle. The canvases are hung at various heights on the walls of the Galerie Laage-Salomon.

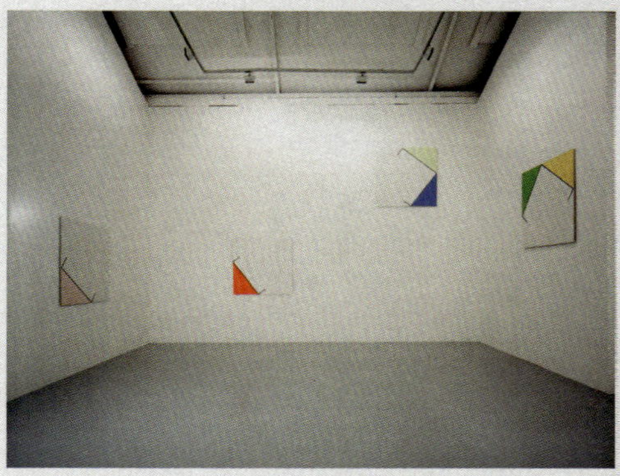

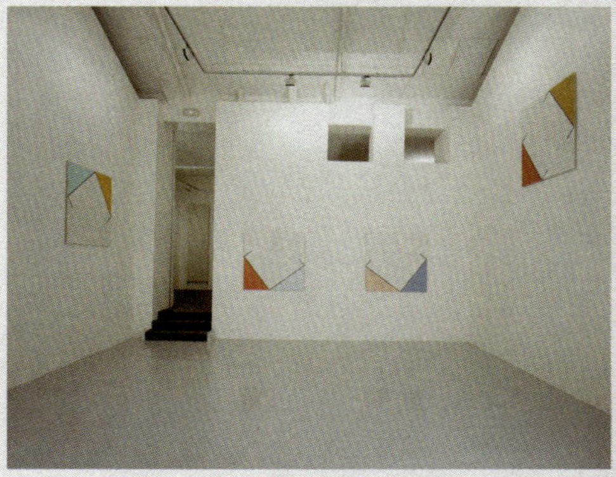

Exhibition views, Galerie Laage-Salomon, Paris, 1987

- Exhibition *Martin Barré. Œuvres des années 50–60*, Galerie Jacques Barbier, Paris, and presentation at FIAC 87, Grand Palais, Paris (works from 1956–62, Galerie Jacques Barbier; works from the 1970s–1980s, Galerie Laage-Salomon).
- Articles by Hindry in *Galeries Magazine*[58] and Anne Tronche in *Opus International*.[59] Interview with Jean-Marie Floch in *Actes sémiotiques. Bulletin*.[60]

- Starts the final series. Preeminent role of color. New geometric figures attached to the edges of the canvas and surrounded by different borders in each series. Disappearance of any markings of the space. White background, showing different shades, from one series to another.

1988

- Solo exhibitions: Galerie Vega, Liège; Galerie Jacques Girard, Toulouse.
- *Art français contemporain. 1960–1987*, Salle Chipka, Sofia (touring to Bucharest, Iaşi); *Les Années 50*, Centre Pompidou, Paris (*59-120×110-B*, under the title *Peinture*)
- Publication of a section in *Eighty Magazine* with articles by Catherine Flohic and Jean-Luc Chalumeau.[61]
- Moves to Rue du Bourg-Tibourg.
- Is awarded the Grand Prix National des Arts.

1989

- Retrospective exhibition *Martin Barré*, showing sixty-one works from 1954 to 1987, Musée des Beaux-Arts, Nantes, curated by Marcel-André Stalter (touring to the Musée des Beaux-Arts, Tourcoing; Galeries des Ponchettes and Galerie d'Art Contemporain, Nice): catalogue with texts by Stalter, Bois, Hindry, and Stoullig.

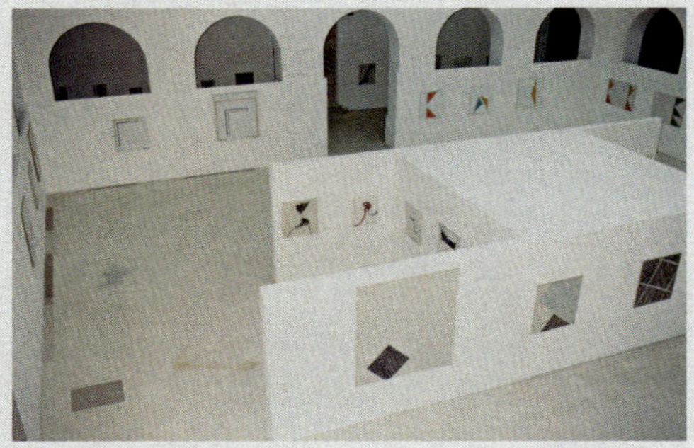

Exhibition view, Musée des Beaux-Arts, Nantes, 1989

- Exhibition of the fourteen paintings from the "87-89" series, Galerie Laage-Salomon, Paris. Rectangular formats (one of which is very elongated horizontally, reminiscent of a predella) and a square. On each canvas, four colored squares with a truncated corner are placed on two edges of the painting. Four bright colors but a maximum of three per canvas, usually two. For each color, the square is cut at a different angle. The presentation of the canvases at different heights transposes the rhythmic effect of the color sequences on each canvas to a larger scale (catalogue with text by Hindry).

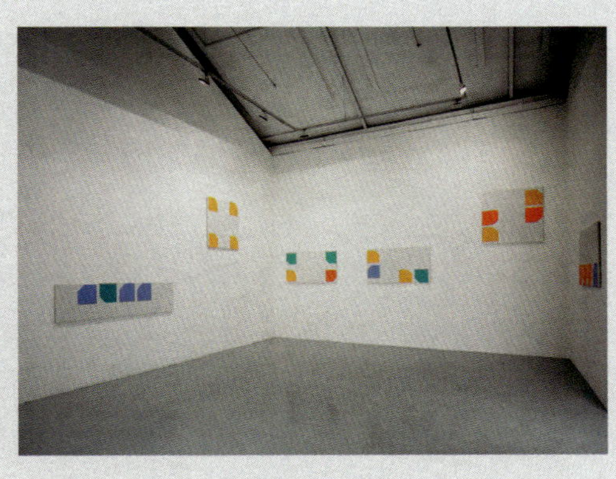

Exhibition view, Galerie Laage-Salomon, Paris, 1989

In the context of a solo exhibition, I don't like someone to do the hanging for me, first of all because I really like to do it—I think I do it well, that's how it should be done and not any other way—and then because it's really an "installation."[62]

- Parallel solo exhibitions: Galerie Barbier-Beltz, Paris (*Œuvres anciennes*), and Galerie Daniel Templon, Paris (*Œuvres des années 60*).
- *Permanence et vitalité de l'art abstrait*, issued by Maeght, Montrouge, to accompany the publication of *L'Art abstrait. Tome 5: 1970–1987* by Ragon and Marcelin Pleynet;[63] *Liberté et Égalité. Freiheit und Gleichheit. Wiederholung und Abweichung in der neueren französischen Kunst*, Museum Folkwang, Essen, and Kunstmuseum, Winterthur, curated by Erich Franz and Dieter Schwarz; *Exposition inaugurale*, Fondation Daniel Templon, Fréjus; *Profils d'une collection*, Musée d'Art Moderne, Villeneuve-d'Ascq.
- Commissioned for the Grande Arche de la Défense, the large polyptych *89-175×350* uses the same pattern as the "87-89" series, enlarged and painted in all four colors.

1990

- Exhibition of the eight paintings from the "89-90" series, Galerie Laage-Salomon, FIAC 90, Grand Palais, Paris. Rectangular formats. The motif is a rectangular trapeze moored to the upper or lower edges of the canvas, which is to be found in the following three series. Here, trapezes of identical dimensions and similar to truncated triangles. Same limitation of colors per canvas as in the previous series, but according to a distribution by zones: at the top the warm hues, at the bottom the cold ones.
- *Polyptyques. Le tableau multiple du Moyen Âge au vingtième siècle*, Musée du Louvre, Paris (*60-T-45*); *L'Art en France. 1945–1990*, Fondation Daniel Templon, Musée Temporaire, Fréjus.
- Publication of an interview with Catherine Lawless in *Les Cahiers du Musée national d'art moderne*[64] on the occasion of the acquisition of two spray paintings by the Centre Pompidou (*65-H-L-78×74*, *67-Z-26-70×53*).

1991

- Exhibition of the fourteen paintings from the "90-91" series, Galerie Interface, Nîmes. Rectangular formats and one square. Two colors: blue and yellow. Half of the paintings are horizontal, showing only one row of figures. Two different sizes of trapeze. For the hanging, figures of the same color are aligned from one canvas to another on the wall to create a kind of frieze.
- Exhibition of the ten paintings from the "91" series at the 1st Lyon Contemporary Art Biennale, *L'Amour de l'art. Une exposition de l'art contemporain en France*. Rectangular formats precisely conceived for the exhibition space, two kinds of predella, two colors: blue and red.

I work less and less with violent colors. . . . There is a soothing effect as if to calm things down. Indeed, I now want form and background to be more and more on the same plane. But if the colors are too bright and the backgrounds too light, it creates different grounds. . . . For me, painting is flat and I don't try to move away from that aspect.[65]

1992

- Exhibition of the twelve paintings from the "91-92" series, Galerie Laage-Salomon, Paris. "Predella" formats and one faux-square, three colors: blue, yellow, red.

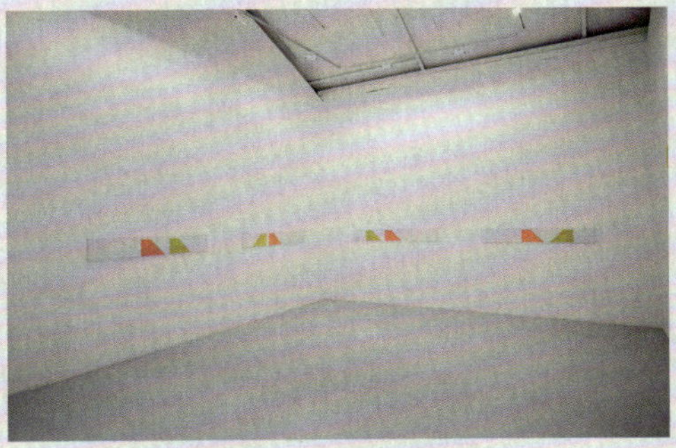

Exhibition view, Galerie Laage-Salomon, Paris, 1992

- Publication of Stalter article, "Martin Barré: tableaux '90-91' et '91'," *Revue du Nord*.[66]
- Makes the "92A" and "92B" series, respectively four paintings, three colors: yellow, red, green, and eight paintings, three colors: blue, yellow, red. Both feature faux-square formats and the rectangle replaces the trapeze. Presentation of the "92A" series in the exhibition *Das offene Bild. Aspekte der Moderne in Europa nach 1945*, Westfälisches Landesmuseum, Münster, touring to the Museum der Bildenden Künste, Leipzig, 1993 (catalogue with text by Hindry).
- French Pavilion of the Universal Exposition of Seville.

1993

- *Martin Barré. Les années quatre-vingt*, curated by Alfred Pacquement, Galerie Nationale du Jeu de Paume, Paris. Sixty-four paintings from 1979 to 1992, including the "92B" series. The hanging of the works is orchestrated by Barré, in collaboration with the architect Antoine Stinco. Barré relates the space of the paintings to the architectural space. Catalogue with texts by Pacquement, Millet, and Schwarz.

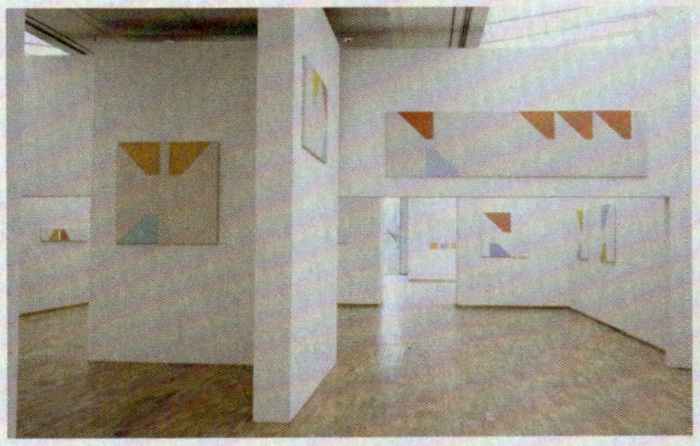

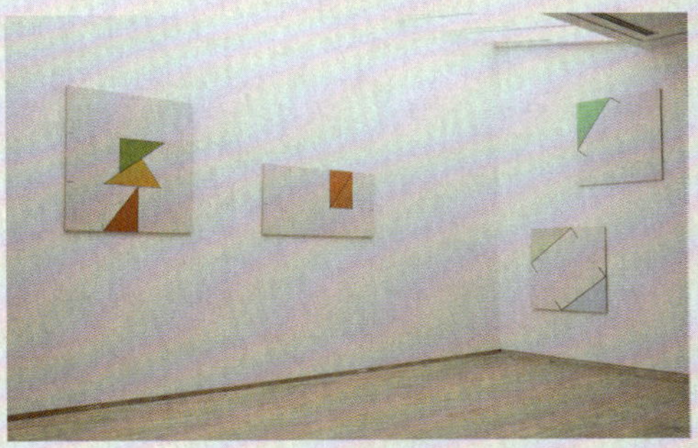

Exhibition views, Galerie Nationale du Jeu de Paume, Paris, 1993 (see p. 204)

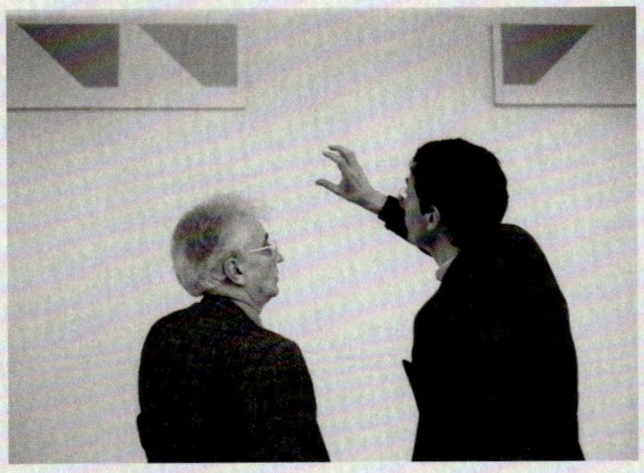

Martin Barré and Alfred Pacquement, Paris, 1993

Inviting Martin Barré to exhibit at the Jeu de Paume was, for this new institution, in keeping with the logic of a program partly devoted to abstraction. And more particularly to a certain family of painters oscillating between intuitive geometry and sensitive pictoriality such as Ellsworth Kelly, James Bishop, and Helmut Federle, who succeeded one another in these rooms. When it came to Martin Barré, the option of an exhibition devoted to the 1980s, and thus following on neatly from the ARC exhibition, was decided by mutual agreement between us. In addition to the coherence of the presentation of the different series, it resulted in an "unruly" hanging designed by Martin Barré and work on the exhibition space, designed in collaboration with the architect Antoine Stinco.

*Particularly remarkable
were the horizontal "predellas"
presented on lintels.*
—Alfred Pacquement, spring 2020

- Publication by Flammarion of the monograph *Martin Barré* by Yve-Alain Bois.

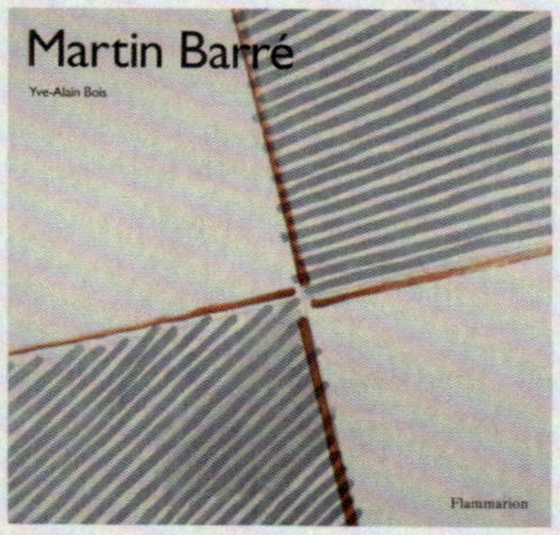

Cover of Yve-Alain Bois, *Martin Barré*, Flammarion, Paris, 1993

The artist dies on July 8.
Among the homages, Hervé Gauville in *Libération* ("Martin Barré jusqu'à l'effacement") and tributes from the artist's friends in *Art press*.[67] For Schefer: "Over the years, I realized that Martin was part of his painting; that he was even its character and figure; managing these angles, admitting little by little colors with this combination of nobility, matured science, gentleness, and a distinctly childlike charm: his body was there. I can no longer understand his painting in any other way"; for Stalter: "For this man who was apparently so non-physical, and who had very simple tastes, hidden from all ostentation, painting was an extraordinary playground, from the most finely intellectualized to the most sensory at times, and this is true for all periods. The quality of the adjustments, the variety of which is in no way tainted, is the major distinction of his work; one feels at ease there, as in Martin's own home, where nothing was left to chance."

Manifeste. Une histoire parallèle, 1960–1990, Centre Pompidou, Paris.

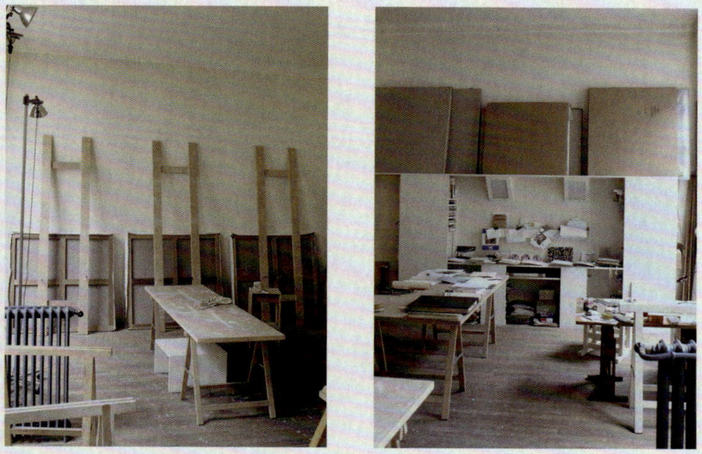
Martin Barré's studio views, Rue du Bourg-Tibourg, Paris, 1993

1994

- *Martin Barré*, Galerie Laage-Salomon: works from the 1980s–1990s.

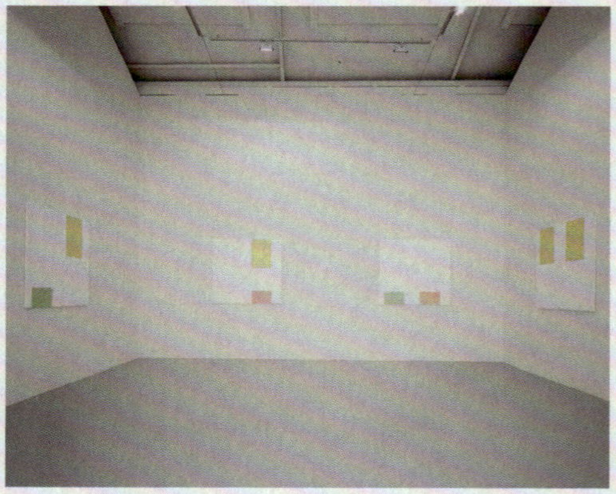
Exhibition view, Galerie Laage-Salomon, Paris, 1994

- Yasmina Reza's successful play *Art* is premiered at the Comédie des Champs-Élysées, Paris. The white monochrome painting on stage used as a pretext for a quarrel between three friends is inspired by *76-77-B-147,5×140* (see p. 131), belonging to a collector friend of the author. The mockery targeting the work in the play provokes perplexity and consternation among art lovers.

1995

- Three paintings from the "92B" series enter the Centre Pompidou collection, Paris.
- *Les Bords de l'œuvre*, Musée Matisse, Nice; *MNAM-CCI. Acquisitions 1993–1995*, Centre Pompidou, Paris; *Passions privées. Collections particulières d'art moderne et contemporain en France*, Musée d'Art Moderne de la Ville de Paris (exhibited painting in the collection of Serge Aboukrat).

1997

- Joint exhibitions *Martin Barré. Peintures des années 60*, works from the 1960s with some from the 1950s, Galerie Denise René – Espace Marais, and *Martin Barré. Peintures de 1972 à 1992*, Galerie Laage-Salomon, Paris.

1998

- *Rendezvous. Masterpieces of the Centre Georges Pompidou and the Guggenheim Museums*, curated by Bernard Blistène and Lisa Dennison, Guggenheim Museum, New York; *L'École de Paris? 1945–1964*, curated by Bernard Ceysson and Jean-Luc Koltz, Fondation Musée d'Art Moderne Grand-Duc Jean – Musée National d'Histoire et d'Art, Luxembourg.

1999

- Solo exhibition, *Martin Barré. Pintura*, Galeria António Prates, Lisbon: works from 1957–67.
- *La Peinture après l'abstraction. Martin Barré, Jean Degottex, Raymond Hains, Simon Hantaï, Jacques Villeglé, 1955–1975*, curated by Alain Cueff and Béatrice Parent, Musée d'Art Moderne de la Ville de Paris.

2000

- *Le Musée du xxe siècle de Michel Ragon*, Hôtel du Département de la Vendée, La Roche-sur-Yon.

2001

- *As Painting. Division and Displacement*, Wexner Center for the Arts, The Ohio State University, Columbus: an exhibition that revived interest in Barré's work in the United States.

2002

- *Ils sont aussi de grands Maîtres*, Galerie Applicat-Prazan, Paris.

2004

- *Beyond Geometry. Experiments in Form, 1940s–1970s*, Los Angeles County Museum of Art, Los Angeles, touring to Miami Art Museum, Miami.

2005

- Foundation of the Association des Amis de Martin Barré, responsible for the preparation of the artist's catalogue raisonné under the general editorship of Bois and Hindry (to be published in 2021–22).
- Solo exhibitions: *Martin Barré*, Galerie Guislain–États d'Art, Paris, works from the 1950s–1990s; *Martin Barré. Works from 1960–1967*, Sutton Lane Gallery, London.

2006

- *Idées de la peinture. Hommage à Martin Barré*, curated by Jean-Pierre Criqui, first exhibition dedicated to Barré at the Galerie Nathalie Obadia, Paris: works from the 1960s–1990s, exhibited together with paintings by Christian Bonnefoi, Raoul De Keyser, Peter Halley, On Kawara, Robert Mangold, Albert Oehlen, Bernard Piffaretti, Pascal Pinaud, and Christopher Wool (catalogue with text by Criqui).

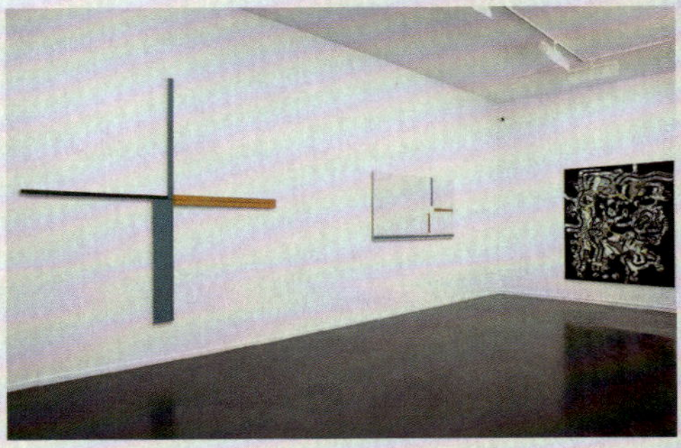

Exhibition view, Galerie Nathalie Obadia, Paris, 2006

- *L'Envolée lyrique. Paris 1945–1956*, Musée du Luxembourg, Paris; *La Force de l'Art*, curated by Blistène (chief curator), Grand Palais, Paris.

2007

- *Martin Barré. Peintures 1960–1992*, Galerie Daniel Buchholz, Cologne.
- *Bajo la bomba. El jazz de la guerra de imágenes transatlántica, 1946–1956*, curated by Serge Guilbaut and Manuel J. Borja-Villel, MACBA, Barcelona.

2008

- *Works by Martin Barré*, works from 1962–91, organized by Thea Westreich and Ethan Wagner, Andrew Kreps Gallery, New York, on the occasion of the publication of the English edition of Bois's 1993 monograph on Barré.
- *Oranges and Sardines. Conversations on Abstract Painting*, Hammer Museum, Los Angeles: Wade Guyton, one of the six curator-artists of the exhibition, includes Barré among his reference artists in a room where his work is exhibited next to that of Felix Gonzalez-Torres.

2010

Martin Barré, "91" ("91" series), Galerie Nathalie Obadia (catalogue with text by Erik Verhagen). *Le Tableau. French Abstraction and Its Affinities*, curated by Joe Fyfe, Cheim & Read Gallery, New York, based on an idea formulated in his article "Martin Barré. A French Alternative," *Art in America*, 2009.[68] *61-T-41* and *76-77-B-102,5×100* enter the Städel Museum collection, Frankfurt; *60-T-26* enters the Musée Fabre collection, Montpellier.

2011

Martin Barré, "91" ("91" series), Andrew Kreps Gallery, New York.

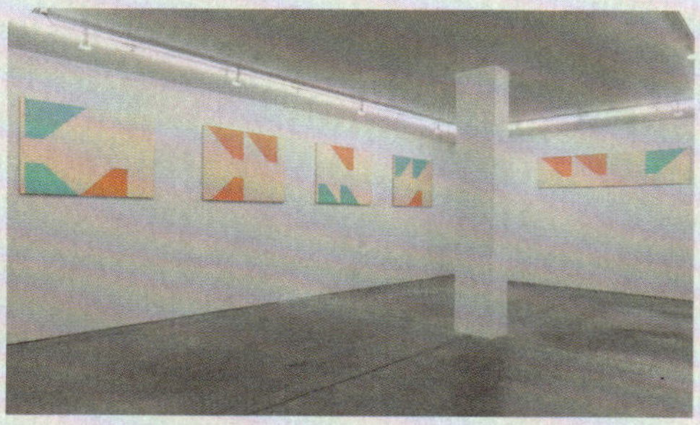

Exhibition view, Andrew Kreps Gallery, New York, 2011

Les Sujets de l'abstraction. Peinture non-figurative de la seconde École de Paris, 1946–1962. 101 chefs-d'œuvre de la Fondation Gandur pour l'Art, curated by Éric de Chassey, Musée Rath, Geneva, touring to the Musée Fabre, Montpellier. Publication of Bois, "Leap Year. Martin Barré's *Greenwich* and *60-T-44*," (works in the Guggenheim Museum collection), *Artforum*.[69]

2012

Déplacer, déplier, découvrir. La peinture en actes, 1960–1999. Simon Hantaï, Martin Barré, Marc Devade, Jean Degottex, Michel Parmentier, LaM – Lille Métropole Musée d'Art Moderne, d'Art Contemporain et d'Art Brut, Villeneuve-d'Ascq (review in *Artforum*, vol. 51, no. 2, by Molly Warnock); *Art of Another Kind. International Abstraction and the Guggenheim, 1949–1960*, Guggenheim Museum, New York.

2013

- *Martin Barré. 1972–1977: les années décisives*, Galerie Nathalie Obadia (catalogue with texts by Hindry and Paul Galvez); *Martin Barré. Paintings and Photo-Conceptual Works, 1967–1976*, curated by Galvez, Galerie Daniel Buchholz, Cologne: first presentation of the conceptual works since 1970; *Martin Barré/ R.H. Quaytman. Arrhythmia (A Tale of Many Squares)*, curated by Galvez, Galerie Nathalie Obadia, Paris; *Martin Barré, Fred Sandback*, curated by Bois, Galerie Hubert Winter, Vienna.

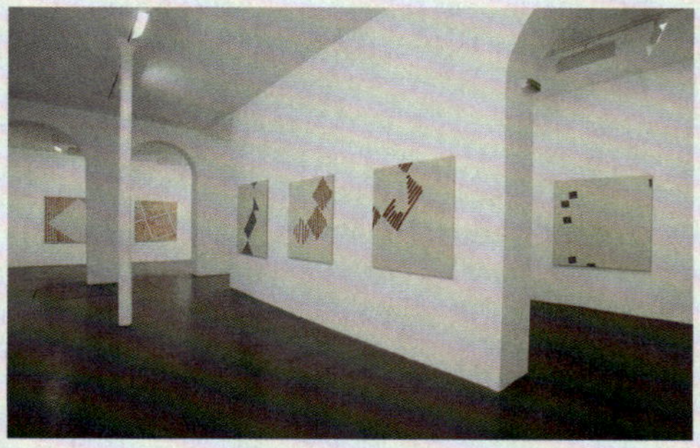

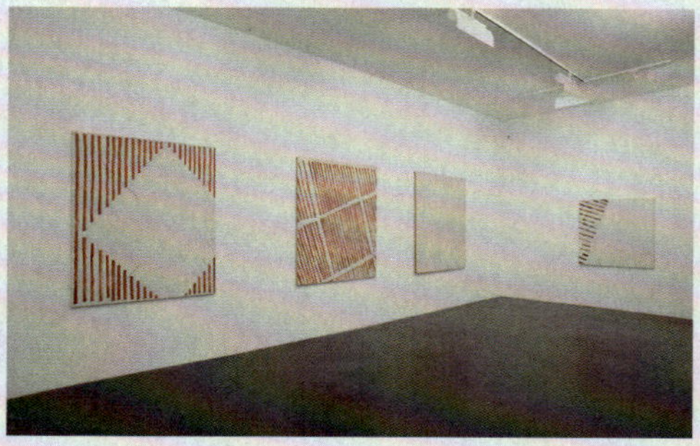

Exhibition views, Galerie Nathalie Obadia, Paris, 2013

- *Steven Parrino/Armleder, Barré, Buren, Hantaï, Mosset, Parmentier, Toroni*, Gagosian Gallery, Paris.

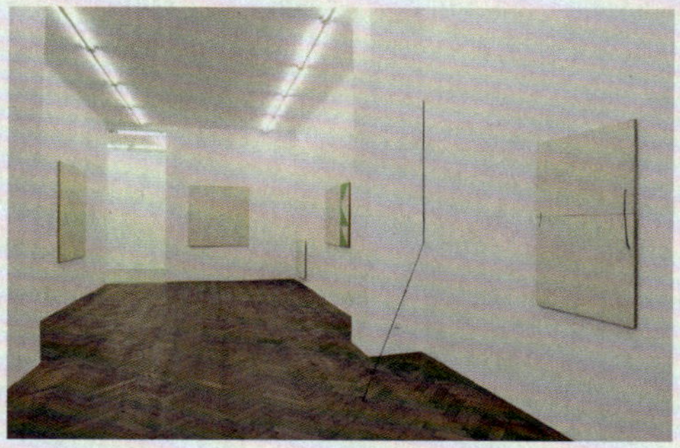

Exhibition view, Galerie Hubert Winter, Vienna, 2013

2014

- *La Peinture ou comment s'en débarrasser* (Martin Barré, Marcia Hafif, Fabio Mauri, Olivier Mosset), curated by de Chassey, Villa Medici, Rome (catalogue with text by de Chassey)
- Acquisition of *67-F-13* by the Art Institute, Chicago.

2015

- *Martin Barré et Bernard Piffaretti*, curated by Blandine Chavanne and Alice Fleury, based on an idea by de Chassey, Musée des Beaux-Arts, Nantes.

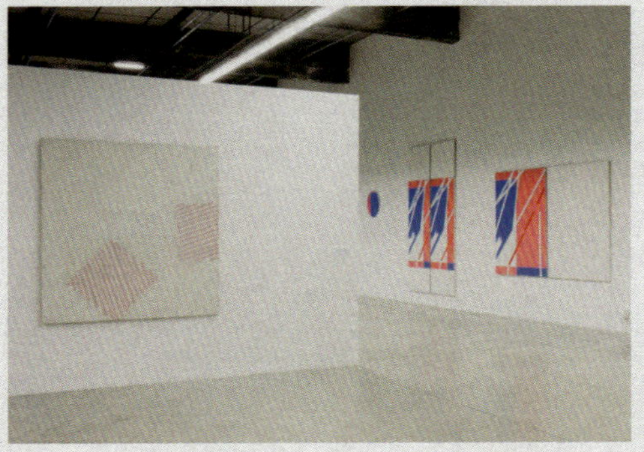

Exhibition view, Musée des Beaux-Arts, Nantes, 2015

I see the exhibition in Nantes in 2015 that brought together my works with those of Martin Barré as a "pas de deux" with this current one. One work in particular (Untitled, *2014), created specifically for that encounter, bears witness to it, in a sign of complicity. This painting in three elements constitutes a single painting, composed of different framings. More than a series of paintings, here it is the series that makes a painting; each piece in it is still unfinished. Barré said he was confronted with unfinished paintings that he was trying to bring to a different unfinished state. The pictorial situations chosen in this triptych refer to the hatching and dotting practiced by Martin Barré in the 1970s. The white lines are negative reminders of his spray paintings of the mid-1960s. The painting continues outside the surface, "inducing" movement and displacement. The triangular shapes could be the tracings of the perimeters of the triangulations of the 1990s. Finally, the blue/pink bichrome painting alludes to the divisions of those same years. A title—related to Jacques Demy, also a native of Nantes—proposed for this exhibition had been discarded. However, the clues for me went further than the Demy and Nantes pairing: one should look again at the credits of* Umbrellas of Cherbourg*, which casually "illustrates" the fundamental figures of Martin Barré's oeuvre—plane, place, displacement, and play, all crowned by the colored "triangulations" here represented by the umbrellas. In my opinion, in this exhibition, Martin Barré's paintings had all the ingredients of a "moving image."*

—Bernard Piffaretti, spring 2020

- *Collected by Thea Westreich Wagner and Ethan Wagner*, Whitney Museum, New York; *Dead Line. Mosset, Barré, Tinguely*, dialogue between the collections of the Musée d'Art et d'Histoire, Geneva, and the Fondation Gandur pour l'Art, Musée d'Art et d'Histoire, Geneva.

2016

- *La Collection Thea Westreich Wagner et Ethan Wagner*, Centre Pompidou, showing six paintings by Barré.
Gift and promised gift from Thea Westreich Wagner and Ethan Wagner to complement the ensemble of works by Barré in the Centre Pompidou collection.

2017

- *Martin Barré. '57'59'60'65*, Kunsthandel Wolfgang Werner, Berlin.
- *61-T-36* enters the Centre Pompidou collection thanks to a gift of Marie-Aline Prat.

2018

- *Martin Barré*, works from the 1960s–1990s, Matthew Marks Gallery, New York.

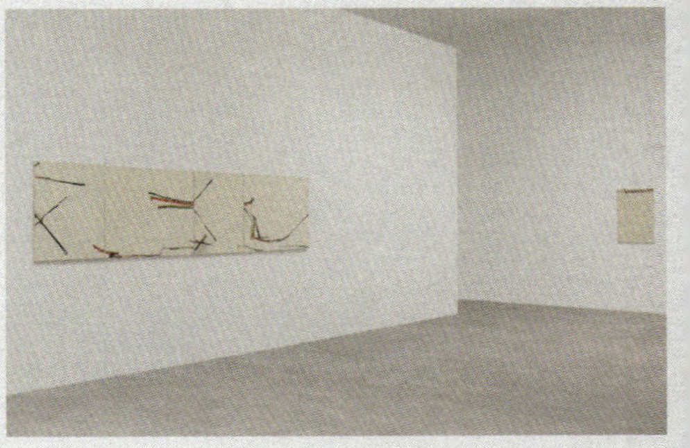

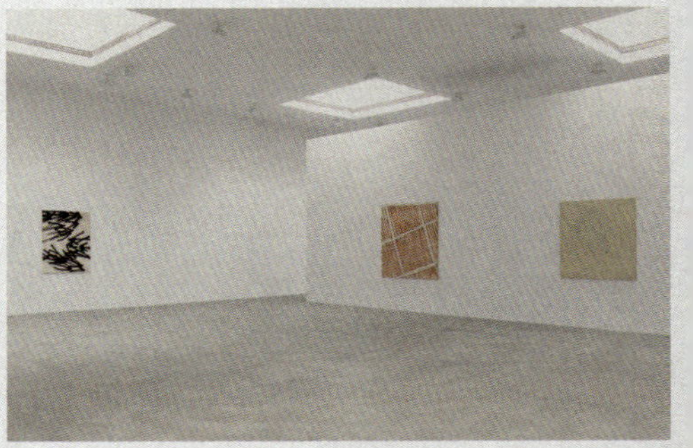

Exhibition views, Matthew Marks Gallery, New York, 2018

2019

Retrospective exhibition *Martin Barré*, curated by Clément Dirié, MAMCO, Geneva.

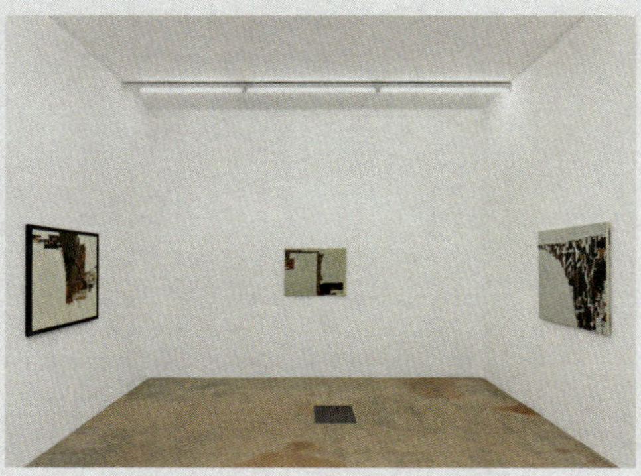

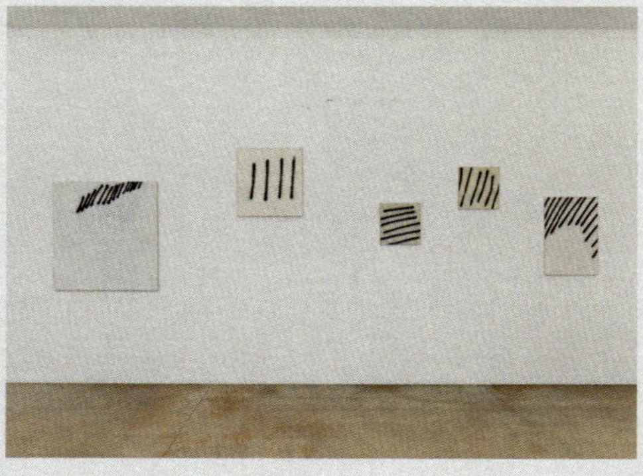

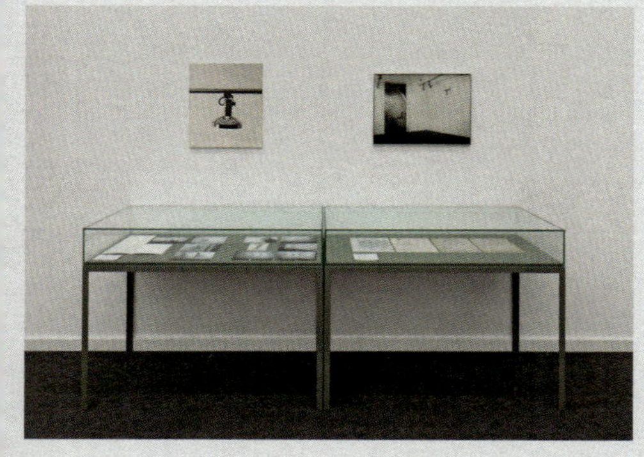

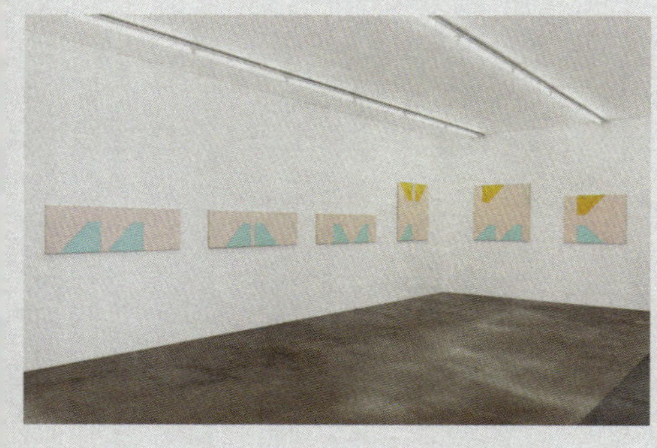

Exhibition views, MAMCO, Geneva, 2019

Artistic Licence. Six Takes on the Guggenheim Collections, Guggenheim Museum, New York: *Greenwich* (1957) features in the selection made by Richard Prince, one of the curators of this show for which each guest artist chose works from the museum's collection.

2020

- Retrospective exhibition *Martin Barré*, curated by Michel Gauthier, Centre Pompidou, Paris. First showing since 1979 of the series *L'Indissociable* at the Musée National d'Art Moderne. Joint catalogue published by MAMCO and the Centre Pompidou, with Flammarion, featuring texts by Bois, Criqui, Dirié, Gauthier, Hindry, and Warnock.

NOTES

1

Catherine Millet, “Interview with Martin Barré” (1974), repr. in Yve-Alain Bois, *Martin Barré* (Cologne, New York, and Paris: Galerie Daniel Buchholz, Andrew Kreps Gallery, Galerie Nathalie Obadia, and Thea Westreich/Ethan Wagner, 2008), 261.

2

Martin Barré, interview with Jean Grenier for RTF, December 1959, quoted in Karl K. Ringstrøm, “Barré,” in *Quatre peintres de l'École de Paris*, exh. cat. (Oslo: Galleri Kaare Berntsen, 1960), 10.

3

Martin Barré, in Millet, “Interview,” 262–63.

4

Martin Barré, in Michel Ragon, “Martin Barré,” *xx*^{e} *siècle* 14 (June 1960): 23.

5

Martin Barré, in Millet, “Interview,” 263.

6

Ibid.

7

Michel Ragon, *L'Aventure de l'art abstrait* (Paris: Robert Laffont, 1956), 205–8.

8

Michel Ragon, in *Seize peintres de la Jeune École de Paris* (Paris: Le Musée de Poche, 1956), 36–37.

9

Annette Michelson, “Paris Chronicle,” *Art Digest* 32, no. 4 (January 1958): 17.

10

Michel Seuphor, *Dictionnaire de la peinture abstraite* (Paris: Hazan, 1957), 127.

11

Martin Barré, in Millet, “Interview,” 264.

12

Ole Henrik Moe, “Corneille og Barré, en ny generasjon,” *Kunsten Idag* 3 (1958): 15–31, 55.

13

Martin Barré, in Catherine Lawless, “Acquisitions. Entretien avec Martin Barré,” *Les Cahiers du Musée national d'art moderne* 31 (Spring 1990): 118.

14

Martin Barré, in Ragon, “Martin Barré,” 23.

15

Martin Barré, in Millet, “Interview,” 263.

16

Ibid., p. 264

17

Pierre Restany, “Martin Barré,” *Cimaise* 51 (January–February 1961): 98.

18

Martin Barré, in Millet, “Interview,” 263.

19

Michel Ragon, *Martin Barré et la poétique de l'espace / Martin Barré and the Poetics of Space* (Paris: Galerie Arnaud, 1960), 45.

20

Bois, *Martin Barré*, 24.

21

Martin Barré, in Millet, “Interview,” 261.

22

Gérard Gassiot-Talabot “Les Métamorphoses nécessaires,” *Aujourd'hui. Art et architecture* 40 (January 1963): 19.

23

Martin Barré, in Millet, “Interview,” 263.

24

Marc Albert-Levin, “Martin Barré ou les malheurs de la vertu,” *Cimaise* 67 (January–February–March 1964): 48.

25

Martin Barré, in Lawless, “Acquisitions,” 117.

26

Martin Barré, in Catherine Millet, “M. B. ‘Elsewhere’” (1985), repr. in Bois, *Martin Barré*, 272.

27

Martin Barré, in Millet, “Interview,” 265.

28

Ibid.

29

Ibid., p. 266

30

Tzvetan Todorov, *Martin Barré*, exh. cat. (Paris: Galerie Daniel Templon, 1969), n.p.

31

Ibid.

32

Martin Barré, in Lawless, “Acquisitions,” 117.

33

Martin Barré, in Millet, “Interview,” 266.

34

Catherine Millet, “Martin Barré,” *Opus International* 17 (April 1970): 46–47; Millet, “L'art conceptuel comme sémiotique de l'art,” *VH 101* 3 (Fall 1970): 3–21.

35

Martin Barré, in Millet, “M. B. ‘Elsewhere,’” 274.

36

Tzvetan Todorov, “Une peinture figurale,” in *Martin Barré*, exh. cat. (Paris: Galerie Daniel Templon, 1973), n.p.

37

Martin Barré, in Millet, “M. B. ‘Elsewhere,’” 272.

38

Martin Barré, in Millet, “Interview,” 266.

39

Catherine Millet, “Martin Barré,” interview, and “Le geste et la règle,” *Art press* 12 (June–August 1974): 6–7 and 8–10.

40

Martin Barré, interview with Christian Bonnefoi, “Entretien avec Martin Barré,” *Documents IV–V, Cahiers d'histoire de l'art contemporain*, March 1976, 70.

41

Christian Bonnefoi, “L'espace, pratique du temps,” *Peinture, Cahiers théoriques* 10–11 (1975): 186–88; Bonnefoi, “Entretien avec Martin Barré,” 67–72.

42

Martin Barré, in Jean Clay, “Questions à Martin Barré,” *Macula* 2 (1977): 78.

43

Jean Clay, “Le dispositif Martin Barré. L'œil onglé,” *Macula* 2 (1977): 67–83.

44

Bonnefoi, “Entretien avec Martin Barré,” 70.

45

Martin Barré, in Millet, “M. B. ‘Elsewhere,’” 273.

46

Suzanne Pagé, introduction, in Pagé et al, *Martin Barré*, exh. cat. (Paris: ARC – Musée d'Art Moderne de la Ville de Paris, 1979), 2.

47

Martin Barré, in Millet, “M. B. ‘Elsewhere,’” 271.

48

Yve-Alain Bois, “Martin Barré, Gal. Ricke, Cologne,” *Artistes* 4 (April–May 1980): 41–43.

49

Martin Barré, in Jacques Sauvageot, ed., *Peindre en 1987*, Supplément au Calendrier des expositions d'art contemporain en Bretagne et Pays de la Loire, no. 8 (Nantes: Artelier-Cas d'urgence, 1987), n.p.

50

Yve-Alain Bois, “Les énigmes de Martin Barré,” *Libération*, November 23, 1981.

51

Yve-Alain Bois, “Martin Barré, Strategies of Concealment,” *Art in America* 70, no. 4 (April 1982): 126–28.

52

Martin Barré, in Millet, “M. B. ‘Elsewhere,’” 274.

53

Jacques Henric, “Martin Barré, peintre de la fin du 2e millénaire après J.-C.,” *Art press* 96 (October 1985): 8–10, here 8.

54

Jean Louis Schefer, “L'espace écarte les figures,” and Catherine Millet, “M. B. ‘Ailleurs,’” *Art press* 96 (October 1985): 11–12 and 13–14 respectively.

55

Ann Hindry, “L'abstraction présente,” *City Magazine* 17 (December 1985): 38.

56

Claire Stoullig, “Martin Barré. Le leurre de la géométrie,” *Artstudio* 1 (Summer 1986): 38–47.

57

Martin Barré, interview with Bernard Lamarche-Vadel, in *Qu'est-ce que l'art français?*, exh. cat. (Labège-Innopole and Paris: Centre Régional d'Art Contemporain Midi-Pyrénées and La Différence, 1986), 33.

58

Ann Hindry, “Martin Barré. L'arrogance discrète d'une peinture absolue,” *Galeries Magazine* 21 (October–November 1987): 83–87.

59

Anne Tronche, “Martin Barré. Une géométrie mentale,” *Opus International* 103 (Winter 1987): 32–33.

60

Jean-Marie Floch, “Un peintre de la non-figuration. Entretien avec Martin Barré,” *Actes sémiotiques. Bulletin* X, no. 44 (December 1987): 46–49.

61

“Martin Barré” section, *Eighty Magazine* 21 (1988): 2–32; articles by Catherine Flohic, “Portrait,” 2–3, and Jean-Luc Chalumeau, “Je ne peins pas des Vénus ou des pommes,” 4–5.

62

Martin Barré, in Lawless, “Acquisitions,” 121.

63

Michel Ragon and Marcelin Pleynet, *L'Art abstrait. Tome 5: 1970–1987* (Paris: Maeght, 1988).

64

Lawless, “Acquisitions,” 117–21.

65

Martin Barré, interview with Henri-François Debailleux, “La géométrie, c'est mon geste,” *Libération*, March 18, 1993.

66

Marcel-André Stalter, “Martin Barré: tableaux ‘90-91’ et ‘91,’” *Revue du Nord* LXXIV, no. 295 (April–June 1992): 355–70.

67

Jean Louis Schefer, “Martin Barré,” and Marcel-André Stalter, “Martin Barré,” *Art press* 183 (September 1993): 93.

68

Joe Fyfe, “Martin Barré. A French Alternative,” *Art in America* 1 (January 2009): 82–85.

69

Yve-Alain Bois, “Leap Year. Martin Barré's *Greenwich* and *60-T-44*,” *Artforum* 50, no. 1 (September 2011).

LIST OF ARTWORKS

CP — Artwork exhibited at the Centre Pompidou

CP (dotted) — Artwork in the collection of the Centre Pompidou, Musée National d'Art Moderne, not exhibited

M — Artwork exhibited at MAMCO

M (dotted) — Artwork exhibited at MAMCO, not reproduced

CP
Peinture, 1955
Oil on canvas, 73 × 60 cm
Mr. & Mrs. Bourbonne Collection
→ p. 10

CP (dotted)
56-40-F, 1956
Oil on canvas, 100 × 81 cm
Centre Pompidou,
Musée National d'Art Moderne,
Paris; acquisition, 1988
→ p. 27

M
Grenam, 1957
Oil on canvas, 81 × 116 cm
Private collection, Paris;
courtesy Applicat-Prazan, Paris
→ p. 28

M
57-50-B, 1957
Oil on canvas, 89 × 116 cm
Fondation Gandur pour l'Art,
Geneva
→ p. 29

CP
57-60-B, 1957
Oil on canvas, 130 × 97 cm
Private collection, Paris;
courtesy Applicat-Prazan, Paris
→ p. 30

M
Peinture, 1956
Oil on canvas, 65 × 81 cm
Private collection, Paris
→ p. 31

CP
57-100×100-A, 1957
Oil on canvas, 100 × 100 cm
Private collection, Paris;
courtesy Applicat-Prazan, Paris
→ p. 33

M
59-116×97-A, 1959
Oil on canvas, 116 × 97 cm
Kunsthandel Wolfgang Werner,
Bremen/Berlin
→ p. 34

M
60-T-20, 1960
Oil on canvas, 140 × 130 cm
Kunsthandel Wolfgang Werner,
Bremen/Berlin
→ p. 35

CP M
59-120×110-C, 1959
Oil on canvas, 120 × 110 cm
[mac] Musée d'Art
Contemporain, Marseille
→ p. 37

M
59-80×75-C, 1959
Oil on canvas, 80 × 75 cm
Private collection, Geneva
→ p. 38

CP
59-140×130-A, 1959
Oil on canvas, 140 × 130 cm
Private collection
→ p. 39

CP
59-120×110-B, 1959
Oil on canvas, 120 × 110 cm
Private collection, Paris;
courtesy Applicat-Prazan, Paris
→ p. 40

CP M
60-T-47, 1960
Oil on canvas, 73 × 120 cm
(diptych)
Loan of the Centre Pompidou
Foundation to Centre Pompidou,
Musée National d'Art Moderne,
Paris, 2016 (Promised gift
of Thea Westreich Wagner
and Ethan Wagner to the Centre
Pompidou Foundation, 2016)
→ p. 43

CP M
60-T-45, 1960
Oil on canvas, 192 × 253 cm
(quadriptych,
one panel: 90 × 96 cm,
one panel: 102 × 110 cm,
two panels: 80 × 86 cm)
Centre Pompidou,
Musée National d'Art Moderne,
Paris; State acquisition, 1978,
allocation, 1981
→ pp. 44–45

CP
60-T-37, 1960
Oil on canvas, 86 × 80 cm
Michel Ragon Collection
→ p. 47

CP
60-T-43, 1960
Oil on canvas, 81 × 330 cm
(quadriptych,
two panels: 81 × 65 cm,
two panels: 81 × 100 cm)
Private collection
→ pp. 48–49

CP
60-T-51, 1960
Oil on canvas, 98 × 88 cm
Private collection, Paris
→ p. 50

CP M
60-T-31, 1960
Oil on canvas, 130 × 89 cm
Private collection, Paris
→ p. 51

CP
60-T-53, 1960
Oil on canvas, 89 × 12 cm
Daniel Templon Collection,
Paris
→ p. 52

CP
61-T-2, 1961
Oil on canvas, 81 × 54 cm
Private collection
→ p. 52

M
61-T-5, 1961
Oil on canvas, 92 × 65 cm
Private collection
→ p. 53

M
61-T-10, 1961
Oil on canvas, 88 × 96 cm
Private collection
→ p. 54

CP
61-T-36, 1961
Oil on canvas, 96 × 88 cm
Centre Pompidou,
Musée National d'Art
Moderne, Paris;
gift of Mrs. Marie-Aline Prat,
2017
→ p. 55

CP
61-T-15, 1961
Oil on canvas, 119 × 81 cm
(diptych)
Private collection
→ p. 56

M
61-T-16, 1961
Oil on canvas, 81 × 119 cm
(diptych)
Fondation Gandur pour l'Art,
Geneva
→ p. 57

CP
61-T-18, 1961
Oil on canvas, 96 × 88 cm
Musée d'Arts de Nantes,
Nantes
→ p. 59

CP
62-F, 1962
Oil on canvas, 96 × 88 cm
Fondation Gandur pour l'Art,
Geneva
→ p. 60

CP

63-C, 1963
Spray paint and acrylic on canvas, 120 × 88 cm
Musée d'Arts de Nantes, Nantes
→ p. 79

CP M

63-O, 1963
Spray paint and acrylic on canvas, 85 × 79 cm
Private collection
→ p. 80

CP

63-Z, 1963
Spray paint and acrylic on canvas, 81 × 54 cm
Private collection
→ p. 81

CP

63-F-A, 1963
Spray paint and acrylic on canvas, 115 × 97 cm
Private collection; courtesy Galerie Georges-Philippe et Nathalie Vallois
→ p. 82

M

65-A-50×50, 1965
Spray paint and acrylic on canvas, 50 × 50 cm
Hall Collection
→ p. 83

CP

65-H-L-78×74, 1965
Spray paint and acrylic on canvas, 78 × 74 cm
Centre Pompidou, Musée National d'Art Moderne, Paris; acquisition, 1990
→ p. 84

CP

65-H-L-113×86, 1965
Spray paint and acrylic on canvas, 113 × 86 cm
Private collection, Rennes
→ p. 85

CP

65-A-73×73, 1965
Spray paint and acrylic on canvas, 73 × 73 cm
Serge Aboukrat Collection
→ p. 86

CP

65-A-73×54, 1965
Spray paint and acrylic on canvas, 73 × 54 cm
Loan of the Centre Pompidou Foundation to Centre Pompidou, Musée National d'Art Moderne, Paris, 2016 (Promised gift of Thea Westreich Wagner and Ethan Wagner to the Centre Pompidou Foundation, 2016)
→ p. 87

CP M

67-Z-7-70×65, 1967
Spray paint and acrylic on canvas, 70 × 65 cm
Fondation Gandur pour l'Art, Geneva
→ p. 88

M

67-Z-18-43×40, 1967
Spray paint and acrylic on canvas, 43 × 40 cm
Hall Collection
→ p. 88

CP

67-Z-1-86×80, 1967
Spray paint and acrylic on canvas, 86 × 80 cm
Musée d'Arts de Nantes, Nantes
→ p. 89

M

67-Z-3-81×54, 1967
Spray paint and acrylic on canvas, 81 × 54 cm
Syz Collection, Geneva
→ p. 90

M

67-Z-19-43×40, 1967
Spray paint and acrylic on canvas, 43 × 40 cm
Private collection
→ p. 91

CP

67-Z-26-70×53, 1967
Spray paint and acrylic on canvas, 70 × 53 cm
Centre Pompidou, Musée National d'Art Moderne, Paris; acquisition, 1990
→ p. 91

CP

67-Z-4-53×49, 1967
Spray paint and acrylic on canvas, 53 × 49 cm
Private collection
→ p. 92

M

67-A-Z-3, 1967
Spray paint and acrylic on canvas, 113 × 105 cm
Private collection
→ p. 93

CP

67-F-2-113×105, 1967
Spray paint and acrylic on canvas, 113 × 105 cm
Loan of the Centre Pompidou Foundation to Centre Pompidou, Musée National d'Art Moderne, Paris, 2016 (Promised gift of Thea Westreich Wagner and Ethan Wagner to the Centre Pompidou Foundation, 2016)
→ p. 94

CP

67-F-4-113×105, 1967
Spray paint and acrylic on canvas, 113 × 105 cm
Centre Pompidou, Musée National d'Art Moderne, Paris; acquisition, 2002
→ p. 95

CP M

67-F-10-86×80, 1967
Spray paint and acrylic on canvas, 86 × 80 cm
Private collection, France
→ p. 96

M

Le Projecteur, "Les Objets décrochés" series, 1969
Silver print mounted on plywood, 55 × 45 cm
Private collection, Paris

CP

72-73-A-200×185, 1972–73
Acrylic on canvas, 200 × 185 cm
Musée d'Arts de Nantes, Nantes
→ p. 103

CP

72-73-F-108×100, 1972–73
Acrylic on canvas, 108 × 100 cm
Private collection
→ p. 104

CP

72-73-D-130×120, 1972–73
Acrylic on canvas, 130 × 120 cm
Thea Westreich Wagner and Ethan Wagner Collection
→ p. 105

M

72-73-E-108×100, 1972–73
Acrylic on canvas, 108 × 100 cm
Private collection
→ p. 106

M

72-73-B-130×120, 1972–73
Acrylic on canvas, 130 × 120 cm
Private collection
→ p. 107

CP

72-73-D-160×148, 1972–73
Acrylic on canvas, 160 × 148 cm
LaM – Lille Métropole Musée d'Art Moderne, d'Art Contemporain et d'Art Brut, Villeneuve-d'Ascq
→ p. 108

M

72-73-B-108×100, 1972–1973
Acrylic on canvas, 108 × 100 cm
Private collection, Paris
→ p. 109

CP

72-73-B-160×148, 1972–73
Acrylic on canvas, 160 × 148 cm
MAC VAL – Musée d'Art Contemporain du Val-de-Marne, Vitry-sur-Seine
→ p. 110

CP

73-74-F-123×114, 1973–1974
Acrylic on canvas, 123 × 114 cm
Private collection
→ p. 112

CP M

73-74-B-149×139, 1973–74
Acrylic on canvas, 149 × 139 cm
Private collection, Paris
→ p. 113

CP

73-74-D-123×114, 1973–74
Acrylic on canvas, 123 × 114 cm
Private collection
→ p. 114

M

73-74-A-149×139, 1973–74
Acrylic on canvas, 149 × 139 cm
Private collection, Paris
→ p. 115

CP

74-75-B-171×159, 1974–75
Acrylic on canvas, 171×159 cm
Musée d'Art Moderne de Paris, Paris
→ p. 117

CP

74-75-C-113×105, 1974–75
Acrylic on canvas, 113×105 cm
Loan of the Centre Pompidou Foundation to Centre Pompidou, Musée National d'Art Moderne, Paris, 2016 (Promised gift of Thea Westreich Wagner and Ethan Wagner to the Centre Pompidou Foundation, 2016)
→ p. 118

CP

74-75-C-139×129, 1974–75
Acrylic on canvas, 139×129 cm
Private collection
→ p. 119

M

74-75-B-139×129, 1974–75
Acrylic on canvas, 139×129 cm
Pierre Brochet Collection, Paris
→ p. 120

CP M

74-75-A-113×105, 1974–75
Acrylic on canvas, 113×105 cm
Private collection, Rennes
→ p. 121

M

75-76-D-145×140, 1975–76
Acrylic on canvas, 145×140 cm
Private collection
→ p. 123

CP

75-76-C-157×145, 1975–76
Acrylic on canvas, 157×145 cm
Private collection
→ p. 124

CP

75-76-D-157×145, 1975–76
Acrylic on canvas, 157×145 cm
Private collection
→ p. 125

CP

75-76-A-157×145, 1975–76
Acrylic on canvas, 157×145 cm
Private collection, Paris
→ p. 126

M

75-76-B-174×164, 1975–76
Acrylic on canvas, 174×164 cm
Private collection, Paris
→ p. 127

M

75-76-C-174×164, 1975–76
Acrylic on canvas, 174×164 cm
Michel Weil Collection, Nice
→ p. 128

CP M

76-77-B-170×160, 1976–77
Acrylic on canvas, 170×160 cm
Private collection, Paris; courtesy Applicat-Prazan, Paris
→ p. 130

CP

76-77-B-147,5×140, 1976–77
Acrylic on plywood, 147.5×140 cm
Private collection
→ p. 131

NOT IN EITHER EXHIBITION

75-A-785×725, 1975
Pencil on paper, 78.5×72.5 cm
Private collection, Paris
→ p. 132

CP

"77-78" series, known as *L'Indissociable*, 1977–78
Polyptych of fourteen paintings, acrylic on canvas
77-78-1-162×81
77-78-2-81×81
77-78-3-81×162
77-78-4-100×62
77-78-5-162×162
77-78-6-81×81
77-78-7-100×162
77-78-8-162×81
77-78-9-81×81
77-78-10-181×162
77-78-11-81×81
77-78-12-81×81
77-78-13-81×81
77-78-14-100×100
Private collection
→ pp. 142–50

CP

79-B-131×124, 1979
Acrylic on canvas, 131×124 cm
Private collection, Paris
→ p. 158

CP

79-A-100×200, 1979
Acrylic on canvas, 100×200 cm
Florence and Daniel Guerlain Collection
→ p. 159

CP

80B-150×140, 1980
Acrylic on canvas, 150×140 cm
Centre Pompidou, Musée National d'Art Moderne, Paris; acquisition, 1982
→ p. 161

M

80B-100×90, 1980
Acrylic on canvas, 100×90 cm
Fondation Gandur pour l'Art, Geneva
→ p. 162

M

80B-120×110, 1980
Acrylic on canvas, 120×110 cm
Private collection, Paris
→ p. 163

CP

80-81-180×168, 1980–81
Acrylic on canvas, 180×168 cm
Musée d'Art Moderne de Paris, Paris
→ p. 165

M

82-84-104×101, 1982–84
Acrylic on canvas, 104×101 cm
Courtesy Galerie Nathalie Obadia, Paris/Brussels
→ p. 166

M

82-84-108×104, 1982–1984
Acrylic on canvas, 108×104 cm
Private collection, Paris
→ p. 167

CP

82-84-108×100, 1982–84
Acrylic on canvas, 108×100 cm
Centre Pompidou, Musée National d'Art Moderne, Paris; acquisition, 1985
→ p. 168

CP M

82-84-128×124, 1982–84
Acrylic on canvas, 128×124 cm
Centre Pompidou, Musée National d'Art Moderne, Paris; acquisition, 1985
→ p. 169

M

84-85-108×156-B, 1984–85
Acrylic on canvas, 108×156 cm
Private collection
→ p. 170

CP

84-85-144×132-D, 1984–85
Acrylic on canvas, 144×132 cm
Private collection, Paris
→ p. 171

CP

84-85-144×132-A, 1984–85
Acrylic on canvas, 144×132 cm
Private collection
→ p. 172

M

84-85-84×168-B, 1984–85
Acrylic on canvas, 84×168 cm
Courtesy Galerie Nathalie Obadia, Paris/Brussels
→ p. 173

M

86-87-120×120-A, 1986–1987
Acrylic on canvas, 120×120 cm
Frédéric Le Clair Collection, Le Vésinet
→ p. 174

M

86-87-120×120-B, 1986–87
Acrylic on canvas, 120×120 cm
Hall Collection
→ p. 175

CP

86-87-120×120-C, 1986–87
Acrylic on canvas, 120×120 cm
Centre Pompidou, Musée National d'Art Moderne, Paris; State acquisition, 1987, allocation, 2008
→ p. 176

CP

86-87-120×120-D, 1986–87
Acrylic on canvas, 120×120 cm
Marie-Aline Prat Collection
→ p. 177

CP M

86-87-120×120-E, 1986–87
Acrylic on canvas, 120×120 cm
Centre Pompidou, Musée National d'Art Moderne, Paris; State acquisition, 1987, allocation, 2008
→ p. 178

M

86-87-120×120-I, 1986–87
Acrylic on canvas, 120×120 cm
Private collection, Paris
→ p. 179

(M)

90-91-54×180-A, 1990–91
Acrylic on canvas, 54 × 180 cm
Private collection
→ p. 180

(M)

90-91-54×180-B, 1990–91
Acrylic on canvas, 54 × 180 cm
Courtesy Galerie Nathalie Obadia, Paris/Brussels
→ p. 181

(M)

90-91-72×144-A, 1990–91
Acrylic on canvas, 72 × 144 cm
Private collection
→ p. 182

(M)

90-91-54×180-C, 1990–91
Acrylic on canvas, 54 × 180 cm
Private collection
→ p. 182

(M)

90-91-72×144-B, 1990–91
Acrylic on canvas, 72 × 144 cm
Courtesy Galerie Nathalie Obadia, Paris/Brussels
→ p. 183

(M)

90-91-96×112-A, 1990–91
Acrylic on canvas, 96 × 112 cm
Private collection, Paris
→ p. 184

(CP)

90-91-96×112-C, 1990–91
Acrylic on canvas, 96 × 112 cm
Loan of the Centre Pompidou Foundation to Centre Pompidou, Musée National d'Art Moderne, Paris, 2016 (Promised gift of Thea Westreich Wagner and Ethan Wagner to the Centre Pompidou Foundation, 2016)
→ p. 185

(M)

90-91-126×126-A, 1990–91
Acrylic on canvas, 126 × 126 cm
Hall Collection
→ p. 186

(M)

90-91-126×126-B, 1990–91
Acrylic on canvas, 126 × 126 cm
Private collection, Paris
→ p. 187

(CP) (M)

91-72×288-A, 1991
Acrylic on canvas, 72 × 288 cm
Courtesy Galerie Nathalie Obadia, Paris/Brussels
→ pp. 188–189

(M)

91-120×160-A, 1991
Acrylic on canvas, 120 × 160 cm
Courtesy Galerie Nathalie Obadia, Paris/Brussels
→ p. 189

(CP)

91-92-42×168-C, 1991–92
Acrylic on canvas, 42 × 168 cm
Courtesy Galerie Nathalie Obadia, Paris/Brussels
→ p. 191

(CP)

91-92-42×168-D, 1991–92
Acrylic on canvas, 42 × 168 cm
Private collection
→ p. 192

(CP)

91-92-42×168-B, 1991–92
Acrylic on canvas, 42 × 168 cm
Private collection
→ p. 193

(CP)

92A-120×126-C, 1992
Acrylic on canvas, 120 × 126 cm
Private collection
→ p. 194

(CP) (M)

92B-124×128-D, 1992
Acrylic on canvas, 124 × 128 cm
Private collection
→ p. 195

(CP) (M)

92B-124×128-E, 1992
Acrylic on canvas, 124 × 128 cm
Fondation Gandur pour l'Art, Geneva
→ p. 196

(CP)

92B-124×128-A, 1992
Acrylic on canvas, 124 × 128 cm
Centre Pompidou,
Musée National d'Art Moderne, Paris; gift in lieu, 1995
→ p. 197

(CP)

92B-124×128-B, 1992
Acrylic on canvas, 124 × 128 cm
Centre Pompidou,
Musée National d'Art Moderne, Paris; gift in lieu, 1995
→ p. 198

(CP)

92B-124×128-C, 1992
Acrylic on canvas, 124 × 128 cm
Centre Pompidou,
Musée National d'Art Moderne, Paris; gift in lieu, 1995
→ p. 199

(M)

92B-124×128-G, 1992
Acrylic on canvas, 124 × 128 cm
Private collection, Paris
→ p. 200

—

The work of Martin Barré is represented by Galerie Nathalie Obadia, Paris and Brussels, and Matthew Marks Gallery, New York.

Under the general editorship of Yve-Alain Bois and Ann Hindry, the artist's catalogue raisonné is currently in preparation. It is due to be published by the Association des Amis de Martin Barré, which can be contacted at associationmartinbarre@orange.fr.

EXHIBITION

MAMCO GENEVA

Director
· Lionel Bovier

Exhibition Curator
· Clément Dirié

Museum Management and Development

Administrator
· Valérie Mallet

Library, Archives, and Museum Resources
· Chloë Gouédard

Digital Communication
· Julien Gremaud

Press and Communication
· Viviane Reybier

Exhibitions and Collection

Chief Curator
· Julien Fronsacq

Honorary Curator
· Françoise Ninghetto

Collection Curator
· Sophie Costes

Curator
· Paul Bernard

Associate Curator
· Fabrice Stroun

Chief of Exhibition Productions
· Cyrille Maillot

Exhibition Productions and Collection Registrar
· Filipe Dos Santos

Registrar in charge of shipping
· Benoît Charron

Associate Restorers
· Pierre-Antoine Héritier
· Caroline Dick

Associate Photographer
· Annik Wetter

Public and Education Services

Public Services Manager
· Yann Abrecht

Public Services Coordinator
· Mathilde Acevedo
· Daniel Maury

Public Services Coordinator
· Charlotte Morel

Education Services Coordinator
· Julie Cudet

Curator in Charge of Publications
· Thierry Davila

Facility Management and Surveillance

Chief of Facility Management
· Antonio Magalhes

Facility Management
· Maria de Fatima Braganca
· Joana Gomes Da Silva

Surveillance
· Matuala Lumeto
· Carlos Martins Fonseca
· Luc Schuwey
· Martine Vaillat De Melo

CENTRE POMPIDOU

Curator
· Michel Gauthier with the collaboration of Rita Cusimano

Exhibition Managers
· Dominique Kalabane
· Bruno Veret

Architect and Scenographer
· Camille Excoffon

Artworks Registrar
· Aude Chaufourier

Management of the Exhibition Space
· Laurent Melloul

Lighting
· Arnaud Jung

Conservation
· Sophie Spalek

Photography
· Valérie Leconte

Documentation
· Odile Rousseau

Cultural Mediation
· Delphine Coffin

Graphic Design
· Lacasta Design

MUSÉE NATIONAL D'ART MODERNE – CENTRE DE CRÉATION INDUSTRIELLE

Director
· Bernard Blistène

Deputy Director, Collections
· Brigitte Leal

Deputy Director, Research and Globalization
· Catherine David

Deputy Director, Industrial Design
· Frédéric Migayrou

Deputy Director, Cultural Programming
· Didier Ottinger

Chief Administrative Officer
· Xavier Bredin

Curator and Head of Department, Bibliothèque Kandinsky
· Nicolas Liucci-Goutnikov

Head of the Collections Department
· Hélène Vassal

Head of the Art Conservation Department
· Véronique Sorano-Stedman

Culture and Creation Department

Director
· Mathieu Potte-Bonneville

Deputy Director
· Nicolas Larnaudie

Head of the Spoken Word Unit
· Jean-Max Colard

Head of the Live Shows Unit
· Chloé Siganos

Production Department

Director
· Anne-Sophie de Gasquet

Head of the Exhibitions Management Unit
· Mina Bellemou

Head of the Artworks Management Unit
· Sandrine Beaujard-Vallet

Acting Head of the Workshops and Technical Resources Unit
· Nathalie Weitz

Head of the Scenography and Museography Unit
· Gaëlle Seltzer

Head of the Audiovisual Production
· Sylvain Wolff

Prevention
· David Martin

Public Programs Department

Director
· Catherine Guillou

Deputy Director, Head of the Cultural Mediation Unit
· Patrice Chazottes

Head of the Public Reception Unit
· Laurence Nida

Head of the Public Development Unit
· Cécile Venot

Head of the Administrative Unit
· Vincent Brico

Communications and Digital Department

Director
· Agnès Benayer

Deputy Director
· Marc-Antoine Chaumien

Head of Public Relations Unit
· Lydia Poitevin

Public Relations Officer
· Caroline Mira

Press Attaché
· Dorothée Mireux

Image Unit
· Christian Beneyton

Head of Digital Unit
· Paul Mourey

Economic and International Development Department

Director
· Gaële de Medeiros

Delegate, International Relations
· Julia de Rouvray

Economic Development
· Marie-Claire Groeninck

Sponsorship
· Jean-Christophe Claude

Sponsorship Officer
· Elisa Vignaud

Publications Department

Director
· Claire de Cointet

Head of Publishing
· Guillaume Grandgeorge

Head of Marketing and Sales
· Élise Albenque

Administrative and Finance Manager
· Marie Savoldelli

PUBLICATION

This publication is co-published by Éditions Flammarion, Éditions du Centre Pompidou, and MAMCO Geneva.

MAMCO GENEVA
AND CENTRE POMPIDOU

Editors
- Clément Dirié
- Michel Gauthier
  with the collaboration of Rita Cusimano

Photo Librarian, MNAM-CCI
- Perrine Renaud

FLAMMARION

Editorial Director
- Julie Rouart

Administration Manager
- Delphine Montagne

Editor
- Mélanie Puchault

Graphic Design
- E+K – Élise Gay & Kévin Donnot

Copy-editing and Proofreading
- Sarah Kane

Translation from the French
- Sandra Reid
- Nicholas Huckle
  (for Yve-Alain Bois' essay)

Production
- Corinne Trovarelli

Color Separation
- Les Artisans du Regard

Print
- Indice (Barcelona, Spain)

—

Papers
- Wibalin Natural Dove Grey (cover)
- Focus Art Natural 135 gsm (inside)

Typeface
- Whyte designed by Johannes Breyer, Fabian Harb, and Erkin Karamemet (Dinamo type foundry)

—

This book has received the support of the Fondation Gandur pour l'Art.

FONDATION
GANDUR
POUR L'ART

Acknowledgments

The editors would like to thank, first and foremost, Michèle Gozland-Barré for her constant support and generous involvement during the elaboration of the two exhibitions, as well as the authors of the essays in this publication, the "witnesses" who were kind enough to recall their relationship with Martin Barré in order to enrich the chronology with personal recollections, public and private lenders, the editorial team at Flammarion, in particular Julie Rouart who immediately agreed to publish a new book devoted to Martin Barré nearly thirty years after the reference monograph published in 1993, and the graphic designers Élise Gay & Kévin Donnot for their sympathetic treatment of the artist's work.

Clément Dirié would like to thank the entire MAMCO Geneva team for its enthusiastic welcome and professionalism, particularly its director Lionel Bovier for his confidence, as well as Anne-Laure Buffard, Henry-Claude Cousseau, Bertrand Dumas, Arnaud Hubert, Zaza and Philippe Jabre, Deborah Najar, Nathalie Obadia, Serge Tiers, and Thea Westreich Wagner & Ethan Wagner.

The Centre Pompidou would like to express its gratitude to the Matthew Marks Gallery and Galerie Nathalie Obadia, to the patrons who wished to remain anonymous, as well as to Paula Aisemberg, Gabrielle Salomon, Bertrand Dumas and Yan Schubert of the Fondation Gandur pour l'Art, and Franck Prazan. It would also like to pay tribute to Michel Ragon, who passed away on February 14, 2020, a longstanding friend of Martin Barré, who was delighted by the organization of this exhibition.

Photo Credits

- Archives Flammarion: 68
- Archives Martin Barré, Paris: 10, 28, 39, 40, 56, 57, 59, 80, 81, 85, 86, 88r, 90, 96, 104, 105, 112, 113, 124, 130, 152–53, 158, 159, 162, 163, 172, 191, 192, 193, 194, 206t, 212, 213, 214t, 215d, 216l, 217–21, 222b, 223, 231l
- Archives Martin Barré, Paris/ Photo Bertrand Huet: 33, 47, 50, 82, 109, 114, 119, 131, 132, 142–50, 170, 177, 180, 181, 182t, 183, 186, 187
- Archives Martin Barré, Paris/ Hans Namuth: 2–3, 222l
- Bibliothèque Kandinsky, MNAM-CCI, Centre Pompidou: 204, 214b, 227r
- Bibliothèque Kandinsky, MNAM-CCI, Centre Pompidou/ Fonds Galerie Laage-Salomon: 206b, 207, 224–25, 226b, 227l, 228r
- Centre Pompidou, MNAM-CCI/ Jacques Faujour/Dist. RMN-GP: 14bl
- Centre Pompidou, MNAM-CCI/ Georges Meguerditchian/ Dist. RMN-GP: 43, 87, 94, 118, 185
- Centre Pompidou, MNAM-CCI/ Philippe Migeat/Dist. RMN-GP: 55, 84, 95
- Centre Pompidou, MNAM-CCI/ Bertrand Prévost/Dist. RMN-GP: 27, 44–45, 91r, 161, 168, 169, 176, 178, 197, 198, 199
- Courtesy Andrew Kreps Gallery: 230l
- Courtesy Applicat-Prazan: 30
- Courtesy Archives Gabrielle Salomon: 126, 127, 166, 167, 171
- Courtesy Galerie Nathalie Obadia: 52l, 229, 230r
- Courtesy Galerie Nathalie Obadia/ Photo Bertrand Huet: 38, 51, 83, 173
- Courtesy Matthew Marks Gallery/ Photo Ron Amstutz: 48-49, 52r, 92, 125, 231r
- Robert David: 63, 67, 215l
- Fondation Gandur pour l'Art/ Photo Sandra Pointet: 29, 60
- Fondation Gandur pour l'Art/ Photo Philippe Migeat, Georges Meguerditchian: 88l
- Claude Gaspari: 110
- Stefan Gierowski Foundation/ Photo Adam Gut: 14br
- International Center of Photography/David Seidner Archive: 228b
- Patrick Jean: 226t
- LaM – Lille Métropole Musée d'Art Moderne, d'Art Contemporain et d'Art Brut, Villeneuve-d'Ascq/ Photo Philip Bernard: 108
- MAM / Roger-Viollet: 117, 165
- MAMCO Genève/ Photo Annik Wetter: 31, 34, 35, 37, 53, 54, 91l, 93, 106, 107, 115, 120, 121, 123, 128, 174, 175, 179, 182b, 184, 188–89, 195, 196, 200, 232
- Max Ottoni: 216r, 240
- The Museum of Modern Art, New York/Scala, Florence/ © 2020. Digital image: 14t
- Ville de Nantes/Photo A. Guillard: 79, 89, 103

—

Legal Deposit
October 2020

Edition Number
L.01EBUN000818

ISBN
978-2-08023-185-7

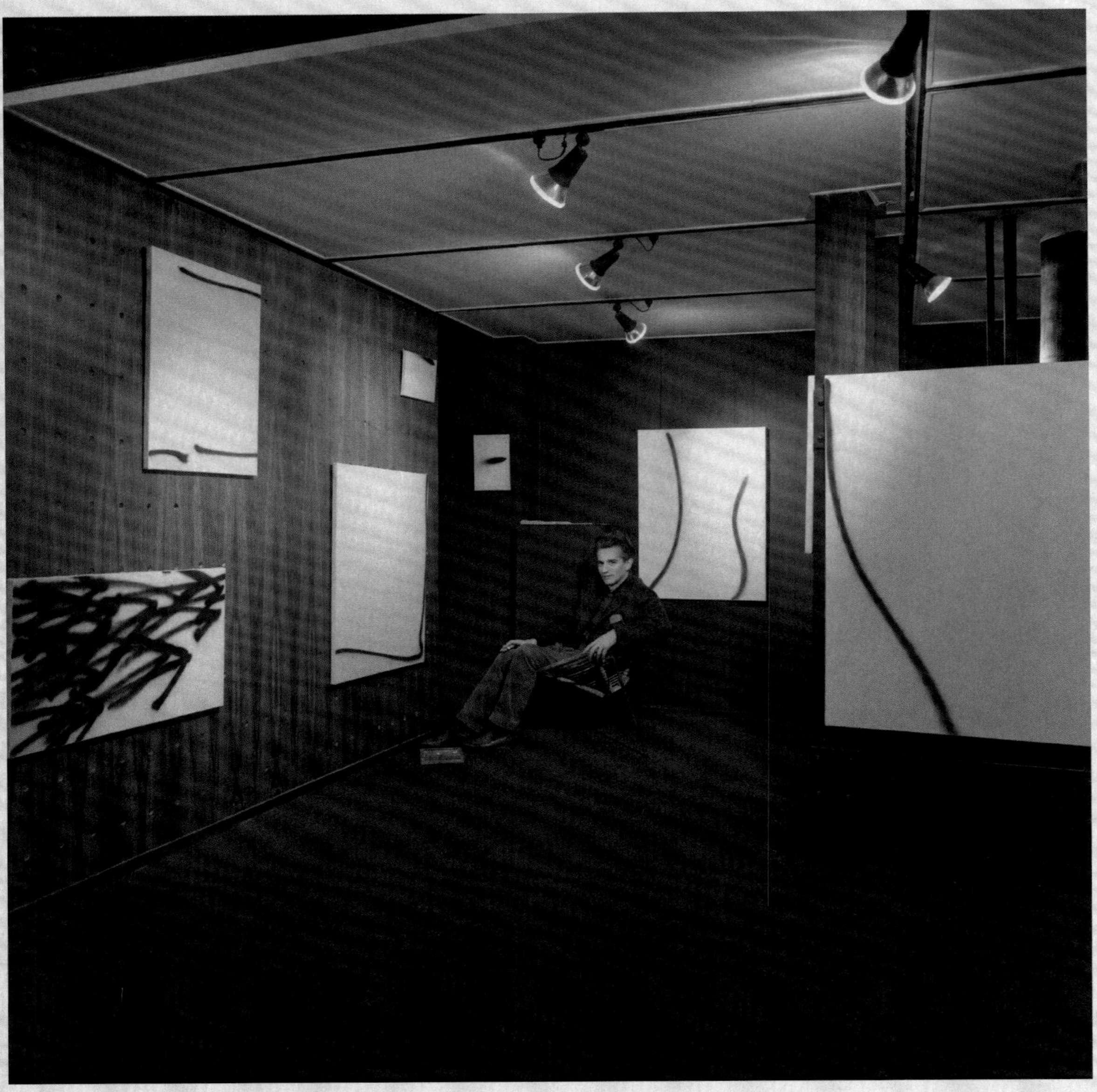

Martin Barré in his exhibition
Peintures récentes de Martin Barré,
Galerie Arnaud, Paris, 1964